Aesthetics as Secular Millennialism

NEW STUDIES IN THE AGE OF GOETHE

New Studies in the Age of Goethe, sponsored by the Goethe Society of North America, aims to publish innovative research that contextualizes the "Age of Goethe," whether within the fields of literature, history (including art history and history of science), philosophy, art, music, or politics. Though the series editors welcome all approaches and perspectives, they are especially interested in interdisciplinary projects, creative approaches to archival or original source materials, theoretically informed scholarship, work that introduces previously undiscovered materials, and projects that re-examine traditional epochal boundaries or open new channels of interpretations.

Titles in the Series

Peter J. Schwartz, *After Jena: Goethe's Elective Affinities and the End of the Old Regime*

Mary Ellen Dupree, *The Mask and the Quill: Actress-Writers in Germany from Enlightenment to Romanticism*

Brian Tucker, *Reading Riddles: Rhetorics of Obscurity from Romanticism to Freud*

Benjamin Bennett, *Aesthetics as Secular Millennialism: Its Trail from Baumgarten and Kant to Walt Disney and Hitler*

Aesthetics as Secular Millennialism

Its Trail from Baumgarten and Kant to Walt Disney and Hitler

Benjamin Bennett

Lewisburg
BUCKNELL UNIVERSITY PRESS

Published by Bucknell University Press
Co-published with The Rowman & Littlefield Publishing Group, Inc.
4501 Forbes Boulevard, Suite 200, Lanham, Maryland 20706
www.rowman.com

10 Thornbury Road, Plymouth PL6 7PP, United Kingdom

British Library Cataloguing in Publication Data Available

Library of Congress Cataloging-in-Publication Data Available

ISBN 978-1-61148-474-8 (cloth : alk. paper)
ISBN 978-1-61148-652-2 (pbk : alk. paper)

For my friends, Jane and Marshall Brown

. . . the only standard for a necessary war is the fight against conditions under which people no longer wish to live—and our experiences with the tormenting hell of the totalitarian camps have enlightened us only too well about the possibility of such conditions. Thus the fear of concentration camps and the resulting insight into the nature of total domination might serve to invalidate all obsolete political differentiations from right to left and to introduce beside and above them the politically most important yardstick for judging events in our time, namely: whether they serve totalitarian domination or not.

— Hannah Arendt

Contents

Acknowledgments

In March 1992 I gave a presentation at Harvard University on "Walt Disney and Hitler," which was the germ of the present book. I remain indebted to the responsive and critical audience there, and to Peter Burgard for organizing that event. For criticism and discussion I am also indebted to Paul Cantor, Jeffrey Grossman, Volker Kaiser, Brett Martz, Larry Rickels, John H. Smith, and Chad Wellmon, to scores of students in graduate and undergraduate classes at the University of Virginia where I developed the material, and especially to Jane and Marshall Brown, to whom this book is dedicated. I am also deeply grateful to Kerstin Steitz for assistance in preparing the manuscript and the index, to Gina Hutton for assistance in practical matters, and to the University of Virginia for leave time in which to work. The English translations of material from Kant's *Critiques* are my own. Chapter Three below was developed from my essay, "The Irrelevance of Aesthetics and the De-Theorizing of the Self in 'Classical' Weimar," in Simon Richter (ed.), *The Literature of Weimar Classicism* (Rochester, N.Y.: Camden House, 2005), pp.295-321. I am grateful to Simon Richter for his permission, on behalf of the copyright holders, to use this material. For all of the following I am grateful to the copyright holders:

Excerpts from *The Origins of Totalitarianism* by Hannah Arendt copyright © 1973, 1968, 1966, 1958, 1951, 1948 by Hannah Arendt and renewed 2001, 1996, 1994, 1986 by Lotte Kohler. Copyright renewed 1979 by Mary McCarthy West. Copyright renewed 1976 by Hannah Arendt, reproduced by permission of Houghton Mifflin Harcourt Publishing Company. All rights reserved.

Excerpts from Theodor W. Adorno, *Aesthetic Theory*, edited by Gretel Adorno and Rolf Tiedemann, newly translated and edited by Robert Hullot-Kentor. English translation copyright © 1997 by the Regents of the University of Minnesota. Original, German language, edition copyright © 1970 by Suhrkamp Verlag. Used by permission of the University of Minnesota Press.

Lyrics from the song *Manhattan*, written by Richard Rodgers and Lorenz Hart, are used by permission of Piedmont Music Company.

Excerpts from *How Novels Think: The Limits of British Individualism from 1719-1900*, by Nancy Armstrong, copyright © 2005 by Columbia University Press. Used by permission of the publisher.

Excerpts from Friedrich Schiller: *On the Aesthetic Education of Man,* edited and translated with Introduction & Notes by Elizabeth M. Wilkinson & L. A. Willoughby (1983). Used by permission of Oxford University Press.

Excerpts from *The Dialogic Imagination: Four Essays,* by M. M. Bakhtin, edited by Michael Holquist, translated by Caryl Emerson and Michael Holquist, copyright © 1981. Used by permission of the University of Texas Press.

Excerpts from Ernst Cassirer, *The Philosophy of the Enlightenment* copyright © 1951 Princeton University Press, 1979 renewed PUP, © 2009- (Pb. Ed.) PUP- Princeton Classic Edition. Used by permission of Princeton University Press.

I am grateful, finally, to P22 and the International House of Fonts for permission to use a special font, P22 St G. Schrift, for quotations from Stefan George in chapter Six.

Introduction

"Secular millennialism" refers to the belief that a millennial or absolutely perfected human condition is achievable by human effort alone, without divine intervention. "Millennium" must here be distinguished from "apocalypse"—even though the two are closely associated in a Christian view of history. For an apocalypse is the sudden uncovering or revelation of some heretofore but indistinctly surmised truth; whereas the secular millennium, as a product of human effort, must in some degree be *known in advance.* How else could we direct our efforts toward it? On the other hand, secular millennialism must be distinguished from utopianism. For if the word is used in accordance with the etymology given it at its birth, a "utopia" is a place or condition that is *not,* however desirable its existence might be; whereas the secular millennium, as I use the term, is understood to be achievable.

In my view, the primary importance of the concept of secular millennialism is that it summarizes the central point made by Hannah Arendt in *The Origins of Totalitarianism:* that neither of the two major totalitarian movements of the twentieth century, in Nazi Germany and in the Soviet Union under Stalin, was in any degree genuinely nationalistic; that each was focused on the achievement of a single total universal world order, an order comparable to the millennium imagined by Christianity. Arendt is very definite on this point, which she uses to distinguish totalitarianism from such relatively simple nationalist dictatorships as fascist Italy. And I think she is correct: not only on the matter of types of absolutism in the twentieth century, but also in her more general suggestion that totalitarianism (or secular millennialist politics) is the most constant and pressing danger that human societies face now and will face in the foreseeable future.

Therefore I consider secular millennialism, as such, a matter of importance. And especially important is the question of how to account for the fact that secular millennialist thinking was embraced enthusiastically by large segments of large populations under Hitler and Stalin. The citation of historical *instances* of secular millennialism does not answer this question—unless one is prepared to show how the upper echelons of totalitarian movements managed to persuade the people under them to become millennialists. (I argue in chapter 9 below that not even the most refined propaganda methods could accomplish this feat without a millennialist predisposition in their audience.) Instances alone—say Marx, Hegel, the

French Revolution, maybe even Francis Bacon—are not enough. In order to explain the secular millennialist character of modern totalitarianism, we require a *tradition* of such thinking which is broadly enough based to account for the susceptibility of large populations to totalitarian propaganda.

My contention is that the new philosophical science of *aesthetics,* in the eighteenth century, provides the impetus for a secular millennialist tradition in European thought which plays a decisive part in twentieth-century totalitarianism. In chapter 1, I will try to give an account of how the aesthetic version of secular millennialism arises: as a displacement mainly of *political* thought, only indirectly related to religious thought. Questions raised in the modern debate on religion and secularity—most recently in Charles Taylor's monumental *A Secular Age*—have no place in my project as presently conceived. If I can show the existence and operation of the tradition I am interested in, then a nuanced criticism of my historical understanding of secularity will only strengthen my position.

I favor the term "aesthetics" because it is used by the originators of the tradition I am trying to trace, especially Baumgarten, Kant, and Schiller. But what I will call "aesthetics" is not exactly what most people understand by the word. I mean, first of all, aesthetics as a philosophical movement, excluding everything one might call practical aesthetics, excluding for instance the study of specific exigencies of production or reception in respect to particular artistic types. I mean aesthetics, in other words, as the study of either beauty in general or art in general—possibilities which mark a characteristic confusion in the supposed science, since it is by no means clear that the two areas of study coincide, or even overlap significantly.

And in a second deviation from common usage, I will continue to designate as "aesthetics" an intellectual tradition which begins under that name but, in the nineteenth and the twentieth century, concerns itself ever less centrally with questions of beauty or art while not losing its secular millennialist quality. I will argue, for example, that modern philosophical hermeneutics, in Dilthey, Heidegger, and Gadamer, belongs to the aesthetic tradition from Baumgarten and Kant. The principal task here will be to show that what I am talking about is a "tradition" to begin with. I think I can make such a showing, with the aid of an argument on the history of the novel; and the crucial connection between that philosophical tradition and practical totalitarian politics will be made by way of considerations belonging to the theory of media and the theory of propaganda.

I have tried to make the argument as easy to follow as possible. Part I covers the origins and the general shape of aesthetics plus the inherent problems in that supposed discipline and the case to be made for regarding the hermeneutics of Dilthey and Heidegger as practically a complete rebirth of the early Kantian-Schillerian phase of the tradition. In chapter

6, the last of Part I, I argue that Heidegger and Adorno, between them, represent something like a logical end to aesthetics, where its relation to totalitarianism also becomes especially clear.

In each chapter of Part I, I aim for as close to a self-contained argument as possible; and Part II is devoted mainly to closing the inevitable gaps that this approach creates in the historical picture. Chapters 7 and 8 contain an extended argument on the realistic novel, which I claim is the main vehicle by which aesthetic tradition maintains itself in the nineteenth century, before its revival as philosophical hermeneutics, and by which it attracts a large popular following. And chapters 9 and 10 deal with relations among the aesthetic tradition, totalitarian propaganda, and the "totalitarian imagination" with its dream of what Arendt calls "human omnipotence." In all of Part II, I try to maintain an attentiveness to avenues by which millennialist ideas are made widely available, and also to instances of *resistance* against the aesthetic impetus in history—hence ultimately against totalitarianism—which include, in my reading, Robert Musil's *Confusions of the Schoolboy Törless*, and Joyce's *Portrait of the Artist as a Young Man*. And chapter 11, at the end, is focused entirely on the ins and outs of such resistance, as it appears, perhaps unexpectedly, in the puppet theater and the animated cartoon.

One final note on basic concepts: Not all secular millennialism is aesthetic. Nazism may be deeply indebted to an aesthetic tradition, but it is not itself a type of aesthetics. And nowhere near all aesthetics is millennialist. It happens that the two concepts both apply to the tradition I am trying to identify, especially in its formative phase. But there is no intrinsic connection between them *as concepts*.

Part I

ONE

Millennial Politics: The Beginning of Aesthetics

Aesthetics, in my view, is an intellectual discipline with very little sense of what it is doing or where it is going. Nowadays—in Hegel's wake, I suppose—we almost always use the term to refer to the general study of art. But in the late eighteenth century it also meant the study of beauty; and the overlap between these two areas of study is not nearly as large as one might suppose. When we go back still further in time, to Kant and then to Baumgarten, we find—in accordance with the etymological sense of the term "aesthetic"—something more like a theory of sense experience, or of "sensory representations" as they were called in an eighteenth-century rationalist psychology. If we try to take aesthetics at its own word about what its business is, then, it seems we find nothing but a constant historical shifting and confusion.

Therefore I propose *not* to take aesthetics at its own word about itself. I will argue that all the principal forms of philosophical aesthetics since Kant—including some philosophical movements that do not call themselves "aesthetics"—belong to a single tradition of secular millennialism, a tradition of understanding history to be oriented toward a millennial goal which must be achieved by human effort alone, without divine intervention. As I have said in the Introduction, an understanding of this tradition is important not only for the light it sheds on the history and confusions of aesthetics. It also helps repair a gap in the thought of one of the most significant historical works of our time, Hannah Arendt's *The Origins of Totalitarianism.* But in the present chapter, I am interested only in the actual birth of modern philosophical aesthetics, a birth in which I claim its millennialist character is already fully established.

3

SECULAR MILLENNIALISM OR ARTISTIC AUTONOMY?

On at least one issue, the question of *where* aesthetics originates, there is a clear consensus. Kant's *Critique of Judgment* (1790) is considered crucial by practically everyone. The term "aesthetics" had been coined in 1735 by Alexander Gottlieb Baumgarten.[1] Kant's contemporary Karl Philipp Moritz is credited with some of the clearest and strongest early formulations of an "aesthetic" view of art. And Schiller's series of letters *On the Aesthetic Education of Man* (1795) is generally regarded as a definitive summation of the new "science" in its first historical phase. All eyes, in other words, are directed toward eighteenth-century Germany.

But things become less clear when we turn to the question of *how* aesthetics originates. Much critical thought is focused on the idea of artistic autonomy.[2] We are told that modern aesthetics arises when, in the eighteenth century, art is recognized as constituting an "autonomous" domain. But it is not hard to see what is wrong with this idea. The supposed nascent autonomy of art is associated with the advent of a bourgeois age; and the typical bourgeois response to art is precisely to insist on the question of its *utility*—not to bypass utility in favor of an idea of art-as-such. Especially the moral usefulness of literature is questioned repeatedly in the seventeenth and eighteenth centuries. Pre-bourgeois art and artistic theory—under aristocratic and ecclesiastic patronage, not directly subject to market forces—will certainly tend to be less worried about proving themselves useful.

Therefore, the fact that the idea of artistic autonomy does still unquestionably arise in the eighteenth century is a fact that requires explanation. Especially Moritz's 1785 essay, "Versuch einer Vereinigung aller schönen Künste und Wissenschaften unterdem Begriff *des in sich selbst Vollendeten*" [Attempt to Unify All Beaux-Arts and Belles-Lettres under the Concept of *That Which Is Complete in Itself*], advances what seems a very strong form of the idea of artistic autonomy. I will argue, however, both in general and with respect to Moritz's thinking in its entirety, that this idea is at best a secondary factor, and that the explanation for its prominence in a bourgeois environment is furnished very neatly by a recognition of secular millennialism as the primary originating force in aesthetics.

My overall argument, on the question of primary and secondary factors in the origination of aesthetics, has two main parts. First, I will show that the idea of artistic autonomy makes good sense and arises naturally in the context of a fundamentally millennialist aesthetics, whereas the reverse is not the case. If one assumes the primacy of secular millennialism, one can account for instances of the idea of artistic autonomy, whereas the idea of artistic autonomy does not account for instances of secular millennialist vision. Of course this argument is useful only if clear instances of such vision can be shown in early aesthetics. But I think I can

assemble enough material here to establish my point at least provisionally. And a good deal more will appear in subsequent chapters.

Second, I will call into question directly the main pieces of evidence
that are adduced in support of the artistic-autonomy hypothesis. I will
argue that the notion of an autonomous aesthetic realm is neither a shaping force in the thought of the *Critique of Judgment* nor a logical consequence of that thought. And I will show the millennialist current in Moritz's thought, to which his assertions on the autonomy of art are in the
end only corollaries.

THE SECULAR MILLENNIALIST MAXIM

I want to begin with some relatively abstract points. The errors in existing
thought on the origin of aesthetics are mainly conceptual, not factual; and
it is therefore important to establish a conceptual framework before dealing with the factual material in detail. I ask patience of my readers. A
detailed discussion of Kant and Moritz follows in the present chapter;
and the remaining gaps in the framework will be filled in later.

To begin with the most important general point: If secular millennialism can be shown to have arisen in eighteenth-century Europe, in a form
broad and strong enough to found a tradition, then it will certainly involve, at least *in posse*, the idea to which Hannah Arendt gives the name
"human omnipotence."[3] The full range of this idea does not appear until
much later in its historical development. Arendt explains how it operates
in twentieth-century totalitarianism:

> In contrast . . . to other despotic forms of government, where frequently
> a clique rules and the despot plays only the representative role of a
> puppet ruler, totalitarian leaders are actually free to do whatever they
> please and can count on the loyalty of their entourage even if they
> choose to murder them. . . . It is not the truthfulness of the Leader's
> words but the infallibility of his actions which is the basis for the struc-
> ture. Without it and in the heat of a discussion which presumes fallibil-
> ity, the whole fictional world of totalitarianism goes to pieces, over-
> whelmed at once by the factuality of the real world which only the
> movement steered in an infallibly right direction by the Leader was
> able to ward off.
>
> However, the loyalty of those who believe neither in ideological
> clichés nor in the infallibility of the Leader also has deeper, nontechni-
> cal reasons. What binds these men together is a firm and sincere belief
> in human omnipotence. Their moral cynicism, their belief that every-
> thing is permitted, rests on the solid conviction that everything is pos-
> sible. It is true that these men, few in number, are not easily caught in
> their own specific lies and that they do not necessarily believe in racism
> or economics, in the conspiracy of the Jews or of Wall Street. Yet they
> too are deceived, deceived by their impudent conceited idea that every-

thing can be done and their contemptuous conviction that everything
that exists is merely a temporary obstacle that superior organization
will certainly destroy.[4]

Without the idea of "human omnipotence" that Arendt suggests here, the
elite formations, composed of relatively intelligent and competent individuals, could never have taken shape under a Hitler or a Stalin. But
without secular millennialism in its eighteenth-century form, I contend, it
is also not likely that the idea of human omnipotence could have been as
available or acceptable in the twentieth century as it was.

If the force for achieving the millennium is not divine (or essentially
so, like the figure of a benevolent "nature"), then it must be human. In
this case it is the duty of enlightened or Enlightenment humanity—part
of our renunciation of what Kant calls "self-imposed immaturity"—to
understand and accept responsibility for transforming the world in accordance with reason. We must have the courage to follow the rightness
of our own reason, and to insist: *as we desire the world, as we envision the
world, so must it be, so shall it be.* This is the secular millennialist maxim,
which in its twentieth-century form, Arendt suggests, asserts power even
over "factuality"; it claims the ability to turn fact itself not merely into
past fact, but simply into non-fact, by organizing it into oblivion. Or is
this arrogant disregard of fact really only a late product of secular millennialism? In Chapter 3 below we will see that Schiller's aesthetic *Letters*
offer two completely different views of Hellenic antiquity: the vision of a
civilization of maximum human integrity and perfection; and the factual
recognition of a society, especially in Athens, whose basic corruption was
unaffected by its artistic achievement. What does this contradiction suggest—at least before Schiller abandons his millennialism altogether—if
not that the alternatives represent a choice for us, that it is our duty to
develop our own civilization so as to realize our *vision* of those Greek
predecessors as a simple truth while crushing the *facts* of ancient history
under the triumphant heel of our own perfected humanity?

With the rise of human-empowering science in the eighteenth century,
along with early forms of social theory and critical historiography, the
notion of factuality becomes in many respects questionable. The place-
ment of the Rock of Gibraltar is a fact that probably neither a Schiller nor
a Nazi will ever take issue with. But there are plenty of facts in the realm
of human affairs—say, the poverty of the lower classes—that change
their very nature as facts depending on the manner in which we accept
them as such. And if it had ever occurred to us to suspect that "everything is possible" (Arendt's phrase), this suspicion is emphatically confirmed for Europeans by the French Revolution. The secular millennialist
maxim is only one logical step beyond this typical intellectual experience,
not only for Schiller, but even more explicitly for Kant—both before the
French Revolution, in the supposedly self-confirming eighth and ninth

propositions of the "Idea for a General History with Cosmopolitan Intent," and afterward, in the whole plan of the *Anthropology from a Pragmatic Point of View.*

WHY AESTHETICS?

It is not unreasonable to expect that in the eighteenth century religious millennialism will be replaced by secular millennialism, that the energy of millennialism will change its character and content. But shall we look for a *direct* metamorphosis of the religious into the secular variety? I will discuss below the influence of theological terminology in aesthetics, an influence that is perhaps clearest in literary studies, where we speak of canonical works, of inspiration, of hermeneutics, and where the enormously subtle and effortful work of editors infuses their texts with something close to sacredness. Still, the argument for a direct historical passage from the religious to the aesthetic has never been made convincingly; and I don't think it can be made. But there is no need of it. The development of millennial aesthetics can be understood perfectly well without any such direct passage.

If we agree, for the sake of argument, that an eighteenth-century secular millennialism exists, then it almost has to have taken the form of a millennial politics, because the association of millennial vision with politics already has a long pre-Enlightenment history: the history of the imperial idea in all its various forms, especially its Christian forms, from Rome onward. Empire is not at first a direct object of millennial vision. But it is a gauge of millennial history; its collapse is meant to signal the proximity of the Christian Millennium. And when empire as an institution is undermined by political reality, empire as an idea becomes its own focus of millennial hope—particularly in France.[5] Against this background, the use of Roman costuming in the French Revolution suggests paradoxically both a post-imperial and a pre-imperial (republican) condition, thus both an invocation of the idea of empire, with its millennial force, and a superseding of that idea by a new and presumably purer eternal (republican) vision of Europe's destiny.

Curiously enough, the idea of an eighteenth-century millennial politics is confirmed by an important case to which it does not apply factually. The creation of the United States was in itself a relatively conservative expedient more or less dictated by circumstances and carried out by a group of intellectuals schooled in British constitutional history. But it is transformed after the fact into a millennialist vision, a revelation of the true political destiny of the whole world.[6] There are various reasons for this retrospective remaking of history. But it could not have happened at all if the perceived character of eighteenth-century political innovation did not suggest thinking in millennial dimensions, if the actual French and the phantom American events did not seem immediately understandable as instances of the secular millennialist maxim: *As we desire the world,* we rational constitution-writers, *as we envision the world,* in our own original political model, *so must it be,* in defiance of the unreasoning inertia of tradition, *so shall it be.*

The American and French experiments, moreover, have both proved in a strong sense successful. But never successful enough. Millennialism and modern politics, especially democratic politics, don't mix. Wherever the millennialist vision surfaces, it gets bogged down in reality, in details, debates, stupidities, confusions, and sheer malice. Surely this inevitable frustration of a basic millennial energy accounts for much of the peculiarity of French patriotism, and especially of American patriotism, which even today, for many people, is wedded not only to fanatical opinions on single words in the Constitution, but also to something called "fundamentalism," which leaps beyond Christianity into a Messianism that finds it hard to distinguish between the Old Testament and the daily newspaper.

And if even the relatively successful instances of a (real or apparent) political application of the secular millennialist maxim are doomed to endless frustration, what can we possibly expect from late eighteenth-century Germany, composed almost entirely of petty absolutist states neither large nor populous enough (nor, as a rule, even oppressive enough) to offer targets for serious political reform? Here, surely, if political millennialism should arise at all, it will meet with a level of frustration hardly imaginable elsewhere. Does this consideration contribute to an understanding of why philosophical aesthetics originates precisely in Germany?

There are many points that have yet to be nailed down before we can call these speculations an argument. But one point is clear, at least in the abstract. If an intellectual domain is needed in which a frustrated political millennialism might redeem itself, then a strictly autonomous aesthetic domain will serve better than any other—because in the aesthetic domain, *the secular millennialist maxim has the quality of simple truth.* In order for any discussion on aesthetic matters to take place, we must first recognize as beautiful, or worthy of aesthetic consideration, the objects or texts we intend to talk about. But this recognition is a matter of arbitrary judgment on our part; in effect that class of objects is whatever we want it to be. Thus we arrive at an aesthetic version of the secular millennialist maxim: *as we desire the collection of aesthetically discussible objects, as we freely decide the contents of that aesthetic "world," so must it be, so shall it be.* I will argue later, against Kant, that the idea of a strictly disinterested judgment is empirical nonsense, as is the idea that a judgment of taste automatically imputes a similar judgment to every human being. But even these opinions do not deny the operation of what we call "canon formation," the process by which we manage to decide and re-decide constantly the contents of the collection of objects and texts that we may use to found or illustrate aesthetic arguments. However blurry and changeable the boundaries of that collection may be.

A principal problem in understanding canon formation, of course, is to identify exactly which "we" represents omnipotent humanity in the aesthetic domain. I will show later that Moritz requires ultimately a unanimity of all mankind, whereas Adorno, like Goethe and Schiller before him,[7] insists that only a small self-selecting group is ever qualified to decide aesthetic matters in our name. But problems of this sort do not affect the main point: that in the aesthetic domain, human omnipotence is a simple fact, the secular millennialist maxim a simple truth. The irresolvable conflicts of the political domain simply vanish.

The trouble with the idea of the autonomous aesthetic domain as a safety valve, for pressures created by political contradictions, is that for most of the eighteenth century that domain did not yet exist as an option. The act or process of discovering it must therefore also have been the act or process of *creating* it—at least if it is as clearly distinguishable and as clearly *new* a domain as the idea of strict artistic autonomy seems to imply. And if these suppositions hold, then we must be able to locate that act or process in specific instances, not merely as a general event that supposedly manages to take place without anyone's actually carrying it out.

But at least one point can be held fast. The idea of an autonomous aesthetic domain, once formulated, is *useful* from a millennialist perspective, whereas it is hard to see how any particular use for millennialism follows from the idea of artistic autonomy. In other words, it is much easier to explain the idea of autonomy in a fundamentally millennialist aesthetics than it would be to derive the millennialist component of aesthetics from the idea of autonomy.

WHENCE AESTHETICS?

But again, where exactly does modern aesthetics come from? An excellent argument on the political origin of aesthetics, on aesthetics as a rationalist response to political frustration, is offered by Jonathan M. Hess in his book *Reconstituting the Body Politic.*[8] Unfortunately Hess accepts the widespread over-estimation of the idea of artistic autonomy. But his argument stays very close to the actual situation in eighteenth-century Germany and covers practically all the significant issues, including matters as subtle and subliminal as the use of specific metaphors in political discourse.

Especially important is his showing that the question of origination really exists, which he accomplishes mainly by a critique (109-18) of the historical narrative suggested by Jürgen Habermas. He points out that aesthetics (considered as the *theory* of autonomous art) is not even an issue for Habermas, who in effect regards it as a "second-order" phenomenon (113), a mere reflection of the supposed "institution of autonomous art" that is called into being by an early-capitalist "commodification of art works" (114). Habermas's argument portrays that commodification—along with the bourgeois appropriation of its "cultural product"[9] —as a single process affecting the whole of what is understood as "art." Thus it falls prey to a fallacious "aesthetic essentialism" (Hess, 118), to the historically untenable conception of "art" as a universal and unchanging category.

The question must first be understood: Where does aesthetic *theory* come from, given that there is no accepted cultural or institutional reality that requires it as an explanation? Then the general shape of an answer is inevitable. Aesthetics arises as the compensatory response to an impasse in some other area of thought—almost certainly politics. Hess's book covers the political side of the situation in admirable detail. It focuses on only three main figures, Moritz, Kant, and Schiller; but the amount of collateral material it adduces—including twentieth-century debates, the culture of literary periodicals in eighteenth-century Germany, and the history of political theory since Hobbes—makes its conclusion thoroughly convincing: that the "emergent concept of autonomous art does more than address problems caused by the expansion of the art market . . . [that it] also responds to fundamental anxieties about the possibility of a politicized Enlightenment [i.e., the possibility of actual political agency for Enlightenment thought] in late eighteenth-century Germany" (18). Especially in absolutist states like Frederick's Prussia, Enlightenment self-consciousness is encouraged in general, but finds that it includes the consciousness of its own political helplessness, its lack of any opportunity to assert rational principles in political life. The aesthetic domain is then invented (Hess suggests) as the setting in which to model a better integrated communal and political form of existence.

But a broadly conceived answer, based on many different kinds of evidence, is not the only kind of answer Hess's question requires. We also need specific instances in which we can actually observe aesthetics being born.

KANT AND HIS SPECTATORS

The most important such instance will probably be the birth of the aesthetic idea in Kant. The thought of the aesthetic part of the *Critique of Judgment*, along with its development by Schiller, is generally taken to be the cornerstone of the whole conception of an aesthetic domain in modern theory.

In order to orient ourselves, we turn again to Hannah Arendt, now to the lectures she gave on Kant's political philosophy at the New School for Social Research in 1970.

> In the center of Kant's moral philosophy stands the individual; in the center of his philosophy of history (or, rather, his philosophy of nature) stands the perpetual progress of the human race, or mankind. (Therefore: History from a general viewpoint.) The general viewpoint or standpoint is occupied . . . by the spectator, who is a "world citizen" or, rather, a "world spectator."It is he who decides, by having an idea of the whole, whether, in any single, particular event, progress is being made [toward freedom, or a durable republic, in every state, and toward a durable arrangement for keeping peace among states]. . . .
>
> Kant's actual theory in political affairs was the theory of perpetual progress and a federal union of the nations in order to give the *idea* of mankind a political reality. Whoever worked in this direction was welcome. But these ideas, with whose help he reflected on human affairs in general, are very different from the "wishful participation bordering on enthusiasm" that caught the spectators of the French Revolution and "the exaltation [of] the uninvolved public" looking on in sympathy "without the least intention of assisting." In his opinion, it was precisely this sympathy that made the revolution a "phenomenon . . . not to be forgotten"—or, in other words, that made it a public event of world-historical significance [i.e. , an event shadowing forth the goal of historical progress]. Hence: What constituted the appropriate public realm for this particular event were not the actors but the acclaiming spectators. [10]

Arendt shows repeatedly the importance for Kant of the figure of the "uninvolved" spectator of history, the "world citizen" whose views are not limited by the interests of any state or party. The non-involvement of such spectators does not imply that they have no effect in history. It is they, for example, who ensure that the French Revolution will be remembered in its true world-historical sense; and that memory will tend in turn to nudge mankind ever closer to the path of its true progress.

But this idea of historical spectating creates problems. Arendt quotes from Kant's *Perpetual Peace* the argument that "[in case the] rights of the people are injured, no injustice befalls the tyrant when he is deposed. There can be no doubt on this point. Nevertheless, it is in the highest degree illegitimate for the subjects to seek their rights in this way. If they fail in the struggle and are then subjected to severe punishment, they cannot complain about injustice any more than the tyrant could if they had succeeded." [11] And she comments: "What you see here clearly is the clash between the principle according to which you should act and the principle according to which you judge. For Kant condemns [on moral grounds, by "practical reason"] the very action whose results he then affirms [assuming the French revolution is meant here] with a satisfaction bordering on enthusiasm" (48). But is it really possible to live and think in the shadow of this contradiction between one's individual morality and one's judgment concerning the progress of mankind?

For Kant even the possibility is not enough. It must be the case that *in actual fact* "spectators" capable of living in the tension between morality and judgment form a relatively large and influential group in any civilization that claims to participate in progress toward the destiny of mankind. I say they must be a group because, as Arendt points out, "Spectators exist only in the plural. The spectator is not involved in the act, but he is always involved with fellow spectators" (63). And I say that group must exist *in actual fact* because if they did not, then there would be no one with an audible voice in the culture who could make valid judgments about human progress; hence there would be in effect no awareness of the existence of human progress as a tendency in history. Nature, on this supposition, would be carrying out mankind's destiny in a manner entirely concealed from us. Which leads to an absurdity, at least for Kant, who says, "Nature has willed that man should produce entirely by his own initiative everything which goes beyond the mechanical ordering of his animal existence, and that he should not partake of any other happiness or perfection than that which he has procured for himself without instinct and by his own reason."[12] Surely the "everything" that "man should produce by his own initiative" must include—once mankind has formed the idea of perpetual progress—precisely that perpetual progress which is our destiny. Nature's manipulation of our development can therefore no longer be *completely* hidden from us, which implies, as I said: Kant's historical "spectators" must exist *in actual fact.*

Perhaps our first inclination is to respond: of course they exist. Their existence is exactly what Habermas means by that of the "public sphere." It thus seems appropriate that 1784, the year of the "Idea for a General History with Cosmopolitan Intent" from which the passage above is quoted, is also the year of Kant's "Answer to the Question: What Is Enlightenment?" where the idea of a scholarly public is developed, whose communication among themselves is subject to no institutional restraints and may perhaps therefore approach the condition of "spectating" that Arendt insists on.

But the question of *possibility* has still not been answered. How is it possible to form an affirmative judgment of events in which one oneself could not have participated actively without violating basic morality? Impartiality and the freedom from institutional compulsion are not enough. One must be able to make a definite positive judgment with no conceptual justification whatever, if need be in defiance of practical reason. (Kant's idea of the ultimate aim of human history is perfectly amenable to conceptual formulation: freedom plus peace. But these concepts are never enough to determine a judgment about the historical significance or effect of any *particular* event. War, we read in the "Idea for a

General History," is often an important step forward; and the "Enlightenment" essay suggests that Frederick's absolutist regime contributes more toward the goal of freedom than a republic could.)[13] A merely impartial observer would say of the French Revolution: The tyrant was in the wrong and the revolutionaries are in the wrong; nothing in this whole struggle is morally right. This, more or less, was Schiller's view. But the historical "spectator" would add: And yet the victory of the revolution fills me with an enthusiastic hope for the future of mankind. How is such a judgment possible without violating the impartiality, the position above the fray, that its ignoring of practical reason presupposes?

THE BIRTH OF AESTHETICS

If we modify the question slightly; if we ask not how that judgment is possible, but rather *what kind* of judgment it is; if we keep in mind, moreover, that such a judgment is accompanied by visionary or millennialist pleasure ("philosophy too may have its *chiliastic* expectations");[14] and if we add the criterion that it must be a type of judgment that people commonly make in reality, at least a certain class of people (a criterion that follows from the need that historical "spectators" exist in actual fact): then the answer becomes reasonably clear. We are talking about judgments of the same basic type as the judgment that some particular object is beautiful.

For Kant this answer will not become valid until the whole theory of such judgments has been worked out in the *Critique of Judgment*. But all the material that is needed, in order to make the possibility of historical "spectating" a crucial question, is already there in the two major essays of 1784, especially in the "Idea for a General History," where the "Fourth Proposition" stresses contradictions between the asymptotically approached goal of human development and some of the means by which we are constrained to approach it. And the suggestion that "spectating" itself may operate as a shaping force in history is also already present: in the sketch, from the "Enlightenment" essay, of a public forum where advanced thinking is encouraged; and in the "Idea," where we read:

> We can see that philosophy too may have its *chiliastic* expectations; but they are of such a kind that their fulfillment can be hastened, if only indirectly, by a knowledge of the idea they are based on, so that they are anything but over-fanciful. . . .
>
> A philosophical attempt to work out a universal history of the world in accordance with a plan of nature aimed at a perfect civil union of mankind must be regarded as possible and even as capable for furthering the purpose of nature itself.[15]

Kant is referring here mainly to the general idea of a natural human destiny; but it is hard to see how that idea can be formed or sustained without judgments concerning particular events. The question of the possibility of such judgments, the possibility of valid historical "spectating," is therefore already implied as a problem in 1784; the experience of the French Revolution in 1789 then certainly raises the stakes for Kant;[16] and the question is answered, finally, in the *Critique of Judgment*. Thus, step by step, modern aesthetics is generated—without the production or influence of a single work of art—by problems in politics and history.

In the course of struggling with issues that are basically political, Kant writes a book that becomes a principal force in establishing the idea of an independent aesthetic domain, a domain in which art, along with its reception and criticism, is not subordinated to any version of metaphysics, any level of morality, any form of utility. Actually, it should have been clear from the outset that in order to establish the possibility of the judgments of historical "spectators," Kant would need to argue indirectly, by showing judgments of a *similar* type. For the historical judgments he has in mind are by definition valid with respect to human history regarded as progress. (They enforce their own validity by being strictly true to type, perfectly disinterested yet enthusiastically human—and capable, in addition, of actually shaping history by influencing how particular events are remembered.) Therefore a direct showing of their possibility would have to include a showing of their validity, which would involve a judgment of exactly the type whose possibility has yet to be shown.

The *Critique of Judgment* turns out to be a book on aesthetics, especially in its effects. But the signs of its nativity, its birthmarks, are easily discerned. The general class of aesthetic judgments—judgments not based on concepts but associated with a disinterested pleasure and made in the name of all humanity—certainly includes all the judgments of genuine historical "spectating." And the idea that the progress of mankind often requires means that seem to contradict the ultimate goal is present in the idea of aesthetic judgments that involve a "negative" component, judgments concerning the "dynamically sublime."[17] As Arendt points out (52-53), the relevant part of the *Critique of Judgment* includes an aesthetic appreciation of war, as an instance of the sublime (§ 28, *KantsWerke*, 5: 262-63), which parallels the frequently called-for positive historical judgment of war that is spoken of in the "Idea for a General History."

Then, at the very end of the aesthetic section of the *Critique of Judgment,* Kant seems to get worried about having focused his work *too* exclusively upon the question of beauty. In § 59 he provides something like a moral justification for his thinking after all, by asserting that beauty is a "symbol of morality"—which implies no inherent connection between the two concepts but only an analogy, involving the immediacy of our pleasure at the beautiful, its separateness from any antecedent interest, the free conformity of imagination with understanding achieved in it, and its claim to universal validity (5: 353-54). Yet even this mere analogy has moral value, by making possible an easy transition from "sensory charm" to an "habitual moral interest."

And in § 60, we come all the way back to the specific concerns of the "Idea for a General History" when we read:

> The propaedeutic to all fine art . . . seems to lie in the cultivation of mental powers by the preliminary study of *humaniora*—presumably so called because "humanity" means a general *sympathy* and also the ability to *communicate* universally and with perfect sincerity, which two qualities, in combination, make up mankind's proper sociability . . . The age and the peoples [that were characterized by] a drive toward *lawful* sociability, by which an enduring community is produced . . . had to invent the art of communicating ideas between their most and least cultivated classes . . . [as] a mean between higher culture and unpretentious nature which then constitutes the standard, derivable from no general rules, for taste as well, considered as a universal human sense. (5: 355-56)

Kant is now careful to limit the independence of art and of taste by tying them to specific achievements in the progress of human society, or even more specifically, to the study of Greek and Roman antiquity (*humaniora*). And in the last paragraph of the section he returns to the analogy of beauty with morality, which has now somehow become a *determining* factor in taste. "Since taste is basically [*im Grunde!*] an ability to judge the sensory manifestation of moral ideas (by way of a certain analogy in the reflection upon both) . . . it is evident that the true propaedeutic to the foundation of taste is the development of moral ideas and the cultivation of moral feeling" (5: 356). The whole problematics of the "Idea for a General History" thus reappears in its progeny, the theory of taste, which now presupposes both elements of its besetting inner conflict, the progress of society and the unbending demands of morality.

It may even be that in these last two sections of the "Critique of Aesthetic Judgment," Kant is toying with the idea that he has found a *solution* to the problem of historical "spectating." For if all taste can be measured against a perfected version of itself that is founded on "moral ideas" and "moral feeling, " then it could conceivably be argued that in all historical judgments (considered as essentially judgments of taste) there is an indwelling moral orientation which compensates for whatever apparent conflicts may arise with the demands of practical reason.

And toward the end of his book's second part, the "Critique of Teleological Judgment," we again have the impression that Kant may be claiming a solution to historical-political problems. For § 83 recapitulates—in condensed form, under the rubric of "Cultur der . . . Geschicklichkeit" [culture of skill] (5: 431-33)—practically the whole content of the "Idea for a General History with Cosmopolitan Intent": especially the argument that nature's "ultimate intention, " with respect to humanity, is "the development of our natural capacities" ("Naturanlagen"), and that this intention can be achieved only by the establishment of "civil society" and a "cosmopolitan" system of cooperating states. But here, in the final pages of the *Critique of Judgment,* this argument is relativized. Alongside the "culture of skill" is placed a more advanced "culture of discipline" whose task is "to make possible for *will* the determination and choice of its own purposes [as opposed to purposes of nature]" (5: 432). And human progress as an intention of nature, accordingly, is overshadowed by "the final purpose of the existence of a world, " which is "man, considered as noumenon . . . as a subject of morality" (§ 84, 5: 434-35).

Thus the progress of humanity has fallen to a lower point on the scale of "purposes." But it has also been made more accessible in the process; its judgments have become less of a problem. For in the "Idea for a General History" we are asked simply to accept the supposition that nature has a purpose for mankind, whereas in the larger context of the *Critique of Judgment,* that supposition is shown to be one which we are entitled to make in the exercise of "reflective judgment" (5: 429)—which must surely entail a gain in substance and probability for individual judgments by the historical "spectator." Of course questions of human progress and historical judgment are not uppermost in Kant's mind at the end of the *Critique of Judgment.* He has other fish to fry. But he comes back to those questions later, and with an energy that certainly owes something to the *Critique* as a re-situating of his political thought.

We have, then, one possible answer to the question of how modern aesthetics is born: almost by accident, in a book which starts out as the circuitous attempt to justify a millennialist theory of historical and political progress and ends up at fundamental questions of theology and belief; a book which in its complicated journey produces what many modern readers consider a definitive statement of the idea of aesthetic autonomy, but whose author then feels morally called upon to rein in exactly that aspect of it. The idea of using judgments of taste to model historical judgments seems harmless enough in itself. But the systematic development of that idea in the *Critique* produces a suggestion of aesthetic autonomy which Kant himself is unwilling to sign onto. Surely the basic structure of ideas in the genesis of aesthetics is evident here: the relation between a primary millennialist vision (displaced from politics) and a derived or secondary idea of aesthetic autonomy.

MILLENNIALISM AND FACT

The relationship between secular millennialism and fact is inherently paradoxical, nowhere more manifestly so than in Kant. On the one hand, since it is not supported by either faith or revelatory scripture, secular millennialism always needs support in the domain of fact. Kant freely admits to being the millennalist (or "chiliast" as he puts in, in Greek) that

I have suggested he was; and his early millennialist idea of progress, as nature's purpose for mankind, requires logically the existence *in actual fact* of a substantial number of thinkers capable of making valid judgments concerning the place of specific events in the course of history. But on the other hand, secular millennialism is also tempted to claim *dominion* over fact, the authority and ability to create its own factuality at the expense of whatever competing facts may confront it. This is the totalitarian move. I am not suggesting that Kant was a totalitarian political theorist *avant la lettre*. But in the next chapter we will observe that in the *Critique of Judgment* he masks the essential millennialism of his argument by presenting it in the form of statements of fact. Millennialism and factuality, for Kant, have a way of acting like two sides of the same coin.

I make this point as justification in advance for a position I will adopt in the next chapter: that Kant's critical project, especially the *Critique of Judgment*, may properly be criticized by arguments concerning fact. It is true that such arguments can never shake off their dependence on *opinion*. If, in your opinion, my argument distorts the facts I claim as its basis, I shall never convince you of the conclusions I draw. The debate between us will tend to become messy. But my point is that precisely this messy ground of facts and opinions—and practical politics—is where Kant's work should be debated, not in a sterile conceptual atmosphere where the value of his thought is meant to follow from its systematic closure. Kant himself, in any case, seems not to have had the foggiest conception of debate, despite his study of Leibniz. Even a staunch defender like Hannah Arendt, in attempting to show his openness to "the testing that arises from contact with other people's thinking" (42), can do no better than cite his supposed "impartiality." But impartiality—for Kant as for anyone else—is not a way of actually encountering the thought of others; it is a way of claiming infallible *rightness*, of occupying the position of judge, not contestant.

It is only on the messy ground of conflicting opinions that fact is fact. (The *concept* of "fact" is not a fact but a concept.) And it is only here, I will argue, that a reasonable judgment can be made concerning the value of Kant's insistence on the factuality of his millennial vision in the *Critique of Judgment*. Secular millennialism, again, has a tendency to defy fact, to claim power over it. And Kant's implied claim to exercise no power whatever in the domain of fact, to take fact simply as it is given, therefore has a peculiar sort of significance in exactly that domain.

ANOTHER BIRTH OF AESTHETICS

The one instance of the origination of aesthetics we have looked at, in Kant, may be central enough to support the whole historical argument of the present book. "Pre-aesthetic" thinking discussed in the next chapter is notable for developing the idea that the activity or experience of the recipient plays an indispensable part in giving a work of art its very nature. But only Kant's addition of a millennial dimension to this thinking makes possible: on one hand, Schiller's grand historical claims, and Hegel's after him; and on the other hand, the idea of an autonomous aesthetic domain, the idea of "art for art's sake" as the later nineteenth century phrases it. And later we will treat in detail Kant's theoretical insistence on the unitary human subject, which has the effect of millennializing the problem of communication and provoking Schleiermacher's anti-millennial venture into hermeneutics, a venture which in turn is picked up and re-millennialized by Dilthey, producing a revival of Schillerian aesthetics. Thus Kant, the originally political "chiliast, "is found at the meeting point of several different strains in the aesthetic project. We might reasonably be tempted to consider him the father of the whole thing.

But still, it will help the argument if we can show that the shift from political to aesthetic millennialism is not just a Kantian idiosyncrasy. And the particular case that suggests itself is that of Karl Philipp Moritz. Jonathan Hess, in the book mentioned earlier, argues that although Moritz is by and large *"not* a political writer" (123), still, it is the free and cheerful (un-Prussian) political life he had observed in England in 1782 that later provides "the context, occasion and ultimately the model for [his] concept of aesthetic autonomy" (126). The argument in detail is lucid, and it is not hard to agree with Hess when he concludes:

> Like statecraft, aesthetic judgment enacts a process in which individuals come together to create a collective body. And the collective body these judging subjects create gives them a form of pleasure Moritz marks [in several essays] as the negation of the bodily pleasure central to the functioning of the absolutist body politic. By setting up art-as-such in opposition to the mechanical arts, Moritz envisions the creation of a social body that has precisely the internal purposiveness and free spontaneity of his vision of the Lockean body politic, a social body whose "true, complete presence" [the "wahres volles Dasein" that Moritz attributes to the *artwork*] derives from the individual acts of judgment that bring it into existence. Unlike the absolutist body politic, which recreated its subjects in its own image as machines, the work of art is created by its judging subjects in such a way as to embody the individual and collective free spontaneity Moritz's political anthropology set up as a political norm. (171-72)[18]

There is an obvious resonance here with my argument earlier that the secular millennialist maxim sheds many of its problems in the aesthetic domain. If Hess is correct, Moritz's thinking offers a clearer and simpler instance of that argument than Kant's.

The trouble is that Hess goes out of his way to organize his thinking around the idea of autonomy, rather than that of millennialism, which leads to unnecessary obscurities. We read, for example, that in making aesthetic judgments, "the human being—which is not an end in itself but only the end of useful objects and the means of the mechanical rationality of the absolutist body politic—is able to construct an objective entity [the artwork] that has the internal purposiveness it [the human being] lacks, an object whose governing laws are antithetical to the instrumental rationality of the absolutist state" (169). I do not think this complicated web of analogies—connecting the individual human being, the art object, and at least two different types of collective—is convincing in itself, as the description of an historical node, or even helpful in Hess's basic argument. There is still room for confusion here. We need to look at Moritz's thinking in detail.

THE QUESTION OF PURPOSE

Let us begin with a passage in Moritz's "Attempt at a Unification of All Beaux-Arts and Belles-Lettres" which is often cited as evidence of the importance of artistic autonomy for its author.

> Wir bedürfen des Schönen nicht so sehr, um dadurch ergötzt zu werden, als das Schöne unsrer bedarf, um erkannt zu werden. Wir können sehr gut ohne die Betrachtung schöner Kunstwerke bestehen, diese aber können, als solche, nicht wohl ohne unsre Betrachtung bestehen. Jemehr wir sie also entbehren können, desto mehr betrachten wir sie um ihrer selbst willen, um ihnen durch unsre Betrachtung gleichsam erst ihr wahres volles Dasein zu geben. Denn durch unsre zunehmende Anerkennung des Schönen in einem schönen Kunstwerke, vergrößern wir gleichsam seine Schönheit selber, und legen immer mehr Werth hinein. Daher das ungeduldige Verlangen, daß alles dem Schönen huldigen soll, welches wir einmal dafür erkannt haben: je allgemeiner es als schön erkannt und bewundert wird, desto mehr Werth erhält es auch in unsern Augen. (2: 945)[19]

[It is not so much that we need the beautiful for our pleasure, as that the beautiful needs us, in order to be recognized. We can exist perfectly well without observing beautiful works of art, but these works cannot exist, as such, without our observing them. The more we can thus do without them, by so much more do we observe them for their own sake, in order as it were to endow them, for the first time, with their own full existence by our contemplation. For by means of our increasing recognition of the beautiful in a beautiful work of art, we increase, so to speak, its own beauty and endow it with more and more value. Hence our impatient desire that everyone should pay homage to beauty where we have recognized it; the more generally it is recognized and admired as beautiful, the more value it acquires in our eyes.]

The similarity of the last sentences to Kant's argument that an aesthetic judgment automatically imputes the same judgment to every human being (*Critique of Judgment*, § 6) is clear, as is the bridge Moritz creates (before the fact) between Kant's argument and the idea that a work of art is *constituted*, brought into full existence, only in the process of its reception. An idea of artistic autonomy also seems to be suggested here, in that any instrumentality of the artwork is denied. But what is the value of this suggestion?

If we look at the essay as a whole, our attention is drawn to Moritz's inability to let go of the concept of "purpose" (*Zweck*). This is bad news for the historian of an "autonomous" aesthetic domain; for if art has a purpose apart from itself, its autonomy vanishes. Moritz does suggest that the individual work of art is constructed and positioned so as to give the impression of having no external purpose. But a very precarious argument by analogy—which Hess makes but Moritz does not—is needed if one wishes to conclude from this point that aesthetics, or art as such, is an autonomous domain.

The essay's dedication to Moses Mendelssohn already signals its focus on the question of purpose. Mendelssohn is credited (by implication) with advances in the discussion of the purpose of beautiful art, especially by comparison with Batteux; yet he is also criticized (by implication) for his failure to go beyond the idea of pleasure *(Vergnügen)* in this regard.[20] Moritz himself, in seeking the "Hauptendzweck" (2: 943) [chief ultimate purpose] of fine art and poetic literature, proposes to take one crucial step further. Pleasure, he says, is not a sufficient criterion because we also receive pleasure from that which is merely useful, not beautiful. The question is: what kind of pleasure? The pleasure I feel in contemplating a useful object, says Moritz, arises from my understanding of how the object can increase my "ease or comfort, " how it can thus make *my* existence more perfect.

> The merely useful object is thus not something whole or completed in itself, but becomes such only by achieving its purpose in me, or by being completed in me.—But in contemplating the beautiful, I roll its purpose out of *my*self and back into the object *it*self; I regard it as something *completed in itself*, not in me, something that makes up a whole in itself and gives me pleasure *for its own sake*—in that I do not assign the beautiful object a relation to myself, but rather assign myself a relation to it. Since, therefore, I cherish the beautiful more for its own sake, the useful merely for my sake, it follows that the beautiful affords me a higher and more unselfish pleasure than the merely useful. (2: 943-44)

This passage gives us problems if we try to read the whole as an assertion of artistic autonomy. Moritz does not say either that the beautiful object has no purpose or that it contains its own purpose. He says that in contemplating such an object, I must "roll that purpose out of myself"—the German verb *wälzen* suggests "roll with effort"—and roll it "back into the object." What exactly is meant by this metaphor?

The beautiful, it appears, requires an action or effort on our part in order to become what it is—which recalls the passage we started with (2: 945). And shortly after the above passage, we receive a fairly clear explanation of what Moritz has in mind.

> Even the sweet astonishment, the *pleasurable forgetting of our self* in contemplating a beautiful art work, is a proof that our pleasure here is something subordinate that we willingly permit to be determined by the beautiful, to which we cede, for a time, a kind of dominion over all our feelings. . . . In that moment we sacrifice our limited individual existence in favor of a higher existence. Our pleasure in the beautiful must therefore approach ever more closely the condition of unselfish *love* if it is to be genuine. (2: 945-46)

Whatever "the beautiful" is in itself—which Moritz doesn't say anything about—its importance for us is that it provides the occasion for an act of self-transcendence on our part, a movement of self-liberation from the individual limitedness that characterizes most of our experience.

Moritz means not merely a passive condition of selflessness or self-abstraction, but an *act* of self-transcendence—which is conveyed by the idea of laboriously rolling away from ourselves the purpose of the object, the idea of resisting forcefully the presumably natural tendency to ask what use it is to us. For if we think of our response to the work of art as a merely passive condition, then we must regard that condition as: (1) a type of pleasure; and (2) the ultimate purpose of the work of art, which would alone be operative in our relation to it. And Moritz reduces these ideas to an absurdity. "How does pleasure arise if not from the intuition of purposefulness [*Zweckmäßigkeit*]? Now if there were something of which pleasure itself were the sole purpose [*Zweck*], then I could only judge the purposefulness of that thing by the pleasure I got from it. My pleasure, however, can arise only from that act of judgment; so my pleasure would have to be there before it could be there" (2: 949). This reasoning is not actually as sound as it wants to be; but it does demonstrate that in Moritz's opinion, my self-transcending response to the work of art must be an act on my part, not a passive response to the object. And it is a natural development of this thought when we read, in "Über die bildende Nachahmung des Schönen," that only the creating genius can experience "the highest enjoyment" of art (2: 974). How are we supposed to derive the idea of an autonomous aesthetic domain from these considerations? Has the beautiful not been subordinated here to a system of psychological or spiritual self-management? or to a hierarchy of strictly subjective achievements culminating in perfect self-transcendence or perfect creativity?

PSYCHOLOGY AND MILLENNIAL VISION

But if we now ask after the millennial aspect of this thinking, and its relation to millennial politics, the answer is not difficult. From very early in his career Moritz is interested in the idea of psychology as a science. And in 1782, the year of his visit to England, he writes a "Prospectus for a Magazine on Experimental Psychology," in which he argues that the new science must be based entirely on case studies, that until "a sufficient number of facts" are collected—concerning *individual* human beings—no attempt should be made at creating "a purposeful whole" (1: 797). Like Schiller after him, Moritz aims at rescuing individual human existence from the generalizing and regimenting tendencies of the age; and like Schiller's, Moritz's thinking on this point has a strong political component. In a little essay called "Einheit—Mehrheit—menschliche Kraft,"[21] which Hess repeatedly calls attention to, Moritz indicates that the most damaging effect of absolutist politics is that it dismantles the human totality of each individual subject and creates a society of humanoid machines whose actions are dissociated from any personal wishes or intentions.

There is no evidence in Moritz's work that he thinks this situation can be ameliorated on the level of practical politics; there is no political bridge from Frederick's Prussia to even as imperfect a parliamentary state as George III's England. But in the "Prospectus" of 1782, with reference to the projected psychological publication, we read:

> What an important work for humanity this could become! It would offer the only way for the human race, by its own efforts, to become more acquainted with itself, to vault upward to a higher degree of perfection, just as an individual person becomes more perfect through self-knowledge. [The *Magazine for Experimental Psychology*] would then become a universal mirror in which the human race might observe itself. And if such a spirit of observation were once brought to life, and if it maintained its focus on this important material of human knowledge, what important steps forward could be made in just a few years. (1: 797)

Given that the new science is meant to be based firmly on techniques for observing people as whole, integrated individuals, it follows that the extravagant hopes Moritz expresses here are at bottom a millennial politics. There is no immediate practical way of opposing the absolutist state. But if humanity's idea of itself is reformed universally, with a newly whole and integrated human individual at its center, then the absolutist politics of anti-individualism will dissolve of its own accord.

In order to make the connection with Moritz's aesthetics, we need only go a few pages further in the "Prospectus," where the question is raised of *how* the factual basis for a new psychology will be assembled.

How will people develop the needful competence for the work of assembling facts? The answer is fairly obvious:

> Whoever wants to train himself as a true observer of the human will have to start with himself. . . . He will have to be attentive to the present reality of his life; he will have to note the ebb and flow in his soul all day long, and the differences between each moment and the next; he will have to take the time to describe the growth of his thoughts and to make himself the object of his own unceasing scrutiny; it is not necessary that he lack strong passions, but he must also master the art, at various times, of lifting himself up suddenly out of the turmoil of his desires in order to act as a cold, completely disinterested observer of himself. (1: 799)

Then, says Moritz, "the observer of the human" will be able to apply his abilities to people other than himself (1: 800-801). But his most important ability is still the "art" of self-transcendence.

> But who will guarantee that the observer of man always has enough coolness and serenity of soul to regard everything that happens as a kind of stage-play, to regard the people who offend him as mere actors? If only he were not himself involved in the play. If only there were no possibility of role-envy.—But what shall one do when one is oppressed by people or by fate and can bear it no longer? What better and nobler expedient than to lift oneself up over this earth and over oneself, so to speak, as if one were a being different from oneself, in a higher region, able to smile at all those troubles, and thus at oneself, at one's own laments and grievances—able to smile—to take it all as a mere play—what ecstasy, what an uplifting to the all-embracing creator of the universe! (1: 801-2)

What is required is exactly the aesthetic self-transcendence spoken of in the "Beaux-Arts and Belles-Lettres" essay, self-transcendence not as an absolute but as an act, an experience one can achieve from time to time by one's own efforts.

In fact it is clear that the unspoken ultimate aim of Moritz's "experimental psychology" is to make *all humans* into "observers of the human" and knowers of themselves. The "magazine," when it comes out, is entitled ΓΝΩΘΙ ΣΑΥΤΟΝ [know thyself], and offers itself to "learned and non-learned readers alike" (1: 1261). The psychology in question is thus a millennial psychology in the service of a millennial politics. And Moritz's aesthetics, in turn, finds its "purpose" in being part and parcel of that millennial endeavor.

The idea of purpose is of course also central in the *Critique of Judgment.* In fact, it seems to me quite likely that a recognition of Moritz's conceptual difficulties prompts Kant's attempt, in §§ 10-11, to dissociate the concepts of *Zweckmäßigkeit* and *Zweck*, so that the idea of a "purposefulness (or purposiveness) without purpose" becomes possible. Kant thus avoids the problem of how to deal with the purpose of the beautiful—which for Moritz must be part of my aesthetic response (since "purposiveness" is not conceptualized independently) and must then be "rolled back" into the beautiful object. But I do not think that Kant's conceptual move here actually accomplishes anything for the idea of artistic autonomy, or is even intended to do so. The notion of "purposiveness" in the *Critique of Judgment* only has the effect of de-aestheticizing the argument by embedding it more firmly in the critique of teleology (the study of ends or purposes)—and in the conditional justification of teleological reasoning—that is ultimately aimed at.

THEOLOGY OF ART?

The idea of artistic autonomy, or of an autonomous aesthetic domain, has its place in the eighteenth century only as a corollary of millennial thinking. Schiller's *Aesthetic Letters* contain the clearest assertion of such autonomy; but we will see that they also carry out a refutation of the whole aesthetic project. The main reason we look for artistic autonomy in the eighteenth century is probably our need to provide a pedigree for the many and varied nineteenth-century versions of what seems to us a religion of art or of beauty: in the Romanticisms, in Cousin, Baudelaire, Arnold, Wagner, Ruskin, Nietzsche's *Birth of Tragedy*, late-century aesthetic "decadence." But my point is that if we try to grasp aesthetics as a connected unfolding in history, we find not a religious tradition but the development of a millennialism at least strongly dissociated from its religious counterpart.

I think this point can be upheld even in Moritz's case. I say "even" because many scholars are of the opinion that Moritz "salvages the rejected religious creed of selfless, disinterested love for God by translating it into a secular theory of the disinterestedness of aesthetic pleasure."[22] That this formulation is Jonathan Hess's is interesting because it produces a contradiction in his own argument.

Hess is correct in asserting (178) that the "quietism" or "separatism" depicted at the beginning of *Anton Reiser* (Werke, 1: 87) is regarded by Moritz as a "psychological disorder" that must be cured "by focusing 'the attention of the human being more on the human being himself' and 'making his individual presence more important to him.'"[23] But when he then understands Moritz's aesthetics as only a secularized version of that quietist selflessness, he is forced to imagine that he has come up against:

> one of the great ironies of public culture in the 1780s . . . Moritz formulates the concept of autonomous art as an attempted solution to the impasse of his political version of the Enlightenment discourse on anthropology in such a way as to diagnose his own aesthetic solution as a psychological disorder of the first degree. He conceives of autono-

mous art as the remedy for the problems of his political anthropology at the same time [as] he offers up a program of moral medicine that subjects this remedy to a rather severe diagnosis. (179)

This is more than just an "irony." It is a simple contradiction, either in Moritz's thought or in Hess's.

I think that the contradiction is Hess's, and that it arises from a very simple misreading of Moritz, which Hess shares with many critics before him. The passages describing the quietism that Moritz rejects read as follows:

> Das ganze Hauswesen bis auf den geringsten Dienstboten bestand aus lauter solchen Personen, deren Bestreben nur dahin ging, oder zu gehen schien, in ihr *Nichts* (wie es die Mad. Guion nennt) wieder einzugehen, alle Leidenschaften zu *ertöten,* und alle *Eigenheit* auszurotten. . . . In allen Mienen glaubte man *Ertötung* und *Verleugnung,* und in allen Handlungen *Ausgehen aus sich selbst* und *Eingehen ins Nichts* zu lesen. (1: 87-88)

> [The whole inhabitancy of the house, down to the lowest servant, consisted of nothing but people whose every effort was (or seemed to be) aimed at going back to their *Nothingness* (as Mme. Guyon calls it), at *extinguishing* all passions and exterminating all *my-own-ness*. . . . In all faces one seemed to read *extinction* and *denial,* in all actions *the going out of oneself* and *going into nothingness.*]

And the main passage from the essay on "Beaux-Arts and Belles-Lettres" with which they are paralleled is:

> Auch das süße Staunen, das *angenehme Vergessen unsrer selbst* bei Betrachtung eines schönen Kunstwerks, ist ein Beweis, daß unser Vergnügen hier etwas untergeordnetes ist, das wir freiwillig erst durch das Schöne bestimmt werden lassen, welchem wir eine Zeitlang eine Art Obergewalt über alle unsre Empfindungen einräumen. Während das Schöne unsre Betrachtung ganz auf sich zieht, zieht es sie eine Weile von uns selber ab, und macht, daß wir uns in dem schönen Gegenstande zu verlieren scheinen; und eben dies Verlieren, dies Vergessen unsrer selbst, ist der höchste Grad des reinen und uneigennützigen Vergnügens, welches uns das Schöne gewährt. (2: 945)

> [Even the sweet astonishment, the *pleasurable forgetting of our self* in contemplating a beautiful art work, is a proof that our pleasure here is something subordinate that we willingly permit to be determined by the beautiful, to which we cede, for a time, a kind of dominion over all our feelings. In that the beautiful draws our observation to itself, it draws it away from our self and makes it seem that we lose ourselves in the beautiful object. And exactly this loss, this forgetting of our self is the highest degree of that pure and unselfish pleasure which beauty affords us.]

Do these passages really suggest a direct line of development from the religious to the aesthetic?

As far as their meaning goes, I don't think the passages are even similar. In the aesthetic essay Moritz is speaking of a type of pleasure *(Vergnügen)*; and nothing could be further than pleasure from "the teachings of Mme. Guyon," which are "strikingly similar to those of the most extreme stoicism" (1: 89). Moritz insists on the temporary quality of aesthetic rapture ("eine Zeitlang," "eine Weile"), whereas the quietists strive uninterruptedly ("in allen Mienen," "in allen Handlungen") for their extinction of self. Above all, the aesthetic rapture attaches itself to the contemplation of an actual physical object, whereas the quietists seek to abandon everything physical in favor of "nothingness." Their favorite posture, says Moritz, is "seated with closed eyes, their heads laid on the table," waiting for "the voice of God or the *inner word*" (1: 87). And if we take into account the essay "On the Artistic Imitation of the Beautiful," the gap becomes even larger. For that essay ends in a paean to the diametrical opposite of "nothingness":

> Even death and destruction are lost in the concept of the *eternally fashioning imitation of the beautiful that is itself uplifted over all fashioning,* the beautiful that cannot be imitated except by *constantly self-rejuvenating existence.*
>
> By this ever self-rejuvenating existence, *we ourselves are.*
>
> That we ourselves *are* is our highest and noblest thought. —
>
> And no more sublime word can be spoken of the beautiful by mortal lips than: *it is!* (2: 991)

How a "salvaging" of quietist religiosity can be attributed to Moritz— even allowing for Goethe's participation in the "Artistic Imitation" essay—is beyond me.

As far as I know, M. H. Abrams was the first to speak of eighteenth-century aesthetic beginnings as a "theology of art." But in fairness to him it must be remarked that he does not actually conflate aesthetics and religion. The question he poses is: "whatever the changing historical circumstances which required, or at least fostered, a new kind of art-theory [in the eighteenth century], was there at hand an intellectual prototype that would satisfy the requirement and whose familiarity to philosophers might explain why the theory of art-as-such, once brought into criticism, developed so rapidly and was accepted so readily and so widely?" (84). And his answer is certainly true as far as it goes: that there was such a prototype "in [various] doctrines of Christian love" (94). The trouble is that by connecting the ideas of aesthetics and religion, that answer opens the way to a confusing of important historical issues.

I think I can clarify my own position on this matter without needing to enter the debate on secularity and secularization that I have resolved to steer clear of. In the case of authors like Matthew Arnold, for instance, the question of degrees and modes of secularity is important. For Arnold, humanity is not only an end in itself; it is also a vessel for quests beyond itself. "At the bottom of both the Greek and the Hebrew notion is the desire, native in man, for reason and the will of God, the feeling after the universal order, — in a word, the love of God." [24] This thinking is obvious- ly religious; but the idea of God is non-specific and broad enough to be worshipped by a culture of beauty, a culture suffused with "aërial ease, clearness, and radiancy . . . sweetness and light" (6: 127). Therefore, in order to find one's way here, one has to imagine a continuum of possibil- ities connecting the religious and the artistic.

No such continuum of possibilities connects the secular millennialist tradition of aesthetics with any specific religious tradition, millennialist or otherwise. As I have pointed out, the millennialist background out of which aesthetics emerges is political, not religious. Perhaps it must be admitted that neither political nor aesthetic millennialism could persist without the supporting analogy, the habit of mind, that is supplied by the history of Christian millennialism. But the relationship in this form is considerably attenuated and permits us to make distinctions. Aesthetics is separable from the general shift of intellectual emphases that we speak of as secularization from the seventeenth century on. It generates its own definite millennialist tradition in the nineteenth century. And if a thinker like Matthew Arnold is affected at all by that tradition, then it is not the religious aspect of his thought that is affected.

It is tempting to think of art—along with the study, cultivation, and enjoyment of art—as a direct substitute for religious feeling in post-En- lightenment Europe, at least among the upper classes. In one specific case, such a mechanism of substitution does operate. When the art of "literature" is created and conceptualized in the eighteenth century as a single category meant to include all of the different and separate poetic arts that we now speak of as its "genres," it very quickly takes the form of *national* literature, and as such assumes a prominent role in Europe's developing public schools, which in turn gradually displace churches as the single social institution that practically everyone participates in. Liter- ature thus becomes, in each national case, something very like a state religion, which goes a long way toward accounting for the editorial and exegetic practices that give its texts the aura of holy scripture.

But even though there is a political component in literature's preser- vation of religious terms and ideas, its situation is entirely different from that of aesthetics. The new art of literature serves as a substitute in relig- ion's long history of relations with politics; a new faith in the nineteenth- century nation-state is now meant to arise after the model of religious faith, as either a supplement or a substitute. But the process of substitu- tion does not operate in the genesis of aesthetics. Aesthetics is forced into existence, at a point of political impasse, in the form of a *project*: for Moritz psychology, for Kant the reform of political thinking, for Schiller, presumably, the "education" named in the title of his *Letters*. In the following chapters we will experiment with various ways of characterizing this project as a single whole. But a project it always is, a plan of action, despite its millennialist dimension, despite what most judicious minds would consider the unattainability of its aims. Its ambition is millennial; but it is still, precisely, ambition, not faith or hope or prophecy. This is what I mean by calling it "secular."

NOTES

1. Alexander Gottlieb Baumgarten, *Meditationes philosophicae de nonnullis ad poemapertinentibus: Philosophische Betrachtungen über einige Bedingungen des Gedichtes*, ed. and trans. Heinz Paetzold (Hamburg, 1983), § 116, where aesthetics is called the "science of perception." English translations of Baumgarten's *Meditationes* are taken from *Reflections on Poetry: Alexander Gottlieb Baumgarten's* Meditationes philosophicae de nonnullis ad poema pertinentibus, trans. Karl Aschenbrenner and William B. Holther (Berkeley, 1954).

2. See especially Jonathan M. Hess, *Reconstituting the Body Politic: Enlightenment, Public Culture and the Invention of Aesthetic Autonomy* (Detroit, 1999), and Martha Woodmansee, "The Interests of Disinterestedness: Karl Philipp Moritz and the Emergence of the Theory of Aesthetic Autonomy in Eighteenth-Century Germany," *MLQ,* 45 (1984), 22-47. Woodmansee's ideas are developed in her book, *The Author, Art, and the Market: Rereading the History of Aesthetics* (New York, 1994).

3. Parallels to this idea occur frequently in thinking on secularity. Charles Taylor, for instance, in discussing post-Darwinian secularity, insists, "What happened here was not that a moral outlook bowed to brute facts. Rather we might say that one moral outlook gave way to another. Another model of what was higher triumphed. And much was going for this model: images of power, of untrammeled agency, of spiritual self-possession (the 'buffered self')." See Taylor, *A Secular Age* (Cambridge, Mass., 2007), 563.

4. Hannah Arendt, *The Origins of Totalitarianism*, New Edition with Added Prefaces (San Diego: Harvest Books, 1985), 387.

5. On this point see Frances A. Yates, *Astraea: The Imperial Theme in the Sixteenth Century* (London: ARK, 1985; orig. 1975), especially Part I, "Charles V and the Idea of Empire" (1-28).

6. One has to distinguish here between millennialism and religion. Robert N. Bellah published a controversial article on "Civil Religion in America," *Dædalus: Journal of the American Academy of Arts and Sciences,* 96, no. 1 (Winter, 1967), 1-21, in which he argued that the United States has never been without its own "civil religion" (in more or less Rousseau's sense), a religion that has much of its terminology, imagery, ethics, and idea of eternity in common with Judeo-Christian tradition, but is still itself definitely not either Jewish or Christian, nor yet strictly deist. This religion, at least in its early phases, was not millennial—certainly not for the framers of the Constitution, whose experience of laborious horse-trading and compromise would have clashed drastically with any idea of their document as an ultimate political revelation. And American political millennialism, as it develops later—especially in the Second World War and then in the Cold War, the idea of the American political and economic system, and "way of life," as a model for mankind's destiny—is not necessarily religious, in either a Christian or a "civil" sense.

7. See, for example, Goethe's description of the people who are "serious" about "world literature" as "eine stille, fast gedrückte Kirche, "*Goethes Werke,* "Weimarer Ausgabe," 143 vols. (Weimar, 1887-1918), 42, 2: 503; and see Schiller on the question of whether the ultimate aesthetic polity really exists: "Dem Bedürfnis nach existiert er in

jeder feingestimmten Seele, der Tat nach möchte man ihn wohl nur . . . in einigen wenigen auserlesenen Zirkeln finden." See Friedrich Schiller, *Sämtliche Werke*, 5 vols., ed. Gerhard Fricke and Herbert G. Göpfert (Munich, 1959), 5: 669. The Goethe edition quoted here will be abbreviated "WA" henceforward.

8. See n2.

9. Hess, 114. It must be noted that Hess is not strictly fair to Habermas in detail. As far as I can see, Habermas never actually speaks of an "institution" of art, autonomous or otherwise, at least not in the section Hess is referring to. See Jürgen Habermas, *Strukturwandel der Öffentlichkeit: Untersuchungen zu einer Kategorie der bürgerlichen Gesellschaft* (Frankfurt/Main, 1990; orig. 1962), 96-100. Indeed the phrase "cultural product" belongs to the English translation of Thomas Bürger and Frederick Lawrence (Cambridge, Mass. , 1989), where Habermas himself (98) has simply "das Werk." But in its broad outlines, Hess's criticism is entirely justified. How do the people in Habermas's by now proverbial coffee-houses decide *what* to use their newly liberated reason on? How can they even identify "art" as a possibility? And where such a choice is in fact made, is it not a sign that art or literature has already acquired (from aesthetic theory) a new kind of "aura"?

10. Hannah Arendt, *Lectures on Kant's Political Philosophy*, ed. Ronald Beiner (Chicago, 1982), 58, 61. In the first passage, the phrases "History from a general viewpoint" and "world citizen" allude to the title of Kant's "Idee zu einer allgemeinen Geschichte in weltbürgerlicher Absicht." The quoted phrases in the second passage belong to a long excerpt from the second essay of Kant's *Conflict of the Faculties* that Arendt had reproduced earlier (45-46) from a volume of translations, Immanuel Kant, *On History*, ed. Lewis White Beck (Indianapolis, 1963), 143-48.

11. Arendt, 47-48, quoting from Kant, *On History*, 130. The original is found in *Kants Werke*, Akademie-Textausgabe, 9 vols. (Berlin, 1968; rpt. of 1902ff.), 8: 382.

12. The "Third Proposition" of Kant's "Idea for a Universal History with a Cosmopolitan Purpose," quoted from Hans Reiss, ed., *Kant's Political Writings* (Cambridge, 1970), 43. See *Kants Werke*, 8: 19. In the body of the text I prefer to translate this title, "Idea for a General History with Cosmopolitan Intent."

13. See proposition 4 of the "Idee zu einer allgemeinen Geschichte" and the last paragraph of "Beantwortung der Frage: Was ist Aufklärung, " in *Kants Werke*, 8: 20-22, 41-42.

14. "Idea for a Universal History," in *Kant's Political Writings*, 50. See *Kants Werke*, 8: 27.

15. *Kant's Political Writings*, 50, 51; *Kants Werke*, 8: 27, 29.

16. The chronology is not as neat as I have suggested, since the *Critique of Judgment* was being worked on before the French Revolution. And the immediate effect of the Revolution on Kant is not easy to gauge. On the one hand, it is difficult to imagine that his insistence later, in *Der Streit der Facultäten*, on the morally significant "enthusiasm" with which the Revolution was greeted *(Kants Werke*, 7: 85-87), does not contain an autobiographical element. But on the other hand, I cannot find any trace of such enthusiasm in his letters from 1789-90. Arendt claims to discern the effect of the Revolution in a change in Kant's "interest" — from "the particular . . . history . . . human sociability" toward "what we today would call constitutional law" *(Lectures*, 15) — and finds a "first indication of this change" in the note to § 65 of the *Critique of Judgment* (16).

17. See *Critique of Judgment*, § 29, *Kants Werke*, 5: 269.

18. The inner quotation from Moritz is found in Karl Philipp Moritz, *Werke*, ed. Heide Hollmerand Albert Meier, 2 vols. (Frankfurt/Main: Deutscher Klassiker Verlag, 1997-1999), 2: 945.

19. Woodmansee, in her book (see n2) and Hess both attribute *originary* significance to this text. Aesthetics, in their view, does not come into its own, does not really begin, until it is de-instrumentalized by Moritz, an event that Woodmansee describes as a "radical departure" (12), while Hess sees Kant's version of Moritz's supposed innovation as marking a "paradigm shift" (159), which idea he claims to borrow (265) from

Manfred Frank, *Einführung in die frühromantische Ästhetik* (Frankfurt/Main, 1989), 38. (In fact, Frank is much more circumspect. He first suggests the idea of a "Paradigmenwechsel" in discussing Novalis's debt to Kant [30]; but in the passage Hess refers to [38], he is still only *asking* whether this idea is justified, and continues to suggest doubts even later [50]. His decision seems to be, finally, that there is after all a radical change in the idea of art from the eighteenth to the nineteenth century, but that this change takes considerable time to develop, in the works of Schiller and the post-Kantian idealists [103], not that it is suddenly all there in Kant and Moritz.) But is Moritz's notion of the de-instrumentalized self-containment of art really unprecedented? The example of Lessing is instructive; for surely the basic argument of *Laokoon*, that the artistic medium radically determines a work's fictional or representational content, asserts artistic autonomy (art's giving itself its own laws, regardless of anyone's inclinations or needs) in much more specific terms than Moritz ever arrives at. In any case, the assertion that an idea on the scale of artistic autonomy is invented, or originates, in one particular text, is always ill-advised; for it presupposes a reliable interpretive knowledge of all other contemporary texts in which the idea might conceivably be found. Klopstock's essay "Von dem Range der schönen Künste und der schönen Wissenschaften" (1758), for instance, is full of obviously "instrumentalist" statementsabout art. But when the arrival of "Tanzkunst" at the end overthrows the essay's whole order of concepts, how deep does the irony cut? Perhaps to the very idea of art as instrument?

20. Moritz, *Werke*, 2: 943. The basic relations among Batteux, Mendelssohn, and Moritz are laid out very neatly in Woodmansee's article, 25-30 (see n2).

21. In Karl Philipp Moritz, *Schriften zur Ästhetik und Poetik*, ed. Hans Joachim Schrimpf (Tübingen, 1962), 28-31.

22. Hess, 178-9. Woodmansee, in her article (31-33, 35), makes the same basic suggestion. And M. H. Abrams, "Kant and the Theology of Art, " *Notre Dame English Journal*, 13 (1981), 75-105, though he publishes earlier, seems to have gotten his version of the idea about Moritz from a lecture by Woodmansee. See Abrams, 92, 104. Hess borrows the idea of "salvage" from Abrams, 92.

23. The inner quotes are from the little preface to *Anton Reiser* (*Werke*, 1: 86).

24. Matthew Arnold, *Culture and Anarchy*, chap. 4, in *The Works of Matthew Arnold*, 15 vols. (New York, 1970; reprint of London, 1903-1904), 6: 124.

TWO

The History and Problems of the Idea of Aesthetics: The Issue of Communication

In order to give more shape and content to the idea of secular millennialism as it characterizes aesthetics, we must start beyond the beginning of aesthetics in the background of that beginning, where our attention is caught by the issue of intersubjective communication. For the sake of compactness I will use the admirably focused argument of Ernst Cassirer's *The Philosophy of the Enlightenment* (1932) as a guide here, and also as a foil.

THE GAME AND ITS PLAYERS

The tradition of secular millennialism that I associate with aesthetics includes a number of figures not usually regarded as aestheticians: especially Schleiermacher, Dilthey, and Heidegger, who form what we usually think of as a hermeneutic tradition. And if we include Hegel in the picture, then the "tradition" we are talking about is moved at least into the vicinity of the whole main stream of post-Kantian European philosophy. Therefore, if it is true that this tradition is a necessary enabling condition for the development of twentieth-century totalitarianism, we might be tempted to conclude that totalitarianism was a normal manifestation of Western intellectual culture as a whole—and perhaps still is.

I think this ascription of a kind of fatality to totalitarianism would be both dangerous and erroneous. But in order to avoid the error, we need a clear understanding of at least three things: (1) the exact boundaries of the "aesthetic" tradition we are talking about; (2) the availability, past and present, of alternative intellectual positions, positions not involved in the aesthetic tradition and its political consequences, or indeed directly opposed to it; and (3) the historical and social conditions under which the secular millennialist tradition of aesthetics finds itself in the academic mainstream, to the exclusion of alternative or oppositional initiatives.

Among the adherents of alternative positions are Leibniz (before the fact), Lessing, Klopstock, Hamann, Herder, and Goethe. The thought of these figures is often very subtle and difficult; but their position with respect to the tradition of aesthetics is fairly clear, once the existence of that tradition is understood. In a sense more interesting are a few figures whose position is in some way ambiguous. I will argue in the next chapter that Schiller starts out as an impassioned millennialist partisan of aesthetics and ends up quite suddenly in the opposite camp. Friedrich Schleiermacher, by contrast, is never himself a millennialist, secular or otherwise, despite the links in his thought to both Kant and Hegel; but his development of a secular hermeneutics nevertheless operates indispensably in shaping the aesthetic tradition. And finally, Ernst Cassirer, in the early 1930s, takes care to separate himself both intellectually and geographically from the Nazis; but he does so as an advocate of precisely that aesthetic tradition without which Nazism could not have arisen—at least not in the form it actually took. We will trace this process, in all its exemplary contradictoriness, in the present chapter.

AESTHETIC HUMANISM: AESTHETICS *AVANT LA LETTRE*?

The chapters of Cassirer's Enlightenment book, with page lengths, are: "The Mind of the Enlightenment" (34); "Nature and Natural Science" (56); "Psychology and Epistemology" (41); "Religion" (63); "The Conquest of the Historical World" (37); "Law, State, and Society" (41); and "Fundamental Problems of Aesthetics" (86).[1] Aesthetics thus forms the culmination of his account of the period; and its discussion in the book's longest chapter occupies more than double the space of each of four other chapters. What can be so important about aesthetics in a book that concerns itself with such a wide range of intellectual and historical material?

Cassirer in effect responds to this question by starting with what he claims are empirical observations, matters of fact:

> The union of philosophy and literary and aesthetic criticism is evident in all the eminent minds of the [eighteenth] century; in no case is it simply an accident; it is inevitably based on a deep and intrinsically necessary union of the problems of the two fields of thought. . . . It is as if logic and aesthetics, as if pure knowledge and artistic intuition, had to be tested in terms of one another before either of them could find its own inner standard and understand itself in the light of its own relational complex. (275, 277)

And when he reaches the climax of his argument, in discussing Baumgarten, he subjects these observations to a single cohesive interpretation:

> Baumgarten's aesthetics goes beyond the sphere of mere logic. It seeks to be a logic of the "lower cognitive forces"; by means of this logic it strives, however, to serve not only the system of philosophy, but above all the doctrine of man. . . . The development of particular talents, especially the talent of the analysis of concepts, may be becoming to the scholar and laudable in the specialist; but the task of philosophy can never be realized in this way. This task requires that no field of knowledge lie fallow and that no gift of the mind go unnourished. . . . The new discipline of aesthetics is thus not only logically validated, but so to speak ethically postulated and justified. For the "beautiful sciences" now form no longer simply a relatively independent province of knowledge; they "activate the whole man" and are indispensable to man's realization of his true destiny. (352-53)[2]

In Cassirer's view, the founding of philosophical aesthetics is thus "characteristic of the entire culture of the eighteenth century," by belonging to the development of a new "philosophical anthropology" (353), a form of philosophizing shaped not by abstract concepts or ideals but strictly with respect to human beings as they actually are.

Cassirer is probably better known as a student of the Renaissance than as an eighteenth-century expert; and his emphasis on aesthetics shows a desire on his part to find a kind of second Renaissance in the Enlightenment, a second great humanist initiative, a second and now definitive liberation of philosophy from its theological shackles, or from the systematic habits in which those shackles had led a stubborn afterlife. There are certainly things wrong with this historical picture; and I think there are things not only historically wrong, but also ethically wrong, with any argument that makes Kant as much a hero of human development as Cassirer's does. But on the other hand, it is hard to imagine an historical view that would cast a more favorable light on the whole aesthetic project; and it is hard to imagine a simpler and more cogent defense of the role of aesthetics as a sub-discipline of philosophy.

In the passages quoted above, Baumgarten is seen as a culmination of the process by which aesthetics is founded, not as its inception. And while this view may not be as crassly unhistorical as the view that makes aesthetics coeval with philosophy itself—so that Aristotle becomes an aesthetician in the same sense as Edmund Burke or Schiller—still it creates definite chronological difficulties. Aesthetics, says Cassirer, arises directly from a Cartesian belief in the "absolute unity" of knowledge (279). And "in the sphere of the arts," the resulting need for unity is satisfied "only when we succeed in reducing the various and apparently heterogeneous forms in which the arts manifest themselves to a single principle." But the text that he then immediately mentions (280) as evidence of this supposedly Cartesian impulse in aesthetics is Charles Bat-

teux's *Les Beaux-Arts réduits à un même principe* [The Fine Arts Reduced to
a Single Principle] which did not appear until 1746, eleven years after the
Meditationes in which Baumgarten had coined the term "aesthetic" and
only four years before his *Aesthetica*. If Cartesian philosophy is really the
principal generating force in aesthetics, surely there should be clear evidence of its operation at an earlier date.

The problem here resides not in Cassirer's view of Descartes' methodological influence, but in the question: influence upon what? It is all very
well to speak of a Cartesian need for "unity" in knowledge; but before
one can apply this idea in a particular area, one must have a reasonable
conception of the object of the knowledge in question. Cassirer speaks of
"the *apparently* heterogeneous forms in which the arts manifest themselves." But for the seventeenth century, and for most of the eighteenth,
that heterogeneity is by no means merely "apparent." Batteux still uses
the common plural term *beaux-arts* to describe his subject matter. And
Cassirer himself, in his detailed discussion of "classical aesthetics"
(278ff.), acknowledges that in *L'Artpoétique* of 1674, Boileau does not have
a unified conception of poetry as such, but is concerned with "implicit
laws which are based on the nature of the various poetic genres" (290),
thus in effect with a *collection* of different arts. (Boileau's singular title
refers to Horace and ultimately quotes the title traditionally given to
Aristotle's treatise, which is also focused more upon genre differences
than upon a synoptic notion of the poetic.)

Like the modern notion of "literature," the modern notion of "art"
does not yet exist in the early eighteenth century—"art" understood as
everything that is produced, in whatever medium, more or less in the
spirit of "fine arts." (The *word* "art," in English or French, does not appear
to be used in this sense until the nineteenth century; but the growth of the
conception can be followed in certain texts, like Batteux's, and in the use
of the German word "Kunst.")[3] And without at least the beginnings of
that unified modern conception of "art" as its object, I cannot see how we
are justified in speaking of "aesthetics" in anything like its modern meaning. It is fairly clear, in fact, that the two ideas—of "art" and of its philosophical study in the form of "aesthetics"—need to be understood as
arising and taking shape together, in a relation of reciprocal influence,
and cannot be separated historically.

HUMAN FINITUDE AS A TRANSCENDENT GOAL

Historical specificity is crucial to Cassirer's project—especially in the
form of his tacit but I think unmistakable idea of a second Renaissance.
And his insistence on anchoring aesthetics in a Cartesian seventeenth
century therefore tends to unbalance his argument. Does this unbalanc-
ing impede his advocacy of aesthetics as an opening of philosophy to the

actual finitude of human life? He makes his basic point with great conviction:

> [Baumgarten] demands of poetic thought that it convey not only form but color; not only objective truth but sensitive force; and not only correct but vital insight. . . . Abstraction, which shows us the way to higher classes of things, always means impoverishment and depletion as far as direct perception is concerned . . . generality and definiteness lie in opposite directions. Aesthetics bridges this chasm; for its "truth" cannot be found beyond or in opposition to concrete qualities, but it can be realized only amid and by virtue of such qualities. Beauty requires not only intensive clarity, as do scientific concepts; it possesses also extensive clarity . . . [which] does not tolerate . . . conceptual reduction and concentration. (347-48)

But can such a position be maintained without falsifying the historical situation?

Cassirer begins with "classical aesthetics" — in English we would normally speak of "neoclassicism" — and is at pains to give this movement its due. He insists that Boileau is not opposed to imagination or individuality but simply recognizes a need to contain these qualities within rational limits for the sake of making each work a finished instance of its type. But his judgment concerning the principal fault of neoclassicism is less expectable:

> Paradoxical as it may seem, it can be said that . . . one of the main shortcomings of classical doctrine was not that it went too far with abstraction but that it did not maintain its abstractions with sufficient consistency. For on every hand in the foundation and defense of the theory, intellectual factors enter which can by no means be strictly derived from its general principles and premises, but which have their origin in the particular situation of the problem, in the intellectual and historical structure of the seventeenth century. . . . At this point [in the doctrine of the "three unities," which is derived not from "the ideal of reason" but from "a merely empirical standard"] classical aesthetics clearly departs from its scientific concept of "universal reason" to take on characteristics of the philosophy of "common sense." . . . Boileau not only treats "nature" and "reason" as equivalents, but he also equates nature with a certain state of civilization . . . [with] forms which life in society has brought to their highest stage of refinement. (292-94)

What has happened to the idea of aesthetics as an opening of philosophy to the finite and contingent (which surely includes the "empirical"), thus as the application of reason in an area where precisely the "ideal" is not to be sought?

It is clear that when Cassirer later talks about human finitude and contingency as the domain of aesthetics, he does not mean human *society* in any of its particular forms. But then, does he mean individual human psychology? In fact psychology is the next possibility he explores in his chronological presentation. He finds the first major statement of a new "subjectivist" phase of aesthetics in Jean-Baptiste Dubos's *Réflexions critiques sur la poésie et sur la peinture* of 1719, about which he asserts, accurately enough:

> Dubos is the first to establish introspection as the specific principle of aesthetics and to defend it against all other merely logical methods as the real source of all sound knowledge. The nature of the aesthetic cannot be known by mere concepts, and the theorist in this field has no other means of communicating his insight to others and convincing them of its truth than to appeal to their own inner experience. The immediate impression, with which all formulation of aesthetic concepts must start and to which it must constantly refer, cannot be replaced by any deductions. (303)

And it is more or less in this empirical spirit, as an appeal to experience, that Cassirer also reads such authors as Hume and Diderot.

But as in the case of neoclassicism, the "empirical" turns out to be what is *wrong,* in Cassirer's view, with psychological aesthetics:

> Wherever Diderot seeks not only to describe but also to explain the beautiful, he finds this possible only if he considers the beautiful as dependent on the "true" and merely as a disguised form of the latter. Only now the norm of truth has changed; its content is no longer based on *a priori* propositions, on general and necessary principles, but on practical experience, on daily routine and utility. Both types of explanation fail, however, to account for the peculiar meaning and value of the beautiful; for the standard employed in both cases is on a different plane from that occupied by the pure phenomenon of beauty. (311)

The advantage of aesthetics is that it eschews the "ideal" in favor of human finitude and contingency. But now it appears that this finitude and contingency must be "pure," or somehow non-empirical, yet without rejoining the ideal. At the very least, a conceptual tightrope is being walked here.

A decisive conceptual move is obviously needed, and is supplied by Cassirer in the assumption that genuine aesthetics depends on "autonomy of the beautiful and self-sufficiency of the imagination" (311). The needful "intellectual impulse" for realizing these qualities, he continues, "could only come from a thinker who neither attempted to analyze beauty theoretically and to reduce it to rules, nor to describe it psychologically and explain it genetically, but who is completely immersed in the contemplation of the beautiful. Such a thinker first appeared in the eighteenth century in Shaftesbury" (312). In particular:

> Rational analysis and psychological introspection, according to Shaftesbury, leave us on the periphery of the beautiful, not at its center. The center is not to be found in the process of enjoyment, but in that of forming and creating. The receptive act of enjoyment is insufficient and

powerless since it does not lead us back to spontaneity, to the real source of the beautiful. But once this source has been discovered, the true and the only possible synthesis has been accomplished not only between subject and object, between the ego and the world, but also between man and God. For the difference between man and God disappears when we consider man not simply with respect to his original immanent forming powers, not as something created, but as a creator. (316)

The thought here, considered as thought, may belong to Shaftesbury, but the accents are more those of Pico della Mirandola on the one hand, and on the other ("*back* to spontaneity") perhaps of Rousseau. In any event, Shaftesbury stands at the very center of Cassirer's aesthetic vision.

And if we ask why this should be, we find that we can also answer, at last, the question of why Cassirer takes the risk of insisting upon an aesthetics *avant la lettre*. For he concludes:

> Shaftesbury . . . deliberately raises the concept of genius above the realm of mere sensation and evaluation, above the sphere of propriety, sentiment, delicacy . . . and reserves it entirely for the productive, formative, creative forces. Shaftesbury thus created for the first time a firm philosophical center for the future development of the problem of genius. He gave this problem a definite fundamental direction which is henceforth pursued unswervingly by the real founders of systematic aesthetics, despite all the deviations to be observed among popular philosophical and psychological studies. From now on a direct path leads to the basic problems of German intellectual history in the eighteenth century — to Lessing's *Hamburg Dramaturgy* and to Kant's *Critique of Judgment*. (318-19)

What is interesting about this passage is how evidently untenable its claims are. Can an idea of genius really be taken as the primary focus of either the *Dramaturgy* or the *Critique of Judgment*? And can such an idea, in turn, be understood as the key to "basic problems of German intellectual history"? Why does Cassirer go so far out on this particular limb?

I suggested in Chapter 1 that aesthetics is not an objective study, but always has an agenda, an ulterior motive. Cassirer's thought is no exception; and the motive behind it is a clear instance of secular millennialism. Aesthetics resolutely renounces the ideal, yet is also profoundly unsatisfied with the empirical. Inspired by a new surge of Renaissance humanism, it aims at a thoroughly finite and fleshly humanity, but a humanity that does not yet exist except occasionally in the form of "genius," its harbinger. Human finitude and contingency is now set up as a transcendent goal, as the aim of history — a humanity grown perfect by having turned away resolutely from its erstwhile ideal pretensions. A resurrection of the flesh is thus envisaged, but not in a Christian sense. Therefore it is of paramount importance to Cassirer that he be able to regard the "founders of systematic aesthetics" as *inheritors* of a tradition of thought (aesthetics *avant la lettre*) that is marked by a radical humanism like Shaftesbury's. Otherwise his whole secret vision of a second Renaissance in the German eighteenth century collapses, since that radical humanism cannot be read out of Kant and Baumgarten directly. (Lessing in fact mocks Baumgarten for being pedantically systematic, hence for *not* meeting what later become Cassirer's criteria.)[4]

Or does his vision collapse? Oddly enough, the idea of a belated German Renaissance in the eighteenth century, on which Cassirer stakes everything, is in itself not at all misguided. Jacobi studies Bruno; Winckelmann reincarnates figures like Cesare Ripa; Herder preaches "Humanität"; Lessing explores all sorts of obscure Renaissance material in the library at Wolfenbüttel; the admiration for Shakespeare includes practically everywhere a sense of obligation to regenerate German poetry in something like a Shakespearean spirit. And then there is Goethe. Harold Jantz concludes his chapter on Goethe's response to Cusanus and Pico, in which he uses Cassirer as a Renaissance authority, with a moment of what seems to me inspired speculation: "It is possible that Cassirer, perhaps unwittingly, learned from Goethe how to see what was central about these early Renaissance philosophers from Cusanus onward."[5] But the more or less respectable Renaissance philosophers and artists and politicians are only the tip of the iceberg. Goethe also practices a modern form of the Renaissance blend of science and magic; he relives the age of exploration in his assimilation of the German language to exotic foreign cultures; and in *Faust*, considered as an esoteric parody of Dante's *Commedia*, he perhaps even imagines the inauguration of post-Christian Europe.

There is, in other words, plenty of material for Cassirer to work with, and material with which he was thoroughly familiar. But his Enlightenment book was published in 1932, the very year he left Germany for good. The trouble with a general and detailed treatment of Germany's delayed humanist Renaissance, at that time, would have been its exposure to nationalistic interpretation. At least partly in order to prevent this, Cassirer focuses on aesthetics and works out the idea of an aesthetics *avant la lettre* which integrates eighteenth-century German thought into a larger European development. But this move leads him onto slippery ground.

MONADOLOGICAL AND PSYCHOLOGICAL DISCOURSE

Let us look at the founding documents of "systematic aesthetics" and ask how far Kant's admiration of Baumgarten, and Cassirer's admiration of both, is justified. In the scholium to §3 of his *Meditationes* of 1735, Baumgarten suggests a position related to Leibniz's doctrine of monads. He speaks of an "appetitus [qui] quam diu ex confusa boni repraesentatione manat, sensitivus appellatur"[6] [appetite which, as long as it proceeds from a confused representation of the good, is called sensitive]. A similar notion of "appetite" is found in the "Monadology." In no. 7 of that short treatise, Leibniz insists famously that "Les Monades n'ont point de fenê-tres, par lesquelles quelque chose y puisse entrer ou sortir" [Monads have no windows by which anything could come in or go out].[7] But monads must also be able to change (no. 10), through temporary states that are known as "perceptions" (no. 14); and since they cannot be made to change by external influences, it follows that an "internal principle" must be at work in the "passage from one perception to another," a principle which Leibniz calls "appetition" (no. 15). Baumgarten goes a step beyond Leibniz by suggesting that a monad's appetition is always oriented to-ward "the good"; but even this is a reasonable interpretation of no. 3 of Leibniz's "Principes de la Nature et de la Grace, fondés en raison," where we read, "The perceptions of the monad spring from one another accord-ing to the laws of the appetites or [of] the *final causes of good and evil.*"[8]

By thus implying an appeal to the doctrine of monads, Baumgarten gives a specific meaning to his central concept "repraesentatio." We will now tend to understand it in relation to no. 2 of the "Principes," where *"perceptions"* are defined as "les representations du composé, ou de ce qui est dehors, dans le simple" [the representations in the simple (i.e. in the monad) of the compound or of that which is outside]. This does not mean that the monad receives an impression (a perception) from without and then forms an inner "representation" of it. Monads have no windows for receiving anything whatever. From the point of view of the monad, there-fore, the "representation" in effect simply *is* the object represented; and it is this idea of representation that is suggested in Baumgarten's §3, quoted above. But at the same time Baumgarten also insists repeatedly that dis-course *(oratio)* is composed of "representations," in that representations are "signified" by words (§1) and are available to be "recognized" *(reprae-sentationes cognoscendae sunt)* by someone who hears or reads the words (§2). Which gives the notion of "repraesentatio" a completely different meaning—a psychological, not a monadological meaning—since the monad, as such, neither speaks nor is spoken to.

Baumgarten is not simply mistaken or vague here. He is being dishon-est. A short while later, in the scholium to §12, we read, "Possunt quide-meiusdem rei repraesentationes huic obscurae, illi clarae, tertio denique distinctae esse" [Of course representations of the same object can be ob-scure for this person, clear for that one, and yet further, distinct for a third]. Thus, in attempting to give the impression of being scrupulous— by responding to a possible objection against his argument—Baumgarten takes the opportunity to emphasize an entirely non-monadological sense of "repraesentatio" by speaking of *different* "representations" of *the same* "object" *(res),* which cannot make sense unless "representation" is under-stood in a psychological sense, as the mind's direct response to an external stimulus. What does he hope to gain from establishing two conflicting definitions of the concept "repraesentatio"?

Once we recognize that there is a question here, we do not have to go far to find an answer. First, even in Leibnizian philosophy, there is no reason why Baumgarten should not employ the sort of psychological discourse implied by the scholium to §12.[9] Leibniz's monad, in its higher instances, is associated with sense organs that exist entirely within the material plenum (the world of efficient causes); and the "impressions [those organs] receive" in the material world are "represented" in the monad by "perceptions" which, under certain circumstances, can rise to the level of "sensation" (French "sentiment"), meaning perception plus memory ("Principes," no. 4). Considered metaphysically, the statement "one may see a dog"—or "one may respond to visual stimuli by forming the mental representation of a dog"—is a completely mistaken way of describing the process in question; but it is perfectly allowable as long as one recognizes it as an instance of psychological (hence non-monadological) discourse and understands its limits. Why does Baumgarten refuse to remain within those limits? Why does he insist on using "repraesentatio" in *both* a monadologically exact *and* a psychologically relaxed manner, without differentiating the two uses?

The answer can only be that he means to smuggle into his psychological discourse the idea of *the intra-monadic indistinguishability of representation and object*. A "representation," as it arises intra-monadically, cannot possibly be compared with its "object" in the sense that that object is part of the material world. The material object, like the Kantian "thing in itself," is simply not available in such a way that we might make that comparison. It follows that my "representation" of an object (in the monadological sense) can never be exposed as wrong or inadequate. It may be an obscure or confused representation—it may lack the clarity and distinctness that would enable me to define the object or derive it from its causes—but it cannot possibly be mistaken about any external "object." At least there is no way ever to convict it of this fault. And by mixing his discourses illegitimately, Baumgarten contrives to suggest the transposition of this theorem into the psychological realm, where it would take the following form: sense impressions (Greek *aistheta*) produce in the mind *adequate* representations of themselves, unmistaken representations, which can be signified by words and verbally communicated in their entirety to other minds (§§ 2, 7).

Considered as psychology, and judged as such empirically, this theorem is nonsense. What could possibly be meant, psychologically, by the adequate mental representation of a sense impression? If I could possess as representation the experience of drinking wine or having sex, in the same way I possess, say, my knowledge of which way is north, why would I ever bother to repeat the experience? My reason for repeating those experiences is that I know they will *seem new* to me—precisely by being different from representations—however often I may already have had them. And what could we possibly mean by the idea of stuffing a sense experience into words and then somehow inserting it into someone else's mind? Would the recipient actually have the experience upon reading the words, or be placed in the condition of remembering it without ever having had it? These considerations explain why neither Baumgarten nor anyone else would ever be foolish enough to state the above theorem in the form I have given it. But then what purpose is served by its lurking submerged beneath the mathematically structured argument of the *Meditationes?*

THE PROBLEM OF COMMUNICATION

I think I know the answer to this question; but I realize that the argument of later chapters is needed to support that answer convincingly. Therefore I state my position with the reservation that it should be taken, for the time being, as an heuristic move, not a conclusion. Baumgarten, I suggest, along with most other eighteenth-century thinkers on aesthetics, is concerned ultimately with *the problem of intersubjective communication,* with the question of how I can make my own intimate experience of things known to others, and how I might gain access to others' subjective experience in turn. On the level of clear and distinct ideas communication is not a problem. Even monads can be understood to communicate on this level, by co-occupying the mind of God. But the bulk of anyone's actual experience involves ideas that are at least confused and most often obscure as well. How can I possibly communicate, how can I relieve my loneliness as an introspective subject, on this level? Baumgarten's conceptual legerdemain manages to convey the suggestion that subjective isolation may not be a problem after all, that even the gross sensory material of our experience can perhaps be represented adequately in discourse, whence it would follow that perhaps our deepest joys and sorrows can be shared by this route as well. His argument contrives to convey this suggestion, but only by concealing the actual theorem, which could not survive in the light of day.

My hypothesis is that intersubjective communication is always a problem in aesthetics and, because of its unresolvability, is always a source of confusion, always a reason (or excuse) for illegitimate conceptual moves by which even the honest ambition to conduct an objective philosophical study of art repeatedly finds itself maneuvered into serving an agenda that has little to do with the ostensible subject matter. In the early eighteenth century, in fact, I would be inclined to use the issue of communication as a touchstone for deciding which writings or theories about art may really be counted as belonging to the prehistory of aesthetics in the modern sense. Dubos, in a well known passage from his *Réflexions,* stakes everything on successful intimate communication: "je ne saurais espérer d'être approuvési je ne parviens point à faire reconnaître au lecteur dansmon livre ce qui se passe en lui-même, en un mot les mouvements les plus intimes de son cœur" [I should not hope to be commended if I did not succeed in my book at making the reader acquainted with what goes on within himself, in a word, with the most intimate inclinations of his own heart]. [10] And the idea of poetry as a kind of painting, in Bodmer for instance, suggests an ability of language to transmit specific sense impressions. But on the other hand, despite Cassirer, I do not see how Shaftesbury can be claimed for pre-aesthetics in this definition by any stretch of the imagination.

The problem of communication has two important characteristics that contribute to its quality as a source of confusion. First: Communication cannot possibly arise as a problem to begin with, it cannot be experienced as a problem, until after our existence has been marked by the experience of *failure* to communicate. As long as our individuality understands itself primarily as the member of a social body, the very idea of "communication" is outshone by the simple awareness of communal existence, like the stars in daytime. Only a sense of *lonely* individuality can bring communication into focus as a problem, which implies that communication does not become a problem until it has become an insoluble one.

And second: The problem of communication is never a single problem, but has a different character for different types of content. Communication seems not a problem at all with respect to strict logical chains of inference, which the recipient can reproduce for him- or herself; and probably also not in the case of most verbal clichés, where the recipient is not interested in forming more than the vaguest idea of what had precipitated the utterance. Nuanced or exceptionally deep emotion is probably the type of content whose communication is most often felt to be a problem. And here, given the differences in our emotional constitution as individuals, not to mention the variability of emotional life from instant to instant, it seems obvious that there can be at least no general solution to the problem. But Kant makes a remarkable effort in this area—untenable as it may be in the final analysis.

KANT AND THE ISSUE OF COMMUNICATION

Communication and communicability become issues especially in the *Critique of Judgment*. Kant is honest enough to concede that sense impressions are not communicable (§ 39); but he still insists that "our presumption in making judgments of taste" (§ 22) requires that we presuppose a "Gemeinsinn" [common sense], as the medium in which the "Gefühl" (§ 21) [feeling] by which we find something beautiful can be communicated. ("Common sense" means here not simple reasonableness, as in English, but rather a non-physical perceptive ability that we have in common, which consists in "the effect proceeding from the free play of our cognitive faculties" [§ 20].) It then follows from the operation of the cognitive faculties ("imagination" and "understanding") in shaping our experience that "a person who makes a judgment of taste" is entitled to assume that "his or her feeling is universally communicable, and is so without the mediation of concepts" (§ 39)—as long as there is no mistake about the nature of that judgment. The further Kant pursues this line of thought, the more central becomes the idea of communicability: "Taste is thus the ability to judge *a priori* concerning the communicability of the feeling connected (without a mediating concept) to a given representation" (§ 40). In other words, we know that something is beautiful, or fails to be, *by* knowing that our feeling about it is communicable. The communicability of nuanced or powerful feelings in general remains questionable. But the experience of the beautiful opens the possibility of easing our subjective isolation at least on certain occasions.

In Kant's presentation, the theorems on taste, feeling, and communicability are derived from the proposition that aesthetic pleasure includes the belief "that one has reason to impute a similar pleasure to everyone else" (§6), which follows in turn from the definition of a judgment of taste as a judgment involving no personal interest whatever (§§2, 5). But I think it is likely that his actual thought process moved in the opposite direction, beginning with the need to make plausible the communicability of feelings as such and working backward toward the empirically dubious idea of a strictly disinterested pleasure.[11] "Cognitions and judgments," he says, "along with the condition of being convinced of them, must be universally communicable, because otherwise . . . they would be a merely subjective play of representational forces, just as skepticism insists" (§21). Thus we suddenly find ourselves at the beginning of the whole critical system, which is erected in large part as an avoidance of skepticism. And when Kant now infers: that the "subjective precondition" of cognition must also be communicable; and that that precondition in turn involves, for any particular object, a specific "attunement" ("Stimmung") of the cognitive powers that can be determined only by "feeling" ("Gefühl"); and that that feeling must consequently also be communicable—it follows that in a strong sense the whole project of transcendental philosophy stands or falls with the assumption that feelings are communicable in certain crucial cases.

In any event, the possibility of attaching a clear positive *value* to the communicability of feeling is later made explicit: "If one could assume that the mere universal communicability of one's feeling must of itself bring with it a value or interest ['Interesse'] for us (which one is not, however, justified in inferring from the character of a merely reflective judgment), then one could explain why, in a judgment of taste, feeling is imputed to all people as a kind of duty"(§40). The mood here is subjunctive, but the constellation of concepts perhaps reveals more about the background and genesis of the *Critiques* than even Kant himself was aware of.

FEELINGS AND FEELINGS

Baumgarten suggests subliminally the communicability of sense impressions; and Kant asserts the communicability of feeling, but construes feeling to exclude sense impressions. Is there a connection between these two ideas of "feeling"? In language, there is such a connection. "Feeling," like German "Gefühl," has to do etymologically with the sense of touch—Latin *palpare* is cognate—which means that the words received the meaning "emotion" by way of metaphor. And in the eighteenth century, particularly in Germany, this metaphorical association between feeling and feeling is still *alive*. The association between sense impressions and intra-subjective movements in general—including the metaphor of "taste," which Kant discusses in § 33 of the *Critique of Judgment*—is still open to question and confusion.

Even Kant, who makes a point of distinguishing clearly between sense impressions and strictly internal subjective conditions, unwittingly provides evidence of this situation. For he uses the word "Sinnesempfindung" (§ 39) to refer to a sense impression—as opposed to "Gefühl" meaning an inner movement or sentiment—even though the general concept of "Empfindung," for most of the eighteenth century, had tended much more strongly to mean emotion. [12] But the case of Baumgarten is stranger still. For he carries out in his *Latin* treatise a blurring of the border between sense experience and the emotions that reflects his situation as a German speaker of his time. The crucial passage in the *Meditationes* reads as follows:

> § XXIV. Repraesentationes *mutationumrepraesentantis praesentium* suntsensuales eaeque sensitivae, § 3, adeoque *poeticae,* § 12.
>
> § XXV. Affectus cum sintnotabiliorest aedii et voluptatis gradus, dantur eorum repraesentationes sensuales in repraesentante sibi quid confuse, ut bonum et malum, ergo determinant repraesentationes poeticas, § 24; ergo *affectus movere est poeticum,* § 11.
>
> [§ 24. Representations of present changes in the person (or mind) representing are sensual (?), thus also sensitive and to that extent poetic.
>
> § 25. Since affects are the more striking degrees of displeasure and pleasure, their sensual (?) representations are given, to someone who is representing anything to himself confusedly, as good and bad; therefore those affects determine poetic representations; therefore it is poetic to stir up affects.]

What exactly is meant by the adjective "sensualis" here, and how does it differ in meaning from "sensitivus"?

Neither "sensualis" nor "sensitivus" occurs in classical Latin; and as far as I can see, there is no clear record of later usage that would enable us to distinguish the terms unambiguously. But we can get an idea of what Baumgarten has in mind from his own text. The term "sensitivus," as applied to a "repraesentatio," is defined in § 3: "Repraesentationes *per partem facultatis cognoscitivae inferiorem comparatae* sint sensitivae" [Representations furnished by the lower part of the cognitive faculty shall be called sensitive]. In a Wolffian context, we associate "lower" cognition with historical or practical knowledge, knowledge derived *a posteriori* from facts that are ultimately traceable to sense impressions. But in § 24 a type of "sensual" representation is identified that belongs to the general category "sensitivus" (the text says this), yet without being derivable from the operation of the physical senses. It is rather a primitive form of *reflection,* the representation of a change affecting the representing agent in the very moment of its representing. The qualification "praesens" is necessary and needs to be understood in a strict sense; otherwise Baumgarten could simply be talking of memory. He is not talking of memory; he is describing a strictly instantaneous, thus quasi-spatial and quasi-sensory form of inward self-awareness which serves to bring emotion (literally, inner motion or change in oneself) into the domain of the physically sensate, thus to create a bridge between feelings and feelings.

(How does Baumgarten hope to get around the psychological implausibility of this idea of instantaneous self-representation, given that self-consciousness is the very definition of inner or experienced time? We need only recall his flirting with monadology, his illegitimate mixing of discourses. For the monad is driven by an internal "appetition" to undergo "changement" ["Monadology," no. 10; Latin *mutatio,*] which is the passage from one "perception" to another, each perception being a new "representation" ["Principes," no. 2]. In the monad, therefore, a *mutatio* and the generation of a *repraesentatio* are strictly simultaneous. The only extra step required by Baumgarten's definition is that we regard the new representation as a representation *of* the change that generates it, which it perhaps even is [monadologically], in the sense of belonging to that change as an aspect of it. But none of this justifies the *psychological* argument he is advancing in the passage under discussion.)

The connection between sense experience and emotion is then exploited in the next proposition, § 25. The logic of that proposition is perhaps not immediately transparent, but it is sound nonetheless, given its premises. What Baumgarten means is: If I am in the process of representing something (say, object X) to myself confusedly, and if my representing is accompanied here and now by a strong inward movement or change, either pleasure or displeasure, then my "sensual" representation of that affect (the possibility of which is asserted by § 24) will attach itself to the representation of object X as the attribute of either goodness or badness. This "sensual" representation, moreover, again by § 24, is confused, hence poetic;[13] and in being added to my representation of object X it therefore makes that representation extensively clearer (by § 16), hence more poetic (by § 17). Therefore "affects" (the subject of the verb "determinant") can be said to determine poetic representations, by resetting their content, whence the last clause of the proposition follows easily.

The only question that is not asked is *how* poetry is supposed to "stir up affects." Or rather, it is asked only subliminally. Baumgarten emphasizes not affects themselves so much as their "sensual representations," which belong to the larger class of "sensitive representations." And if we are taken in by the flirting with monadology, we shall now regard these representations as communicable in language, so that affects themselves must also be in some sense communicable, or perhaps we might say, linguistically contagious. In exactly what sense? Neither this question itself nor any likely answer to it would pass what lawyers call the laugh test. Which is why it is not asked explicitly.

Both Baumgarten and Kant are citizens of what we might call the nascent age of lonely individuality, a type of individuality we can call "Cartesian," but which is in truth the product of a long developing interaction of religious and philosophical thought with social reality. The idea of the individual as an absolute atom of human existence makes it appear necessary now to *explain* how human society can have come about, how a Hobbesian original egoism can have been overcome either by a basic social need (as already in Grotius) or by a social contract of the form postulated by Locke or Hume or Rousseau. But society alone is not enough for the increasingly isolated individual of this period. Communication also becomes an imperative, in the sense of a sharing among individuals of the intimate contents of each one's emotional experience. I think it is in response to this imperative that Baumgarten resorts to a juggling of discourses, and Kant to the idea of a strictly disinterested pleasure, in order to demonstrate that communication does after all happen. As if such a demonstration, and the implied need for it, were not itself already proof of the contrary proposition.

Baumgarten and Kant live in a Germany where the metaphorical association of sense impressions with inner feelings is still available for manipulation. Baumgarten, in the *Meditationes*, simply takes advantage of this situation, using it as a quasi-factual background against which his illegitimate Latin argument aimed at the communicability of feeling might gain the feeling of plausibility—as indeed it did, in some quarters. Kant would never have dreamt of doing anything so dishonest, and resists the pull of his native language by distinguishing scrupulously between sense impressions and emotions. But he is not strong enough to resist the imperative of communication when it whispers into his ear the delusion of disinterested pleasure.[14] And just how strong the seductive power of that imperative is, finally, can be measured by Cassirer's willingness, a century and a half later, to buy into not only Kant's but even Baumgarten's thinking. For a soon-to-be German exile in the early 1930s, the need for communication leading toward a universal human community is perhaps decisive—as opposed to propaganda for a national community. But however understandable and estimable the motives behind it, Cassirer's complicity in the conceptual untidiness of aesthetics turns out to be a bargain which I contend had already in effect backfired on him.

THE IDEA OF BEAUTY

In discussing Kant we have drifted away from the question of art. For Baumgarten, in the *Meditationes,* the problem of communication attaches itself mainly to questions of art, especially the art of poetry. But for Kant, beauty is by far the more central concern of aesthetics. What makes the idea of beauty attractive as a project for the intellectual wing of lonely individuality?

The answer to this question can already be read out of Plato's *Phaedrus,* in Socrates' "palinode" after the manner of Stesichorus:

> Now, as we have said, every human soul has, by reason of her nature, had contemplation of true being; else would she never have entered into this human creature; but to be put in mind thereof by things here is not easy for every soul. Some, when they had the vision, had it but for a moment; some when they had fallen to earth consorted unhappily with such as led them to deeds of unrighteousness, wherefore they forgot the holy objects of their vision. Few indeed are left that can still remember much, but when these discern some likeness of the things yonder, they are amazed, and no longer masters of themselves, and know not what is come upon them by reason of their perception being dim.
>
> Now in the earthly likenesses of justice and temperance and all other prized possessions of the soul there dwells no luster; nay, so dull are the organs wherewith men approach their images that hardly can a few behold that which is imaged, but with beauty it is otherwise. Beauty it was ours to see in all its brightness in those days when, amidst that happy company, we beheld with our eyes that blessed vision, ourselves in the train of Zeus, others following some other god; then were we all initiated into that mystery which is rightly accounted blessed beyond all others; whole and unblemished were we that did celebrate it, untouched by the evils that awaited us in days to come; whole and unblemished likewise, free from all alloy, steadfast and blissful were the spectacles on which we gazed in the moment of final revelation; pure was the light that shone around us, and pure were we, without taint of that prison house which now we are encompassed withal, and call a body, fast bound therein as an oyster in its shell.

There let it rest then, our tribute to a memory that has stirred us to linger awhile on those former joys for which we yearn. Now beauty, as we said, shone bright amidst these visions, and in this world below we apprehend it through the clearest of our senses, clear and resplendent. For sight is the keenest mode of perception vouchsafed us through the body; wisdom, indeed, we cannot see thereby—how passionate had been our desire for her, if she had granted us so clear an image of herself to gaze upon—nor yet any other of those beloved objects, save only beauty; for beauty alone this has been ordained, to be most manifest to sense and most lovely of them all. [15]

And in something close to a stroke of genius, Cassirer restates in just two words practically the whole content of the above passage when he speaks of "the pure phenomenon of beauty." [16]

By a "pure phenomenon" Cassirer certainly does not mean a *mere* phenomenon, nothing but an appearance; nor does he seem to be referring to the purified result of a phenomenological reduction like Husserl's. The phrase, therefore, is practically a contradiction in terms: because "pure" has to mean essential, simple, unalloyed, whereas in a "phenomenon" (literally an "appearing") that which appears is necessarily affected by the conditions of its appearing and so is no longer "purely" itself. Or at least—as Socrates suggests in the passage above—this is true of every pure essence with the single exception of beauty. For beauty is the unique instance of an ideal's showing itself directly in the sensible world, thus the only possible "phenomenon" to which the attribute "pure" might properly be applied. Cassirer positions himself on a conceptual tightrope by insisting that aesthetics eludes any strictly ideal definition of itself, yet is also not correctly understood as an empirical pursuit. It turns out that this tightrope is a version of the Platonic definition of beauty.

And the importance of such an idea of beauty from the point of view of the post-Cartesian problem of communication has to do with the dualism and the nominalism that characterize Cartesian philosophy. For a philosophical realist (meaning the opposite of a nominalist) communication can be a demanding task, but not the kind of desperate problem that it is in the eighteenth century. If such universal notions as justice, temperance, wisdom, and beauty (those that Plato mentions in the passage above) correspond to real entities, if they are instances of what Socrates calls τὰ ὄντα (*Phaedrus,* 249E) [those things that truly are], then all of my personal thought and feeling will necessarily *position* me with respect to those entities, in such a way that my position, hence my inner condition, can be disclosed to another person. It may happen that I or my interlocutor, or both of us, do not yet understand those ideals clearly enough to locate each other in relation to them, in which case we must talk the matter through until clarity has been achieved. Which is exactly what is accomplished in the Platonic dialogues. But barring some form of morbid delusion, it cannot happen that I find myself desperately alone, that I become a Werther, in such a world.

A basically nominalist view—that abstract ideas or universals are really only words, whose meaning may shape itself differently in each individual's mind—therefore makes *possible* the eighteenth century's increasingly lonely individual. And Cartesian dualism finishes the job by making that loneliness *inevitable*. For dualism, as the strict separation of soul or mind from body and matter, thus strictly separates that which needs to be communicated (the nominalistically conceived contents of my inner experience) from the material world in which all the available means of communication are situated, including spoken and written language. Communication is thus made *necessary*—how can a soul, strictly excluded from material nature, subsist without at least intersubjective commerce?—by exactly the factors that make it *impossible*.

Under these conditions, the unique attractiveness of the idea of beauty is understandable. For if beauty exists more or less in the Platonic sense, it must bring about a salutary relaxation of any strict dualism, by being the one and only ideal entity that also has a direct effect in the material world; or conversely, by being the single form of materially conditioned experience that is directly traceable to an ideal cause. And philosophical nominalism is also undermined by beauty considered as a universal conception which has an inseparable real component, albeit not on the ideal plane.

Strictly speaking, the Platonic notion of beauty is incompatible with either a consistent nominalist or a consistent dualist position. But logic is not the issue here. Communication, especially of emotional experience, is recognized as a problem and a need from the seventeenth century on. The development and popularity of the novel is clear evidence on this point. But where will someone influenced by the Cartesian or Leibniz-Wolffian school be inclined to seek a method of dealing with this problem? The idea of beauty suggests an answer: not in a strict Platonic sense, but in that it calls attention to an area of recorded human experience that eases the constraints of nominalism and dualism and can also perhaps be studied fruitfully with eighteenth-century intellectual tools. What is needed, in other words, is a new *science of beauty,* which is pretty much what was soon understood as "aesthetics."

But how can a new, presumably objective science hope to have any effect upon the *personal* problem of communication? Here another advantage of the idea of beauty appears. For one result of the incommunicability of feelings is that we cannot say exactly what those feelings are, exactly what needs to be communicated. When we speak of the basic affects of pleasure and displeasure, we seem to know what we are talking about; but the nuances of those affects, their gradation and intermixture—comparable to nuances in our experience of touch and taste and smell—are understood at best only by metaphors that involve exactly those physical senses. At this juncture a science of beauty, which must deal with *direct* connections between sense impressions and corresponding inward movements, might be expected to get us somewhere in the matter of communication.

SOME SPECIFIC USES OF BEAUTY

Thus, so to speak, starting with only the nominalist and dualist limitations of Cartesian philosophy plus the Platonic idea of beauty, we have logically constructed Alexander Gottlieb Baumgarten. For Baumgarten begins with a book about communication, the *Meditationes,* which aims at understanding "perfect sensate discourse," a discourse in which everything classifiable as αἰσθητά (including, but not restricted to, sense experience, § 116) can be adequately communicated. But that book does not even raise the question of the *possibility* of such discourse, which is the problem of communication. And Baumgarten at last opens this question of possibility in his *Aesthetica* by taking up the question of beauty, "pulchritudo," which he defines as "perfectio cognitionis sensitivae" (§ 14)[17] [the perfection of sensate cognition]. Such perfection is made up of three types of "agreement" ("consensus")—that of the thoughts or things thought ("rerum et cogitationum") among themselves (§ 18), that of the order of thought with itself and with its objects (§ 19), and that of signs among themselves and with their order and objects (§ 20). If the empirical existence of these "agreements" could be ascertained, their communicability would certainly follow and the idea of a perfect or perfectible discourse would be justified.

For Kant, as for Baumgarten, the idea of beauty anchors aesthetics with respect to the task of human self-orientation in the world. Whatever the case may be with particular aesthetic judgments, Kant insists that aesthetic theory as a whole is not by any means disinterested. We have, he says, not only an "empirical interest in the beautiful," based on the importance of the communication of feelings in human society (*Critique of Judgment,* § 41), but also an "intellectual interest" (§ 42), having to do with the inferred moral temper of a mind to which we might attribute certain types of judgment. We even have a kind of representational interest, insofar as beauty, by way of an analogy between types of free mental activity, may be regarded as a "symbol of morality" (§ 59). To an extent, then, Kant concedes the proposition I have suggested, that aesthetics always has ulterior motives; except he implies that such ulterior motives arise only after the fact and so do not cast doubt on the immediate validity of aesthetics itself—which seems to me a shaky position.

But what of Cassirer? What advantage does he hope for from his adamant insistence on the "pure phenomenon" of beauty? In *An Essay on Man,* written in 1944, a year before his death, he is even more definite than in his earlier work: "Beauty appears to be one of the most clearly known human phenomena. Unobscured by any aura of secrecy and mystery, its character and nature stand in no need of subtle and complicated metaphysical theories for their explanation. Beauty is part and parcel of human experience; it is palpable and unmistakable." [18] This statement is not an assertion of fact or truth so much as an appeal to the reader, a statement that will achieve meaningfulness only to the extent that we, all of us, agree with it. Like Dubos's *Réflexions*, it stakes everything on the possibility of the adequate communication of feelings. It hovers on the verge of saying: If you do not instantly and instinctively assent to what I am stating, then read no further, for you are not truly an instance of the "human" in my sense of the term. Here, as in the eighteenth century, the idea of beauty is a device by which the question of communication can be drawn out into the open and at least thrown down as a challenge.

But for Cassirer himself, the situation is more complicated than it had been for the thinkers treated in his Enlightenment book. The function of the idea of beauty is now not merely to remove the sharp edges of philosophical nominalism and dualism, but to attenuate the whole idea of system so as to enable a serious philosopher to write a book like *An Essay on Man*. Cassirer of course never loses his respect for Kant's "systematic edifice," which he says "overshadows the Enlightenment even while it represents its final glorification" (*Philosophy of the Enlightenment*, 274). But the relatively broad and relaxed focus of *An Essay on Man* makes clear that he considers the time for making philosophical systems to be over, that now philosophers must communicate rather than construct. And how shall this understanding itself be communicated without bringing the important philosophical systems of the past, especially Kant's, into disrepute? At least part of the answer to this question is for Cassirer the idea of beauty, that "pure phenomenon" whose incarnation of a logical impossibility seems able to undermine system as such, but to do it gently, humanly, without disrupting precisely our aesthetic appreciation of those actual systems, like Kant's, without which our own preter-systematic perspective could never have been achieved.

THE CASE OF LESSING

Is Cassirer's project feasible? Can we really retain the benefits of systematic philosophy—its soundness, its structural completeness—yet also move beyond system into an emphatically unshackled and "human" mode of thought? My own answer to this question is no. The promise of aesthetics is always delusive; its apparent tempering and humanizing of philosophical systematics is never in the end anything but a device— however innocent the intentions of its practitioners—by which we are subjected to systematic constraints far more rigid than those we had hoped to avoid, constraints that affect not only our intellectual activity, but our political and our day-to-day practical life as well.

This matter resists treatment in general terms and must be debated case by case. (Who will be foolish enough to take a position *against* the idea of beauty?) And the case suggested most strongly by Cassirer himself is that of Lessing, about whom he says, in the very last words of the Enlightenment book, that it was "because of him that the century of the Enlightenment, to a very great extent dominated by its gift of criticism, did not fall prey to the merely negative critical function—that it was able to reconvert criticism to creative activity and shape it and use it as an indispensable instrument of life and of the constant renewal of the spirit" (360). If by "criticism" here we understand a conceptual scrupulousness that easily degenerates into pedantry and intolerance, then Cassirer is crediting Lessing with a special intellectual flexibility, doubtless aesthetically schooled, that is willing to accept logical or conceptual incongruences for the sake of living, of being open and human and creative. And as attractive as this view of Lessing may be, it is completely wrong.

Far from advocating or permitting a relaxation of conceptual strictness, Lessing insists on making that strictness absolute, on carrying it even beyond the point at which a completed system might offer us some comfort, on practicing the most implacable and incorruptible "criticism" imaginable. Cassirer, for instance, is very fond of Lessing's *Die Erziehung des Menschengeschlechts* [The Education of the Human Race], which he reads as "nothing but a theodicy of history, a justification of religion not through a being which has existed from the beginning of time but through religious growth and the goal of this growth" (192). You can interpret Lessing's text this way only if you stop reading soon enough to avoid the argument's final logical step, the derivation from that "theodicy of history" of the doctrine of metempsychosis, which you must now either accept (you Christians) or else rethink the whole matter from square one. [19]

And as far as the theory of art is concerned—let us not say "aesthetics," a word he himself avoids—Lessing adheres unswervingly to the idea of imitation. But for him, *imitation does not imply communication.* The crucial point in *Laokoon* is that both poetry and painting are irreparably deficient considered as representations of experience, poetry because it cannot adequately represent the material or spatial aspect of our experienced world, painting because it fails to represent adequately the temporal aspect or the quality of action. It happens, says Lessing, that the imagination of the reader or observer is inclined to supply the missing component of experience in each case, so that we get the impression of receiving from the work of art a total imitation of experience, all the more so since the combination of objective and subjective elements in that impression mimics a similar combination in our ordinary direct experience of reality. [20] But it is never implied in this argument that art communicates a *specific* experience to us, that there is ever any necessary degree of similarity between what I experience in my reading or viewing and what you do. Communication is in fact eliminated as an issue at the very outset, since the imitative efficacy of art depends precisely upon its communicative deficiency.

If Lessing, then, avoids the issue of the communication of feelings or experience, my inference would be that it is because of the conceptual compromises that inevitably attend that issue. And one might expect, in turn, that Lessing would also have no use for the idea of beauty. But in *Laokoon*, especially chapter 2, he insists not only that "for the ancients beauty was the highest law of the visual arts,"[21] but that painting and sculpture, by their nature, *should* be restricted to the depiction of the beautiful. The trouble, from an "aesthetic" point of view, is that the notion of beauty is used here in such a way as to defeat any idea of an "idea" of beauty that might have satisfied Baumgarten or Kant or (by rights) Cassirer. When Lessing speaks of an "Ideal" of human beauty (6: 19), he means something like the rule of Polyclitus, a canon of bodily and facial proportions. And otherwise he is careful not to let the word "beauty" suggest anything more than: what you and I, especially if we were ancient Greeks, might consider beautiful; or more specifically, the quality that makes it possible for us to look at something repeatedly or for a long time without finding it either tedious or disgusting or ridiculous. He even justifies the use of beauty as a criterion in legislation limiting what works of art may be shown in public (6: 18-19). At every turn, he de-Platonizes beauty; he dissociates artistic beauty from anything we might recognize as an aesthetic argument or project.

I will have more to say about Lessing further on. But for the time being I offer the relation between him and Cassirer, Cassirer's compulsion to invoke him and to invoke thereby a refutation of his whole valorizing of aesthetics, as a symbol of the contradictoriness and confusion of the aesthetic project as a whole.

NOTES

1. These page counts, and all subsequent references to the book, are from Ernst Cassirer, *The Philosophy of the Enlightenment* (Orig. pub. 1932), trans. Fritz C. A. Koelln and James P. Pettegrove (Princeton, 1951).

2. "Beautiful sciences" translates the German "schöne Wissenschaften," which in the eighteenth century is the standard German translation of French "belles-lettres." See section C 2b α of the article on "Wissenschaft" in Grimm. Georg Friedrich Meier, *Anfangsgründe aller schönen Wissenschaften*, 3 vols., 2nd ed. (Halle im Magdeburgischen, 1754-1759; reprint Hildesheim: Olms, 1976), whom Cassirer mentions in a footnote (353), exploits the apparent combination of the ideas of beauty and science in this locution to suggest the idea of aesthetics. The idea of "activating the whole man" is also from Meier, vol. 1, § 15: "Die schönen Wissenschaften beleben den ganzen Menschen."

3. For the situation in English I find the *OED,* atypically, rather unhelpful. It does not set off the aesthetic meaning of "art" very clearly, except in following the phrase "art for art's sake" ("l'art pour l'art") from Victor Cousin (1818)—other sources give Benjamin Constant precedence—through a number of English instances. The aesthetic meaning of French "art" is certainly well established by 1865, in Hippolyte Taine's *Philosophie de l'art,* but the process leading to this point is gradual, including the instances I have mentioned plus a suggested instance, curiously enough, from Grimm, on "Kunst," II, 4, c, ε, who finds "l'art" in the singular with modern meaning in Voltaire's "Essay sur la poésieé pique." French sources, e.g. Alain Rey, *Dictionnaire historique de la langue française* (Paris: Le Robert, 1992), 119, generally credit the influence of German "Kunst" on French. For the modern meaning of "Kunst" Grimm, II, 4, d, credits mainly Winckelmann, Lessing, Herder, Goethe, and Schiller, but curiously does not mention Moritz, even in the article on "Kunstwerk."

4. In the "Vorrede" to *Laokoon.* See Gotthold Ephraim Lessing, *Werke,* ed. Herbert G. Göpfert, 8 vols. (Munich, 1970-9), 6: 11.

5. Harold Jantz, *Goethe's Faust as a Renaissance Man: Parallels and Prototypes* (Princeton, 1951), 45.

6. For the Latin/German and Latin/English editions used here, see chap. 1, n1. Aschenbrenner and Holther, the English translators, in an editorial note (81) on Baumgarten's § 3, refer to Christian Wolff, *Psychologia empirica,* § 580, which uses "appetitus" in very much the same way; and it may be in fact that the confusion of monadological and psychological discourses that I discuss below begins with Wolff. But the exploitation of this confusion to suggest an aesthetic theorem on the verbal communicability of sense impressions is strictly Baumgarten's. In any case, as far as I can judge, it has not been established that Baumgarten or Wolff had studied directly either the "Monadology" or the "Principes de la Nature et de la Grace," which are the Leibniz texts that I use below. But both Baumgarten and Wolff were aware of the theory of simple and complex substances, and of Leibniz's notion of "pre-established harmony," which presupposes a strict separation of the realm of final causes from that of efficient causes; and these ideas in turn are sufficient to imply logically most of the doctrine of monads. Moreover, in my own argument, the doctrine of monads is not strictly necessary as such; I could have spoken of a "metaphysical" discourse strictly separated by Leibniz from psychological discourse. In other words, I am using those two very clear and succinct texts of Leibniz to make the abbreviated version of what would be a very cumbersome argument about Baumgarten if I attempted to identify exactly the source of every Leibnizian echo. Interestingly enough, the secondary literature on Leibniz, Wolff, and Baumgarten tends to be a good deal less circumspect on this matter than I am. Perhaps I am underestimating the extent to which manuscript material was passed around at the time. See e. g. Walther Arnsperger, *Christian Wolff's Verhältnis zu Leibniz* (Weimar, 1897), 46, who speaks of a direct reference on Wolff's part to the Leibnizian monad but without citing his source; Jürgen Nieraad, *Standpunktbewußtsein und Weltzusammenhang: Das Bild vom lebendigen Spiegel bei Leibniz und seine Bedeutung für das Alterswerk Goethes* (Wiesbaden, 1970), 71n6, who speaks of how Wolff's understanding of the Leibnizian monad is incomplete; Ursula Franke, *Kunst als Erkenntnis: Die Rolle der Sinnlichkeit in der Ästhetik des Alexander Gottlieb Baumgarten* (Wiesbaden, 1972), who has a whole chapter on "Die monadologische Komponente der Sinnlichkeit" in Baumgarten (51-61); and Friedhelm Solms, *Disciplina aesthetica: Zur Frühgeschichte der ästhetischen Theorie bei Baumgarten und Herder* (Stuttgart, 1990), 109, who speaks of Wolff's "systematizing" of an "axiom" derived from the "Monadology." But still, I think circumspection is called for. There is, in any event, a certain amount of confusion about facts. Consider, for example, Catherine Wilson, "The Reception of Leibniz in the Eighteenth Century," in *The Cambridge Companion to Leibniz,* ed. Nicholas Jolley (Cambridge, 1995), who, in the very midst of an argument that attempts to show "clear echoes of the *Monadology* in Wolff" (446), also says that "Wolff never used the term 'monad,'" which is of course not true. See e. g. the *Discursus praeliminaris de philosophia in genere,* § 160, where we read, "*Leibnitius* elementa

rerummaterialium statuit esse monades sive substantias simplices, quae gaudeant vi repraesentandi universum limitata. "
Some of these considerations may also apply, *mutatis mutandis,* to the discussion of Kantian and Leibnizian "apperception" in chap. 4.

7. The original is quoted from *Die philosophischen Schriften von Gottfried Wilhelm Leibniz,* ed. C. J. Gerhardt, 7 vols. (Berlin, 1875-90), 6: 607-23. The translation used is Gottfried Wilhelm Leibniz, *Philosophical Writings,* ed. G. H. R. Parkinson (London: Everyman, 1995), 179-94.

8. This text is found in the original on 598-606, in the translation on 195-204.

9. For Leibniz's willingness to accept psychological discourse, see no. 27 of the *Discourse on Metaphysics* of 1686.

10. The original is from Abbé Du Bos, *Réflexions critiques sur la poésie et sur la peinture,* reprint of the posthumous edition of 1755 (Paris, 1993), 1. The translation is from Cassirer, 303.

11. In Kant's own view, all the material of the *Critique of Judgment* is generated systematically by the structure of the whole critical project. But it is fairly clear that in fact the idea of disinterested pleasure is part of a general European quest (mainly in response to Hobbes) for fundamentally unselfish elements in human psychology. Interestingly resonant with Kant's thought is Francis Hutcheson's idea of "the moral sense," in *An Inquiry concerning Moral Good and Evil* (1725-26). See Hutcheson, *Collected Works,* facsimile ed., 7 vols. (Hildesheim: Olms, 1969-1971), 1: 107-24. The evidence for the existence of this moral sense is found primarily in certain instances of *pleasure* (here the resonance with Kant), and Hutcheson contends, "Our *Sense* of Pleasure is antecedent to *Advantage* and *Interest,*" (103).

12. In J. C. Adelung, *Grammatisch-kritisches Wörterbuch* (Vienna, 1807-8; Orig. pub. 1774-86) the difference between *fühlen* and *empfinden* is still strongly marked; the former in fact is still associated with its etymological sense referring to the use of the fingertips. But the clearest and best known piece of evidence that *empfinden* and words derived from it are felt to have to do with emotion is Lessing's suggestion, in 1768, that "empfindsam" (he thought he was coining the word) be used to translate English "sentimental." See the article on "empfindsam" in Friedrich Kluge, *Etymologisches Wörterbuch der deutschen Sprache,* 18th ed., rev. Walther Mitzka (Berlin: de Gruyter, 1960), 164.

13. Aschenbrenner and Holther, 83, cite another parallel with Wolff, *Psychologia empirica,* this one in § 605, which has "affects" arising *from* "a confused representation of good and evil." One can see here how Baumgarten is taking basic concepts from Wolff and reconfiguring them entirely.

14. Dante, interestingly enough, whom Kant would doubtless have dismissed as a dogmatist, recognizes (*Purgatorio,* 21. 73-75) that even our obvious interest in possessing *knowledge* poisons our ability ever to be confident about such possession.

15. Plato, *Phaedrus,* 249-50, as translated by R. Hackforth, in *The Collected Dialogues of Plato Including the Letters,* eds. Edith Hamilton and Huntington Cairns (New York: Pantheon, 1961), 496-7.

16. Cassirer, 311. The phrase in the original is "das reine *Phänomen* der Schönheit" (Cassirer's emphasis), in Ernst Cassirer, *Die Philosophie der Aufklärung,* 2nd ed. (Tübingen, 1932), 417.

17. I refer to the partial edition, Alexander Gottlieb Baumgarten, *Theoretische Ästhetik: Die grundlegenden Abschnitte aus der "Aesthetica" (1750/58),* ed. Hans Rudolf Schweizer, 2nd ed. (Hamburg, 1988).

18. Ernst Cassirer, *An Essay on Man: An Introduction to a Philosophy of Human Culture* (Garden City, NY: Anchor Books, n. d. ; Orig. pub. 1944), 176.

19. .For more detail on this point, see my "Reason, Error, and the Shape of History: Lessing's Nathan and Lessing's God," *Lessing Yearbook,* 9 (1977), 60-80.

20. For full details of this argument, see the Lessing chapter in my *Beyond Theory: Eighteenth-Century German Literature and the Poetics of Irony* (Ithaca, 1993), 116-61.

21. Lessing, *Werke,* 6: 20.

THREE

The Irrelevance of Aesthetics as Discovered in "Classical" Weimar

Chapter 1 treated the beginning of aesthetics, particularly in Kant and Moritz. Chapter 2 followed Cassirer through what I should prefer to call pre-aesthetics (before the millennialist moves of Kant and Moritz), and tried to throw light on the background and the besetting problems of aesthetics. The present chapter discusses a text that by rights should have marked the end of aesthetics. That aesthetics nevertheless continued to operate for at least a century and a half after its demise in Schiller's thinking, is a problem that we shall have to deal with.

THE EXISTENCE AND INTEGRITY OF THE SELF

If there is any reason for saying "German classicism"—rather than simply saying what these words really refer to, the works of Goethe and Schiller produced during the period of their association—if there is a coherent spirit in those works that justifies the value-laden notion of the "classical" otherwise than by nationalistic convenience,[1] then in view of the high level of abstraction in the two authors' correspondence on poetry and art, we should expect to find such a spirit describable in terms of aesthetic theory. For by the time that classical collaboration gets started, an aesthetic *movement* had long been building in European and especially German thought. The term introduced by Baumgarten in 1735 is adopted by an extraordinary variety of thinkers, including Hamann, Mendelssohn, Kant, and Schiller; and even where the term "aesthetic" is not prominent, the practice of bringing questions of beauty and art, of artistic judgment and artistic production, into the erstwhile preserve of school philosophy, becomes ever more common, in thinkers like Lessing, Herder, Moritz, and Goethe. Political millennialism and the problem of communication are two sources of this movement's energy. But there is much left to be said on the question: *What is at stake* in the general intellectual tendency that includes the emergence of aesthetics as a discipline?

This question is asked in exactly these terms, and an answer is proposed, by Andrew Bowie:

> Baumgarten's *Aesthetica,* part one 1750, part two 1758, and Hamann's *Aesthetica in nuce,* of 1762, already begin to suggest what is at stake in the emergence of aesthetics as an independent branch of philosophy. Despite their obvious differences, Baumgarten and Hamann share a concern with the failure of the Rationalist traditions of the eighteenth century to do justice to the immediacy of the individual's sensuous relationship to the world which is part of aesthetic pleasure. [2]

And a bit further on, Bowie puts his finger on what becomes a crucial dilemma for Schiller. "Revaluing the sensuous particular," he says, "and giving it primacy in one branch of philosophy poses problems: how does one abstractly grasp the particular without abolishing its value as particular?" (5). "The particular," problematic as it may be, is not problematic enough as long as it is regarded as a possible object of investigation. The particular, strictly conceived, can never be "regarded" at all, but is irrevocably *hidden* from philosophy. *Individuum est ineffabile* (the individual is inexpressible) is a truth not only for Herder, Goethe, and Dilthey.

Still, Schiller nevertheless gives something close to a complete statement of what is at stake in aesthetics in letter no. 4 of *Über die ästhetische Erziehung des Menschen* [On the Aesthetic Education of Man—henceforward called *Aesthetic Letters*], the work that forms the summary and culmination of his struggle with aesthetic questions in the 1790s.

> Aber eben deswegen, weil der Staat eine Organisation sein soll, die sich durch sich selbst und für sich selbst bildet, so kann er auch nur insoferne wirklich werden, als sich die Teile zur Idee des Ganzen hinaufgestimmt haben.Weil der Staat der reinen und objektiven Menschheit in der Brust seiner Bürger zum Repräsentanten dient, so wird er gegen seine Bürger dasselbe Verhältnis zu beobachten haben, in welchem sie zu sich selber stehen, und ihre subjektive Menschheit auch nur in *dem* Grade ehren können, als sie zur objektiven veredelt ist. Ist der innere Mensch mit sich einig, so wird er auch bei der höchsten Universalisierung seines Betragens seine Eigentümlichkeit retten, und der Staat wird bloß der Ausleger seines schönen Instinkts, die deutlichere Formel seiner innern Gesetzgebung sein. [3]

> [But precisely because the state is to be an organization formed by itself and for itself, it can only become a reality inasmuch as its parts have been tuned up to the idea of the whole. Because the state serves to represent that ideal and objective humanity that exists in the heart of each of its citizens, it will have to observe toward those citizens the

same relationship as each has to himself, and will be able to honor their subjective humanity only *to the extent* that this has been ennobled in the direction of objective humanity. Once man is inwardly at one with himself, he will be able to preserve his individuality however much he may universalize his conduct, and the state will be merely the interpreter of his own finest instinct, a clearer formulation of his own sense of what is right.][4]

The question here is not merely whether philosophical systematics can "do justice" to a human "particularity" or "immediacy" understood as pre-existing. What is at stake is whether—in a practical and therefore a political sense—we human beings shall be able *to have in the first place*, each of us, his or her own truly particular, individual being.

The very condition of the self is in question. In no. 6, in his discussion of the difference between ancient Hellenic civilization and its modern European descendants, Schiller insists that the self, in the sense of our experience of our own being, is not an absolute, but is historically and culturally contingent; that it is in fact possible for "the individual concrete life" to be "destroyed"; that a mode of individual experience can be *annihilated* ("so wird denn allmählich das einzelne konkrete Leben vertilgt" [5: 585]) by developments in the cultural and political sphere. And the task of aesthetics is to restore the "concrete" self: to restore a condition in which my strict "Eigentümlichkeit," the unrepeatable particularity of my being as myself, can be preserved even in the face of universal moral and social claims made on me; a condition in which we, like the Greeks, will be "at once individual and genus," namely *representatives* of the human genus" (5: 668; T, 177).

Actually Schiller presents this restoration of human selfhood as the task of beauty itself, not that of aesthetics. But if the effect he hopes for can be expected from the simple operation of artistic beauty upon contemporary sensibilities, why does he bother to write his treatise? The very existence of the *Aesthetic Letters* implies that beauty alone, or the practice of art alone, is insufficient, that an advance in the understanding of beauty, an advance in aesthetics, is also needed.[5] And in Schiller's historical view, this implication makes sense. For the modern corruption of my experience of the individual self, the destruction of my "concrete life," is the result of a process of abstraction, a submission to the power of "the abstract idea of the whole" (5:585; T, 101). It follows that I can be led back to a more fully human condition only by a process that begins where I after all find myself, on a high level of abstraction, and proceeds *toward* the particular and immediate.

Which is exactly what aesthetics, as represented by Schiller's *Letters*, seems to be doing. The actual logical argument of the *Letters* begins in no. 11 with the words:

> Wenn die Abstraktion so hoch, als sie immer kann, hinaufsteigt, so
> gelangt sie zu zwei letzten Begriffen, bei denen sie stille stehen und
> ihre Grenzen bekennen muß. Sie unterscheidet in dem Menschen et-
> was, das bleibt, und etwas, das sich unaufhörlich verändert.Das Blei-
> bende nennt sie seine *Person,* das Wechselnde seinen *Zustand.* (5: 601)

> [When abstraction rises to the highest it can possibly attain, it arrives at
> two ultimate concepts before which it must halt and recognize that
> here it has reached its limits. It distinguishes in man something that
> endures and something that constantly changes. That which endures it
> calls his *person,* that which changes, his *condition.* (T, 115)]

We are offered not merely abstraction, but the highest possible abstraction. Every reader, no matter how thoroughly corrupted by abstraction,
can therefore be reached by this argument. And only five letters later, at
the end of no. 15—by a process Schiller costumes as the strict logical
development of his initial abstraction—we arrive at the idea of a state of
utter emotional immediacy, an aesthetically aroused state in which we
find ourselves

> zugleich in dem Zustand der höchsten Ruhe und der höchsten Beweg-
> ung, und es entsteht jene wunderbare Rührung, für welche der Ver-
> stand keinen Begriff und die Sprache keinen Namen hat. (5:619)

> [at one and the same time in a state of utter repose and extreme agita-
> tion, and there results that wondrous stirring of the heart for which
> mind has no concept nor speech any name. (T, 132)]

Individuum est ineffabile. Yet aesthetics claims to open through logic an
avenue by which that ineffable condition might be communicated and
shared after all.

   Moreover, Schiller's initial abstract notions obviously summarize Cartesian dualism, which suggests an *historical* idea of aesthetics. The intellectual corruption of the experiencing self, we infer, reaches a kind of
climax in Descartes, who claims to derive the self logically (as the domain
in which I cannot doubt) and so exposes it utterly to the universal. Thus
the task is set for an opposed philosophical movement, the development
of aesthetics, that is aimed at restoring our immediate humanity. We can
now give a more exact name to the goal of aesthetics: it is not merely "the
human," in the sense of Cassirer's second humanist Renaissance, but the
restoration of total, unalienated humanity in every individual.

AESTHETIC RECEPTION AND THE RESTORED SELF

Can we make the same claim with respect to Kant and Moritz, the originators of modern aesthetics? The case of Moritz is clear, given that his
millennialist psychology, aimed at restoring an integrated individual, is

the root of his aesthetics. Nor does the case of Kant give us much difficulty, even though the *Critique of Judgment* is concerned hardly at all with art. Its topic is the faculty of judging as such, including judgments of taste which are made "byway of an *entirely disinterested* pleasure or displeasure" (§ 5). But if we press the question of what is at stake in the *Critique,* sections III and IX of the Introduction [Einleitung] bring us back to an idea of reintegration of the self, in the assertion that judgment makes possible a transition between the otherwise radically separate faculties of "Verstand" and "Vernunft" [understanding and reason].

Schiller, then, has accurately detected and adopted an entirely central idea in the early development of aesthetics. But the *artistic* dimension of this idea requires the notion of aesthetic reception that is found in Moritz's 1785 "Beaux-Arts and Belles-Lettres" essay:

> It is not so much that we need the beautiful for our pleasure, as that the beautiful needs us, in order to be recognized. We can exist perfectly well without observing beautiful works of art, but these works cannot exist, as such, without our observing them. The more we can thus do without them, by so much more do we observe them for their own sake, in order as it were to endow them, for the first time, with their own full existence by our contemplation. For by means of our increasing recognition of the beautiful in a beautiful work of art, we increase, so to speak, its own beauty and endow it with more and more value. Hence our impatient desire that everyone should pay homage to beauty where we have recognized it; the more generally it is recognized and admired as beautiful, the more value it acquires in our eyes.[6]

Moritz claims in effect that a work of art is *constituted,* brought into full existence, only in the process of its reception.

This idea is central in aesthetics from the outset. The implication, in Baumgarten's *Meditationes,* that a "perfect sensory discourse" is possible, would have as a consequence that sensory "representations" can be adequately incorporated into discourse and fully reconstituted by a reader. Baumgarten himself does not develop this thought; but the decisive aesthetic move is evident nonetheless, the idea that the work of art is not coextensive with the material of which it is made, but is first fully constituted, first comes into existence, in its communication to a sensitive recipient.

The idea is not new in Baumgarten, and is related in an obvious way to the development of social and economic conditions in Europe in the seventeenth and eighteenth centuries. As various forms of the middle class gain standing and leisure and cultural importance, and as the value of works of art must therefore be justified, more and more, from the point of view of a purchaser or a paying audience, the study of art will naturally orient itself more toward the work's reception than toward its production. The primacy of the concept of beauty in artistic studies shows this orientation. But such socio-economic considerations by no means imply

that the focus of aesthetics upon reception lacks a philosophical dimension—unless we are willing to believe that Lessing's and Schiller's analy-
ses of the process of reception, as well as Moritz's in "On the Plastic
Imitation of the Beautiful," are motivated solely by a need to accommodate the same contemporary society against which much of their argument is directed.

Thus our attention is drawn again to the question of what is at stake in
aesthetics. And the answer remains the same. When Schiller speaks of the
"destruction" of the concrete experiencing self, he is speaking of a condition that in the following century would be known as "alienation." The
sensate self has ceased to exist not literally, but only in the sense that it
lacks any guarantee or confirmation of its existence. It exists in a kind of
isolation, cut off from its Cartesian counterpart that "thinks and therefore
is," cut off from the ego that is constituted by reflective thinking. It is
exiled, in particular, from the common human world-girdling network of
discourse, in which it might conceivably have found itself reflected and
confirmed. Baumgarten appears to understand the situation when he
notes in his *Metaphysica* (§ 512) that in respect to the lower cognitive
faculties, those faculties engaged by the work of art, a person is limited
absolutely by the position of his or her body in the world. But he does not
carry out the aesthetic implications of this thought. For if the strictly
limited sensate self not only perceives the beautiful in art, but is the site
where the work of art, or the perfect sensory discourse of poetry, *first
achieves its full being*—or even if we merely have reason to form this
impression (which is what Moritz actually suggests)—then the alienation
of that sensate self has been overcome. It now receives an indispensable
function in the world of communicable representations and so is reintegrated into that world, into the universe of discourse, hence is confirmed
and reconnected with the rational (discursive) self in a newly whole person. (Since Baumgarten does not go into these ramifications of his subject
matter, his treatment of it does not yet qualify as "aesthetics" in Schiller's
or Moritz's sense, but remains only a theory of sensate cognition and a
dream of verbal communication.)

I contend, then, that Schiller's view of what is at stake in aesthetics
reflects a clear understanding of the historical situation. But if we can
assume that it is precisely this historical situation, that it is *the question of
aesthetics* that interests Schiller, rather than any particular aesthetic questions, then we are tempted to conclude that the *Letters* arrive at a *reductio
ad absurdum* of the whole aesthetic project. For if what is at stake in
aesthetics is the reintegration of the self, which means the rehabilitation
of the strictly particular sensate self by way of a de-theorizing of the self
as a whole, how can this task ever be accomplished by aesthetics, which
is itself a theoretical discipline? In letters 11-15 Schiller creates a logical
bridge from maximum "abstraction" to emotional immediacy. But in order actually to travel this bridge (to *experience* the immediacy it arrives

at), we would have to be reading by some vehicle other than discursive logic, which would mean that the bridge itself (as an instance of discursive logic) is no longer there for us.

There is still nothing for it. If aesthetics is to have any validity, it must assign the task of accomplishing its anti-theoretical project to art alone, or to beauty. But what reason is there for confidence that art, or beauty, is suited to that project? The historical evidence, as Schiller himself points out, tends in exactly the opposite direction. "And indeed it must give pause for reflection that in almost every historical epoch in which the arts flourish, and taste prevails, we find humanity at a low ebb, and cannot point to a single instance of a high degree and wide diffusion of aesthetic culture going hand in hand with political freedom and civic virtue, fine manners with good morals, refinement of conduct with truth of conduct" (5:598-9; T, 113). Even our judgment of the Greeks is poisoned by this reflection upon history.

> As long as Athens and Sparta maintained their independence, and respect for the laws served as the basis for their constitution, taste was as yet immature, art still in its infancy, and beauty far from ruling over the hearts of men. . . . When, under Pericles and Alexander, the golden age of the arts arrived, and the rule of taste extended its sway, the strength and freedom of Greece are no longer to be found. Rhetoric falsified truth, wisdom gave offence in the mouth of a Socrates, and virtue in the life of a Phocion. (5:599; T, 113-14)

And even without these historical worries, the very existence of aesthetics continues to call its own project into question. If beauty alone were sufficient to improve the human condition, why would aesthetics be necessary?

SCHILLER'S ARGUMENTS ON HISTORY AND EDUCATION

Is Schiller really suggesting a *reductio ad absurdum* of aesthetics in this sense? This question contains two parts. (1) Can we adduce further interpretive evidence in support of such a negative reading of the *Letters*? (2) Can we form a plausible conjecture about why Schiller should want to develop that negative position, what end he has in mind? In response to (1) I will offer a reading of the *Letters* alongside *Wallenstein* and *Maria Stuart*. And question (2) will lead us to *Wilhelm Tell*, and to both the person and the work of Goethe.

The thought of the *Aesthetic Letters* is very complicated and pretends to a high degree of technical philosophical refinement.[7] For this reason, some simple interpretive questions about the text are hardly ever asked. The whole historical dimension of the argument provokes such a question. Why does Schiller insist so strongly upon the assertions: (1) that the Greeks represented a clear maximum of aesthetic culture (5:586); (2) that the further development of civilization in Europe necessarily entailed a disintegration of that human wholeness; and (3) that the disintegration can be repaired, our wholeness restored, only by an ennobling of character in the present age (5:592)? Why does he suggest in letters 11 through 15 that the development of aesthetics represents a reversal of the whole historical unfolding of philosophy that culminates in Descartes? He himself points out that perfect Greek humanity never actually happened in history (5:599); and in the very midst of his historical presentation, he reminds us that we are not bound by our historical circumstances:

> But can man really be destined to miss himself for the sake of any purpose whatsoever? Should nature, for the sake of her own purposes, be able to rob us of a completeness that reason, for the sake of hers, enjoins upon us? It must, therefore, be false that the cultivation of individual powers involves the sacrifice of wholeness. Or rather, however much the law of nature tends in that direction, it must be open to us to restore by a higher art the totality of our nature that the arts themselves have destroyed. (5:588; T, 104)

When he speaks later of the need for an "ennobling of character," he is invoking a concept (in German, "Charakter") that can refer either to individuals themselves or to a general level of individual development. But the context, especially the comparison with the Greeks, makes clear that "Individuen" themselves (5:583) are at issue; and the passage just quoted implies that precisely as individuals we are *not* subject to the historical forces that have supposedly corrupted our "character."

There is perhaps not an actual inconsistency here; but there is enough vagueness, ambiguity, conceptual slippage, to cause us concern about the integrity of the whole edifice. Why does Schiller raise the question of history in the first place? Why not simply set forth the abstract idea of beauty, and that of the "ästhetischer Zustand" (5:633-36) [aesthetic state or condition] in which perfect freedom is restored to us, and then show how these ideas suggest possibilities for dealing with the corrupt political and cultural situation of Europe in the 1790s? Or to look at it the other way around, why does he mention "aesthetic education" in his title, and then not say anything about ways in which people might *actually* be educated, about practical possibilities for propagating aesthetic culture? As the text stands, the idea of "education" in the title serves no purpose except to call attention to the bind we get into when we ask whether the educative task is assigned to beauty alone, or to aesthetics. At the end of no. 9 there is a long exhortation to enthusiastic young readers about how to keep themselves pure in the present age (5:595); but no practical educative advice is offered.

It appears that either the thought of the *Letters* is fundamentally disordered or something is going on beneath the surface that unifies the endeavor.[8] I think there is some truth in both possibilities. And once we understand the subsurface unifying tendency, in all its logical and rhetorical complexity, we will also understand why Schiller can be forgiven some confusion in his argument.

In the very last letter, no. 27, Schiller turns away from the mainly psychological discussion of the "aesthetic state [of mind]," or aesthetic "Bestimmbarkeit" (5:632-36) [determinability], which had occupied him in nos. 20-25, and comes back to the question of politics and history. Now he defines three types of polity (or "state").

> If in the *dynamic* state of rights it is as force that one man encounters another, and imposes limits upon his activities; if in the *ethical* state of duties man sets himself over against man with all the majesty of the law, and puts a curb upon his desires; in those circles where conduct is governed by beauty, in the *aesthetic* state, none may appear to the other except as form, or confront him except as an object of free play. *To bestow freedom by means of freedom* is the fundamental law of this kingdom. (5:667; T, 176)

The task of history, obviously, is to realize the third, "aesthetic" political type. But the immediately preceding letter, no. 26, has poisoned this historical suggestion at its root. "In whatever individual or whole people we find this honest and autonomous kind of [aesthetic] semblance, we may assume both understanding and taste, and every kindred excellence. There we shall see actual life governed by the ideal, honor triumphant over possessions, thought over enjoyment, dreams of immortality over existence. There public opinion will be the only thing to be feared, and an olive wreath bestow greater honor than a purple robe" (5:659; T, 169). For this passage directly contradicts the factual discussion of the Greeks in no. 10, and so calls attention to the manner in which historical fact makes nonsense of the very idea of an "aesthetic" polity. Why does Schiller return to historical argument in the first place—and then why in so transparently illogical a fashion?

I can see only one possible answer, provided we agree that the question exists. The last two letters, nos. 26 and 27, are a *gesture*, indicating that we must somehow *pass beyond* the psychological argument that is, after all, the work's logical culmination. Indeed, it follows from Schiller's idea of the goal of aesthetics that the idea of a psychological state of "aesthetic determinability" must mark the culmination of *aesthetics as a whole*: the idea of a mental state in which "an actual *union* and interchange between matter and form, passivity and activity, momentarily takes place, so that the *compatibility* of our two natures . . . hence the possibility of sublimest humanity, is thereby actually proven" (5:654; T, 164-5). Surely, once this "proof" is established, the goal of all aesthetics, the reintegration of the self, has been achieved. Why does Schiller now distract us by reopening the treacherous question of history? Why should it be necessary to pass beyond the goal of all aesthetics?

THE ABSURDITY OF AESTHETICS

The trouble with the idea of the aesthetic state of mind is that while it *is* logically the culmination of aesthetics, it cannot legitimately be *thought of* as a goal or culmination. For in the aesthetic state of mind, "die Selbsttätigkeit der Vernunft [wird] schon auf dem Felde der Sinnlichkeit eröffnet" (5:642) [the autonomy of reason is already opened up within the domain of sense itself (T, 153)]. But "Selbsttätigkeit" here means "autonomy" in the sense of an *active* faculty, which cannot establish itself except *by acting*, by taking "[den] Schritt von demästhetischen Zustand zu dem logischen und moralischen" [the step from the aesthetic to the logical and moral state]—which means that the ultimate proof of aesthetic determinability is furnished only after the fact, only by the act of self-determination that proceeds from it. When aesthetic determinability, or freedom from determination, is desired for its own sake, as a goal, then a perversion of its very nature occurs. This argument is not made in the *Letters* themselves; but it emerges clearly from Schiller's treatment of the figure of Wallenstein and of the figure of Leicester in *Maria Stuart*. Wallenstein complains:

> Wärs möglich? Könnt ich nicht mehr, wie ich wollte?
> Nicht mehr zurück, wie mirs beliebt? Ich müßte
> Die Tat *vollbringen*, weil ich sie *gedacht*,
> Nicht die Versuchung von mir wies—das Herz
> Genährt mit diesem Traum, auf ungewisse
> Erfüllung hin die Mittel mir gespart,
> Die Wege bloß mir offen hab gehalten?—
> . . .
> Wars unrecht, an dem Gaukelbilde mich
> Der königlichen Hoffnung zu ergötzen? (*Wallensteins Tod,* 139-51)

> [Is it possible? That I can no longer do as I wish, can no longer go back if I feel like it? I have to *carry out* the deed just because I *thought* of it, didn't banish temptation, nourished my heart with this dream, stored up the wherewithal just in case, just because I kept my paths open?— . . . Was it wrong to enjoy the delusive image of royal hope?]

And like Wallenstein, Leicester also suggests a travesty of the aesthetic state of mind in that his intentness on keeping his options open, his taking of free determinability as a goal, only plunges him all the more helplessly into a determination over which he has no control.

The true aesthetic state of mind (if it exists) can never be a goal, only the way toward a goal.[9] Hence the last two historical numbers of the *Letters:* which make the gesture of superseding the concept of the aesthetic state of mind; but also, in their contradictoriness, reveal that such supersedure *cannot possibly occur in a work of aesthetic theory,* where that concept is the culmination of the whole discipline. Thus the possibility of a *reductio ad absurdum* of aesthetics as a whole arises—a showing that aesthetics, in its quality as theory, cannot help but take as a goal or culmination the concept whose very nature is perverted thereby. In fact, given that what is at stake in aesthetics is the rescue of the human self from the disruptive powers of theoretical abstraction, the indictment suggested by the *Letters* cuts even deeper. For of all the possible types of philosophical anthropology—disciplines of thought that have humanity as their object—aesthetics now turns out to be the most pernicious, by subjecting to abstract dismemberment precisely the need for a complete and integrated idea of humanity. On this view, aesthetics is thus a symptom, if not indeed a cause, of exactly those problems in history against which it is supposedly erected.

And yet, a direct critical exposé of the self-contradiction in aesthetic theory would itself still inevitably *be* a work of aesthetics. By showing the fault of aesthetics in the disintegration of the self, it would still be advocating an integration of that self; and by thus advocating what it is unable to take the responsibility for achieving, it would only be repeating the hypocritical procedure of the aesthetics it criticizes. Therefore the only possible method of dealing with the problem of aesthetics is the one that seems to be employed in the *Letters:* not to attack aesthetics, but to affirm it, to develop it to a level of conceptual completeness at which it cannot help but destroy itself by its own contradictions—especially the two incompatible views of human history that are required in its unfolding. The *Letters* are thus an *unreadable* text. One cannot possibly learn anything by reading them because they bring about the self-overthrow of exactly the generic or disciplinary presuppositions that make their statements intelligible. If this conclusion seems outlandish, we need only recall that the same idea is implied by the gratuitous mention of "education" in the title. Only when we ask about the educative content of the book are we faced with the absence of any such content, and thus nudged toward the understanding that in the end this text is nothing but a kind of pantomime, an essentially mute performance of the emptiness of aesthetics as a whole. It does not follow that the *Letters* are a useless work, or that the reintegration of the self is a worthless project. By undermining aesthetics as a theoretical discipline, the *Letters* can in fact perhaps be said to liberate that project from its theoretical shackles, thus to make it a real possibility after all.

GOETHE AS READER

The fact that an unmasking of the absurdity of aesthetics was certainly not part of Schiller's original project does not invalidate this interpretation. It is possible that Schiller wrote practically all of the *Letters* without having a clear idea of where he was headed. After all, the difference between a positive reading of that text, as if it were a straightforward contribution to aesthetics, and the negative reading I have outlined, is very small; the negative reading asserts that the *Letters* undermine aesthetics simply by developing its concepts to the last possible degree. In fact, the difference between these two possible readings boils down to how we visualize *the mind of the reader*. And fortunately we have a very good idea of how Schiller visualizes his reader from about 1794 on. His model reader is Goethe; and he specifically appoints Goethe as his principal reader for the *Letters*.

The *Letters* are not discussed in great detail in the two men's correspondence; but the discussion that exists is very interesting. It is clear, above all, that Schiller has great difficulty in justifying to himself and to Goethe the quality of the *Letters* as theory. In his letter of 7 January 1795 he complains:

> I cannot express how much it pains me to turn away from [your novel, *Wilhelm Meisters Lehrjahre*] and look back at philosophical matters. There everything is so cheerful, so alive, so harmoniously relaxed and humanly true, while here everything is so strict, rigid and abstract, so extremely inhuman, since all nature is synthesis and all philosophy antithesis. True, I can claim to have been as true to nature in my speculations as the concept of analysis permits . . . but still I feel no less vividly the infinite distance between life and reasoning.

And then, a short while later, in the letter of 27 February, he pulls himself together and asserts, "I am getting more and more in control of my material, and I discover, with every forward step that I take, how solid and certain the ground is on which I have built. From now on I shall no longer fear any objection that might overturn my structure of thought." But precisely this vacillation shows how deeply the questions of system and abstraction concern him—particularly in his relations with Goethe, whom he regards as a prime example of the non-abstract mentality of "Genie" (23 August 1794) [genius], which, without benefit of philosophical labor, knows more and knows it better than any philosopher.

The one thing genius supposedly cannot know about, however, is *itself*. Schiller, with a kind of adolescent tactlessness, cannot resist making this point directly to Goethe: first in the letter of 23 August 1794 where he says, "und nur weil es als ein Ganzes in Ihnen liegt, ist Ihnen Ihreigener Reichtum verborgen . . . (weil das Genie sich immer selbst das größte Geheimnis ist)" [and only because it resides in you as a totality, is your own wealth of knowledge hidden from you . . . (for genius is always, from its own point of view, the greatest mystery)]. And then he sends to Goethe, with a request that he read it and respond, an early partial manuscript of the *Letters*, exactly the type of systematic, abstract work that a genius should not be expected to profit from. He goes even further in his letter of 20 October 1794: "As different as the tools may be with which you and I take hold of the world, as different the offensive and defensive weapons that we employ, still I believe that we aim for the same principal point. In these letters you will find your own portrait, under which I would gladly have written your name if I did not hate to anticipate the feeling of thoughtful readers." The concept of ambivalence does not begin to cover what is expressed here. Schiller insists that his thought is radically different from Goethe's, except perhaps in its ultimate goal. But then he claims that he has observed and understood and *recognizably* portrayed Goethe in (of all things) his work of systematic aesthetic philosophy—he means presumably that Goethe is an example of aesthetically whole mankind—and would Goethe now please respond to this claim. Goethe does respond, politely, on 26 October:

> Das mirü bersandte Manuskript habe sogleich mit großem Vergnügen gelesen, ich schlurfte es auf Einen Zug hinunter. Wie uns ein köstlicher, unsrer Natur analoger Trank willig hinunter schleicht und auf der Zunge schon durch gute Stimmung des Nervensystems seine heilsame Wirkung zeigt, so waren mir diese Briefe angenehm und wohltätig, und wie sollte es anders sein? da ich das, was ich für recht seit langer Zeit erkannte, was ich teils lebte, teils zu leben wünschte, auf eine so zusammenhängende und edle Weise vorgetragen fand.

> [I have read the manuscript you sent me with great pleasure. I drank it all down in one draft. Just as a delicious drink, one that is analogous to our nature, slips easily down our throat and on our tongue already shows its wholesome effect by harmonizing our nervous system, thus these letters were pleasant and beneficial to me; and how could they have been otherwise? since I found what I have long recognized as right, and what I have in part lived and in part wished to live, set forth in such a cohesive and noble manner.]

Evidently Goethe had read Schiller's letter very carefully; he talks about the *personal* resonance that Schiller had suggested. But it is not at all clear that he had read any of the *Aesthetic Letters* themselves. And my claim is that Schiller eventually *accepted* this form of non-reading as the correct response to his text. If a reader is not seduced into the text's abstract speculation; if, like Goethe, a reader seems not even to notice the work's rigid, forbidding systematicity: then, by his instinctive resistance to abstraction, such a reader demonstrates exactly that wholeness of humanity which is "portrayed" in the text as the goal it can never truly be. For such a reader, moreover, that human wholeness is *not* a goal, but is simply the ever-repeated precondition of reading (or observing) and understanding.

To look at it differently, the *Letters* engage a reader's abstract reasoning power, but do so only in order to exhibit their own unreadability and therefore abandon each reader to his or her own strict immediate particularity. The text thus offers itself, as Schiller offered it, to an audience of

Goethes, and does as much as possible toward the inherently aesthetic end of encouraging and perhaps even producing such an audience.

There are many things in the story of Wilhelm Tell that attracted Schiller; but not least among them was the image of Tell as a radically non-speculative spirit. Tell neither has nor needs an abstract grasp of the idea of freedom; simply by being who he is, he becomes the place where freedom *happens as a fact.* Thus he is a fairly clear image of Goethe as reader with respect to the idea of free human wholeness that is always aimed at, but can never be achieved, by aesthetics as an intellectual discipline. Such human wholeness can *happen as a fact* only in something like Goethe's non-reading of the *Letters.* Tell also shares with Goethe the virtue of analytic blindness. He can accept Parricida man to man ("Ihr seide-in Mensch—Ich bin es auch" [*Wilhelm Tell,* 3224]); but his self-integrated being is utterly unreceptive to any conception of the depth at which Parricida mirrors him and in effect indicts him. He is thus a development of the figure of Goethe as he is portrayed (and now identified by name after all) in the essay "On Naïve and Sentimental Poetry": Goethe, the naïve poetic spirit who in *Werther* achieves representational mastery over a sentimental story that by rights ought to lie beyond his ability even to conceive of it (5:738). And my point is that this figure, this Goethe, who accomplishes the paradox of unsentimentally imagining the sentimental, is already present behind the scenes in the aesthetic *Letters,* as the reader of the unreadable, the reader who somehow manages to understand the book by a route that is entirely incommensurate with the book's own aesthetic systematics—a reader for whom aesthetics can therefore perhaps retain a certain validity even in the process of being reduced to the absurd.

THE IRRELEVANCE OF AESTHETICS

What Schiller eventually recognizes, in other words, is that the loss or corruption of the self—if it ever actually happens—belongs to the process of *reading.* In reading, more than anywhere else, we attempt to leave behind our immediate, particular self for the sake of an experience by which we hope our mental horizon will be significantly changed. Hence, once again, the self-contradiction in aesthetics. In reading a work of aesthetics we embrace precisely the move of alienation (separation from the particular self) against which aesthetics is erected. Or at least we do this if we read as we normally assume we are expected to. Even without reading the *Aesthetic Letters* in detail, Goethe understands this problem and responds by suggesting not that the work had broadened his mind, but that it had nourished him corporeally, by suggesting thus that an entirely new type of reading is required in order to rescue the work from its contradictions. And Schiller, I think, eventually accepts this suggestion—

probably before finishing the *Letters* in June 1795 (which would explain the change of subject in the last two numbers) and certainly before finishing the more affirmatively paradoxical essay on naïve and sentimental poetry.

But where does this leave our argument? In the *Aesthetic Letters,* Schiller creates an unreadable text, a text that does not so much assert as perform a reduction to absurdity of the whole aesthetic project as he had received it, especially from Kant. But he does not appear to be aware of his own accomplishment until Goethe calls it to his attention obliquely by intimating that the only adequate reader of that text is one who does not need aesthetics in the first place, a non-alienated reader for whom reading is nothing but an assimilation of the text to immediate personal needs. Thus we arrive at two widely differing ideas of aesthetics. Either aesthetics (as practiced by Schiller) is at once both necessary and futile, humanity's tragic protest against a radically alienated condition from which there is no escape, since the protest itself only exacerbates it; or aesthetics (as dismissed by Goethe) is a hypochondriac dramatizing of humanity's supposedly alienated condition, which in fact only creates the problems it pretends to respond to.

But if we look back at the path we have followed to this point, we recognize that the negative or tragic reading of the *Letters* is established only by Schiller's *ceding authority,* in aesthetic matters, to Goethe, the presumably alienationless reader. Thus the *Letters* are shown to be an even more paradoxical document than we had thought: a detailed aesthetic argument by which not merely the contradictoriness, but the irrelevance or pointlessness of aesthetics is established—to the extent that an aesthetic argument can "establish" anything at all. Schiller's ceding of authority in aesthetics is evident from the fact that he never again writes a systematic treatise on the subject—even though there are plenty of loose ends to be tied up in the *Letters,* especially the idea of "education." And the one major essay he does still write, on naïve and sentimental poetry, is not on aesthetics, but is a continuation of his struggle with the figure of Goethe, which Goethe himself acknowledges in his letter of 29 November 1795. Indeed, in view of the critical and paradoxical, non-systematic quality of this last essay, one fancies that Schiller has here ceded to Goethe not only authority, but authorship itself.[10] It is true that later on, from time to time, Schiller continues to insist that the *Letters* mark his own methodological position vis-à-vis Goethe—for instance, in his letter of 9 July 1796. But such passages only remind us how difficult and painful Schiller found that ceding of authority to Goethe, that inevitable acceptance of the irrelevance of aesthetics.

GOETHE AND LEARNING NOT TO LEARN

Only one question remains. Is Goethe's position, as Schiller accepts it, really Goethe's position? Is it even really a "position," not merely an involuntary manifestation of Goethe's "genius"? We can be guided on these points by Goethe's later clearer pronouncements in the little essay "Nachlese zu Aristoteles Poetik" [Another Look at Aristotle's *Poetics*] from 1827. If the poet does his duty, says Goethe, if the work of poetry is constructed and rounded off as a complete object, then the reader or spectator *will not be changed by it,* will not experience the slightest long-term effect upon his or her character or behavior or perceptions.[11] The educative effect of poetry, including the aesthetic notion of a rehabilitation of the self, is simply denied.

In order to see how this denial operates in poetic practice, we might consider a text that critical tradition has long considered one of Goethe's most obviously educative endeavors, *Iphigenie auf Tauris*. In Act Two, Scene One, Pylades apparently succeeds in dispelling for a moment Orest's deadly despair by reminding him of how they had once dreamt together of great deeds (lines 662-79). But he does not encourage this reminiscence. He now admonishes Orest:

> Unendlich ist das Werk, das zu vollführen
> Die Seele dringt. Wir möchten jede That
> So groß gleich thun als wie sie wächs't und wird,
> Wenn Jahre lang durch Länder und Geschlechter
> Der Mund der Dichter sie vermehrend wälzt.
> Es klingt so schön was unsre Väter thaten,
> Wenn es in stillen Abendschatten ruhend
> Der Jüngling mit dem Ton der Harfe schlürft;
> Und was wir thun ist, wie es ihnen war,
> Voll Müh' und eitel Stückwerk!
> So laufen wir nach dem, was vor uns flieht,
> Und achten nicht des Weges den wir treten,
> Und sehen neben uns der Ahnherrn Tritte
> Und ihres Erdelebens Spuren kaum. (680-93)

[The work that our soul strives to complete is infinite. We would like to do each deed right now on as large a scale as it assumes over time when the song of poets has long propelled and magnified it through various lands and peoples. It sounds so beautiful, what our fathers did, when, resting in the quiet evening, a young man drinks it in with the sound of a harp; and what *we* do is, as their deeds were to them (our fathers), full of effort and mere patchwork. Thus we run after what flees from us, and pay no attention to the road we are traveling, and barely see *next to us* the footsteps of our ancestors and the traces of their earthly lives.]

The thinking here is straightforward in itself. The deeds from the past that we celebrate, while they were actually being done, were as effortful and clumsy and fragmentary, and as *insignificant* (lacking the completed form of achievements), as our own actions are. The significance of our forefathers' deeds, their exemplary quality, is solely a result of their having been magnified and perfected in poetic representation. Poetry therefore has a damaging effect, since it teaches us to expect our own deeds to appear to us in a poetically monumental form, which cannot happen, and so discourages us from undertaking anything at all. "Ich halte nichts von dem, der von sich denkt/Wie ihn das Volk vielleicht erheben möchte" (697-98) [I have no respect for the person who thinks of himself in the form in which his people might one day exalt him], says Pylades a bit further on.

But problems arise when we consider this passage in relation to our reading, here and now, of the poetic work *Iphigenie auf Tauris.* For Pylades is arguing *in general* against the poetic magnification of past events for purposes of edification. Or more precisely, he is arguing against our habit of *reading* poetic works in this manner. Thus, unless we dismiss his words as merely an expression of his character, with no claim to validity, we are faced with a dilemma. If we accept his basic assertions, that poetry tends to universalize its content and that such universalizing is morally damaging for a reader, then Goethe's text, *Iphigenie,* has become unreadable in the same way as Schiller's *Aesthetic Letters.* The meaning of *Iphigenie* reduces the reading of *Iphigenie* to a moral absurdity. And the only way to avoid this dilemma is to find a way to read *Iphigenie* without buying into its universalizing educative quality as poetry, just as Goethe suggests the possibility of reading the *Aesthetic Letters* without buying into their procedure as systematic aesthetics.

Indeed, the relation here between *Iphigenie* and the *Aesthetic Letters* may be more than mere analogy. For the aesthetically reintegrated self is certainly one of those delusive poetic magnifications of existence that Pylades is talking about, illusions by which we are induced not to strive but merely to despair over our own condition. And when Goethe responds to the *Letters* by saying he has received them not as a systematic challenge but as a soothing drink, he is not preening himself on possessing the natural "genius" Schiller has credited him with. On the contrary, he is saying (as Pylades would say) that the idea that mankind once possessed a more perfect self than ours is a poetic delusion, that our mode of individual being is neither more nor less disintegrated than the Greeks', and that we need only read as the people we *are*—without looking for truths or lessons that might change us—in order to leave the specter of aesthetics, the aesthetic Furies who torment us with our supposed degeneracy, behind us.

The lesson of *Iphigenie* is that we must not seek any lesson in *Iphigenie.* The speech of Pylades that suggests this inference merely underscores a quality of the play that is already fairly clear from the general disposition of motifs and incidents. If the play is really about an eighteenth-century notion of "humanity"—as many speeches in it suggest—then why was this particular work of Euripides chosen for adaptation, in which the whole plot rests on a supernatural premise, a divine action that cannot be reduced to the "human" by any stretch of reasoning? This incongruity operates not only in general, but also more pointedly in Act Three, Scene One, where Orest has perfectly good reason to think that the priestess has gone mad (1188-99)—which interferes with the motif of his own supposedly irrational despair. And why does Goethe handle the riddling oracle as he does? Why not let the riddle be solved, the true "sister" be identified, *before* Iphigenie's climactic plea for reconciliation (2064-94)? As the scene stands, Iphigenie's humane pleading *fails* to solve the plot's problems, and a verbal gimmick is needed to take up the slack. And what about Thoas? The play's politically experienced audience has a very good idea of what is likely to happen to a lame-duck ruler, a king for whom no clear line of succession exists. His court breaks down into factions, intriguing against one another with a view to producing the *next* king, and he himself is lucky if he does not get assassinated in the process. For all her humane sentiments (2152-74), this is the situation in which Iphigenie is leaving her royal benefactor.

The more one looks at this work, the more one recognizes that it is practically made of incongruities. And what purpose can this kind of structure have if not to thwart a reader's or spectator's universalizing appetite, to deny us anything that might be regarded as a general lesson? Many Goethe scholars would counter this suggestion by referring not to the text of the play itself, but to a poem of Goethe's from 1827, addressed to the actor Krüger and sent with a copy of *Iphigenie.*

> Was der Dichter diesem Bande
> Glaubend, hoffend anvertraut,
> Werd' im Kreise deutscher Lande
> Durch des Künstlers Wirken laut.
> So im Handeln, so im Sprechen
> Liebevoll verkünd' es weit:
> Alle menschliche Gebrechen
> Sühnet reine Menschlichkeit. (WA, 4:277)

[What the poet, in faith and hope, has entrusted to this volume, let it become public in the circle of German lands through the artist's agency. Thus in acting, thus in speaking, lovingly proclaim it abroad: . . .]

The last lines (not yet translated above) are normally read as Goethe's idea of the lesson to be learned from the play *Iphigenie.* But in my opinion those lines are normally not "read" at all, they are merely garbled. Do they really state that "all human weaknesses" are atoned for, or made good, or excused, or cancelled out, by "pure humanity"?

First of all, there is a word play here. A much more expectable object than "Gebrechen" (faults, lacks, afflictions), for the verb "sühnen" (assuming it really means "atone for"), would be "Verbrechen" (crimes). In order to atone for something, one must first be responsible for it, and "Gebrechen" are primarily faults that one is *not* responsible for. Does "sühnen," then, really mean "atone for"? This question turns out to be trickier than one might expect, since in the whole huge corpus of Goethe's utterances (including letters and conversations), the present poem is the *only* place where Goethe uses that verb.[12] The verb he normally uses to denote the expiation or cleansing of guilt is "entsühnen," which appears four times in *Iphigenie* itself (1617, 1702, 1969, 2138). Moreover, if a two-syllable verb is needed, a trochee, with roughly the meaning of "entsühnen," why does Goethe not use "heilet" or "tilget" ("heals" or "cancels")? Or if the meaning tends more toward "alleviate," why not "mildert" or "lindert"? At least one of these suggestions has a parallel in Goethe's *Maskenzug* of 1818 where we read:

> O, warum schaut er nicht, in diesen Tagen,
> Durch Menschlichkeit geheilt die schwersten Plagen! (WA, 16:271)

> [Oh why does he not see, these days, the greatest ills being healed by humanity.]

But in the poem on *Iphigenie* Goethe chooses a *strange* verb, a verb he has never used before and will never use again. Surely he has a special purpose in mind.

The verb "sühnen" does not necessarily mean "atone for" or "make good," although it does suggest responsibility with respect to its object, and even suggests the idea of paying or making reparation for a wrong.[13] But "Gebrechen," unlike "Verbrechen," are faults for which one is normally not responsible. The meaning of the last lines of the poem, therefore, must be that "pure humanity" *assumes* the responsibility for "all human faults"—which produces a paradox. "Pure" or presumably perfect humanity accepts responsibility for, thus receives within its domain, "all" possible "human imperfections." Which implies that pure or perfect humanity does not exist in the form of a humanity cleansed or emptied of faults, a universal virtue that cancels out human afflictions. It follows, in fact, that "pure humanity" is not even the same thing in different circumstances. What it is in any particular situation depends on the particular faults (the *specific* configuration of imperfections) that it embraces there. It is a quality that can only be known locally, in immediate experience, and cannot be abstracted from those individual peculiarities of character ("Gebrechen") for which it assumes responsibility in the one case we happen to be looking at.

What is "lovingly proclaimed," in the poem as in the play *Iphigenie,* is thus in effect immediate experience itself, the irreducible particularity of what I actually am—except that even to make the statement in this form is to abstract illegitimately from the immediacy it means. To state this idea as a theorem is inescapably to take the first step toward an "aesthetics," which cannot engage the immediate local particularity of human life without seeking to incorporate it into the illusion of a reconstituted ideal human nature. "Pure humanity," unlike that supposedly reconstituted humanity, does not transcend temporary human failings, but is indissolubly bound to them—an idea which is also reflected in Goethe's playing (WA, 5/1:230, 279) on "Menschlichkeit" ("humanity," singular) and "Menschlichkeiten" ("human failings," plural).

Like the spectator of tragedy in Goethe's reading of Aristotle, we must learn to dispense with the expectation of being edified or even changed by what we read. Or rather, we must *have* dispensed with that expectation, since even our "learning," as an act, would violate its own object. For the same reason, it would be incorrect to say that Schiller is confirmed by Goethe in an understanding of the *contradictoriness* of aesthetics, which he had been groping toward in the *Aesthetic Letters* without fully knowing it. Aesthetics does not become contradictory until *after* one has committed oneself to the method of abstraction that brings about its contradictions. With respect to the domain and content of poetry, rather, with respect to the strict immediacy and particularity of life as it is actually lived—with respect, in other words, to its own avowed object—aesthetics must be recognized as *irrelevant*.

And finally, if the paradox seems overstrained when we speak of a work whose ultimate lesson is that it has no lesson, let us recall that *Iphigenie* is only a first step toward realizing this idea. The most important and obvious instance is the book Goethe was actually working on when he claimed to have imbibed Schiller's *Letters* as a soothing drink, *Wilhelm Meisters Lehrjahre*. For any lesson learned from this novel becomes significant only to the extent that we apply it to our own lives; and what Wilhelm's experience demonstrates is precisely that such searching for general lessons in life inevitably misleads us. Again, we are presented with the problem of learning how to read without taking the aesthetic step of attempting to derive from the text some human essence, some radical liberation, some cure for our supposedly damaged existential integrity. As Goethe says later of Laurence Sterne:

> So sehr uns der Anblick einer freien Seele dieser Art ergötzt, eben so sehr werden wir gerade in diesem Fall erinnert, daß wir von allem dem, wenigstens von dem meisten, was uns entzückt, nichts in uns aufnehmen dürfen. (WA, 42/2: 204)

> [As much as we enjoy the sight of this kind of free soul, to the same extent, precisely in this case, we are reminded that of everything that delights us here, or at least of most of it, we may absorb no part into ourselves.]

NOTES

1. If it was ever excusable to be blind to the nationalistic dimension of the concept of German "classicism"—"Klassik," which implies undying value and is strictly distinguished from "Klassizismus," which does not—then it stopped being so with the publication of *Die Klassik-Legende*, ed. Reinhold Grimm and Jost Hermand (Frankfurt/Main, 1971). Three of that book's essays are important in this particular regard. Wilfried Malsch, "Die geistesgeschichtliche Legende der deutschen Klassik" (108-40), suggests fundamental intellectual oppositions between the thinking of authors in the "classical" period itself and the image of that period in later writing. Max L. Baeumer, "Der Begriff 'klassisch' bei Goethe und Schiller" (17-49), summarizes lucidly eighteenth-century usage of the notion of the "classical," including its decidedly nonnationalistic use by Goethe. And above all, Klaus L. Berghahn, "Von Weimar nach Versailles: Zur Entstehung der Klassik-Legende im 19. Jahrhundert" (50-78), shows how the development of German nationalism co-opts the idea of the "classical" and in the process distorts and obscures the actual history of writing in Germany. Other important early works in the demystifying of German "Klassik" include René Wellek, "Das Wort und der Begriff 'Klassizismus' in der Literaturgeschichte," *Schweizer Monatshefte*, 45 (1969), 154-73, and Eva D. Becker, "'Klassiker' in der deutschen Literaturgeschichtsschreibung zwischen 1780 und 1860," in *Zur Literatur der Restaurationsepoche 1815-1848*, eds. Jost Hermand and Manfred Windfuhr (Stuttgart, 1970), 349-70. But why, then, does the idea of a German "Klassik" persist even today? If we worry about this question enough, we begin to get a feel for the central concept in W. Daniel Wilson, *Das Goethe-Tabu: Protest und Menschenrechteimklassischen Weimar* (Munich, 1999). There are certain things people just plain don't want to think about Goethe. And while Wilson's specific concern is human rights, his arguments also highlight, more generally, Goethe's complete *lack of principle*, a trait which, even in his own time, people (like Schiller) euphemized by speaking of his "natural genius." Part of what I hope to show here is that with respect to aesthetics, precisely this character trait supports an historically significant move on Goethe's part, and Schiller's along with him.

2. Andrew Bowie, *Aesthetics and Subjectivity: from Kant to Nietzsche* (Manchester, 1990), 4.

3. Schiller, *Werke*, 5:578. See chap. 1, n7.

4. The translation (which I occasionally modify) is that of Elizabeth M. Wilkinson and L. A. Willoughby, in Friedrich Schiller, *Essays*, ed. Walter Hinderer and Daniel O. Dahlstrom (New York, 1995), 94-5. Cited as "T" below.

5. Compare Terry Eagleton, *The Ideology of the Aesthetic* (Oxford, 1990), 2-3: "With the birth of the aesthetic, then, the sphere of art itself begins to suffer something of the abstraction and formalization characteristic of modern theory in general; yet the aesthetic is nevertheless thought to retain a charge of irreducible particularity, providing us with a kind of paradigm of what a non-alienated mode of cognition might look like. Aesthetics is thus always a contradictory, self-undoing sort of project, which in promoting the theoretical value of its object risks emptying it of exactly that specificity or ineffability which was thought to rank among its most precious features."

6. Moritz, *Werke*, 2:945, see chap. 1, n18.

7. Consider, for example, in letter no. 19, the paragraph beginning, "Hier müssen wir uns nun erinnern . . ." (5:629), which states that the "transcendental philosopher," unlike the "metaphysician," does not have to worry about contradictions that occur in his conceptual edifices: ". . . so stellt er beide [sich scheinbar widersprechenden] Begriffe mit vollkommner Befugnis als gleich notwendige Bedingungen der Erfahrung auf, ohne sich weiter um ihre Vereinbarkeit zu bekümmern." It almost seems that Schiller is parodying himself here, or even parodying Kant. And curiously enough, this whole passage is found reproduced in Kant's own posthumous papers. See *Schillers Sämtliche Werke: Säkular-Ausgabe*, 16 vols. (Stuttgart and Berlin, 1904), 12:372. In fact, in the balance of this paragraph, where he insists on a strict *distinction* between "the

mind itself" and the two drives that after all constitute that mind (a textbook example of *petitioprincipii*), I think Schiller has to be aware of the logical skullduggery he is engaged in.

8. Woodmansee argues in her book (57-86; see chap. 1, n2) that the *Letters* show a kind of hypocrisy, that the "expressly political" aim asserted at the beginning turns out only to mask "the very material existential considerations of a professional writer in Germany at the end of the eighteenth century" (58-59). Wolfdietrich Rasch, "Schein, Spiel und Kunst in der Anschauung Schillers," *Wirkendes Wort*, 10 (1960), 2-13, advances the radical suggestion that Schiller is seeking to create an "aesthetic" effect with the *Letters* themselves.

9. For much of this same argument, but oriented differently, see my "Trinitarische Humanität: Dichtung und Geschichte bei Schiller," in *Friedrich Schiller: Kunst, Humanität und Politik in der späten Aufklärung*, ed. Wolfgang Wittkowski (Tübingen, 1982), 164-77.

10. On Goethe as in a sense the true author of "Über naive und sentimentalische Dichtung," see my *Goethe as Woman: The Undoing of Literature* (Detroit, 2001), 217-19.

11. Goethe, WA, 41/2:251. See chap. 1, n7.

12. At least this is true if the search function for the on-line WA can be trusted.

13. Especially the phrase "zur Sühne," as Goethe uses it, suggests reparation for a wrong committed. See, for example, Book 6 of *Reineke Fuchs*, 186, and 388-413, where the phrase occurs a number of times. Also, in letters, see WA, 4. Abt., 27:241, 50:90.

FOUR

Kant and His Shadow: The Persistence of Philosophical Aesthetics

Schiller develops and lays bare the secular millennialist tendency in the aesthetics he had inherited mainly from Baumgarten and Kant: the focus of aesthetics upon rehabilitation of the particular human self, upon restoration of a human wholeness that has supposedly been disrupted by alienating forces in society, religion, and philosophy. But in the very process of developing that tendency, he also discredits it, in his and Goethe's recognition of the irrelevance of aesthetics with respect to its own supposed domain in poetry and art. The persistence of aesthetics as a force in European philosophy therefore needs some explaining; and the purpose of the present chapter is to show the significance of Kant and his legacy in this regard.

KANT AND HUMAN CORRUPTION

Let us remind ourselves of the three principal characteristics of aesthetics in the Kantian tradition: (1) its quality as a secular millennialism; (2) its insistence on the insoluble problem of communication; and (3) its conviction that the work of art is fully constituted as itself only in the process of its reception. The first, the idea of secular millennialism, has a crucial logical consequence that will attract our attention repeatedly as we go on. If one is a secular millennialist in the aesthetic sense; if one believes in the project of human rehabilitation, of restoring an unalienated form of existence that has been lost in the course of human history: then one *must* also believe in the existence, even today, of some definite element or component of the perfected humanity one hopes for. Either a vestige of our original perfection or a harbinger of our eventual perfection must be identifiable even in the corrupt present. For if the present human condition were uniformly corrupt, then all our projects and efforts could not possibly escape the general corruption, and we should have no hope of gaining our end. This point marks a significant difference from Christian millennialism, in which intimations concerning the end of history may take the form of God's free gift to an otherwise hopelessly benighted humanity.

Aesthetics, however—assuming Schiller's diagnosis is correct—arises in the eighteenth century as a distinctly non-Christian millennialism. And it is usually not difficult to identify the element of uncorrupted humanity on which it pins its hopes. In Schiller's own case—before he bows to necessity and concedes the irrelevance of aesthetics—it is the "play drive," the metaphysical root of our sense of beauty; for Cassirer it is the "pure phenomenon" of beauty itself; for Moritz it is the "work of art," once we recognize its true mode of existence. But the case of Kant seems to present a problem. How can there be a vestige of uncorrupted humanity in his thought if he never attaches his aesthetics to the project of human rehabilitation in the first place? Communication is definitely an issue in the *Critique of Judgment.* But Kant seems to resist the tendency of that issue to associate itself with the idea of a present human degeneracy that needs to be repaired.

This appearance is delusive. Kant is every bit as fascinated by the image of a restored humanity as Schiller is; the difference is that he projects that image onto contemporary humanity as if it were an empirical fact. I refer to the two principal qualities by which he defines a judgment of taste, the type of judgment that can declare something beautiful: that no personal interest whatever be involved in the feeling on which it is based; and that in the very act of making it, we automatically impute a similar judgment to every other human being. These two qualities work smoothly in the mechanism of the *Critiques,* which accounts for their seductive power. But they are empirically vacuous; they correspond to nothing whatever in actual human experience.

There is no such thing as judgment without personal interest. There is not even any such thing as a feeling without personal interest—for example, a feeling of satisfaction or approval, Kantian "Wohlgefallen."[1] Certainly not if that feeling is expressed in a communicable judgment. The mind does not work that way. Except perhaps in moments of complete surprise, our feelings never arise innocently, but are always supervised and guided as they develop; because it always seems advantageous for us to feel (or be thought to feel) a particular way. The specific personal interest in operation when a feeling becomes manifest as a judgment, as an inclination or affection, may be obscure; but it is never absent. Look at the admiring crowd in an art museum or a concert hall, or at the lip of the Grand Canyon, and tell me that those people are not all making sure, for whatever reason, to be *seen* finding the object beautiful. Moreover, taste is not a natural ability—whatever even an Edmund Burke might urge to the contrary. One learns taste, perhaps in formal education, perhaps as part of one's upbringing or part of a deliberate change of persona in later life. Taste therefore always has a component of *exclusivity*. In any particular case one knows there are people who could not possibly share or reproduce or understand one's aesthetic judgment; and one inevitably derives satisfaction from such knowledge. This applies as much to the aficionado of NASCAR as to a connoisseur of wines.

I am arguing, it is true, from what seem to me the empirical facts of human psychology, which means I am opposing an *opinion* to Kant's strictly systematic conclusions. But in chapter 1, I argued that precisely the factualness of the implied psychology of the *Critique of Judgment* is logically required by that book's political dimension, hence that a discussion of opinions is unavoidable. And it remains my opinion that there is a significant gap between Kant's "critical" thinking and the manner in which human beings actually manage their existence on this planet. His thinking on morality, especially the notion of a categorical imperative, requires before it can operate that every ethically significant intention be associated with a generalizable "maxim"—as if maxims were ever unambiguously associated with intentions except after the fact. It is true that in the *Groundwork for the Metaphysics of Morals,* he offers plenty of illustrative examples. But they all seem to me remarkable for how completely they lack the feel of reality.

The instance of aesthetic judgment and the idea of beauty is even more clear-cut. For here Kant's thinking involves not merely a practical error or inconvenience, but a practical impossibility. He himself points out—we noted in chapter 2—that his system implies an *interest,* on our part, in the existence of the beautiful, an empirical interest, an intellectual interest, and what I called a "representational" interest. But if this theorem is true, then it can be known; and if it is known, then given the psychological constitution of our species, there is no way to imagine its not having an effect upon our aesthetic judgment in every particular case. For now, in every case, we have a specific interest in finding objects or scenes or actions or ideas beautiful. (And especially in the "empirical" sense, where communication is at stake, the interest in question is strongly personal.) Precisely the logic of the *Critique of Judgment* thus has as a consequence that it is now impossible for me to believe confidently in any actual instance of uncorrupted aesthetic judgment, any instance of judgment without interest—since our interest (and my personal interest) in the existence of the beautiful, hence in finding beautiful the particular thing we happen to be faced with, can always be known.

Does it follow that Kant's aesthetic thinking is *wrong?* No. The thought of the *Critique of Judgment* leads to a practical impossibility, not a logical contradiction; and our recognition of that impossibility depends on our knowledge of actual human psychology. In order for Kant's aesthetic thinking *not* to be wrong, therefore, it need only be true that actual human psychology is wrong in the sense of being deeply corrupt, of conflicting with its own rational possibilities. Once we grasp this point, it follows immediately that Kant's aesthetics, no less than Schiller's, is aimed at the establishment of an uncorrupted human condition, a better, simpler psychology, a humanity in whose existence and behavior and thinking and actualized intersubjectivity the "critical" system of concepts might be empirically justified.[2]

It is exactly in this sense that Schiller develops, and so exposes, Kant's aesthetics. For Schiller takes as his starting point not metaphysics as such but rather a metaphysical psychology, a system of drives or instincts by which the human mind and the human world are constituted. Actual present-day human psychology, on this model, is marked by a fundamental imbalance and corruption. And the millennial vision of aesthetics is focused accordingly on the task of re-balancing the drives so as to liberate the human potential of the play drive and make possible an aesthetic polity.

KANT'S "ORIGINAL APPERCEPTION"

If the *Critique of Judgment* thus obeys the general rule that aesthetics is never merely a study of existing conditions but always a millennialist project, aimed at the restoration or rehabilitation of humanity, then where in Kant's system do we find the needful contemporary vestige or harbinger of the envisaged goal? The idea or experience of beauty cannot have this function for Kant. As the object of a judgment unmixed with personal interest, a type of judgment we are in truth not yet capable of, beauty is not directly available to us in the first place.

The answer to the question, I think, is found not in the *Critique of Judgment* but in the *Critique of Pure Reason,* in the central notion of "transcendental apperception," or "pure" or "original" apperception, as Kant also calls it.[3] The concept of apperception is borrowed from Leibniz; and although Kant gives his own meaning to it, I think that what attracts him is the notion of *a strictly original movement of non-contingency or necessity in the self,* a movement of something like reflection that somehow manages not to require the prior existence of reflection in its object.

For Leibniz, "The nature of the monad is representative, and consequently nothing can limit it to representing a part of things only" ("Monadology," no. 60),[4] which means that "every monad is a mirror that is . . . representative of the [whole] universe from its point of view" ("Principes," no. 3). But at the same time, "every monad must be different from every other" ("Monadology," no. 9); and since monads do not differ by representing different objects, it follows that they differ by representing their objects differently. Up to the level of representation, therefore, which is the same thing as "perception" ("Principes," no. 4), every monad is unique, which is to say, every monad is strictly particular or contingent. It is at this point that apperception enters the scheme.

> Ainsi il est bon de faire distinction entre la *Perception* qui est l'état interieur de la Monade representant les choses externes, et l'*Apperception* qui est la *Conscience,* ou la connoissance reflexive de cet état interieur. ("Principes," no. 4)

> [Thus it is well to distinguish between *perception,* which is the inner state of the monad representing external things, and *apperception,* which is *consciousness,* or the reflective knowledge of this inner state.]

The perceptions by which the monad is constituted, in other words, most often happen without the monad's knowledge, so to speak; and the move by which a monad may take cognizance of a perception is called apperception.

Leibniz uses the word "reflexive" to describe that move, since it is after all an operation of the monad with respect to itself. And despite Baumgarten's attempt to muddy the issue, apperception is *not* itself a form of representation (a form of the same operation by which the monad represents the universe), but belongs to an entirely different order of operations. But it is also evident that apperception is *not yet* one of those "acts of reflection" ("Actes reflexifs") that are spoken of in the following passage from the "Monadology":

> 29. But it is the knowledge of necessary and eternal truths which distinguishes us from mere animals, and gives us *reason* and the sciences, raising us to knowledge of ourselves and God. It is this in us which we call the rational soul or *mind.*
> 30. Further it is by the knowledge of necessary truths and by their abstractions that we are raised to *acts of reflection,* which make us think of what is called the *self* ["ce qui s'appelle *Moy*"], and consider that this or that is within *us.* And it is thus that in thinking of ourselves, we think of being, of substance, of the simple and the compound, of the immaterial and of God himself, conceiving that what is limited in us, in him is limitless. And these acts of reflection provide the chief objects of our reasonings.

Apperception is a reflective move, but it is definitely not yet reflection in the lofty sense of these two paragraphs. It is, we might say, a move at the brink of reflection, perhaps even the move by which reflection could be said to originate. And even in Leibniz it seems to be a *transcendental* move, a move that is always one step beyond the contingency (dependence on point of view) of each monad's perceptions, a move that is essentially *the same move* in every particular instance, in every monad, in every mind.

Kant is careful in his use of this thinking. He distinguishes between what he calls "empirical" apperception—meaning presumably Leibnizian apperception—and his own idea of "pure" or "original" apperception.[5] But I think it is obvious that he is attracted to the concept by the transcendental possibilities that are already there in Leibniz's version. He opens the matter by arguing that in a "multiplicity of representations" ("Das Mannigfaltige der Vorstellungen") which in itself can be purely sensate, any "connection" (any knowable order or structure) must be a spontaneous act of the understanding. Such an act, however, presupposes "the concept of the unity of that multiplicity"—this concept being that of which the "connection" is a representation. And Kant now calls that unity, which is original apperception, "the *I think.*"

> The *I think* must *be able* to escort ["begleiten"] all of my representations, for otherwise something would be represented in me that could not be thought, which means: the representation would be either impossible or, at least, nothing for me. That representation that can be given prior to all thinking is called *intuition* ["Anschauung"]. Therefore [since the "I think" must *be able* to escort all representations, even if in a particular case it does not actually do so] all multiplicity of intuition has a necessary relation to the *I think* in the same subject in which that multiplicity happens to be found. This representation [the "I think"], however, is an act of *spontaneity,* i.e. it cannot be seen as belonging to sense impressions. I call it *pure apperception,* in order to distinguish it from the *empirical* type, or also *original apperception,* because it is that self-consciousness which, in bringing forth the representation *I think* (which must be able to escort all others and is one and the same in all consciousness), can itself not be escorted by any further representation. (§ 16, 108-9)

I use "escort" to translate "begleiten," rather than the more usual English "accompany," because the above passage clearly implies a *hierarchy* of representations according to whether one representation can take another under its wing, so to speak. Every representation or mental image that is *mine* must be susceptible to my thinking it, to being escorted into the scope of my reflective consciousness; whereas the representation that does the escorting, the "I think," is never itself in need of escort, since it already *is* a form of self-consciousness; there is no further representation of mine that can be imagined as guiding or controlling it. Original apperception, or the "I think," is therefore not contingent; it does not depend on *whose* "I think" it is, which would be precisely that further guiding representation that cannot be there. It is "one and the same in all consciousness" ("in allem Bewußtsein"), which I take to mean in *everyone's* consciousness.

In other words, the thing that makes me myself, the very gateway to my particular contingent conscious being, is transcendental in character, not strictly mine at all. If I am the particular person I am, then it is only by way of a transcendental "I think" that I am that. Or we might say, *sum ergo cogito.* But when Kant speaks of the "I think" as a representation (an idea, a "Vorstellung"), is he not playing the same illegitimate game as Baumgarten when the latter speaks of "representations of present changes in the person representing"? In fact he is not. Baumgarten is simply mixing incompatible discourses, whereas Kant, in discussing "original apperception," is talking about something that by its nature *must* have three distinguishable aspects: (1) it must be a representation that attaches itself to other representations as a limiting or determining factor; (2) it must be a spontaneous act, since it cannot possibly be accounted for by the operation of sense impressions alone; and (3) it is also the "self-consciousness" in which the act is carried out that produces the representation, a self-consciousness whose unity can be accounted for only *by* the originary act "I think."

Original apperception, in having these several aspects, facing in these several directions, is thus a kind of *hinge* between sense experience and reflective consciousness (as is suggested in Leibniz), a hinge whose absence Kant views as the principal fault in Locke's theory of mind. In accordance with the quality of hinge, moreover, it is also true that "the first pure cognition of the understanding ['Verstandeserkenntiß'], on which all the rest of its use is based, and which is also independent of all conditions of sensate intuition, is the principle of the original *synthetic* unity of apperception" (§ 17, 111).

THE MILLENNIALIST INVENTION (I)

We saw in reading nos. 29 and 30 of the "Monadology" that for Leibniz the establishment of the "self," beginning with the primitive move of apperception, opens for us a way that leads directly to the highest possible truths, including knowledge of God. The same is not by any means Kant's view. Original apperception (the *I think*) not only throws ourselves and our world open to us; it also imposes a *limit* on our mode of being and understanding.

> All *my* representations in any given intuition must be subject to that sole condition under which I can count them as *my* representations for my identical self, and can thus group them together as connected in an apperception by way of the general expression, *I think.*
>
> This principle, however, does not hold for every possible type of understanding, but only for one through whose pure apperception in the representation *I am* no multiplicity is yet given. That understanding through whose self-consciousness the multiplicity of intuition could be given at the same time, an understanding by way of whose representation the objects of that representation could also receive their existence, would not need a special act synthesizing [a given] multiplicity for the unity of consciousness, whereas human understanding, which only thinks but does not receive intuitions, requires that act. (§ 17, 112)

The need for original apperception is thus a fault in human understanding. And in case we are tempted to follow Leibniz and Descartes, and argue that precisely our faults lead us toward knowledge of God, by enabling us to imagine those faults removed, Kant immediately continues:

> But for human understanding, it [the subjection of *"my* representations" to the condition of original apperception] is unavoidably the first principle, so that our understanding *cannot form the slightest conception [sich nicht den mindesten Begriff machen kann,* my emphasis] of another possible understanding, either of one that could have intuitions itself, or of one that could possess sensate intuitions, but of a kind different from those limited to space and time. (§ 17, 112)

Our faults are such, Kant insists, that they offer us no direct way of thinking beyond them. We can speculate about the existence of an understanding freed of human limits, but we cannot form a usable or workable idea; we cannot approach anything like knowledge.

Indeed, the limits of human understanding, as Kant expounds them, are such as practically to guarantee that our thinking, especially about ourselves, will succumb to error and corruption. He argues, in particular, that our knowledge of ourselves is not fundamentally or structurally different from our knowledge of objects.

> If we agree concerning the latter [external senses in space] that by way of them we know objects only to the extent that we are externally affected, then we have to admit concerning the internal sense [domain of time] that by way of it we have intuition of ourselves only so far as we are inwardly affected *by ourselves,* so that, as far as inner intuition is concerned, we know our own subject only as a phenomenon, not according to what it is in itself. (§ 24, 122)
>
> I exist as an intelligence that is conscious of its ability to connect, but, with respect to the multiplicity that it is to connect, is subject to a limiting condition that it calls the inner sense, which requires that that connection be intuitively available only by way of temporal relations that are entirely separate from actual concepts of the understanding. That intelligence can therefore know itself only as it merely appears to itself by an intuition (which cannot be intellectual and given by the understanding directly), not as it would know itself if its *intuition* were intellectual. (§ 25, 124)

The trouble here is not logical but practical. If I know myself only as a "phenomenon" or an "intuition of the inner sense," thus as a kind of *object* (and as belonging ipso facto to a "multiplicity"), then I must also experience that knowledge as a *loss* of myself, as a defect, a move of self-alienation—as the condition of being distanced from myself in a manner that is incompatible with the notion of *unity* that attends the very idea of a self as established (precisely) in original apperception.

If I could become a kind of god, if my intuition were intellectual, if my representations guaranteed the existence of their objects, the defect in question would be repaired. But a crucial result of the aesthetic half of the *Critique of Judgment* is that it is not necessary to go that far to find a solution to the problem of self-knowledge — which is the problem of lonely individuality. It is sufficient if I am assured that my feelings, events in my strictly subjective life, are universally communicable. Such an assurance cannot fail to relax the painful opposition between subject and object which is the problem of self-knowledge. By being assured that my sense of other people's feelings is valid, and by being assured that my own feelings are known to other people in turn, I find myself living in a world where the subject has learned to avoid closing itself off from its "outside." Or perhaps the subject has recognized that it was never in truth closed off to begin with. Even in such an aesthetically relaxed world, I still cannot know myself directly as myself, as a subject. But that type of knowledge need no longer tantalize me as a goal. For now, in the world I share with other human beings, neither my subjectivity nor subjectivity in general is any longer absolutely excluded from the domain of knowledge.

This world of communicable feelings is the world whose actual existence (in the sense that we are justified in assuming its existence) Kant attempts to demonstrate in the *Critique of Judgment.* And the failure of that demonstration — the *empirical* failure, I have argued — only has the effect of shifting his thought from the real to the millennial, making it a description of the better humanity that needs to be erected in place of our present episode of morbid, self-corrupting self-consciousness — the episode of a humanity that cannot think of its own being without finding itself defective. And if we now ask after the necessary contemporary vestige or harbinger of that better humanity, the answer is clear: it is pure or original apperception itself, the founding moment of self-consciousness which is repeated in all self-consciousness, the single moment of self-consciousness that is transcendental in character (not subject to the constraints and sufferings of lonely individuality) and therefore offers itself, in all self-conscious existence, as a model and promise of achieved communication.

Kant himself would not have described his thought in this manner. But my point is that his aesthetics conforms *in structure* to the general pattern of aesthetics as Schiller understands it in the original plan for the *Aesthetic Letters.* The *Critiques,* in spite of themselves, thus offer a strong corroboration of Schiller's thought. But there is one point at which Kant goes further than Schiller. His thought, understood as a Schillerian aesthetics, locates the contemporary harbinger of perfected humanity not in the idea of beauty or in a postulated "drive" equivalent to that idea, but in the founding moment of our self-consciousness itself, which models communication by being present in the same way for all of us. This device, the location of a promise of restored humanity in the founding moment of exactly the process that corrupts our humanity, is what I call a "millennialist invention." It is the type of move by which aesthetics is eventually induced to overflow its boundaries and become a political infection in the whole fabric of Western civilization.

Millennialist invention is the technique of using a problem as its own solution. It associates itself especially with the problem of communication, where the only possibility for a solution is often found in the sophistry of taking failure to communicate as itself a communicable experience. This is what Hermann Broch does in his essay on "collapse of values," and what Friedrich Schlegel does in his idea of a new mythology. The most influential use of the invention is probably Hegel's development of the idea of self-consciousness. And perhaps the most pernicious instance is Heidegger's attempt to understand the hermeneutic circle as a guarantee of knowledge. I have already shown that Lessing avoids the millennialist maneuver when he understands art's failure to communicate as a vehicle of imitation, but *not* of communication. Even the artistically imitated experience, in Lessing, is an experience we undergo alone, except perhaps to the extent that "Mitleid" limits the very possibility of aloneness. In the next section, I will try to put these ideas into perspective by coming back to Lessing in a context that also has to do with Schlegel's application of the millennialist invention to ancient and modern sensibilities.

EXCURSUS: ALTERNATIVES TO THE KANTIAN VIEW

I call Kant's original apperception an "invention"—not a "discovery"—because there is no reason why a transcendental ground for self-consciousness needs to be given in the first place. Must there be a single focus to which all of "my" representations are automatically referred? Is it necessary to understand human existence (or my particular existence) as founded upon a unified something, a "self"? Even if there were undoubtedly such a thing as the self, would it be legitimate to assume with Kant that that self is constituted by a move of self-consciousness? If the medium of the "inner sense" is time, does it not follow that self-consciousness always posits the *prior* existence of precisely itself, including its consciousness?

Freud, if these questions had been put to him, would have answered in a thoroughly non-Kantian manner. And even in Kant's time, there are plenty of Germans, and other Europeans, who suspect that the individual thinking mind is not so much the seat of consciousness as an illusory *product* of consciousness. In coming to grips with literature of the period, one is often moved to ask decidedly un-Kantian questions, such as whether it might make sense philosophically to regard the actual material theater as a primary organ of human understanding—an idea that resonates with the suggestion in Diderot's *Paradoxe sur le comédien* that what we think of as "natural" human individuality may be radically histrionic. Or in connection with both Goethe and Hölderlin, or both Herder and Hamann, the question of the ontological priority of the individual, in relation to various forms of collectivity, is at least an open one. And in Heinrich von Kleist's work there are several attempts to discredit any general conception of the human that might require a transcendental grounding of the individual as its privileged instance.[6]

But possibly the most significant of the available alternatives to Kant's invention, and easily the simplest, is suggested by Lessing. It is true that for Lessing, "Mitleid," or "sympathy," is an important concept in understanding art and literature. In his famous letter to Friedrich Nicolai, we read: "The single task of tragedy is this: It must expand *our ability to feel sympathy*. Not merely should it teach us to feel sympathy toward this or that unfortunate; rather it should impress upon us that unfortunate people at all times and in all forms must move us and enlist our sympathy. . . . *The most sympathetic person is the best person*, the readiest to practice all social virtues and all types of magnanimity."[7] Does "sympathy" here refer to the communication of feelings between selves in the sense of strict Kantian subjects? How could we reconcile this idea with our recognition in chapter 2 that art and literature, understood in *Laokoon* as techniques for "imitating" the human, are founded precisely upon the *impossibility* of communicating the immediate content of experience.

Lessing does not live in a Kantian universe. Kant begins with a strictly insoluble problem: how I might know my subjectivity without making it an *object* of knowledge and so losing hold of exactly the subjective (transcendentally unified) quality I had been looking for. But if subjective feelings are communicable in certain fairly common instances, then my failure to know myself may be compensated for by the experience of intersubjective commerce. For Lessing, on the other hand, the importance of sympathy, of learning to feel other people's feelings, is that it develops in us the knowledge that our "self" has never been transcendentally unified in the first place, that the suffering of other people, in an ethically crucial sense, simply *is* our suffering, and is so "at all times and in all forms," without needing to be based on communicable experiences. Later, in no. 75 of the *Hamburgische Dramaturgie*, Lessing expands this thought by arguing that for Aristotle, fear and sympathy (fear and pity, in the usual translation) are not entirely distinguishable from one another, that in fact "[Aristotelian] fear is sympathy directed toward ourselves" (4:579)—which suggests not only that other people's suffering is ours, but also that even our own personal suffering stands in the same relation to us (by attracting our sympathy) as other people's.

EXCURSUS CONTINUED: ANCIENTS AND MODERNS

The purpose of this excursus is to show why the persistence of secular millennialist aesthetics should be considered a *problem* in European intellectual history, not a natural occurrence. And Lessing's position relative to this matter is important because of its simplicity, which emerges again in relation to the question of ancients and moderns. One immediate effect of the association of self-consciousness with corruption is historical nostalgia, if not ancestor-worship. Dead people and dead civilizations (the deader the better) have the advantage over us that their lives, seen from our point of view, possess *completeness,* exactly the quality of integral unity that we miss most desperately in our own lives. Therefore those ancients are the objects of a senseless but insuppressible *envy* on our part. (The senselessness of such envy is what Goethe's Pylades emphasizes in the speech to Orest that was discussed in chapter 3.) And this feeling is operative in modern Europeans' constantly increasing conviction, from the seventeenth century on, that an unbridgeable gulf separates them from classical antiquity, especially Greece, considered as a mode of satisfying human experience.

It follows conversely that where the envious idea of a gulf of incomprehension between ourselves and the ancients is absent, there also the hypochondriac nightmare of our corrupt self-consciousness has either been undone or has never existed to begin with. The text I am thinking of in this regard is *Laokoon,* where the argumentative invocation of Winckelmann already places our relation to classical antiquity in the foreground, and where in the first chapter Lessing uses the question of Laocoon's screaming to position himself as follows:

> Screaming is the natural expression of bodily pain. It is not uncommon for Homer's wounded warriors to fall screaming to the ground. . . . I know, we more refined Europeans from a shrewder posterity know better how to control our mouths and our weeping. Good manners and decency forbid screams and tears. The active bravery of that earlier crude age has been transformed with us into a passive bravery. And yet, in this latter bravery, even our own forefathers were greater than we are. But our forefathers were barbarians. To bite back even the worst pain, to face the mortal stroke without lowering one's eyes, to die laughing at the adders' bites, to weep neither for one's own sin nor for the loss of one's best-loved friend, these are traits of ancient Nordic heroism. (6:14)

Thus a first step is taken in demystifying ancient Greece. It is not the ineluctable passage of time, from age to age, that separates us from the Greeks, so much as a simple difference in culture, a "barbarian" difference from the Greeks that had obtained even for the ancient form of our own culture. But Lessing continues:

The Greek was not so [not heroic in the Nordic sense]! He had feelings and experienced fear; he gave expression to his pain and his misery; he was not ashamed of any of his human weaknesses; but no such weakness was permitted to hold him back from the path of honor or from the performance of his duty. What arose for the barbarians from wildness and self-hardening [namely, the virtues of honor and duty] was produced in the Greek by principles *[Grundsätze]*. (6:14-15)

In order to have an experience of the world not fundamentally different from that of the ancient Greeks (Lessing implies) we need do only two things, neither of which is impossible or even particularly difficult: we must let go of the artificial inhibitions we impose on the expression of our feelings; and having learned, by study, the "principles" on which the Greeks based their actions, we must resolve to act in accordance with them ourselves.

But this position is not easy to set forth in discourse. In the form of a statement it is exposed to endless quibbles. Does the expression of "feeling" never conflict with duty or honor? Whose interpretation of Greek "principles" of activity shall we accept, and an interpretation based on which Hellenic subculture? The conclusion, by being stated, quickly becomes a problem, a problem of authority which is only the problem of subjectivity turned inside out—and we are back where we started. How does Lessing deal with this difficulty?

This question turns out to be the same as the question: what is *Laokoon* really about? Much of chapter 1 is about Greek culture by way of Homer, whereupon chapters 2-10 appear to justify the book's title by concerning themselves more or less centrally with the Laocoon statue and the corresponding story in Vergil—although there is a long discussion of Sophocles' *Philoctetes* in chapter 4, and the polemic in chapters 7-10 against Joseph Spence's *Polymetis* (1747) brings up theoretical issues that quickly leave the original examples behind. But in chapter 11, with the transition to a polemic against the *Tableaux tirés de l'Iliade, de l'Odyssée, et de l'Enéide* (1757) of Count Caylus, and with the question of whether one can speak properly of "pictures" in Homer, Lessing (in my view) finally gets down to business. Chapter 12 is on the visible and the invisible in Homer; chapter 13 on senses other than sight in Homer; chapter 14 on Milton and Homer; chapter 15 on kinetic subject matter in Homer. Chapter 16 is mainly theoretical, on the idea of poetry's imitating action alone, but the point is illustrated from Homer; and if chapter 17 seems to change direction by taking up the question of descriptive poetry, it is only in order to ask dramatically, in chapter 18, if Homer can possibly be regarded as a descriptive poet, which leads to a brilliant treatment of the Homeric epithet and an opening of the comparison of Achilles' shield with that of Aeneas in Vergil. Chapter 19, then, is mainly on Achilles' shield; chapter 20 on Helen's beauty in Homer; chapter 21 on Helen and the Trojan elders; chapter 22 returns to the topic of Caylus's distorted view of

Homer; chapter 23 justifies the ugliness of Homer's Thersites; and chapter 24 continues the discussion of ugliness with further remarks on Homer. Chapters 25-29 conclude the book with a treatment of various matters, including the phenomenon of disgust and several relatively narrow issues raised by Winckelmann. And the very last quotation in the book, like a kind of coda, is the quotation (from a pseudo-Herodotus) *of a* quotation from Homer (6:185).

Lessing's book is thus, above all, about *how to read Homer*. It therefore asks by implication whether a modern European can possibly read Homer adequately. And its answer to this question, while never stated, is bodied forth by every line of its exegesis, the answer: Yes, it is possible for us to read Homer adequately. The question alone, like the question of our relation to Hellenic antiquity in general, becomes pointless when asked directly; *by* being asked, it steers the mind toward a timid, problem-seeking attitude that cannot but produce a negative answer. Lessing's positive answer, by contrast, is asserted in the simple carrying out of an adequate relation to Homer, and thence to Hellenic antiquity in general.

If this reading of the *Laokoon* project seems devious, let us recall that only a few years later Lessing carries out the same procedure again, and now even more compactly and perspicuously, in *Wie die Alten den Tod gebildet* [How the Ancients Represented Death], published in 1769. Like *Laokoon*, this little book costumes itself as something quite other than what it is—in this case as a polemical response to Klotz (6:409-10)—which enables it to suggest a host of interesting and difficult questions without actually formulating them. If the ancients represented or allegorized death in a manner significantly different from that to which modern Europeans are accustomed (we ask ourselves), does this not imply that death simply *was* something different for them? Death is not a kind of object that can be distinguished from other objects and then defined; in order to say what death "is" in a given cultural situation, one expects to have to carry out an extensive analysis of the culture in question. And the ancients were heathens. Between Christians and heathens, if anywhere, surely there will be a difference in the conception of death at its most basic.

But for practically all of his essay, Lessing does not even hint at this larger question. He confines himself to analyzing in detail the iconic representations of death in classical antiquity—and while he is at it, the lexical representations as well: Κῆϱ / Θάνατος, *letum* / *mors* (6:446-49). And the effect of this analysis, as in *Laokoon*, is to make by example a point that could not have been made by assertion: that the ancient conception of death is not inaccessible to us after all, because precisely the inherent obscurity of death as a concept, which is what causes difficulty in identifying its allegorical representations, implies that for practical purposes the concept is simply identical with those representations. To understand how death is represented is to understand as fully as possible how death is *understood* (in effect, what death *is*) in any given cultural situation. With respect to classical antiquity, the whole trick is to identify the relevant images and allegories correctly, and to demonstrate the correctness of our work by showing that it makes sense in the larger scheme of our knowledge of ancient culture—a demonstration, a making sense, that now constitutes retroactively the accessibility of the conception we had started with.

It follows now, moreover, at least in principle, that there is nothing to stop us from actually adopting the ancient representations of death for our own use, and hence the ancient conception as well. (Where could the difference possibly be located?) It is at this juncture that the book's submerged argument finally comes to the surface, in the very last paragraphs:

> In this respect [with regard to the Judeo-Christian idea of death as a punishment for sin], it would probably be our religion that expelled the ancient cheerful image of death from the precincts of art. But since this same religion has revealed that terrible truth not for us to despair at, since it too assures us that the death of the pious cannot be otherwise than soft and refreshing: I do not see what should keep our artists from discarding the hideous skeleton and laying claim once again to that better image [the one used by the ancients]. Even scripture speaks of an angel of death, and what artist would not prefer an angel to a skeleton as his subject?
>
> Only a misunderstood religion can estrange us from beauty; and it is a proof of the true, of the correctly understood true religion, if it always brings us back to the beautiful. (6:462)

There are several levels of irony here; but most important for our purposes is the suggestion that Christianity, for all these centuries, has misunderstood *itself*, which makes nonsense of the whole idea of cultural closure within a unique mode of self-understanding, and so removes, yet again, any basis for denying our direct intellectual access to classical antiquity. And the possibility of such access, as I indicated above, presupposes a radically un-Kantian view of the individual self.

ACCIDENTAL HISTORICAL PROMINENCE IN PHILOSOPHY AND AESTHETICS

It is not strictly accurate to speak of "alternatives" to a Kantian view of the self when referring to Lessing as a principal instance. Lessing, after all, died in 1781, the year of publication of the first *Critique*. The actual historical situation is better described as follows: In Kant's time, a variety of reasonable views of the self are available, views that in effect avoid a Kantian problematics—as Leibniz's notion of apperception also does, by observing scrupulously a distinction of psychological from metaphysical discourse. When Kant makes his basic critical move with the idea of "transcendental apperception," and then completes it in 1790 by the idea of an aesthetically founded assurance of communication, his achievement is therefore not a solution but the *creation* of a problem, the asking of an unnecessary and arguably wrong-headed question.

And yet, in the accepted academic version of the history of philosophy, the Kantian view clearly prevails over all its eighteenth-century rivals. In Fichte, and then in Hegel, the problem of personal self-consciousness, of a subjectivity struggling to overcome built-in errors in its self-understanding, becomes the principle on which a whole world is constructed, or a total system of history. (Fichte's move, in the *Wissenschaftslehre*, is to discard the Kantian thing-in-itself and derive the possibility of experience from mind alone in the process of self-consciousness. Hegel's is to imagine the struggle and triumph of spirit in history on the model of individual self-consciousness, as a process of recollection that eventually finds its end in "the consummation of the beginning" [Löwith].)[8] And the inevitable anti-Hegelian reaction only has the effect of re-problematizing the self in more or less Kantian terms, by exposing the manner in which a Hegelian linking of the personal and the universal must end by obscuring the situation of an actual contingent individual in the world—just as Kant himself had imagined his work the exposure of a baseless optimism in Leibniz's leap from self-knowledge to knowledge of God.[9]

No matter how the history of these ideas has played out, however, it is still wrong to think of the human self as a given quantity concerning which there can be specific advances (Kantian or otherwise) in knowledge or understanding. Nor was Kant himself even really aiming at such an advance. He practically admits later in *The Conflict of the Faculties* that his purpose in the *Critiques* was to set forth an intellectual position by which the Faculty of Philosophy might be catapulted into a commanding role with respect to the other three better-connected faculties of the university. This purpose is served primarily by the theorem that "the first pure cognition of the understanding" concerns a self-consciousness that is always potentially corrupt. Thence arises a *problematizing* of reason and understanding, of those faculties of mind that up to then had generally been regarded as combining by nature into a relatively simple instrument for intellectual tasks. It seems to follow from such problematizing that now neither medicine nor law, nor even theology, can begin to operate without first having its instruments critically inspected and cleansed of corruption by philosophy.

This academic corridor war does not explain the historical success of the Kantian problem of the self any better than the idea of an advance in understanding does. But it shows how accidental the history of philosophy is—at least the history of prominent philosophical systems in the West. Kantian critical philosophy is in truth as irrelevant to my management of either my life or my reason as aesthetics turns out to be with respect to the artistic and literary practices it claims as its domain. Just as aesthetics is obliged to manufacture for itself the problem of a corrupt humanity in need of rehabilitation, the problem that justifies its existence, so also, in Kant, the quest for a solution to the dilemma of the self-seeking self is what creates the dilemma in the first place. The enduring prominence of Kantian philosophy and of aesthetics is attributable to nothing but their having been formulated at a time when social and political conditions made it convenient for large numbers of people to imagine themselves in possession of a lonely individuality alienated from its fellows and from all the determining factors of its condition. Not that Kantian philosophy actually helps anyone afflicted with that feeling of self; it lives, rather, by flattering professional philosophers with a delusive sense of remaining in touch with the large mass of humanity. And aesthetics does not actually rehabilitate any individual or group; it flatters the flatterers of the great uncreative mass of humanity with the delusion that art and literature exist for the sake of pleasing and in the end benefiting them.

WHAT THE NINETEENTH CENTURY WAS LIKE

The question of which philosophical systems or ideas gain prominence at which points in history is decided not by the unfolding of an inner logic in the discipline, but by extraneous circumstances. Even if this proposition is not as universally valid as I think it is, it certainly applies to the prominence of Kantian philosophy in the nineteenth century, along with its development in Schillerian aesthetics and the project of human rehabilitation. In order to understand the history of post-Kantian aesthetics, therefore, we must be able to say something about the nineteenth-century cultural situation in which it unfolds. I will do what I can in Part Two below; but for the time being, we can get a sense for where we are headed by reminding ourselves of the millennialist invention and the closely related problem of communication.

Secular millennialism cannot operate without identifying a definite vestige or harbinger of the restored humanity it seeks. This vestige or harbinger may be located either externally or internally with respect to the process of corruption that must be overcome. In Schiller and Moritz, and later in Cassirer, the former applies. The play drive or the work of art or the "pure phenomenon" of beauty becomes efficacious only by standing apart from the corrupting processes we are enmeshed in. In Kant, on the other hand, the millennialist invention is needed; the harbinger of redemption is identical with the source and origin of corruption. There is a resonance here with the idea of the fortunate fall in some Christian thinking. But in Kant and his successors the paradox is more pointed, since the source of corruption is not merely the occasion for a redemptive move on God's part, but is itself the very engine of redemption.

And if, for Kant himself, human redemption still seems a relatively modest affair, requiring only our ability to assure ourselves of the communicability of our feelings, the German Romantics quickly find more ambitious uses for his invention. Fichte enthrones self-consciousness itself, in place of Kant's Reason, as the ground of free human self-determination.[10] Friedrich Schlegel applies the invention to questions of art and mythology, suggesting that the historical process by which true mythology has been lost, once it reflects on itself in philosophy, becomes itself the source of a new mythology and a rebirth of poetry and art. And the idea of historical process as a form of initially self-corrupting but ultimately self-perfecting reflection is itself then perfected by Hegel, whose actual *Ästhetik*—as if his whole system were not originally that—relegates all historically significant artistic practice to the past, and so avoids the nasty question of why art or beauty alone is not sufficient for the aesthetic project.

It seems reasonable now to infer that the acceptance of aesthetics as a legitimate intellectual endeavor, along with the development of ever more paradoxical versions of Kant's invented identity of corrupting and redemptive forces, reflects a civilization that regards itself as abandoned to its corruption, in contact with no transcending level of truth or tradition, hoping therefore to find redemption here and now, in the very bosom of corruption. If we consider further the association of aesthetics with issues of communication, we shall perhaps also suspect a link to the popularity and stature of *the novel,* considered as that literary form which is focused, with ever greater sophistication, upon the disclosure to its readers of the strict subjectivity of its characters.[11] By the early nineteenth century, most European novels can be read (even if their authors had never heard of Kant) as supplements to the *Critique of Judgment,* attempts to provide in particular instances the same assurance of the communicability of subjective conditions and contents that Kant had claimed to provide on a general level. In academic philosophy, the secular millennial vision rises to dizzying heights. But even outside Hegel's lecture hall, in European society as a whole, it appears that at least the basic Kantian desideratum of profound intersubjectivity retains its power and so supports the persistence of aesthetics.

Obviously there is a great deal more to be said here; and at the present stage of the argument, it is still hard to see how we can say anything at all without incurring the obligation to carry out a comprehensive cultural history of nineteenth-century Europe. I will come back to the matter later on when it can be organized more compactly.

CONFUSION AND DISCONTINUITY: THE HISTORY OF AESTHETICS

The sense in which I use the term "aesthetics" is tightly circumscribed. Aesthetics, for my purposes, is the particular form of secular millennialism that is derivable from Kant's critical philosophy by way of its development in the theory of art and history that Schiller first constructs and then is persuaded (by Goethe) to dismiss. Its goal is the satisfaction of our supposed need for intersubjective communication and for the restoration of unity in each individual self. Its method is presumably some form of education in matters of beauty and art. The historical significance of this form of secular millennialism is fairly clear. It is a seminal form of the widespread millennialist tendency in nineteenth-century thought. But this tendency as a whole cannot reasonably be characterized as "aesthetics," because the focus on questions of beauty and art is only sporadically maintained. If aesthetics, in the sense I propose, has a history, then it is a discontinuous history, but in my view still a very important one. For aesthetics is much more directly involved than nineteenth-century philosophy as a whole in the twentieth-century totalitarian destiny of secular millennialism.

The history of aesthetics, in its early phase, runs roughly as follows: Aesthetics has its roots in a Cartesian problematics. For Schiller it is Descartes' theorizing of the individual self that marks the historical extreme from which aesthetics takes its direction and impetus as the uncovering of philosophical significance in a re-particularized self. And the combination of nominalism and dualism in Cartesian thought provides the logical basis for a sense of lonely individuality that operates beneath the surface in such pre-aesthetic thinkers as Dubos and Baumgarten, and then especially in Kant. I do not mean that early aesthetics is Cartesian in spirit. On the contrary, I use "Cartesian" as a convenient designation for the general European intellectual and cultural situation *against* which aesthetics is eventually erected. And I offer the conceptual connection of Cartesian nominalism and dualism with what Cassirer calls Platonically the "pure phenomenon" of beauty as an indication of why that situation should call forth precisely aesthetics as an adversarial move.

But that move is confused from the outset. It is never clear whether the emerging discipline will be primarily a study of beauty or a study of the fine arts, or whether or how these two areas of study are related. The concept of nature is often invoked to provide a larger philosophical context: with respect to the idea of beauty in Batteux, with respect to the fine arts in a developing notion of genius from Shaftesbury and Young to Kant. But nature itself is differently contextualized, hence has different meanings, in its different uses. And when something close to a logically complete aesthetics is finally formulated, in Kant's critical philosophy, it does everything it can to avoid presenting itself as such. Its quality as an aesthetics—its vision of a corrupt humanity in need of fundamental rehabilitation—does not become apparent until Schiller works it out in detail. And Schiller, in turn, accomplishes this crucial systematic clarification only at the cost of recognizing its irrelevance to any actual social, political, or cultural problems.

One could be forgiven for concluding, therefore, that aesthetics simply does not exist as a significant strain in European philosophy from the seventeenth century on. At least one or two of its defining components seem to be missing in practically every instance. Where, for example, is the question of communication raised in Schiller's *Aesthetic Letters?*

I think this particular question can be answered, but the answer does not help matters. In the very last letter Schiller suggests that our aim must be to establish an *"aesthetic* polity" in which every person will confront every other person "only as an object of free play." *"Freiheit zu geben durch Freiheit* ist das Grundgesetz dieses Reichs,"[12] he says, *"To bestow freedom by means of freedom* is the fundamental law of this kingdom." That communication is at issue here becomes clear a bit further on where we read: "All other forms of communication [*Mitteilung*] divide society, because they relate exclusively . . . to that which distinguishes man from man; only the aesthetic mode of communication unites society, because it relates to that which is common to all" (5:667; T, 177). And "that which is common to all," the single quality that is present in every human subject *constitutively* (as that which makes it a subject), is precisely freedom. Thus Schiller in a sense perfects the system of the *Critique of Judgment.* In Kant the aesthetically assured communicability of feelings—apart from its political dimension—is not much more than a therapy for individual loneliness. But Schiller, having opened the millennialist aspect of aesthetics that Kant suppresses, will settle for nothing less than absolute or total intersubjectivity: intersubjectivity on a level where individual freedom still has the quality of "play" and so is not yet subject to determination (hence separation) in any form; intersubjectivity that therefore transcends itself in the direction of ideal community.

This vision, however, is arrived at only in the deeply self-questioning coda of Schiller's argument, which develops the recognition that aesthetics is by nature obliged to deny its own inherent goal. Schiller makes a more ambitious leap, but in the end his thought confuses itself as much as Kant's does. And when we take the next historical step, the notion of "aesthetics" seems to evaporate altogether. Schiller, in his philosophical works of the 1790s, is a scrupulous follower of Kant; and the *Aesthetic Letters,* in turn, are an important factor in the background of Hegel's *Phenomenology of Spirit.*[13] But if Schiller works out the aesthetic and millennialist dimension of Kant's *Critiques,* Hegel, while retaining Schiller's millennialism, seems to have dispensed with any recognizably aesthetic questions. Art, as an activity of Spirit, has a place in the *Phenomenology,* but is restricted to the phase of "religion" in Spirit's progress toward Absolute Knowing.

What I think happens is this: Schiller eventually understands the irrelevance of aesthetics, the internally contradictory process by which the study of beauty (and of art in the broadest sense) renders itself pointless with respect to its own object. Art therefore becomes an *insoluble* problem. (Not necessarily a hopeless problem: the mission of art, the de-theorizing of the self, may still be achieved. It may in fact already be achieved in some individuals [like Goethe], but can never be achieved in a manner that we might grasp theoretically.) Now Hegel, of all people, must certainly have been aware of the self-conflicting tendency in Schiller's thought; but he was also constitutionally unable to imagine a problem without a solution. He recognizes the problem in Schiller, therefore, and proceeds to solve it by subsuming it, and with it the whole question of art, under a larger millennialist structure which does have an identifiable culmination in the form of Absolute Knowing. I offer this speculation not as an interpretation of the *Phenomenology* in its entirety, but as an attempt to understand Schiller's place in the process of its conception and composition.

Aesthetics, in the sense I have tried to give to the term, thus seems to be inherently self-canceling, hence necessarily short-lived. It is first fully developed by Kant, but without recognizing itself, then recognizes itself in Schiller, but only at the cost of also recognizing its pointlessness, and is then mercifully done away with by Hegel. Bits and pieces of it live on, but only as bits and pieces. Secular millennialism becomes a philosophical template for Hegel and Marx and many less prominent thinkers. The project of deep intersubjective communication is explored by the developing form of the novel. The terms "aesthetic" and "aesthetics" are still used, but for most of the nineteenth century—apart from Hegel's *Ästhetik* and such post-Hegelian systems as that of Friedrich Theodor Vischer—attach themselves mainly to questions of artistic production and reception in the modern bourgeois age.

But in the next chapter I will argue that at the end of the nineteenth century and in the early twentieth, the bits and pieces manage to reassemble themselves into Kantian-Schillerian aesthetics all over again, except that now it calls itself not "aesthetics" but "hermeneutics." This reassembly of aesthetics—once we agree that it actually happens—is a phenomenon that cries out for explanation, yet obviously defies any explanation that presupposes the internally regulated unfolding of an intellectual discipline.

NOTES

1. "Das Wohlgefallen, welches das Geschmacksurtheil bestimmt, ist ohne alles Interesse" is the heading of § 2 of the *Critique of Judgment*.

2. Kant himself can be called as a witness on this point, for with the idea of "radical evil" he formulates his own version of what is fundamentally wrong with

human psychology. But this thought is not fully worked out until *Die Religion innerhalb der Grenzen der bloßen Vernunft* (1793). Indeed, a reluctance to venture too far into matters of religion—at least until he felt himself better prepared—may account in part for his resistance to the millennialist tendency in his own aesthetic thought.

3. The term "transcendental apperception" is used in the first edition of the *Critique*. See *Kants Werke*, 4:81-83 (full reference in chap. 1, n11). In the second edition it is called "pure" or "original" apperception, *Kants Werke*, 3:108.

4. Editions and references as in the notes to chap. 2.

5. In the second edition, this part of the *Critique* is divided into sections (§§). Each quotation below is located by section number and page in *Kants Werke*, vol. 3. The present reference is § 16, 108.

6. This is, one might say, a *pro domo* paragraph. Critical arguments supporting the implied assertions in it can be found in my *Beyond Theory* and *Goethe as Woman*, in my *All Theater Is Revolutionary Theater* (Ithaca, 2005), in my *The Dark Side of Literacy: Literature and Learning Not to Read* (Bronx, NY, 2008), and in my "The Thinking Machine," *Revue internationale de philosophie*, 65, no. 255 (=1/2011), 7-26.

7. Lessing, *Werke* (see chap. 2, n4, for full reference), 4:163. Letter of Nov. 1756.

8. Karl Löwith, *From Hegel to Nietzsche: The Revolution in Nineteenth-Century Thought* (Garden City: Anchor, 1967; orig. German, Zürich, 1941), 30. What Löwith calls, in Hegel, "the eschatological design of world history" (29), is called by M.H. Abrams "The Circuitous Journey: Through Alienation to Reintegration," in Fichte, Hegel, and others. See Abrams, *Natural Supernaturalism: Tradition and Revolution in Romantic Literature* (New York, 1971), 197-252.

9. For Hegel and the reaction, see Löwith, especially Part Two, section IV, "The Problem of Man," 304-22, on Hegel, Feuerbach, Marx, Stirner, Kierkegaard, and Nietzsche.

10. Abrams, 358-59, locates this aspect of Fichte's thought at the center of more than just a German revolutionary movement in the early nineteenth century. He refers mainly to Fichte's letter to J.I. Baggesen, April 1795, about the *Wissenschaftslehre*.

11. The best commentator I know of, on this aspect of the novel as a form, is Dorrit Cohn, *Transparent Minds: Narrative Modes for Presenting Consciousness in Fiction* (Princeton, 1978), whose thought we will come back to in Part II. The novel as a vessel of "private experience" (Ian Watt, *The Rise of the Novel: Studies in Defoe, Richardson and Fielding* [Berkeley, 1964; orig. 1957], 174-207) is accounted for ordinarily, in large part, by appealing to "the rise of individualism" (Watt, 177) in the seventeenth and eighteenth centuries. In Part II below, we will find that certain refinements in the idea of individualism enable us to understand the novel and aesthetics as two aspects of a single basic historical move. Abrams has a good deal to say about the *Bildungsroman* in connection with his "circuitous journey." And Lynn Hunt, *Inventing Human Rights: A History* (New York, 2007), 35-60, assigns the novel a central role in the development of individual rights.

12. 5:667; T, 176. Full references in chap. 1, n7, chap. 3, n4.

13. Walter Kaufmann, *Hegel: A Reinterpretation* (Garden City, NY: Anchor, 1966), devotes a whole subchapter (18-31) to the influence of the *Aesthetic Letters* on Hegel and specifically on the *Phenomenology*. One can quibble about various pieces of his evidence, but it is hard to disagree with the main point. Hegel first takes note of the *Letters*, admiringly, in a letter to Schelling (16 April 1795) at the time of their original publication. And in the "Einleitung" to his *Vorlesungen über die Aesthetik*, he still admires what he sees as their epoch-making grasp of an *"Einheit* nun des Allgemeinen und Besonderen, der Freiheit und Nothwendigkeit, der Geistigkeit und des Natürlichen." See Georg Wilhelm Friedrich Hegel, *Sämtliche Werke*, ed. Hermann Glockner, 20 vols. (Stuttgart, 1927), 12:98.

FIVE

Aesthetics and Hermeneutics

If philosophical aesthetics persists into the twentieth century in the form of a tradition of secular millennialism, then its persistence must be attributed to what I have called extraneous factors. One such factor is Friedrich Schleiermacher, who plays a crucial role in that tradition, but without himself being an aesthetician, in my sense or in any other. He employs the millennialist invention, and in a way that prefigures its use in all future hermeneutics, but without himself being a millennialist, secular or otherwise. And he is, I think, the first Kantian to apply the master's thought in a discussion of language.

THE ISSUE OF LANGUAGE

In order to grasp Schleiermacher's position and significance, we need to go back to the question of the unity of the self. I have said that there are plenty of alternatives to Kant's absoluteness on this question, including especially the position suggested by Goethe, who manages to be completely open and impenetrably cryptic about it at the same time.

> Freuet euch des wahren Scheins,
> Euch des ernsten Spieles:
> Kein Lebendiges ist ein Eins,
> Immer ist's ein Vieles. (WA, 3:88)

[Rejoice in the true illusion, in the serious play: No living thing is a One, it's always a Many.]

The applicability of these lines to the question of the unity of the human self or subject is made clear by their association with the larger poem "Die Metamorphose der Pflanzen" (WA, 3:85-87), where the intellectual and personal condition of human observers is understood to be closely analogous to the structure of what they observe.

But Goethe is an exceptional case. Lessing is much more typical in needing a submerged argument in order to establish a position at variance with what was to become Kant's insistence on the problematic and corruptible unity of the human subject. Grammar itself seems to obstruct us in this matter. How shall we use the pronoun "you" or "he" or "she," or especially "I," without implying, for practically every reader, the integral unity of the person to whom it refers? Language is a problem for anyone attempting a non-Kantian account of the self; and language therefore becomes a principal issue for the actual opponents of Kant.

Especially the *Critique of Pure Reason* is attacked for its use of German in a manner so entirely detached from common practice that it becomes meaningless. This point is made not only by Herder and Hamann, who both lived in Kant's shadow and had bones to pick with him, but also by relatively disinterested parties like the poet Friedrich Gottlieb Klopstock.[1] And although Goethe professes gratitude toward Kant, for helping him clarify his own thinking, he does so only in the process of shifting Kant's propositions into an idiom with which the philosopher would have been decidedly uncomfortable. I refer to the series of four little essays in vol. 1, no. 2 of *Zur Morphologie* (WA, pt. 2, 11:45-57). In the piece "Anschauende Urtheilskraft" [Intuitive Judgment] (54-55), Goethe even makes something close to a Herderian move. He quotes a passage from § 77 of the *Critique of Judgment* where Kant distinguishes carefully between *intellectus archetypus* and *intellectus ectypus*, between a hypothetical understanding *(Verstand)* that could have its own intuitions and actual human understanding which must proceed "discursively."(The idea of a possible but not conceptualizable intuitive understanding, presumably a godlike understanding, which appears in the *Critique of Pure Reason,* was discussed in chapter 4 above.) And then he suggests, outrageously, that the reason for Kant's strict distinction is merely to indicate by irony a way of getting around it, a way of achieving intuitive or archetypal understanding after all, by dint of long training and long study of nature to the point where we become "worthy of participating intellectually in nature's productions."

Kant sets up a strict, abstract, and static opposition; Goethe interprets it into a biographical narrative, ostensibly hypothetical but evidently personal. And then he embeds that narrative in a huge idea of evolutionary natural history that Kant, in a footnote to § 80 of the *Critique of Judgment,* had called a possible "adventure of reason" but without according it any actual validity. Thus, in effect, Kant is accused of imposing artificial, static structures upon a living, fluid, developing subject matter (our actual life) which can be understood adequately only from within, from the point of view of a participant, not that of a detached observer. For all the difference in tone here, there is not much difference in substance from the little fable of the spider and the bees with which Herder closes his *Meta-kritik* against Kant.[2] A spider (representing the "critical" Kant) descends on a beehive, whose inhabitants he sneers at as "low businesspeople, downward looking, bustling empiricists"; he then spins over them a web which he declares is the "moral world order." Luckily the web is blown away, and the bees resolve: "Let him spin spiderwebs who has nothing better to do; we fly and gather godly sustenance, refreshing food, and a brighter flame for the light of day."

At base, the issue is language. By a participatory or "empirical" atti-tude Herder means primarily a willingness to operate within the histori-cally evolved and generally recognized possibilities of the German lan-guage. He is fond of quoting Leibniz against Kant in this regard: on the philosophical usefulness of German's rich non-abstract, reality-oriented vocabulary (*Werke*, 8:371-73), and on the advisability of avoiding an in-vented, non-idiomatic metaphysical terminology in philosophy (8:619-22). And even though Goethe, in the little essays mentioned above, shows no antagonism toward Kant—Herder's antagonism, he claims (49), em-barrassed him—still he too keeps the issue of language constantly in view and clothes it with the kind of irony we have come to expect. He says he has managed to "grow accustomed gradually to a [Kantian] language that had been completely alien" to him (53); but he cites as his guide in this learning process the essay "On Naïve and Sentimental Poetry" (52), which is by far, in style and in thought, the least Kantian of Schiller's aesthetic-critical works of the 1790s. He thus leaves plenty of room for suspicion that what he says about Kant concerns after all "only what had been stirred up in me, but not what I had read [in Kant]" (51), not Kant's own actual meaning or procedure or idiom.

The question of the unity of the subject is always present, if not always explicit, in this discussion of language. Herder devotes one energetic and engaging section of his linguistically oriented *Metakritik* to a "rational" dismantling of the Kantian "I think" (8:518-22). But is there an intrinsic connection between the question of language and that of the unity of the self?

SENDING AND RECEIVING

To show such a connection, and how it affects our understanding of Schleiermacher and hermeneutics, we can begin with a simple general proposition: *The producer of an utterance, the speaker or writer, tends to oper-ate as a multiple subject, a plurality, whereas in receiving or understanding an utterance, the subject tends to operate as a single unit.* No one, in speaking or writing, can hope to maintain anything close to complete control over the implications of the utterance. Every word or phrase we use brings with it a history, a huge collection of prior instances, some more prominent or audible than others but all pointing uncontrollably in different directions, a cacophonous chorus of ghostly voices from the past which inhabit and splinter the voice of the present speaker. I am not only "myself," but also all those other people, when I speak or write. But when I understand an utterance, even an utterance of my own, I am by definition making a decision; I am reducing the spoken or written cacophony to a single meaning or pattern of meanings. I am therefore asserting the singularity not only of the speaker's subject, but also of my own. For by being arbitrary, which it always is in the final analysis, that act of decision is strictly "my" act, hence presupposes my unique self as its vehicle. [3]

But aesthetics is never separate from the question of communication; and the question of communication is always a *hermeneutic* question, a question of understanding, not a question of verbal or semiotic production. Given our experience of understanding an utterance, of registering the effect of an utterance upon our own mental inventory, the question of communication must take the form: Can understanding be verified, can it be distinguished from misunderstanding, established as more than just the listener's personal fancy? Thus we arrive at a linguistic contextualization of Kant's basic philosophical stance. His aesthetic focus on the problem of communication leaves him no choice logically but to insist upon the strict unified integrity of the individual self.

But we can go further by asking: Is it possible to have a theory of language that is not focused upon communication or understanding, an idea of language as nothing but sending, nothing but productive activity? One version of such a theory is Herder's. In his prize-essay on the origin of language, Herder never even raises the question of how or whether language communicates. (When he speaks of the ability of sounds to awaken sympathetic emotional reactions in the creature hearing them, he is referring to *animal* communication [*Werke*, 1: 697-8].) Nothing matters for him about language but the effects of its *practice*, in creating first an articulable human world and then a fabric of human societies in that world, a practice which includes our acting as if we understood one another, but without any basis for such an assumption. In fact, when he comes to the matter of how a plurality of languages arises, he states categorically: "Im eigentlichen metaphysischen Verstande ist schon nie eine Sprache bei Mann und Weib, Vater und Sohn, Kind und Greis möglich" (1:791) [In the strict metaphysical sense it is never possible for there to be a single language for man and woman, for father and son, for child and codger]. If we look at the matter with "metaphysical" exactness, that is, we must conclude that communication never happens, for the simple reason that no two of us are ever even using the same language. And if we believed in the efficacy of linguistic communication, how could we explain the splintering of older languages into multiplicities of modern ones? By decisions *not* to communicate?

Nor is Herder alone in this approach to linguistic questions. That both Goethe and Klopstock, for example, think in terms of linguistic productivity rather than linguistic communication, can be argued easily enough.[4] But perhaps a more interesting case is that of Hamann, who does not actually formulate a theory of language in Herder's manner, but nevertheless makes his position clear by dramatizing it in his style, which is built out of practically nothing but quotations, so much so that in reading even his simplest statements we find ourselves worrying about whether we have failed to recognize a source. Hamann, that is, actually stages for us the uncontrollable cacophony or multiplicity that in truth characterizes the condition of the speaking subject.

And in relation to this idea of productive language, Herder's idea or Hamann's, Kant must be convicted of avoiding the question of language for the sake of preserving the possibility of communication. If he had understood how completely our existence is embedded in language as a productive activity, he could never have imagined that transcendental basis for communication (the unity of the "I think") upon which the whole system of his philosophy depends. This is where Schleiermacher comes in.

KANT RESCUED

As far as I can tell, the main problem Schleiermacher was concerned with was how to read the New Testament in an age of historical criticism without sacrificing one's use of it as a vehicle of truth. But his grappling with this problem took him on a huge detour which turned out to be a philosophical project in its own right, the founding of modern secular hermeneutics.

When we first open Schleiermacher's notes on hermeneutics, we might be inclined to place him on the side of Hamann and Herder in their criticism of Kant. For he does not by any means avoid the question of language. In his so-called "compendium-like exposition" of hermeneutics from 1819, we read:

> 5. Since every utterance has a double relation, to the totality of the language and to the total thinking of its originator, all understanding includes two moments, understanding the utterance as a distinct part of its language and understanding it as a fact in the thinking person. . . . In this respect, every person is on the one hand a place in which a given language shapes itself in a unique way, and his utterance can only be understood against the totality of the language. But the person is also a steadily developing intellect, and his utterance must be understood as one fact among others in this connection.
>
> 6. Understanding can happen only with the mutual interpenetration of these two moments.[5]

Clearly the recognition that our existence is embedded in our language is not nearly as foreign to Schleiermacher's thinking as Herder considered it foreign to Kant's.

But Schleiermacher remains nevertheless a Kantian philosopher in the sense of being committed to the idea of a unified self. He defines hermeneutics as "the art of understanding" (75); and understanding is the domain of the strictly singular subject. When he writes on aesthetic matters, he avoids the problems we have discussed by concentrating entirely on the question of how to define "art" in relation to its "theory," rather than on the notion of the beautiful;[6] but his work still contains a (Kantian) millennialist tendency whose presence appears most clearly in the resoluteness with which he resists it in the end—as if he were attempting to rescue Kantian philosophy, at the last minute, from its aesthetic confusion. He adopts an approximation of the position on language of Kant's most determined critics, but then shows in effect how even that position can be developed in a Kantian manner.

I do not claim that this was actually Schleiermacher's project. But it is a project which can reasonably be read into his work's historical tendency, a project for which he positions himself by avoiding the suggestion that communication is an established fact (essentially Baumgarten's position) or that it is an accomplishment which reason herself entitles us to consider ourselves capable of (Kant's position). He treats communication not as an object of philosophical longing, but as a manageable practical task, a task requiring "art," which includes not only systematic discipline but natural talent as well (78).

Kant is interested in the *communicability* of subjective conditions. He does not worry about how such communicability will be realized as actual *communication*, which is the avoidance of the question of language for which his critics attack him. And that fault is then made good by Schleiermacher, who concerns himself with the practical communication of "thought"—which means subjectively conditioned thought, the form in which Kant's "feelings" would need to be communicated. In place of Schiller's vision of a corrupt humanity requiring rehabilitation, Schleiermacher suggests the idea of a humanity that will never communicate perfectly, but can still be trained to communicate more effectively than it has heretofore. Thus the historical pretensions of aesthetics (explicit in Schiller, implied but suppressed in Kant) are abandoned, and the problem of communication is brought down to earth, where it after all belongs, since even for Kant the communicability of feelings is significant primarily for counteracting the experience of subjective aloneness.

THE HERMENEUTIC CIRCLE

But communication is still a problem. To rescue Kant, Schleiermacher must still show how verifiable communication can be achieved, or at least approached; and he begins by making this problem as difficult as possible. He requires that understanding involve the "mutual interpenetration of two moments," the totality of the language and the total thinking of the utterance's originator. But this creates a complicated situation. Immediately after proposition no. 6 in the quotation above, he comments:

> 1. The utterance is not yet even understood as a fact of the intellect if it is not understood in its relation to the language, because the quality of being born into a particular language modifies the intellect.
> 2. The utterance is also not understood as a modification of the language if it is not understood as a fact of the intellect, because the intellect contains the basis of all influence of the individual upon the language. (77)

In other words, we cannot carry out the psychological aspect of understanding without first having completed the linguistic aspect; and we cannot complete the latter without the former as a basis. This is a version of what has come to be known as the hermeneutic circle.

The circular structure, in fact, is replicated even within its own individual elements. Proposition no. 5 (quoted above) is commented upon as follows:

> 1. Every utterance presupposes a given language. Of course one can also turn this around the other way . . . because a language only becomes what it is by way of utterances. . . .
> 2. Every utterance rests upon an earlier thinking. This can also be turned the other way around . . . (77)

Treating the utterance as part of its language always involves a certain inaccuracy, since if the utterance is non-trivial or worth understanding to begin with (cf. 78-79), it generates its own linguistic change. And convenient as it may be to imagine the individual as thinking *before* he or she speaks, this too is obviously inaccurate. How could thinking ever find its way into an utterance without first being linguistically conditioned, situated relative to existing utterances?

These conceptual difficulties or slippages explain why Schleiermacher must insist that understanding is an "art," not a systematic discipline. And in connection with the opposition between grammatical (language-oriented) and psychological (speaker-oriented) interpretation, he gives a provisional idea of how that art might work. "If the grammatical side were to be completed for itself alone, a perfect knowledge of the language would have to be given; in the case of the other [psychological] side, a complete knowledge of the person would be required. Since neither of these conditions can ever be met, it is necessary to go back and forth between the two sides; and it is impossible to set rules for how this must be done" (78). It appears that we must feel our way into any given utterance, so that each small advance in grammatical understanding helps us with the psychological side, and vice versa. But how can we be confident that understanding is possible in the first place, that we are not just playing a kind of subjective solitaire when we interpret?

THE MILLENNIALIST INVENTION (II)

The hermeneutic circle arises for Schleiermacher because he attempts to be a Kantian philosopher without avoiding the issue of a subject's embeddedness in language; because he insists on conceiving the subject as: (1) a strict unity, fully enclosed and inaccessible from without, which at the same time, however, (2) is radically conditioned by linguistic particulars and therefore not open to transcendental analysis. And then, in a move comparable to Kant's use of original apperception (the root of subjective isolation) as an anchor for the possibility of a rehabilitated and communicative humanity, he uses precisely our embeddedness in language as an avenue for verifying our understanding of given utterances, thus establishing the communicability of subjective conditions after all. As in Kant, the problem itself (here a different problem) is employed as its own solution.

The crucial passage from 1819 has terminological difficulties. The word "divinatory," for instance, is written in place of a crossed-out "prophetic." But the substance is clear:

> The art [of understanding] can develop its rules only out of a positive guiding formula, and this formula is: "the historical and divinatory, objective and subjective reconstruction of the given utterance."

1. "Objectively historical" means grasping how the utterance operates in the totality of the language and how the knowledge it contains operates as a production of the language. — "Objectively prophetic" means surmising how the utterance will itself become a developmental node for the language. Without both of these, material and formal misunderstanding is unavoidable.
2. "Subjectively historical" means knowing how the utterance arises as a fact in the mind, "subjectively prophetic" means surmising how the thoughts contained in the utterance will continue to operate on and in that mind. Without both of these, misunderstanding is likely.
3. Our task can be expressed thus: "To understand the utterance, first, just as well, and then better than its originator does." For since we have no unmediated knowledge of what is inside him, we must seek to bring many things into consciousness that can remain un-

conscious for him except to the extent that he reflects and himself becomes his own reader. On the objective side, in this case, he has no data beyond what is available to us. (83-84)[7]

The question that troubles readers here is: How can Schleiermacher speak of understanding an utterance "better" than its originator does?

In the above passage, "objective" and "subjective" refer to what we called the grammatical or linguistic side of understanding and the psychological side. And since Schleiermacher remains clear about our having "no unmediated knowledge" about what goes on "inside" the originator, no access to the subjectivity that has brought forth the utterance, it must be true that our "better" knowledge of the utterance's meaning emerges from the movement "back and forth" between objective and subjective interpretation that is made possible by the embeddedness of the speaking subject in the language being used. How else, if not by a detour through the linguistic realm, could we find our way to "unconscious" motivations in the speaker? Embeddedness in a particular language is indispensable to the argument. When Schleiermacher suggests that a speaker who "reflects and himself becomes his own reader" can also draw forth hidden motivations in the utterance, he reminds us (in a Herderian or Hamannian vein) of how little control we have over our utterances *as speakers*. Only the reader or interpreter, the unified intellect who weighs possibilities and makes decisions about meaning, can be said to exert any control over the utterance. In this sense it is almost automatically true that I understand your utterance "better" than you do.

But this point does not yet justify Schleiermacher's assertion. For if you now "reflect and become your own reader," then you and I are again on an equal footing and my "better" understanding has evaporated. Everything hinges, therefore, on what is meant by a "prophetic" or "divinatory" understanding. What makes it possible for us to "surmise" (German "ahnden") how an utterance will operate in the *future* development of its language or in the *future* of the mind that has produced it? Once the question is put in these terms, only one answer suggests itself. It is *our* embeddedness in the language (either from childhood or acquired later by study), it is *our* immediate participation in the language's developing condition, that enables us (if we have a talent for it) to surmise "prophetically" where the language is headed; and it is *our* sharing with the speaker the condition of embeddedness in the particular language that enables us (if we have a talent for it) to surmise or "divine" the subsequent unfolding of that speaker's mind. It is this quality of surmise or prophecy, this following of the utterance *beyond* the moment it is made, that measures the extent to which we understand it "better" than its originator. Is the originator thus strictly excluded from "our" understanding in this sense? Of course not. There is no reason why the originator should not carry out the same move of divinatory understanding that we do, whereupon he or she would achieve a knowledge different from, and "better" than, that of an originator *as* originator.[8]

Against the background of Kant's *Critiques,* this thinking is a clear instance of the millennialist invention. It begins by abandoning the idea of a transcendental pathway for communication, and then recognizes that the problem thus created, the absence of transcendental factors in communication, implies the communicating subject's *complete* embeddedness in a particular language. But such embeddedness, properly considered, is the problem's solution. This move, this seeking out of problems in order to treat them not as obstructions but as intellectual catapults, is what I think reflects a millennial tendency in Schleiermacher. But it is a tendency he succeeds in resisting.

VERSIONS OF KANT AND CHRISTIANITY

What is gained by Schleiermacher's hermeneutic argument? Its usefulness is at least limited by the fact that it rests upon one large assumption: that the *object* of understanding exists, and exists in a highly specific way. It must be true that with every movement "back and forth" between the objective and the subjective side of interpretation I come at least one small step closer to a valid understanding of the utterance. The sequence of provisional understandings by which I grope my way forward must converge toward a single goal (even if that goal is itself subject to continuing development), a goal which I will probably never reach but which still gives contour and purpose to my endeavor. And there is nothing in the nature of language or of any utterance that might guarantee the existence of such a goal. For all I know, every shift between objective and subjective interpretation is leading me further astray, producing ever greater incongruities in my thought. As an interpreter, I have no choice but to *assume* the contrary of this possibility.

This assumption includes at least the assumption of strict unity and singularity in the human subject. Whence else could the needful object of understanding, the self-identity and coherence of the utterance, receive its own unitary existence? (Even as a kind of asymptote it would be characterized by unity.) It is true that Schleiermacher, like Hamann and Herder, understands that a speaker, as speaker, lacks control over his or her utterance. But that speaker must nevertheless still be constituted as a singular Kantian subject which asserts itself as a central, perhaps "unconscious" unity in the utterance's meaning, the hermeneutic object. Otherwise the whole hermeneutic project is hopeless.

But not only the unity of the subject who speaks is assumed; that of the interpreting subject is required as well, my own subjectivity. For without a fundamental internal unity, without an unchanging level of structure, my mind would have no leverage to prevent incongruities from infecting its "prophetic" activity. I pointed out above that we will attribute a stronger unity to a subject in the process of understanding than to one in the act of speaking. But Schleiermacher simply assumes (with Kant) that strict unity is the subject's condition. Thus he adopts the idea of the subject's embeddedness in language without accepting what Hamann and Herder (and Goethe and Klopstock) would regard as the concomitant, radically speaker-oriented linguistic theory.

In effect, if not in intent, Schleiermacher wants to have it both ways, to embrace the positions of both Kant and his adversaries. The assumption of singularity and unity in the thinking subject is already inherent in Kant's setting of his critical task: to show what is implied by the situation of a singular subject confronting multiplicity in the object world and having only discursive understanding by which to establish an orderly relation to that world, an experience of it. In carrying out his task he produces essentially an aesthetics, the vision of a corrupt humanity that requires from the experience of beauty a restoration of intersubjective communication. But this aesthetics depends on a transcendental origin for the subject, in "pure apperception," entirely apart from the manner in which reason and understanding may be conditioned by language. And this defect is in a sense repaired by Schleiermacher, who thus provides us with a new version of Kantian philosophy, a de-transcendentalized version which is perhaps no longer an aesthetics.

If this is Schleiermacher's achievement, it is only accidentally such. His main concern was to devise a method of reading the New Testament that would accommodate both a modern historical approach, focused on the texts' embeddedness in their authors' actual culture and language, and a traditional Protestant approach reflecting and supporting the present reader's personal faith. How successful he was in that endeavor does not concern us here. What matters for our purposes is that his was a decidedly Kantian Christianity, dependent (for the operation of its hermeneutics) on the idea of a singular and unified subject.

This idea is by no means dominant in the history of Christian thought—however closely it may seem related to the notion of a soul exposed to judgment. In Augustine, in fact, and in neo-Platonic theology, and later in Scholasticism, we can trace a habit of recognizing in the human subject's experience of itself a mysterious combination of unity with multiplicity, which serves to present constantly to our introspective view a symbol of the Trinity.[9] And in Schleiermacher's immediate cultural neighborhood there is the case of Hamann, who begins his *Aesthetica in nuce* with the outcry: "Not a lyre!—nor an artist's brush!—a winnowing fan for my Muse, to sweep the threshing floor of holy literature!"[10] A discourse is needed, in other words, by which the author does not seek individual control over his material (as it were with his fingers), but rather casts it aloft indiscriminately, entrusting its articulation to the wind. The key to this discourse is a motto apparently from Erasmus,

"Rede, daß ich Dich sehe" (2:198)[11] [Speak, that I might see you]. Ostensibly this motto refers to what we receive from God in "Creation, which is a speech addressed to the creature by way of the creature." But cryptically, in Hamann's "Rhapsody in Kabbalistic Prose" (2:195), it also describes what God *wants from us.* The human soul must express itself, as best it can, in indiscriminate multiplicity, so that it may be "seen" by God, in whose vision alone, if anywhere, its unity and singularity are achieved.

Schleiermacher's, by contrast, is a Kantian Christianity, in which unity and singularity simply belong to the subject's own necessary mode of being and being conscious. For Kant this state of affairs is manifest as an unfulfillable need to experience directly our subjective unity—thus as an inability to carry out Hamann's move of self-abandonment—which in turn produces the problem of self-consciousness and the sense of deep corruption in our nature. But Schleiermacher tends to move Kant toward the earthbound and conciliatory. For in his hermeneutics, the unity of the subject is necessary to guarantee the existence of any object of understanding, which implies that the experience of understanding, if we ever achieve it, includes an intimation of subjective unity more direct than anything Kant ever envisages.

The same applies to Schleiermacher's Christianity as Christianity. There is plenty of room for Christianity in the system of the *Critiques,* as long as one does not associate with it the wrong type of knowledge or justification. But Christianity in this form, as a *permissible* belief, is a relatively bloodless philosophical religion, whereas Schleiermacher's Christianity, without ceasing to be fundamentally Kantian, is evangelical in nature, steeped in a reading of the New Testament. Thus, again, it is as if Schleiermacher were engaged in stripping Kantian philosophy of its quality as an aesthetics, stripping it of the Schillerian claim to promote a radical reformation of humanity, and steering it in a simpler, more earthbound and (one might say) more wholesomely parochial direction.

WILHELM DILTHEY AND THE REBIRTH OF AESTHETICS

If this attenuation of Kantian thought is an actual tendency in Schleiermacher's work, as I think it is, then it is one which never caught on in the broad development of European philosophy. We have already had a brief look at the accidental formation of a philosophical mainstream in the nineteenth century, a mainstream, in its Hegelian and counter-Hegelian currents, which was clearly not in the market for a simpler, more earthbound and wholesomely parochial philosophy. What the nineteenth century wanted, in those philosophical systems that it favored with historical prominence, was exactly what it got: aesthetic leftovers in the form of promises for a rehabilitated or perfected mankind.

And at the end of the nineteenth century, Wilhelm Dilthey is still catering to his time's thirst for greatness and epochality. But he is doing so in a new way. In an essay on "The Emergence of Hermeneutics," published in 1900, he says:

> Therein lies the immeasurable importance of literature for our understanding of intellectual life and history: that only in language does human interiority find its complete, exhaustive and objectively understandable expression. Therefore the art of understanding [Schleiermacher's phrase!] has its center in the explication or *interpretation of the residue of human existence that is contained in language.*
>
> The explication, and the inescapably associated critical treatment, of this residue was consequently the starting point for *philology*, which is at base a *personal art and virtuosity in such treatment of what is preserved in writing.* And only in connection with this art and its results can any other interpretation of monuments or historically recorded actions be successful. We can be mistaken about the motives of people's actions in history; the people themselves can put them in a deceptive light. But the work of a great poet or discoverer, of a religious genius or a genuine philosopher, can never be anything but the true expression of that person's inner life. Even in this fundamentally mendacious human society of ours, such a work is always the truth, and unlike any other expressive use of fixed signs, it is inherently open to a complete and objective interpretation, indeed it is a source of interpretive illumination for the other artistic monuments of its time and for the historical actions of its contemporaries.[12]

Obviously Dilthey is a firm believer in past greatness, and in our ability to achieve something close to a complete knowledge of such greatness, a re-experiencing of it, a "Nachfühlen" (5:317). Which seems to imply that we ourselves, in turn—we nineteenth-century latecomers—are also capable of producing great revolutionary instances of the human.

But Dilthey's vision of human rehabilitation or perfection is not focused on the future, like that of Hegelians or Marxists. The systematic initiative to which he devoted much of his life was what he called "Geisteswissenschaften"—usually translated "human sciences," but meaning more exactly: sciences concerned with "Geist," with human intellectual ability and production. These sciences do not claim to be historically predictive. Their attention is directed primarily not at the large structures and movements of history, but rather at the smallest discernible historical units, the human individuals who happen to have made a difference; and up to the limiting point where "Individuum est ineffabile" (5:330), they attempt to understand those individuals *from within* (5:317-18). Whatever "general law-like conditions and comprehensive relationships" (5:317) the human sciences are able to describe must be based on that repeated internal study of individuality.

Hence Dilthey's interest in Schleiermacher, who had de-transcendentalized Kantian philosophy and infused it with techniques for improving
our understanding of individual human instances. But Dilthey always
pushes Schleiermacher's thought a step further than the latter would
have considered permissible. Schleiermacher intends his interpretive
techniques only for what he considers significant utterances, utterances
that make an appreciable difference in the expressive or indicative range
of their language as a whole. In Dilthey, this relatively modest attempt to
give shape to the hermeneutic endeavor reappears as the idea, quoted
above, that the utterances of truly "great" individuals evince a uniquely
interpretable form of "truth." Evangelical Christianity had been religion
enough for Schleiermacher; but Dilthey pushes hermeneutics itself (and
with it the "Geisteswissenschaften") even beyond religion toward the
possibility of an institutionalized perfection of the human.

Another instance of Dilthey's tendency to overstrain Schleiermacher's
thinking has to do with the idea of individuality. Schleiermacher needs
the Kantian assumption of a unified and singular self as a basis from
which to infer the existence of the hermeneutic object; but he does not
make an issue of it, he simply takes it as given and works with it. For
Dilthey, on the other hand, the singularity and strict uniqueness of the
individual is not merely a given fact. It is a culmination of the whole
process of the universe, which is structured by "individuation." In his
"Contributions to the Study of Individuality" of 1895-6, Dilthey asserts
that reality exhibits to our intellect two fundamental properties *(Grundei-
genschaften)*: the first is "uniformity"; and then, "on the basis of all these
uniformities [in nature], the singular arises," in the sense that "every
singular thing is [strictly] different from every other" (5:270). From a
scientific point of view, what matters principally in inorganic nature, and
even in most of organic nature, is the detection of uniformity. But "the
singular" is present everywhere, and becomes ever more prominent as
one ascends the ladder of essences from inorganic matter toward human
interiority. Until finally:

> The highest stage at which these tendencies toward individuation in all
> reality appear is human-historical life. Even at this stage, homogeneity
> and uniformity form the basis for individuation; but individuation ar-
> rives here at its culminating point. For it is now the object of an inde-
> pendent interest. Whereas what we seek in nature are its general laws,
> here the singular becomes itself the object of scientific inquiry. When I
> observe how heated liquid lead, dripped into water, assumes various
> strange forms, these forms as such awaken only a fleeting interest in
> me; the attention of the natural scientist is focused exclusively on the
> laws that determine those forms. . . . But on the other hand, new biogra-
> phies are constantly striving to lay hold of the great singular fact of
> Frederick the Great or Goethe. The study of the gradations, relation-

ships, types that appear in this area is therefore of the greatest interest. (5:271-72)

It is not enough that the "human sciences" carry out in practice the study of individual instances of the human. Dilthey insists that that study be justified by a theory of individuation with cosmic dimensions.

His project is thus not merely to understand significant instances of human individuality, but *to rescue individuality as such,* to preserve imme-diate, experienced human particularity in an historical situation where it is threatened by the abstract systematicity of philosophy and science. In other words, despite a whole century's separation, his project is almost exactly the same as Schiller's in the *Aesthetic Letters.* And like Schiller, he recognizes that his rescue mission must begin where the threat itself is located, in the domain of the abstract and systematic. I have suggested that systematic idealist philosophy, in the wake of Kant, is originally aesthetics. But in the course of the nineteenth century, its systematic qual-ity overwhelms the original aesthetic interest in immediate human partic-ularity. And Dilthey's project, reaching back to the attenuation of Kant's transcendental systematicity by Schleiermacher, is in effect an attempt to rescue aesthetics, to re-establish it in its original eighteenth-century char-acter. Dilthey himself is not unaware of the aesthetic tendency in his work. About two-fifths of the "Contributions to the Study of Individual-ity" is taken up by a long chapter on "Art as the First Representation of the Human-Historical World in Its Individuation" (5:273-303).

But the problems in Schiller's work are also there for Dilthey, especial-ly the question of what purpose can possibly be served by aesthetics or the "human sciences" if art alone, or our sense of beauty or "play," is not sufficient to defend human particularity against the generalizing, system-atic tendencies of the age. And Dilthey, as far as I can tell, for all his study of Goethe, never learns the lesson of ironic withdrawal that eventually impressed itself upon Schiller. He thus overstrains not only Schleier-macher's thought, but that of the *Aesthetic Letters* as well. He in fact at-tempts to *institutionalize,* as "human sciences," exactly the systematic as-pect of aesthetics that Schiller had found embarrassing from the outset. He bears a significant share of the responsibility, therefore, for a *rebirth* of aesthetics in the twentieth century—an insidious rebirth, costumed as what by rights should have been the fundamentally critical and (as for Schleiermacher) practical pursuit of hermeneutics.

THE MILLENNIALIST INVENTION (III)

But a greater share of the same responsibility is borne by a later figure whose status as a significant contributor to Western thought has to do in large part with his appropriation of Dilthey. Martin Heidegger, namely, in the "hermeneutic" argument of §§ 31-34 of *Sein und Zeit,* carries out an intransitivization of the verb "understand." In ordinary parlance we use "understand" to invoke what Heidegger calls "the as-structure of interpretation," "die Als-Struktur der Auslegung."[13] We understand something "as" this or that; in fact we usually do so in exactly the manner that he scornfully dismisses as the "throwing of a 'meaning' over nakedness that is present" (150). And he deals with this problem in our use of concepts by distinguishing "interpretation" as the vehicle by which the otherwise only potential transitivity of "understanding," hence the object of understanding, is first developed. "In [interpretation] understanding appropriates understandingly to itself that which is understood" (148).

Understanding itself, considered apart from interpretation, is what Heidegger calls an "existential," meaning a "fundamental mode of the *being* of Dasein" (143, § 31).[14] Existentials are the first or primary results of "the analysis of Dasein" (44, § 9). In the case of understanding, this condition follows from the point that "Dasein is ontically distinguished in that, in its being, this being itself *matters* to it," so that "Dasein, in some manner and some form of explicitness, understands itself" (12, § 4). And understanding, in this still basically intransitive sense, is the source or vehicle of what appears in interpretation as a "fore-structure," the consistent description of which becomes very complicated—involving a "fore-having," a "fore-seeing," and a "fore-grasping" (150). But in my imperfect terminology, that notion boils down to the idea that the identification of the object of interpretation is always already the interpretation itself, in advance of itself. This is the route by which Heidegger approaches the question of the hermeneutic circle.

But the intransitivizing of understanding is also the device by which he *solves* the problem of the hermeneutic circle, for his purposes, once and for all. How does the hermeneutic circle arise—as we experience it in interpretive practice, especially in "philology" (152)? Is it simply an "ultimate" phenomenon (151), marking a place where there are no more questions to be asked? No, replies Heidegger. Understanding as an "existential," as a constitutive mode of being of Dasein, receives its fore-structure as "the expression of the existential *fore-structure* of Dasein itself" (153)— the fore-structure that arises from Dasein's being an entity whose being matters to itself and must therefore matter to itself (in order to be precisely Dasein's being) before it can matter to itself. (This formulation violates Heidegger's admonition [153] at the end of § 32 about "ontologically characterizing" Dasein; but I can't help that.) It therefore makes no sense to try to avoid the hermeneutic circle. We must, rather, "find our way into it in the correct manner" (153), in order to discover there "a positive possibility of knowledge in the most primordial sense." Precisely our failure to achieve "scientific" precision in "philology" (152), our failure to achieve objectivity in "exact textual interpretation" (150), can thus itself be realized as a significant *philosophical* achievement if we take it the right way. This is an extreme form, and I think a culmination, of the millennial-ist invention.

And yet it is hard to see what the point of the invention is, in Heidegger's version. In Kant the transcendental grounding of the self in pure apperception is a response to the experience of lonely individuality, and threatens only to exacerbate that experience until the theory of aesthetic judgment rescues it as a promise of communication. For Schleiermacher the invention shadows forth the importance of not only understanding the self's embeddedness in language, but learning to experience it direct-ly. For Hegel the invention represents the only possible way to make sense of history. But what experience or concern motivates Heidegger?

With the other figures we can be even more specific. Schleiermacher responds to the possibility of an actual death of religion. Kant needs to find a significant role in civilization for the Faculty of Philosophy. Hegel is concerned with academic matters even more concretely, in an attempt to situate his actual physical lecture hall so that the stream of history runs not alongside it, as if in a window or on a big screen, but right through the middle of it, in the presumed interaction of speaker and listeners. And it is true that there is something of this dramatizing of the lecture hall in Heidegger as well, in the opening of *An Introduction to Metaphysics* for instance. But here the feeling is derivative and perfunctory, in a text that is much more fundamentally a book than most of Hegel's are.

What does Heidegger really want? Has he no ulterior motives? If we try to understand him, are we reduced to using only his own terms and concepts, his own self-understanding? Has self-understanding been per-fected in his case to the point where there is no more getting behind it?

KANT'S SHADOW STILL

I think we can form a critical understanding of Heidegger's project after all, if we look at the unspoken side of his relation to Kant and Dilthey. The first chapter of the first main interpretive part of *Sein und Zeit* opens with what I regard as a fairly straightforward rewriting of Kant, perhaps not exactly the kind of rewriting envisaged at the end of the "Vorrede" to the second edition of the *Critique of Pure Reason*,[15] but also not an irrepa-rable undermining of Kant's system. I mean Heidegger's notion of the "Jemeinigkeit" of Dasein (42, § 9), the quality or "character" of Dasein according to which the being of Dasein is "in each case mine." There are any number of connections to be made here with earlier Western philoso-phy: with the quasi-subjective manner of history's operation in Hegel; with Dilthey's need to rescue immediate personal experience. But most directly and significantly, Heidegger is here reworking what had been Kant's insistence on the unity and singularity of the self. Especially Kant's notion of the "I think" as a specific representation raises the question of why the human self should be configured in just this one of a number of possible ways—a difficulty which is presumably overcome by situating the predicate of mine-ness (the predicate otherwise created by "I think") in a primary analysis of Dasein itself.

Another instance of this type of repair work on Kant is Heidegger's use of *Verstehen* [understanding] to replace what Kant had called *Verstand* ("understanding" construed as "*the* understanding"). The depth of the relation between these two concepts is apparent in the association of both with the notion of possibility. Heidegger is emphatic on this point:

> In understanding *(Verstehen)* lies existentially the being-type of Dasein as ability-to-be. Dasein is not something just present that possesses in addition some ability, but rather it is in the first instance being-possible. . . . Possibility as an "existential" is the most primordial and the ultimate positive ontological determinateness of Dasein; like existentiality in general, it can at first only be set up as a problem. The phenomenal basis for seeing it at all is offered by understanding as an ability-to-be that discloses. (143-44, § 31)

And in Kant, the understanding *(Verstand)* is the source of "the possibility of any connection at all" in intuitions, hence of the possibility of experience.[16] In fact there are passages in the section of *Sein und Zeit* just quoted that could almost have been written by Kant: "The total state of affairs reveals itself as the category-based totality of a *possibility* of order in what is given [which in Kant would be 'intuitions']. But even the 'unity' of what is present as multiplicity, namely nature, is only discoverable on the basis of the disclosedness of a *possibility* of itself" (144-45, § 31). As in Kant, the question of a possible order in multiplicity (Kant: "Verbindung"; Heidegger: "Zusammenhang") leads directly to the question of "unity," which Kant answers with the notion of the "I think," Heidegger with the concept "nature."

The trouble with *Verstand,* however, as Kant conceives of it, is that it has the quality of an unexplained human faculty or power, a "Vermögen,"[17] which exposes it to the unanswerable criticism formulated by Nietzsche in no. 11 of *Beyond Good and Evil*—a criticism which Heidegger is certainly aware of:

> How are synthetic judgments a priori *possible?* Kant asked himself. And what was his answer in reality? *Vermöge eines Vermögens*["by the power of a power," or "by virtue of a virtue," or archaically, "by dint of a dint"]: unfortunately not in these words, but so long-windedly and dignifiedly, with such an expenditure of German profundity and intellectual ornament, that people were deaf to the jolly *niaiserie allemande* in such an answer.[18]

And again, Heidegger solves the problem by taking what for Kant had been a separately thinkable faculty in human nature and moving it into the very definition of Dasein, as the "existential" *Verstehen,* on a level that no longer harbors faculties or "categories." (Of course it is not certain that Nietzsche would not have taken the complicated terminology by which Heidegger accomplishes this repair as yet another instance of "niaiserie allemande.")

But Heidegger's work constantly situates itself in an extensive web of relations with ancient and modern thought. With what justification do I focus exclusively here on Kantian echoes or parallels?

THE ISSUE OF LANGUAGE STILL

Let us review some of the arguments made above. The modern type of individual, for whom aesthetics becomes both possible and necessary, may be regarded as a Cartesian invention; "beauty," in Cassirer's sense, responds to a Cartesian problem, as does aesthetics (temporarily) for Schiller. The same Cartesian individuality is experienced by both Baumgarten and Kant as a lonely individuality, which gives rise to the sense of communication as a *problem*. Baumgarten's response is that of a charlatan. But Kant is the first honest philosopher of lonely individuality in the modern sense; and as such he becomes, if unwittingly, the father not only of aesthetics, but also of hermeneutics considered as a grappling with the problem of communication. In Schleiermacher we can see the direct connection between hermeneutics and Kantian philosophy; and by Dilthey's example we recognize the possibility of a hermeneutic rebirth of aesthetics in the spirit of Kant via Schiller.

But what gives us the right to include Heidegger in this history? It is accurate to say that there is an element or aspect or phase of Heidegger's thought that is connected with the history of hermeneutics and thence at least distantly with aesthetics in the sense of what I have called Kant's shadow. *Sein und Zeit* does concern itself with the hermeneutic circle—perhaps more centrally than Heidegger lets on, if that little argument can be read as a justification of the book's "interpretive" procedure as a whole. Heidegger does recognize a significant debt to Dilthey, which he dilutes by including Count Yorck in its acknowledgment (397-404, § 77). And his most prominent disciple, Hans-Georg Gadamer, seems to have been guided by the master to a position where philosophy and hermeneutics are practically indistinguishable.

Given this much, the question we are faced with is easy to formulate. Can we locate in Heidegger's work as a whole, not only in *Sein und Zeit*, the characteristic *structure* of philosophical aesthetics, the vision of a rehabilitation or perfection of humanity along with the identification, in our present condition, of definite vestiges or harbingers of the more perfect human state we are bound for? If this question is answered in the affirmative, then I think we can generalize from Heidegger's Kantian echoes and argue at least plausibly that aesthetics in the sense of Kant's shadow, or secular millennialism, is what he is really up to.

Once the question is formulated, however, the answer is obvious. Humanity for Heidegger is, and has always been, and will always be, "on the way to language." Is this idea definite enough to be a goal for humanity in the Kantian-aesthetic sense? I don't see why not. Schleiermacher's work, in focusing on communication, demonstrates by implication how damagingly indefinite Kant's aesthetic ideal of communicability had been. And Schiller prepares us for an idea of education, perhaps even a program, about which he then never says a word. It appears that indefiniteness is one of the besetting faults with how ideals are visualized in the Kantian-aesthetic tradition. Heidegger himself, in the very process of praising Dilthey's energy and ambition as a thinker, also dismisses rather abruptly what he calls a vague "tendency" in the direction of "philosophical anthropology" (47, § 10), a tendency, a goal or vision, on which Dilthey had staked practically everything.

In fact, Heidegger is rather less indefinite about humanity's fundamental aim or need than the other writers we have discussed—although he remains cryptic enough. In the last part of his book *On the Way to Language,* the essay (actually a lecture) "Der Weg zur Sprache," he offers what he calls a "Wegformel,"[19] a "formula" having to do with the "way" to language, which reads: "Die Sprache als die Sprache zur Sprache bringen" (242-43, 250, 261). Idiomatically, this formula can be translated, "To bring language, as language, up for discussion." But there is more to it than that. By saying "language, as language," the formula implies that in most discussions of language it is not in truth language that is being discussed. And part of how this problem arises is suggested by the fact that the German expression for "to bring up for discussion" uses the concept "language" itself, instead of English "discussion." We are thus reminded that we cannot discuss language except through the use of language; and if the language we use is not yet language as it is in truth, not yet "language, as language," how can it possibly encompass that truth? And how will we know, except by discussion, whether the language we are using fulfils the necessary condition for discussing language? Which leads to the possibility of a non-idiomatic reading of "zur Sprache bringen," to the idea that language might be brought to the condition of becoming itself an act of language, a speaking out of *itself.*

Heidegger's formula is thus three different things: a sign for the goal toward which humanity needs to be headed; a sign for the "way" toward that goal; and a direction for how we might first find our way to that way, to the condition of being "on the way." This is a complicated situation. Its complications might even be resolvable into a "circle" (243) of the hermeneutic type we are familiar with; and at one point Heidegger himself seems worried about his convoluted terminology, which "sounds like the speech of an egoistic solipsism" (262). (What other kind of solipsism is there?) But his thought is not fundamentally more complicated, for example, than Kant's *Critiques* considered as the aesthetics they really are. The transcendental grounding of the self in pure apperception is a truth anchored in reason; but it is also a truth which, even in knowing and understanding it, we somehow manage not to be convinced of, and which we can experience only as the promise of a still unrealized human community. Or we think of Schiller, who suggests that we learn from the Greeks something the Greeks were never in a position to teach, or of Dilthey, who requires of "human sciences" the systematic capture of a radically non-systematic perspective on existence. And what are all of these complications if not versions of the single central paradox of aesthetics, which teaches us what its own operation, as aesthetics, shows us to be incapable of learning, yet therefore all the more fundamentally in need of learning?

But for Heidegger, again, the issue is language, and had been even early in his career, even in *Sein und Zeit,* where we read at the very beginning that "the object of questioning here ('das *Erfragte*'), the sense ('Sinn') of being, will require its own conceptuality ('eine eigene Begrif-flichkeit'), which in turn will, on the level of essence, set itself off clearly against the concepts in which things that are attain a determinate meaning" (6, § 2). By "conceptuality" Heidegger of course does not mean merely "vocabulary" or "terminology," for both of which there are unambiguous terms in German. He has to mean something closer to a fundamental rethinking of the way concepts are produced and ordered in language. And he cannot simply describe that rethinking at the beginning of his book, in a language which itself has not yet been rethought. He and his reader, in other words, even at this point in *Sein und Zeit,* already find themselves "on the way to language."

GREEKS AND GERMANS STILL

The structural feature that most clearly marks Heidegger's work as aesthetics, however, is its attempt to show vestiges or harbingers of the better human condition it is aimed at—which means, in Heidegger, instances of past or present *linguistic* operation that reveal possibilities for language not yet fully realized in modern Europe. The three principal sources for these prophetic instances of language are: ancient Greek, German etymology, and the overall category of the poetic, of *Dichtung,* usually referring to German poetry. But no instance from any of these three sources can become prophetic, can assume its station "on the way to language," except by being *interpreted.* Heidegger's philosophy, then—if we understand it as a millennialist aesthetics, as thought always "on the way to language"—is radically hermeneutic after all; it stands or falls with the soundness of its interpretive practice, including the practice of *interpreting texts.* Thus, as Heidegger intimates in "The Way to Language," we are faced again with the problem of the hermeneutic circle.

I have suggested that the significance of any instance of hermeneutic thought can be measured by how seriously the hermeneutic circle is taken, how deep a problem it is. For Schleiermacher the problem is serious enough to make necessary a de-transcendentalized version of the Kantian unitary self, an "I think" that guarantees the existence of an object of interpretation which can at least be approached. Dilthey appears to go a step further when he agrees only "to accept for the time being" (*zunächst gelten lassen*) Kant's term "transcendental" (5:246) as applied to criticism of the relation between consciousness and its contents. For it is clear that he means ultimately to dispense with the last shreds of "transcendental" thinking, the last remnants of any general template for the individual self, and to rescue the object of interpretation only *historically,* in the idea of privileged instances of individual greatness that become interpretable precisely *by* being great, by shaping our own historical existence at its core. (Gadamer's later "hermeneutic conversation" is in essence a generalization of this idea.)

But in Heidegger, finally, the object of interpretation vanishes altogether, except to the extent that it is a product of interpretation, and nothing is left for interpretation to aim at but the hermeneutic circle itself. Heidegger's version of the Kantian "I think," the "Jemeinigkeit" of Dasein, means not simply "mine-ness" but "mine-ness in every particular case." Therefore I experience it not as a given self-unity in either myself or others—which might anchor interpretation—but always as a potentially limitless multiplicity. And while it is true that there are certain figures in history, including Heraclitus and Hölderlin, to whom Heidegger assigns special significance in humanity's confrontation with the question of being, the crucial point is precisely that these figures' thinking has *not* shaped our immediate historical existence (as it had for Dilthey), that their influence must now, and always, be rescued by interpretation.

Interpretation is therefore everything for Heidegger, yet lacks any firm external relation by which its soundness as interpretation might be substantiated. The only possible basis for a final judgment on any interpretation, says Heidegger in *Sein und Zeit,* is the question of whether it "enters the hermeneutic circle correctly," in such a way as to expose the circle's metaphysical dimension in "the fore-structure of Dasein itself." Do we ask whether an interpretation is correct or incorrect in the exegesis of its text? Heidegger, in *Sein und Zeit,* is openly scornful of the pretensions of "philology" to exactness; and in any case, the absolutizing of the hermeneutic circle renders such questions trivial.

If one wanted to be unkind, one could suggest that by eliminating the particular object of interpretation and installing everywhere in its place the hermeneutic circle alone, Heidegger avoids all responsibility for dealing faithfully with the texts he talks about. The way would then be open—as if it were "the way to language"?—toward an authoritarian or absolutist regime of interpretation, a regime in which adherence to a prescribed terminology (if costumed as a *Begrifflichkeit* or "conceptuality") would be the sole touchstone of an interpretation's rightness. This would not be entirely fair to Heidegger. His readings of ancient Greek, in such works as *An Introduction to Metaphysics,* are open-minded, imaginative, and for my money often deeply illuminating. And his readings of etymology, of the metaphors that operate behind simple stems like *Griff* or *Ort,* or the various verbs that are combined in modern conjugations of the meaning "to be," are succinct, eloquent, and strongly evocative of *our* particular situation in language as an unfolding complexity. But the case of German poetry is different.

I argued above, in connection with Lessing, that it does not make much sense to deny categorically the possibility of a valid understanding of classical antiquity. But it is also true that with respect to the interpretation of ancient Greek philosophy and poetry there is a good deal of room for imaginative perceptions of the sort Heidegger proposes, as there is also with respect to interpretation of the metaphorical aspect of Indo-European etymology. In the case of modern German poetry, however, texts written more or less in *our* language, there is a narrower domain of exegetic plausibility that limits interpretation. It is much easier for an interpretation to be obviously wrong. If the absolutized hermeneutic circle now operates as an excuse to ignore that limit in favor of a philosophically correct way of speaking and reading, then I think we will have entered the realm of authoritarian interpretation, and the effect on Heidegger's system will be crippling.

THE HISTORY OF COMMUNICATION

There is one more issue that needs to be looked at before we attempt a decision on this matter. Aesthetics, in the sense of the present argument, is always associated with the problem of communication. But that problem has a history of its own within the discontinuous history of aesthetics. Baumgarten juggles incompatible discourses in such a way as to give the impression of having shown that the communication of feelings is possible in language and maximally so in poetry. Kant hedges on this point and claims only that in relation to certain types of judgment we are entitled to assume that our feelings are communicable. Schiller does much to clarify matters when he suggests that the communicability of feelings, especially of the experience of freedom, must be regarded not as a present possibility, but as a component of the millennial goal toward which even Kantian aesthetics is oriented—although Kant did not know it.

Then Schleiermacher develops Kantian philosophy in another direction by replacing the question of communicability with the practical question of communication. The possibility of communication is now based on our sharing the condition of embeddedness, as thinking subjects, in a particular language. But the aesthetic and millennial dimensions in Schiller's development of Kant are missing in Schleiermacher; and aesthetics is not completely reassembled on a hermeneutic basis until Dilthey's secular millennialist vision of the destiny of the human sciences. The possibility of communication is still based (as in Schleiermacher) on a shared shape in our existence, except that that shape is now due to the influence of great individual minds of the past.

From this perspective we can understand Heidegger's position as a summary and culmination of the whole of aesthetics. As in both Schleiermacher and Dilthey, the possibility of communication, the hope for a fruitful discussion of philosophical issues, is based for Heidegger on our sharing a condition of embeddedness; and as in Schleiermacher, it is language that thus enfolds us. But for Heidegger the role of the *particular* language is not exactly the same as for Schleiermacher. One chapter of *Unterwegs zur Sprache*, entitled "Aus einem Gespräch von der Sprache," consists of a dialogue between Heidegger himself and a Japanese visitor. In the course of this dialogue it is made clear that the use of German as a medium for discussion impedes the understanding of "East Asian" literature, religion, culture, and philosophy. The condition of being embedded in a particular language is therefore not without importance. But on the other hand, the dialogue between Heidegger and the Japanese does take place and does in the end seem to get somewhere. It follows that there is also a sense in which our embeddedness in language transcends any particular language and may be regarded as an embeddedness in language as such.

This point is significant because it implies that communication can never be sufficient for Heidegger if it depends on our shared embeddedness in a particular language; that communication at the depth striven for by philosophy is never a fully realizable condition in our lives but always only beckons from the distance, as part of what we are "on the way" to, as a millennial goal. Thus Heidegger combines Schleiermacher's hermeneutic communication and Schiller's vision of deferred aesthetic communication in a single idea.

The idea of our constant embeddedness in language as such might even be regarded as Heidegger's repair of Baumgarten's clumsy attempt to smuggle into logic the proposition that every level of human experience is transferable into discourse. And in connection with Heidegger's insistence on the importance of poetic practice, of *Dichtung*, in our idea and experience of language, we think not only of Baumgarten, but also of Dilthey and the function of poetic monuments. Thus it seems almost as if

Heidegger were trying to encompass in his system the whole of the aesthetic movement as I have tried to describe it.

Moreover, the quest for vestiges or harbingers of a perfected human condition with respect to language is never far from Heidegger's thoughts. In *Unterwegs zur Sprache* we find the formula:

> Der Mensch spricht nur, indem er der Sprache entspricht.
> Die Sprache spricht.
> Ihr Sprechen spricht für uns im Gesprochenen. (33)

> [A person speaks only by corresponding to (entering into an appropriate relation with) language.
> Language speaks.
> Its speaking speaks for us in the spoken.]

And "the spoken," in turn, has a special relation to poetry, which has to do with poetry's being an original, not a derived or invented, form of language (31). In particular:

> Im Gesprochenen des Gedichtes west das Sprechen. Es ist das Sprechen der Sprache. Die Sprache spricht. (28)

> [In the spoken of a poem, speaking "west" (= "is" in the root sense of "endures," hence becomes able to admit an essence or *Wesen*). It (the poem?) is the speaking of language. Language speaks.]

We do not need to go too far into the subtleties of this utterance to recognize that it identifies "the poem"—that specially palpable and enduring instance of "the spoken"—as a promise, a harbinger, that must encourage us "on the way to language." And again, only interpretation can decide which specific pieces of language qualify as poems in this sense.

In Heidegger, then, we have not only an instance of aesthetics in the form of secular millennialism, but a culmination. And if it is true that the vision of secular millennialism, lacking an anchor in faith, is empty without demonstrable harbingers of the millennium in our present condition, then it follows that everything in Heidegger's philosophy, everything in aesthetics as he summarizes it, depends on the degree of validity that can be attributed to his interpretations—especially his interpretations of modern German poetry, since the question of our *present* condition is all-important.

It is not enough simply to understand his interpretations of Hölderlin, say, or of Trakl, and then relate them to his thought in general. This procedure can have no bearing on our judgment of his whole project— unless we are willing to accuse him (as we might Hegel) of trying to use the existence of his thought as evidence of its own validity.[20] Just as Kant must believe that transcendental apperception is strictly undeniable; just as Schiller, in the beginning, must be mortally certain that no one can be human without forming a conception of his or her humanity and therefore implicitly acknowledging the play drive; just as Moritz can have no doubt about the recognizable factualness of works of art; just as Dilthey envisages a scientific understanding of instances of strict individuality; just as Cassirer is apparently prepared to exclude from the human race anyone who does not *know* beauty: so Heidegger, correspondingly, must offer interpretations of his favored poetic texts that can claim a certain level of recognizable validity.

A PARENTHETICAL WORD ON GADAMER

Gadamer is certainly less dogmatic than Heidegger, and willing to take positions more exposed to criticism. It is in response to criticism that he writes, in the "Vorwort" to the second edition (1965) of *Wahrheit und Methode:*

> Evidently misunderstandings have arisen due to my use of the tradition-loaded expression "hermeneutics." . . . I did not wish to develop a system of technical rules that could describe or indeed prescribe a methodology of the human sciences ["Geisteswissenschaften"]. My intention was also not to study the theoretical bases of work in the human sciences with a view to practical applications. If the present work has practical consequences, then surely not on behalf of unscientific "engagement," but rather on behalf of a "scientific" honesty that acknowledges the pre-engagement operative in all understanding. My actual claim was and is a philosophical one: the question is not what we do or should do, but rather what is happening with us beyond the range of our doing or willing.[21]

There is a certain amount of undeniable truth in this passage. *Wahrheit und Methode* does not offer hermeneutic "rules"; and it does concern itself philosophically with the large historical situation in which understanding happens.

But there is also some twisting of the truth here. If Heidegger simply refuses to admit the possibility of valid criticism, Gadamer's instinct is to squirm out from under it. In particular, he may not (as he says) formulate specific positive "rules" for understanding and interpretation; but his negative points concerning earlier hermeneutics, notably Schleiermacher and Dilthey, are still by implication certainly prescriptive enough to make a legitimate target for such early critics as Betti and Hirsch.[22]

Most interesting for our purposes is his critique of Schleiermacher, who seems to cause him some discomfort. He begins by ascribing to Schleiermacher, unjustly, the project of "a canon of grammatical and psychological interpretive rules" (1:189), and then spends pages and pages discussing the earlier thinker in detail—conceding in the process that his method is not reducible to "the application of rules" after all

(1:193). And in the end, these complications lead nowhere but to the conclusion that Schleiermacher's thinking may have been important in its time, but was insufficiently "historical" to keep from becoming obsolete. "His hermeneutics was directed in truth at texts whose authority was established. . . . He meant to teach how one was to understand speech and written tradition because the one important thing for the doctrine of faith was Biblical tradition. Therefore his hermeneutic theory was still far from any historical attitude ["Historik"] that could serve the human sciences as an organum" (1:200-201). Exactly how valid is either this criticism itself or the "historical attitude" it postulates?

Gadamer's style is diffuse and unfocused, leaving plenty of room for statements with which it is hard to disagree. For instance, as part of his introduction to the notion of "Wirkungsgeschichte" — which I will translate simply as "effect-history," the history of the effects that a fact or event or piece of language has had — he says:

> When we try to understand an historical phenomenon from the historical distance that shapes our own hermeneutic situation, we are always already subjected to the effects of effect-history. That history determines in advance what appears to us as questionable and as an object of study; and we are forgetting half of what is really there, indeed we are forgetting the whole truth of the phenomenon, if we take the immediate phenomenon itself as its own whole truth. (1:305-6)

In other words, our own way of looking at the phenomenon belongs to the history of its effects, and conditions what the phenomenon is from our point of view. But only a few pages earlier, he had smuggled a much larger claim into the discussion.

> Now time [the time separating us from an event in history] is no longer primarily an abyss that must be bridged, but is in truth the supporting basis of events in which present events are rooted. Temporal separation is not something that must be overcome. . . . In truth that separation must be recognized as a positive and productive possibility of understanding. It is not a yawning abyss, but is filled up with the continuity of convention and tradition, in whose light we receive everything from the past. (1:302)

We are reminded of the millennialist invention, particularly of Heidegger's version, in which the hermeneutic circle is made into a guarantee of knowledge. But the element here that sticks in our throat, or ought to, is the concept of "continuity" ["Kontinuität"].

The three central concepts on which Gadamer's hermeneutics is founded are probably: *wirkungsgeschichtliches Bewußtsein* [effect-historical consciousness], *hermeneutisches Gespräch* [hermeneutic conversation], and *Horizontverschmelzung* [fusion of horizons]. And all three depend absolutely on the assumption of *continuity* in historical tradition, an assumption that flies in the face of our actual experience of history. If traditions worthy of the name need to be continuous, in any reasonable sense, then we might as well eliminate the noun "tradition" from our vocabulary. Certainly the tradition I am tracing in the present book would not survive that test, for all its indispensability in accounting for the most monstrous political events of the age. For all we know, it could be true that all tradition is continuous on some level. But our knowledge of historical detail is never sufficient to enable us to experience that continuity as a useful factor in understanding the past, at least not in the case of traditions that are complex enough to be interesting. Traditions as we know them are quirky, unpredictable, reversible, self-contradictory, always reappearing where they have no business. Or so it seems to me.

As with Kant, therefore, so also with Gadamer: an empirical critique of the argument shows the concepts in which it culminates to be millennialist dreams. There are valuable ideas and insights in Gadamer, as in Kant. But an unacknowledged millennialist tendency poisons the thought as a whole, a condition which is compounded in Gadamer's case by the sloppiness of his reading of Schleiermacher. In discussing Schleiermacher, we saw above that the notion of "divinatory" or "prophetic" understanding requires an orientation toward the *future* of an utterance, the future of the speaking or writing mind and the future of the language as a whole. In other words, understanding for Schleiermacher involves a move into exactly the same space where Gadamer situates understanding, the time span between the utterance itself and the interpreter's present. The difference is that Schleiermacher does not reify this time span by endowing it with "continuity," a continuity whose positing by Gadamer shows exactly the same need for "authority" that he himself criticizes, unjustly, in Schleiermacher. In fact, Schleiermacher's thought has all the advantages of Gadamer's—its refusal to let us forget about the possible uses and pitfalls of a tradition of understanding—without Gadamer's leap into an ultimately millennialist regimen of concepts claiming descent from Heidegger's "fore-structure of understanding."

The vicissitudes of the tradition we are talking about, incidentally, become at least amusing at this point. Schleiermacher establishes his credentials as a Kantian by stripping Kant of both his overt transcendentality and his covert millennialism; Dilthey finds Schleiermacher revelatory and rewards him by re-millennializing his work in a spirit that Schiller (a vehemently professed Kantian) had both created and discredited; Gadamer dismisses both Schleiermacher and Dilthey as obsolete, but in doing so only repeats Dilthey's re-millennialization of a now supposedly discredited Schleiermacher. This, I think, is what tradition really looks like as a rule.

NOTES

1. Hamann's little essay, "Metakritik über den Purismum der Vernunft," in Johann Georg Hamann, *Sämtliche Werke,* ed. Josef Nadler, 6 vols. [Vienna, 1949-1957], 3:281-89, was not published in his lifetime but was read in manuscript by Herder and others in 1784. Herder's *Eine Metakritik zur Kritik der reinen Vernunft* (1799), by contrast, is a substantial book in two parts. But a sense for his view of Kant's use of language can be gained from two places where he appeals to Leibniz, one at the beginning, one toward the end. See Johann Gottfried Herder, *Werke,* 11 vols. (Frankfurt/Main: Deutscher Klassiker Verlag, 1985-2000), 8:320-22, 619-22. As far as I know, Klopstock's "Grammatische Gespräche" have not yet appeared in a modern edition, but the passage I am referring to can be found in Friedrich Gottlieb Klopstock, *Klopstocks sämmtliche Werke,* 10 vols. (Leipzig, 1854-55), 9:310-11.

2. Herder, *Werke,* 8:639-40.

3. These considerations are implicitly operative in Leibniz, for whom the vessel of "representing," or understanding at its most basic, is the absolutely unified monad, whereas no such unity can obtain in the real-world production of utterances. Again, the integrity of Leibniz's thinking depends on a strict disjunction (which Baumgarten sabotages) between metaphysical (monadological) and psychological discourse.

4. For specific arguments, see my *Beyond Theory,* esp. 193-216, 264-67.

5. Fr. D. E. Schleiermacher, *Hermeneutik,* ed. Heinz Kimmerle, 2nd ed. (Heidelberg, 1974), 76-77.

6. See Friedrich Schleiermacher, *Schriften,* ed. Andreas Arndt (Frankfurt/Main: Deutscher Klassiker Verlag, 1996), 803-43.

7. In no. 1, the text actually reads, "qualitative and quantitative misunderstanding is unavoidable." The terms I have substituted, however, are Schleiermacher's own from a footnote (83) to the passage in which "qualitative" and "quantitative" are defined.

8. Manfred Frank, in his book *Das individuelle Allgemeine: Textstrukturierung und interpretation nach Schleiermacher* (Frankfurt/Main, 1977), carries out at great length an interpretation of Schleiermacher that I do not think differs much from mine. Understanding a text better than its originator, he says, involves an "Erweiterung seines [des Textes] bisherigen Bedeutungshorizonts," which approaches (in Gadamerian terminology) "die wirkungsgeschichtliche Totalität" of all possible readings (363) and so is always a move into the future of the type I have described. The reason Frank needs as complicated an argument as he does is that he starts out from Gadamer and Heidegger, for whom (as for Kant) the unitary subject is a given. I think it makes more sense, and is more economical, to begin by recognizing the unitary subject as an *issue,* and in any case as an entity (if it exists at all) that does not determine the initial shape of an utterance. The question of the existence of the *object* of understanding, which I take up in the next section, tempts Frank into a lengthy and complicated attempt to *answer* it (e.g., 185-99). My procedure is to regard that object's existence as an assumption and to analyze it as such.

9. See e.g. Augustine, *De Civ. Dei,* 11.26; *De Trinitate,* 15.49; Victorinus, *Adv. Arium,* 1.31-32, 62-64; 3.7; 4.20-21; Thomas Aquinas, *Summa,* 1a, 27.1-2.

10. Hamann, *Sämtliche Werke,* 2:197.

11. The whole apophthegm to which Hamann alludes reads as follows:"Quum dives quidam filium adolescentulum ad Socratem misisset, ut indolem illius inspiceret, ac pædagogus diceret; *Pater ad te, ô Socrates, misit filium, ut eum videres:* tum Socrates ad puerum; *Loquere igitur,* inquit, *adolescens, ut te videam:* significans, ingenium hominis non tam in vultu relucere, quam in oratione, quod hoc sit certissimum minimeque mendax animi speculum." See Erasmus, Apophthegmata, III, 70, in *Desiderii Erasmi Roterodami Opera omnia* (Leiden, 1703-06), vol. 4, col. 162. The context here, a teacher speaking to a pupil, obviously supports my contention that Hamann means not only our request of nature, but also God's request of us, and specifically of Hamann. Sven-Aage Jørgensen, in an excellent popular edition of Johann Georg Ha-

mann, *Sokratische Denkwürdigkeiten. Aesthetica in nuce* (Stuttgart: Reclam, 1958), 86, credits Walter Boehlich with having first pointed out this allusion to Erasmus. But the only work of Boehlich's that he mentions is a review of Nadler's complete Hamann edition in *Euphorion*, 50 (1986), which does not mention Erasmus. I have not been able to find a book or article in which Boehlich points to the allusion. Curiously enough, the phrase "loquere ut te videam" also occurs in Baumgarten, in the scholium to § 92 of the *Meditationes*. Baumgarten seems to regard it as a Latin *commonplace*, suggesting the possibility of judgments directly attributable to the physical senses, the possibility of a "iudicium sensuum." It is entirely likely that Hamann knew this passage; but I cannot see a significant connection with the *Aesthetica in nuce*.

12. Wilhelm Dilthey, *Gesammelte Schriften*, ed. Bernhard Groethuysen et al. (Stuttgart and Göttingen, 1966ff.), 5:319-20.

13. Martin Heidegger, *Sein und Zeit* = *Gesamtausgabe* (Frankfurt/Main: Klostermann, 1975ff.), 2:151. The page numbers refer to pagination in the book's original edition, which is indicated in the margins of the *Gesamtausgabe*. The present reference is to § 32 of the book, as are all the others in this chapter, unless otherwise noted.

14. .I will follow the practice of many translators and leave the word "Dasein" (= more or less "being there") in its German form. Heidegger himself more or less translates the term in passing when he says, "Sciences have, as behaviors of man, the being-type of this entity (man). We grasp this entity terminologically as *Dasein*" (11, § 4). This is not to say that Dasein is man's being, which latter is clearly defined as "existence" (n12, § 4). Dasein, rather, is the entity ("Seiendes") that man is in respect of his being.

15. Kant, *Werke* (see chap. 1, n11), 3:25.

16. Kant, *Werke*, 3:107-8, § 15; see also Einleitung II, 3:28-30.

17. Kant is in general very fond of the notion of a "Vermögen." One significant instance, in the *Critique of Pure Reason*, of the designation of "Verstand" as a "Vermögen" is found in the Introduction to Transcendental Logic, *Werke*, 3:75. Even "Vernunft" is described as a "Vermögen," 3:42-43.

18. Friedrich Nietzsche, *Sämtliche Werke: Kritische Studienausgabe*, ed. Giorgio Colli and Mazzino Montinari, 15 vols. (Munich, 1980), 5:24.

19. Martin Heidegger, *Unterwegs zur Sprache* = *Gesamtausgabe*, 12:242. As above, pages are those of the original edition, indicated in the margins of the *Gesamtausgabe*.

20. As far as I know, Heidegger himself never accuses Hegel in exactly these terms. But in *Sein und Zeit*, as part of his argument against Hegel's notion of the spirit's "falling" into time (§ 82 b), 434, he quotes, from the *Phänomenologie des Geistes*, one of any number of passages in which Hegel tries by implication to situate his own writing in its own system: "die Zeit ist der *Begriff* selbst, der *da ist* und als leere Anschauung sich dem Bewußtsein vorstellt; deswegen erscheint der Geist notwendig in der Zeit und er erscheint so lange in der Zeit, als er nicht seinen reinen Begriff *erfaßt*, das heißt nicht die Zeit tilgt. Sie ist das *äußere* angeschaute vom Selbst nicht *erfaßte* reine Selbst, der nur angeschaute Begriff." See Hegel, *Sämtliche Werke*, 2:612. Full reference in chap. 4, n13.

21. Hans-Georg Gadamer, *Gesammelte Werke*, 10 vols. (Tübingen, 1985-1995), 2:438.

22. See Emilio Betti, *Die Hermeneutik als allgemeine Methodik der Geisteswissenschaften* (Tübingen, 1962); and E. D. Hirsch, Jr., *Validity in Interpretation* (New Haven, 1967).

SIX

The End of Aesthetics: Heidegger and Adorno

I am fairly sure that aesthetics was doomed from the start. Secular millennialism cannot operate without being *right* about certain phenomena in the experience of its readers—its vestiges or harbingers. And this is probably too much to ask of an intellectual discipline, which is what aesthetics claims to be. Intellectual disciplines, unlike propaganda ministries, can flourish only in an atmosphere of relatively unrestricted debate. But forms of secular millennialism live on nonetheless, even forms that are clearly affiliated with aesthetics. It is easy to agree with Walter Benjamin, for example, when he suggests that fascism carries out an aestheticization of politics.[1] It may even be possible to agree with him on a level deeper than that of his own actual intention, a level on which it may make sense, after all, to speak of the end of aesthetics—but not necessarily the end of secular millennialism in its new political form.

HÖLDERLIN'S CONVERSATION

Of all modern poets, the one whom Heidegger regards most confidently as a philosophical ally is Friedrich Hölderlin. His interpretations of Hölderlin are therefore especially important for understanding his interpretive practice in general; and among those interpretations, his reading of the following short passage obviously deserves special attention:

> Viel hat erfahren der Mensch.
> Der Himmlischen viele genannt,
> Seit ein Gespräch wir sind
> Und hören können voneinander.[2]

131

[Man has learned (or experienced) much. Has named a large number of the heavenly ones, since we have been a conversation and can hear of (or from) each other.]

The idea of linguistic activity as a constitutive element in human existence, as what we "are," is already enough to highlight this passage for Heidegger.

(The four lines in the form given above do not belong to the final version of Hölderlin's "Friedensfeier," if there even is a final version. But Heidegger is working with the only text available to him, and I will treat that text as if it were authentic Hölderlin. My aim here is not to understand Hölderlin, but to analyze Heidegger's interpretive procedure.)[3]

To begin with, some simple exegetic points need to be considered. The first has to do with the word "von." In German, "voneinander hören" can mean either "to hear *from* each other" or "to hear *of* each other." Hölderlin's line therefore seems to mean something like: we have been able to hear of each other from each other. The suggestion is perhaps one of synthesis or unity. The source of the information we receive and the content of that information are the same; no third party interferes in the communication. But a suggestion of division or uncertainty also arises. To hear "of" or "about" something, from whatever source, is always to receive knowledge second-hand, not directly. And if we receive information about the "other" *only* from that same "other," then there is no warrant for the accuracy of the information, and we therefore also no longer have a clear idea of where the information is coming from. These concerns are magnified by the idea that we "are" the conversation in which we are engaged, that neither I nor any "other" have a stable identity outside the conversation, an identity against which its operation and content might be measured. The concept "can," moreover, in German as in English, can situate itself either after or before the fact. "We can" can be a conclusion drawn from the fact that "we have done," or it can be an assertion about something we have not yet done, which opens again onto uncertainty.

One further point that goes a bit beyond the exegetic but should certainly be important for Heidegger concerns the relation between "der Mensch" and "wir," between "man" or "mankind" and "we." Why does the poet not say: *we* have learned much in the time that we have been a conversation? Surely the "we" refers to humans, to the individuals who make up "mankind." Hölderlin's procedure here has the effect of profiling the expression "der Mensch" in its quality as a summarizing abstraction derived from the radically plural reality in which "we" have our being. "Der Mensch"—one might infer—does not exist prior to the conversation that "we" are, but rather is coeval with that conversation, if not a product of it. (First *we* are a conversation, and since then *mankind* has experienced much.) For Heidegger this should be by rights a very important point. One of his principal objections to Hegel, as early as § 82 of *Sein und Zeit,* is directed against the idea that the spirit "falls" into time—an idea that could be associated with the line "since we have been a conversation" if one could infer that "we" had been something else beforehand. The relation between "der Mensch" and "wir" could certainly be used to argue against such an inference.

Once we know that Heidegger is interested in this particular passage from Hölderlin, therefore, we can practically write his interpretation for him. To go one more step: why does Hölderlin write "Seit ein Gespräch wir sind" instead of the more natural "Seit wir ein Gespräch sind"? Are we meant to supply mental commas and read "Seit, ein Gespräch, wir sind," which would make "ein Gespräch" an appositive, not a predicate? In English, this possibility could be rendered: "since we (a conversation) have been in existence," which would operate strongly against a Hegelian reading, against the idea that we at some point began being a conversation after having been something else. Surely Heidegger would prefer this alternative.

Any number of interpretive paths now open up for a Heidegger. *Erfahrung* [experience] is a crucial problem in Kantian philosophy and, as a problem, makes transcendental apperception necessary as the possibility of order in representations. Hölderlin might be read as disagreeing with Kant by attributing the possibility of experience not to the "I think" but to the "we converse"—which would fit better with the *je* (each) in Heidegger's "Jemeinigkeit" of Dasein. And if we can infer that only the process of "conversation" creates a general notion of humanity ("der Mensch"), then we can perhaps situate that conversation in the vicinity of Schiller's "play." For Hölderlin, it would then be the radical plurality of human existence ("wir") that produces experience; "man" is the comprehensive (Schillerian) philosophical notion of this process, whereas the myriad mythical "names" uttered by religion are a cryptic but truer representation of it. (One thinks of Heidegger on πόλεμος.)[4]

An interpretation in something like this form would not yet be sufficient to satisfy the inherent need for interpretation in Heidegger's project. No argument on the philosophical content of those verses could possibly be sufficient in itself. One would still need to show that in its manner, as well as its matter, Hölderlin's utterance is the foreshadowing of an ultimate transfiguration of language, a signpost "on the way to language." But certainly something like what I have suggested would be needed to support such a showing.

A FAILURE OF NERVE

The trouble is that Heidegger himself offers nothing at all, not even the rudimentary exegetic beginnings of an interpretation. His commentary on the passage from Hölderlin begins: "We—human beings—are a conversation. The being of man is grounded in language; but this can happen authentically only in *conversation*. This is not only one way in which language is realized, but language essentially is only as conversation. . . . But then what is a 'conversation'? Evidently the speaking-with-each-other *(Miteinandersprechen)* about something. Speaking then mediates thereby the coming-to-each-other *(Zueinanderkommen)*" (36). Hölderlin says "voneinander"—making it clear, incidentally, that his "conversation" is not merely about "something"—and Heidegger jumps to "miteinander" and "zueinander." Then he quotes the passage again, including the words "hören können voneinander," and continues: "The ability-to-hear *(Hörenkönnen)* is not just a result of the speaking-with-each-other, but rather, the other way round, is a precondition of it. But even the ability-to-hear is itself in turn oriented toward the possibility of the word and needs this. Ability-to-speak *(Redenkönnen)* and ability-to-hear are equally primordial." He insists on associating the idea of "can" with *ability*, whereas the immediate suggestion in the idea that "we can *hear of* or *hear from* each other" is not ability so much as *possibility*.

But then he refers to the passage one more time, using the words, "wir können voneinander hören," and continues: "We are a conversation, which always also means: we are *one* conversation. The unity of the conversation consists therein, that in the essential word, in each case, is revealed the One and the Same that we agree about, on the basis of which we are united and so are authentically ourselves. The conversation and its unity is the bearer of our Dasein." Hölderlin, whose words are balanced on a knife edge between unity and division, has been left behind. Heidegger is talking about a text that does not exist and would probably not be worth talking about if it did exist.

Heidegger's commentary continues, and I could continue my commentary on it; but I would only be repeating myself. We must ask not why Heidegger interprets so badly, but rather why he does not even gesture at interpreting what is actually on the page before him. A secular millennialist project like Heidegger's cannot be adequately supported by its own conceptual or formulative structure. It requires external support in the form of vestiges or harbingers of the millennial state envisioned—which in Heidegger's case must come from the interpretation of poetic texts. And if I am not mistaken, precisely Heidegger's understanding of this point makes him *avoid* interpretation.

For there is no such thing as the interpretation of a poetic text that is not debatable. If Heidegger were to carry out interpretations of the sort that I have sketched, he would therefore be exposing not only those interpretations themselves, but his whole philosophical project (which depends on them), to the danger of being rebutted in debate on specific points. He talks a good deal about "danger," even in the same commentaries on Hölderlin in which he discusses the "conversation" that we "are" (33-35). But when the possibility of an *actual* danger arises, one that he would have to face in the real world of intellectual debate, he backs down. Instead of interpreting Hölderlin, he picks a couple of convenient terms from one of the latter's conveniently difficult texts and uses them to construct an easily recognized variant of the thinking of *Sein und Zeit*. Debate thus becomes pointless; it would be a "conversation" in which we hear *of* Heidegger *from* Heidegger. The project is preserved from danger, but only at the cost of any connection it might have had with reality.

The Hölderlin commentary thus shows, at the very least, a failure of nerve. Heidegger is driven by the shape of his own thought toward poetic interpretation; but in the end he cannot bring himself to do what he knows he must. Or perhaps it is worse. Perhaps he is attempting to pass off his commentaries *as* interpretations. Aesthetics, we would be tempted to say, begins with one charlatan in Baumgarten and ends with a corresponding charlatan in Heidegger.

THE PLACE OF POETRY

Evidence in support of my view of Heidegger is offered by Heidegger himself in *Unterwegs zur Sprache,* where he attempts to deal with exactly the issues I have just raised. He begins the essay "Die Sprache im Gedicht: Eine Erörterung von Georg Trakls Gedicht" by indicating what he means by "Erörterung," which would ordinarily be translatable as "discussion" or "discussion in detail."

> *Erörtern* [the verb] means here, first of all: to show or direct [someone?] into the *Ort* [usually = "place"]. Then it means: to attend to the *Ort*. Both, the showing into the *Ort* and the attending to the *Ort,* are the preparatory steps for an *Erörterung*. But we already take enough of a chance if we content ourselves in the following with the preparatory steps. The *Erörterung* ends, as is proper for a journey of thought, in a question. It asks after the *Ortschaft* ["placefulness"?] of the *Ort*. [5]

And when he goes on to explain further, this opening loses a good deal of its obscurity.

> Originally the name "Ort" means the point of the spear. Everything comes together in it. . . . Our task now is to *erörtern* that *Ort* which collects the poetic speaking of Georg Trakl into his Poem *(Gedicht)*, the *Ort* of his Poem.
>
> Every great poet composes only out of one single Poem. Poetic greatness is measured by the extent to which the poet is so fully dedicated to that One Poem that he is able to maintain his poetic speaking unadulterated in it.
>
> The Poem of a poet remains unspoken. None of the individual poetic works *(Dichtungen)*, not even their totality, says everything. And yet, every poetic work speaks out of the totality of the one Poem and says

this totality each time. The *Ort* of the Poem is the source of that surge
that in each case propels the speaking as a poetic speaking. (37-38)

The word "Gedicht," which I have capitalized as "Poem" (as opposed to
"Dichtungen" or "poetic works"), refers to a single radiant center that
Heidegger contends must always be there for each poet in order to make
poetry truly poetry and not mere writing, even though that center is
never directly manifest as itself.

But the crucial point for our purposes is Heidegger's distinction now
between "Erörterung" and "Erläuterung," which latter is normally translatable as "commentary" or "clarification."

> Since the unique Poem remains in the unspoken, we can *erörtern* its *Ort*
> only by attempting to point into the *Ort* from out of what is spoken in
> individual poetic works. But for this purpose each individual poetic
> work requires first an *Erläuterung*. By this means the pure essence,
> which sparkles its way through all that is poetically spoken, is brought
> to a first level of radiant appearance.
>
> It is readily seen that a proper *Erläuterung* already presupposes
> *Erörterung*. Only out of the *Ort* of the Poem do the individual poetic
> works glow and ring out to us. But conversely, an *Erörterung* of the
> Poem requires the preliminary passage through a first *Erläuterung* of
> individual poetic works.
>
> Every thinking dialogue with the Poem of a poet remains within
> this mutual relation of *Erörterung* and *Erläuterung*. (38)

Heidegger's commentaries on Hölderlin had been called
"Erläuterungen." Now they are by implication dismissed, and presumably their mistakes along with them, as *mere* "Erläuterungen."

Moreover, Heidegger has now come back to something very like
Schleiermacher's interpretive method. Just as Schleiermacher finds it necessary to move back and forth between psychological and grammatical
interpretation, constantly correcting each by the other, so Heidegger recognizes a need to move back and forth between *Erörterung* and
Erläuterung. But there is an important difference. Schleiermacher's aim is
to refine and perfect *both* components of his oscillatory interpretive procedure; Heidegger is not especially concerned with *Erläuterung* except to
the extent that it serves the goal of *Erörterung*.

And the whole process, for Heidegger, serves yet a further goal, a
millennial goal of the type that we do not find in Schleiermacher.

> The authentic dialogue with the Poem of a poet must be a poetic di-
> alogue: the poetic conversation between poets. But also possible and at
> times even necessary is a dialogue of *thinking* with poetry, because both
> have a specially marked, if in each case different, relation to language.
>
> The conversation of thinking with poetry is aimed at evoking the
> *essence* of language, so that mortals might learn once more to dwell in
> language. (38)

How important is this idea? If Heidegger, having left the project of commentary *(Erläuterung)* behind, can now make a convincing or even significantly suggestive argument on the place or locus of poetry, the *Ort* of at least one poet's Poem, would a reasonable person's opinion about the history of aesthetics in general be affected?

I don't think so. In the first place, any argument Heidegger offers will hinge on an unmediated recognition of this or that poet's "greatness" — a concept that lacks all honesty except to the extent that it is debatable in the arena of criticism, which it still is even for Dilthey. And in the second place, the argument that Heidegger does offer on Trakl is about as transparently dishonest as they come. It concludes:

> All formulas are dangerous. They force that which is said into the externality of quick opinionating and can easily disrupt one's pondering. But they can also be a help, a spur at least and a handhold for continuing reflection. With these reservations we may say, formulaically:
>
> The *Erörterung* of his Poem shows us Georg Trakl as the poet of the still concealed Evening-Land or Western World *(Abend-Land)*. (81)

No great perceptiveness is needed to see that Heidegger's actual thought moves in the reverse of his essay's direction. It begins with the concept of the West, the Occident (in German, "Abendland"), the supposed cultural organism descended especially from Hellenic antiquity and Christianity. It seeks to imagine this vague entity as having a primordial dimension (77), as a compact and radiant focus of poetic truth — sufficiently self-assured to be open-minded, sincere, and unfailingly polite in the conversation with the Japanese that follows. It then fastens upon the titles of two of Trakl's rather less significant poems ("Abendländisches Lied" and "Abendland")[6] and exploits the difficulty of Trakl's diction and imagery to maneuver its target concept into what looks like a central position. And finally it recognizes in the geographical component of the concept "the West" — in its implication of place *(Ort)* — the opportunity to rechristen its own discursive procedure as *Erörterung*, thus distancing it from the dangerous debatable ground of the Hölderlin commentaries.

AESTHETICS AND THE NEED FOR CERTAINTY

Heidegger's favoring of intellectual procedures that restrict debate is a feature of his thought which we will be inclined to associate with political corruptibility. This association may be valid, but not in so straightforward a manner as might appear at first glance.

To understand what is at stake here, we have to begin with the special need for *certainty* that characterizes the practice of aesthetics. In part this need arises from the requirement that secular millennialism — aesthetic or otherwise — be indisputably right about the vestiges or harbingers of its envisioned goal. But the case of aesthetics is rendered more desperate by the elusiveness of its subject matter. Physics does not need to start by being certain about the existence of the physical world; biology, sociology, psychology, and history do not need to start by being certain about the existence of the objects they inquire into. The question of existence never arises, because eventually the inquiries themselves assume a certain shape that represents, for the time being, their object. (This is also true in most branches of philosophy.) But aesthetics can never put aside the nagging doubt that perhaps, after all, there is no such thing as beauty, or that the distinction of "art" as a particular class of objects or activities does not hold. Aesthetics, therefore—unless some clever way around this necessity is cooked up—must *begin* by making certain of its object, at least of its object's existence.

Otherwise one has to begin by simply admitting that aesthetics does not know what it is talking about—which is actually one way of approaching the subject. In the first paragraph of the "Draft Introduction" to his posthumously published *Aesthetic Theory,* Adorno quotes Ivo Frenzel quoting Moritz Geiger (thus suggesting a kind of tradition) as follows:

> [Frenzel says:] "There is scarcely another philosophical discipline that rests on such flimsy presuppositions as does aesthetics. Like a weather vane it is 'blown about by every philosophical, cultural, and scientific gust; at one moment it is metaphysical and in the next empirical; now normative, then descriptive; now defined by artists, then by connoisseurs; one day art is supposedly the center of aesthetics and natural beauty merely preliminary, the next day art beauty is merely second-hand natural beauty.' Moritz Geiger's description of the dilemma of aesthetics has been true since the middle of the nineteenth century."[7]

This nested quotation mirrors neatly the structure of Adorno's whole book. Rather than develop a positive theory in a single line of argument, it offers a large number of arguments from different directions that are evidently meant to exhaust all the available fruitful approaches to the general topic. It attempts, that is, to accomplish for aesthetics in one sweeping act what only a long history of research and theorizing has done for the other sciences I mentioned: to show a certain shape in the overall inquiry that may then be taken to represent the object of inquiry.

Adorno's project is thus clever enough in its conception. But can it succeed in avoiding the need for a kind of certainty which at the very least must establish an unhealthy disjunction between art "itself" and the domain of unrestricted debate in which criticism operates? (The corruptibility of such a disjunction is most obvious in literary criticism, where it appears as the distinction between "primary" and "secondary" texts.) I think the answer to this question is no; and I think one can show the points at which that need for certainty appears in Adorno's own presentation. But first we have to understand exactly what we mean by "certainty" here.

In Heidegger's case certainty means *agreement*. We are certain about the greatness and the prophetic character (as harbingers) of certain poets because we find ourselves in a cultural situation in which no one whom we might take seriously could possibly be inclined to challenge our certainty. Exactly this idea of certainty is modeled in the discussion of Hölderlin where Heidegger insists that our participation in the *one* conversation of our being presupposes our absolute agreement concerning "the One" and "the Same" on which this conversation (he thinks) must be based. And in his discussions of Trakl, the community within which agreement establishes our certainty is named. The *Ort* of Trakl's Poem, we hear, is "Abgeschiedenheit" ("seclusion," more or less, 76); but the greater mystery, the *Ortschaft dieses Ortes* (76)—"Ortschaft" usually refers a place settled and named by people)—turns out to be that "Abendland" or Western World which Heidegger also cryptically associates (78-79) with the conveniently italicized *"Ein* Geschlecht" (One race or clan; Trakl, 66) that he fishes out of the poetry.

This use of the expectation of agreement comes to Heidegger by way of a history of de-transcendentalizing moves with respect to Kant. Schleiermacher discards Kant's transcendental basis for the communicability of feeling in favor of the hypothesis that verbal communication becomes a reasonable practical goal in the self-structuring tendency of every particular language. That we share with one another our dependent relation to a language is sufficient to ground not certainty, but at least the hope for some success in our hermeneutic endeavors.

But Schleiermacher's thought is not an aesthetics. Not until Dilthey is hermeneutics turned firmly in an aesthetic direction by the idea of the human sciences, which promises a restoration of human particularity in much the same sense as Schiller's *Aesthetic Letters*. Schleiermacher had claimed only that linguistic contours offer a basis on which we might proceed as interpreters. Dilthey asserts that in the case of "a great poet or discoverer . . . a religious genius or a genuine philosopher,"[8] we can be absolutely certain of the existence of the object of interpretation—which had still been a problem for Schleiermacher, making Kantian assumptions necessary. Dilthey, as far as I know, does not explain his reasons for certainty on this point; but I think it is reasonable to infer that agreement is crucial. Greatness, for Dilthey, obviously has to be *undisputed* greatness, the greatness of thinkers, especially writers, whose stature is such that all our lives are shaped by their influence—in much the same way that they are, for Schleiermacher, by tendencies in a language.

For Schleiermacher the question of the possibility of adequate interpretation (which is answered by the contours of a given language) is clearly distinct from the question of the existence of the object of interpretation (which is answered by the doctrine of the unified subject). For

Dilthey the two questions become one, a single question which is now answered by the existence of indisputably great writing: answered in such a way as to guarantee—in the cases that count—both the existence of the object of interpretation and the prophetic quality of just those cases, their quality as harbingers of a new intellectual world-construction (*Aufbau der geistigen Welt*) in the human sciences.

Or to look at it differently: The hermeneutic circle operates in Schleier-macher's thought from its very first steps and so creates an element of uncertainty at every level. Dilthey's thought, by contrast, is not affected by the hermeneutic circle until *after* certainty has been achieved on the matter of poetic or historical greatness and on that of the destiny of the human sciences. Only in the very last pages of "The Origin of Hermeneu-tics" do we read:

> Here the central difficulty of all interpretive art makes itself felt. The totality of a work is supposed to be understood from individual words and their connections, but the complete understanding of individual parts already presupposes an understanding of the whole. This circle repeats itself in the relation of the individual work to the intellectual temper and development of its author, and it comes back again in the relation of that individual work to its literary genre. . . . In theory one arrives here at the limit of all interpretation, which can never carry out its task beyond a certain point. Thus all understanding remains only relative and can never be completed. Individuum est ineffabile. (5:330)

Dilthey's work, unlike Schleiermacher's, is essentially an aesthetics. It presupposes indisputable certainties and is oriented toward a millennial goal. The hermeneutic circle is important primarily because it ensures that even if that goal can be achieved, even in the perfected world of the human sciences, there will still be room for debate about interpretive matters.

Heidegger now goes a considerable distance beyond Dilthey. For him the hermeneutic circle is not a relativizing or limiting factor at all, but rather a cryptic vessel of "the positive possibility of the most aboriginal knowledge."[9] The domain of certainty is therefore even larger than in Dilthey; and debate is in the end simply excluded, at least on matters of genuine significance. Heidegger himself would certainly have objected to this characterization of his thought and work. Philosophizing, he tells us over and over again, is always a form of questioning, never the achieve-ment of answers or formulas or positions. But that questioning, as far as I can see, never cuts deep enough to create the possibility of significant disagreement or debate. It is always a questioning like that of the "Ques-tioner," the Heidegger figure, in conversation with the Japanese: not a debate but a co-operative process in which the interlocutors (like those, supposedly, in Hölderlin's "conversation") are joined much more power-fully by the agreed-upon "One and Same" that grounds their discourse than they could ever be separated by critical disagreement. Kant is honest enough to show his hand eventually—in *The Conflict of the Faculties,* which exposes the sense in which the *Critiques* had been a move in academic politics. But Heidegger goes to his grave without seeming even to recognize, first, that his philosophy had been basically an aesthetics, and second, that it had sustained itself as such by disguising as substantive thought an exploitation of the professor's unappealable prerogative to set discourse-rules in advance.

The need for a certainty that we experience in the form of agreement thus appears to be typical of aesthetics. In Cassirer's appeal for our assent to his idea of beauty it reaches the intensity of desperation. And at one point it even tempts Kant into a moment of explicit millennial speculating. In § 20 of the *Critique of Judgment* he argues that a "Gemeinsinn," a "sense-in-common" (meaning an "effect of the free play of our cognitive faculties" that we have in common with everyone else), must be presupposed in order for us to make judgments of taste; and in § 21 he shows that we have, in general, good reason to postulate such a sense-in-common. This is as far as his argument can carry him, and as far as he really needs to go for the time being. But in § 22 he insists on going a step further:

> This indeterminate norm of a sense-in-common is really presupposed by us, as is proven by our presuming to make judgments of taste. Whether in fact there exists such a sense-in-common as a constitutive principle of the possibility of experience, or whether a still higher principle of reason implies a regulative principle that obliges us first to bring forth in ourselves a sense-in-common for higher purposes; whether therefore taste is an original and natural power or only the idea of a still unattained artificial power . . . this question we will not and can not yet take up.

Even in the midst of an argument that works perfectly well on its own terms, Kant cannot suppress the need for something closer to an absolute certainty of communication, which in turn opens for a moment the millennial dimension of his thought—the idea of a "still unattained" humanity—a dimension which he usually tries to resist or at least conceal.

Schiller, finally, provides something like a defining instance of the aesthetic need for certainty by way of agreement. For of all the concepts about which we might declare ourselves certain on the basis of agreement, surely the most general is "the human." And this is the concept upon which Schiller's abstract argument is focused in the *Aesthetic Letters,* where its logical equivalence to the concept of a play drive is demonstrated, hence its equivalence to a recognition of the centralness of the notion and feeling of the beautiful in all our lives. Of all the aesthetic theorists we have looked at, therefore, Schiller probably has the clearest idea of what is at stake in his theorizing and the best reason to be satisfied with it. But he is also the most definite about accepting, when he must, the absurdity of the whole endeavor.

AGREEMENT: ADORNO AND MORITZ

None of this helps us place Adorno. Does he really manage to circumvent the need in aesthetics for an unsupported preliminary certainty, based solely on agreement, concerning the object of inquiry? For that matter, is his "aesthetic theory" really an aesthetics to begin with, or is it only a survey of possibilities? One indication of where he might fit in the history of aesthetics appears in the section that his editors call "Toward a Theory of the Artwork":

> That the experience of artworks is adequate only as living experience [versus remembered experience?] is more than a statement about the relation of the observer to the observed, more than a statement about psychological cathexis as a condition of aesthetic perception. Aesthetic experience becomes living experience only by way of its object, in that instant in which artworks themselves become animate under its gaze. This is George's symbolist teaching in the poem "The Tapestry," an *art poétique* that furnishes the title of a volume. Through contemplative immersion [on our part] the immanent processual quality of the work is set free. By speaking [to us], it becomes something that moves in itself. (262, trans. 175-76)

(The reference to Stefan George is revealing, and we will return to it.) What Adorno says here about artworks is almost exactly what Karl Philipp Moritz had said in 1785 on the artwork as "that which is complete in itself." Only Moritz had expressed himself in a less technical register:

> It is not so much that we need the beautiful for our pleasure, as that the beautiful needs us, in order to be recognized. We can exist perfectly well without observing beautiful works of art, but these works cannot exist, as such, without our observing them. The more we can thus do without them, by so much more do we observe them for their own sake, in order as it were to endow them, for the first time, with their own full existence by our contemplation. [10]

In both authors, we have an extreme form of "reception" aesthetics. The very existence of the work, as an artwork, depends on our responding to it; the work first becomes what it is in unfolding itself beneath our gaze and is never anything substantially different from just this Becoming. The attribute of "Being," as opposed to "Becoming," is simply never applicable to artworks (Adorno, 263).

Adorno never mentions Moritz, as far as I can tell. And he would probably object that Moritz's notion of "that which is complete in itself" is nothing but an invocation of perfect "consistency" as a criterion for art. [11] This judgment would be unfair. Moritz's grasp of the paradox and aporia of artistic self-consistency may perhaps lack the refinement of Adorno's; but it is no less firm and profound for that lack. The very idea of a thing that is "complete in itself," and yet (for just that reason!) also requires a specific unpredictable act on our part in order to become what it is, already contains most of Adorno's refinement in the form of para-doxical implications. A page or so after the passage quoted above, Moritz continues: "That which is useless or purposeless cannot possibly give pleasure to a rational being. Therefore, whenever an object lacks any external use or purpose, these must be sought in the object itself if it is to awaken pleasure; I must *find in the individual parts of that object so much purposefulness that I forget to ask after the purpose of the whole*" (2:946). Inner consistency is thus, paradoxically, a relative matter, as in Adorno. And surely Moritz, a pioneering psychologist, is aware of the complications in his idea of "forgetting." Which implies an understanding here, as in Adorno, of the immediate aporetic relation between artistic self-sufficien-cy and the artwork's incessant movement outward into the domain of its "other."

Perhaps the most significant aspect of what Adorno and Moritz have in common, however, is the failure of any objective answer to the ques-tion of how we might identify a genuine artwork in the first place. Ador-no, even while insisting that a definition of art or the artwork is impos-sible (11, 263, 267), cannot break free of this question, which he ap-proaches obliquely but incessantly by way of the idea of an exercise of critical judgment—it being understood that "The question . . . of what is and is not an artwork cannot in any way be separated from the faculty of judging, from the question of quality, of good and bad" (246, trans. 164). And I have suggested that the shape of his whole inquiry is meant to represent a possible approach to the same problem. But in the end, for Adorno, there are no unequivocal criteria for judging or identifying art.[12] He himself acknowledges that "What is essential to art is that which in it is not the case" (499, trans. 335),[13] hence that criteria can always be ruled out but can never be established.

In Moritz, the question of how to distinguish true art, or art as the vessel of true beauty, is hardly even touched on—a fact that is significant in its own right. For this question is as crucial in his thought as it is in Adorno's. Without some procedure for identifying genuine artworks, all Moritz's and Adorno's illuminations about the object's "becoming" under our gaze, its "immanent character of being an act" (Adorno, 123, trans. 79), are reduced to empty talk, uninterested in verification. And in the absence of applicable criteria, the only possible procedure for limiting the domain of genuine art is that of *prior agreement*. This is not to say that we must all agree on all the details of a complete catalogue of genuine artworks before we can do aesthetic theory in the manner of Moritz or Adorno. But before we begin, we must have at least a reasonable expecta-tion of agreeing on what is art.

For Moritz this reasonable expectation is enough to open the millennial dimension of his thinking. The identification of genuine artworks is present as an unavoidable issue in all his aesthetic writing; but his closest approach to dealing with it is found in the essay "Über die bildende Nachahmung des Schönen" [On the Artistic Imitation of the Beautiful], where we read: "Taste, or the ability to judge beauty, belongs, like the beautiful itself, among those things that we do not require as soon as we don't know them, things that we do not feel the lack of if we don't have them; things of which the need only arises with their possession, where it satisfies itself by way of itself. If the need for it arises before we possess it, then that need cannot be other than presumptuous and affected" (2:983). You either are or are not in possession of the ability to judge beauty. You cannot strive for that ability or seek guidance in achieving it. The same passage continues:

> Therefore the only path by which we can be educated to a true enjoyment of the beautiful is the same path by which the beautiful itself arose: *the preliminary quiet observation of nature and art considered together as a single great totality*, which, reflecting itself to itself in all its parts, leaves the most perfect impression of itself where all relationship ceases, in the genuine artwork, which, like that totality, in itself complete, has the goal and purpose of its existence in itself. (2:983)

In order to understand true art, the mind must enact, by contemplation and understanding, the *genesis* of the true artwork, which is itself in turn an act of contemplation and understanding vis-à-vis the great totality of nature.

Moritz thus deals with the question of recognizing true art by refusing to answer it, by avoiding all particulars and leaping into the metaphysical. But even here—for all the pre-Romantic feel of these passages—he is not far from Adorno. Immediately after the last quotation above, he begins a discussion of the destructive or damaging quality (*das Schädliche*, 2:983-85) in beauty—of the manner in which beauty implies our destruction, just as the destruction of plant life is implied by the existence of more highly organized forms of animal life that eat it. And yet—as we also learn from a similar passage in Adorno (202), on art as the spear that heals the wound made by itself—art is also the only influence that can fully reconcile us to our mortality.

Again, therefore, the only possible procedure for identifying true art is agreement. True art is what a competent group of judges agrees is true art. But we can now say exactly *who* must be involved in such an agreement. For by offering no particulars, no guidance, in the matter of developing genuine taste, Moritz also sets *no specific limits* to the group of people for whom true taste is a possibility. Ultimately, therefore, identification of true art must be based on the agreement of *all humanity*. Of course such agreement can never actually happen. But Moritz insists that the experience of the beautiful does happen. And if that experience brings with it the reasonable expectation of authoritative agreement, then our eyes are turned in the direction of an eventual unanimity of humankind, which is Moritz's millennial vision. "For by means of our increasing recognition of the beautiful in a beautiful work of art, we increase, so to speak, its own beauty and endow it with more and more value. Hence our impatient desire that everyone should pay homage to beauty where we have recognized it; the more generally it is recognized and admired as beautiful, the more value it acquires in our eyes" (2:945). In chapter 2, I pointed out the relation between this thought and Kant's. But Moritz is more direct and more passionate. He insists that there be real agreement here and now, hence certainty, on the existence of aesthetic experience, for the sake of the infinite multiplication of that agreement in a secular millennium toward which both beauty and humanity are oriented.

ADORNO AND THE AVOIDANCE OF THE MILLENNIAL

The affinities between Adorno and Moritz are useful for understanding the significance of how Adorno's thinking is different, particularly on the matter of whose agreement is necessary for a decision on what is genuinely art. Adorno does not avoid the question of identifying true art. He comes back to it repeatedly, especially by way of the idea of critical judgment and in the discussion of differences between true art and products of the "Kulturindustrie." Thus, unlike Moritz, he does set limits to the group of people who are qualified to participate in the needful (if hypothetical) vote by which the question of true art must be settled. If you cannot follow him (both understanding and affirming) in his specific critical decisions, then you have thereby excluded yourself from the competent group.

Now we can see why Stefan George's poem DER TEPPICH occurs to him immediately when he needs a text that evokes the definitive aesthetic experience, the moment of absolute certainty that one is observing a true artwork.[14] The tapestry described in the poem's first six lines—presumably "The Tapestry of Life" (the title of the volume in which the poem appears)—shows a confusing conglomeration of human, animal, and vegetable forms, plus ornaments and crossing lines, all caught in a "frozen dance." And line seven says that no one grasps the "riddle" of these "entangled" figures—where the word *verstrickt* [entangled] also suggests "woven" or "knitted." But then comes a turning point in line eight:

Da eines abends wird das werk lebendig.

[When (or then) one evening the work comes to life.]

Word order is a problem here. *Da* could mean either "when" or "then." But if it were the conjunction, then the verb "wird" would have to go to the end. And if it were the adverb, then the verb would naturally go into second position, producing "Da wird eines abends . . ." The line immediately following underscores this possibility:

Da regen schauernd sich die toten äste.

The line as it stands therefore hovers between the two meanings. On one hand, it is still connected *(da* as conjunction) to the foregoing description; on the other hand, it is also sharply disconnected, a suddenly *new* "then" *(da* as adverb). Thus something like Adorno's idea of the artwork's immanent "processual" quality is built into the poem's language.

But in order to complete our understanding of why Adorno is attracted to this poem, we need to read it to its end. Stanza three, immediately following the turning point, says that the tapestry's coming to life "brings the solution" we were wondering about, presumably the solution to the tapestry's "riddle."And then the final stanza reads:

Sie ist nach willen nicht: ist nicht für jede

Gewohne stunde: ist kein schatz der gilde.

Sie wird den vielen nie und nie durch rede

Sie wird den seltnen selten im gebilde.

> [It (the solution) is not subject to being willed, is not something for every ordinary hour, is not a possession of the guild (i.e. of any publicly organized group?). It is never available to the Many and never by way of speech; it is rarely available to rare individuals in the guise of a shape or form.]

There is no way Adorno could invoke this poem without invoking, thereby, the idea of the *esoteric,* of a truth or knowledge available only to "rare individuals." (Even the apparently gratuitous "one evening," in the turning-point line, refers to the time of day when secret societies typically hold their meetings.) Agreement is still the only possible basis for certainty in the identification of true art. But for Adorno such agreement cannot be even hypothetically universal. What is required, rather, is unanimity within a highly restricted and presumably self-selecting company of aesthetic adepts.

At least from the present age on, art is never truly the business of any but an extremely small segment of humanity. Which implies further that art, for Adorno, dissociates itself strongly from any form of millennialism. There is a "utopian" side to art, but the utopia in question is inherently self-cancelling.

Each artwork is utopia insofar as through its form it anticipates what would finally be itself, and this converges with the demand for the abrogation of the [non-abrogatable?] spell of self-identity cast by the subject. . . . But because for art, utopia—the yet-to-exist—is draped in black, it remains in all its mediations recollection; recollection of the possible in opposition to the actual that suppresses it; it is the imaginary reparation of the catastrophe of world history; it is freedom, which under the [equally non-abrogatable?] spell of necessity did not— and may not ever—come to pass. . . . Aesthetic experience is that of something that spirit may find neither in the world nor in itself; it is possibility promised by its impossibility. Art is the ever broken promise of happiness. (Adorno, 203-205, trans. 135-36)

Utopia is thus an issue for aesthetics, but not even hypothetically a goal. Erica Weitzman, commenting on the gloomy final paragraph of the *Aesthetic Theory* (386-87, trans. 260-61), lays out the situation in very simple terms.

Even in a world without social violence, alienation, inequity, etc. (and for Adorno, Marxian by profession and humanist by default, these criteria are by and large not subject to debate), art would maintain its negative stance, if [for?] nothing else in remembrance of barbarisms past. To hope to do otherwise would anyway be to set the dialectic in motion once again, and have the pretenses of an affirmative art shown up by a temporality that refuses to be reconciled, and above all, by the logical impossibility of owning one's own freedom from the compulsion of ownership.[15]

Or to look at it from the point of view of a select artistic company united by esoteric knowledge: art, far from being an avant-garde, is now the endless and hopeless rear-guard action covering its own endless retreat from advancing hordes that are armed with its own incessant but hopeless promises.

Adorno's *Aesthetic Theory* is thus not really an aesthetics—at least not in the sense I have been using. But it is also not simply a text of a different type, like Schleiermacher's; it does not simply *lack* a millennial dimension. It contains, under the rubric of the "utopian," a clear sense of its own potential millennial character, and it deliberately repudiates that character. Its fundamental gesture with respect to Schillerian aesthetics is *avoidance of the millennial.*

The question is: why? Why is it so important to get rid of the millennial pretensions of aesthetics? Or if there is a compelling reason to avoid secular millennialism as such, why attempt to preserve aesthetics without it? Especially when a non-millennial aesthetics takes the form that it does for Adorno: a replacement of all millennial hope with nothing but the vision of an endless sad nobility of secret knowledge, knowledge by which nothing of consequence is ever likely to be accomplished. Would Nietzsche not have recognized instantly in this proud esoteric company an ascetic priesthood of the arts? What does Adorno hope to gain by the bargain he has made? [16]

ADORNO AND THE BASIC AESTHETIC PROBLEM

I think, first of all, that Weitzman is right about Adorno's determination to preserve the basic negativity of art at all costs, art's immanent critical function vis-à-vis society. There are very few points in the *Aesthetic Theory* that are as unequivocally insisted upon.

> Art, however, is social not only because of its mode of production, in which the dialectic of the forces and relations of production is concentrated, nor simply because of the social derivation of its thematic material. Much more importantly, art becomes social by its opposition to society, and it occupies this position only as autonomous art. By crystallizing in itself as something unique to itself, rather than complying with existing social norms and qualifying as "socially useful," it criticizes society by merely existing, for which puritans of all stripes condemn it. . . . What is social in art is its immanent movement against society, not its manifest opinions. Its historical gesture repels empirical reality, of which artworks are nevertheless part in that they are things. Insofar as a social function can be predicated for artworks, it is their functionlessness. (335-37, trans. 225-27)

This view of art is obviously incompatible with aesthetic millennialism in anything like the form it takes for Schiller or Moritz or Cassirer, or even Kant, a millennialism which is always aimed at the positive integration of art with society and at a perfected version of exactly the communication that art, for Adorno, necessarily excludes (see 115, 167, 218, 335-36, 360).

But simple avoidance of the millennial does not solve Adorno's problem: If art is immanently critical with respect to society, critical simply by being what it is, then what is the function of systematic aesthetics—with respect to either art or society? Is aesthetics needed as a complement or confirmation of art's critical negativity? Then it would follow that what aesthetics says about art does not hold strictly for art alone, art left to its own devices. And in the particular case we are concerned with, does Adorno's dialectical subtlety—especially on the matter of a "utopian" component in artworks—not overcomplicate matters and so tend to obscure the inherent negative move of art itself?

One of the most interesting things about Adorno's work is that he understands this problem and responds to it—as neither Schiller nor Moritz nor Cassirer had before him.

> Just how little a universal concept of art suffices for artworks is demonstrated by the artworks themselves in that, as Valéry noted, few fulfill the strict concept. Guilt for this is borne not only by the weakness of artists in the face of the formidable concept of their object, but also by

the concept itself. The more single-mindedly artworks devote themselves to the emerging idea of art, the more precarious becomes the
relation of artworks to their other, a relation that is itself demanded by
the concept. But this relation can be conserved only at the price of
precritical consciousness, desperate naïveté: Today this is one of art's
aporia. It is evident that supreme works are not the most pure, but tend
to contain an extra-artistic surplus, especially an untransformed material element that burdens their immanent composition; however, it is
no less evident that once the complete immanent elaboration of artworks, unsupported by anything unreflected that is other than art, has
taken shape as an aesthetic norm, it is not possible willfully to reintro-
duce impure elements. (271, trans. 181-82)[17]

By "the emerging idea of art" *(die hervortretende Idee der Kunst)* I assume
Adorno means, in a Hegelian sense, the increasingly purified idea of art
that arises necessarily in the history of artistic practice. It follows that that
idea is purer now than ever in the past, and so offers itself more readily
for single-minded "devotion" *(Nachhängen)*, which produces the aporia
Adorno refers to: artworks can now be truly art only by not being strictly
art. And it is in the gaps produced by this aporia, gaps between genuineness and purity and between mutually unraveling types or "genres" of
genuineness ("Gattungen . . . [die] sich verfransen," 271), that aesthetics
has its place. Only aesthetics, which recognizes art in all its guises and
can analyze the forces that create its gaps, is in a position to keep those
gaps from dissipating altogether the possibility of a single artistic effect
(however "functionless") in society.

Social good is even more clearly the justification for aesthetics in another passage somewhat further on.

Crudeness of thinking is the incapacity to differentiate within a topic,
and differentiation is an aesthetic category as much as one of understanding. Science and art are not to be fused, but the categories that are
valid in each are not absolutely different. Conformist consciousness
prefers the opposite, partly because it is incapable of distinguishing the
two and partly because it refuses the insight that identical forces are
active in nonidentical spheres. The same holds true with regard to
morality. Brutality toward things [including concepts?] is potentially
brutality toward people. The raw *[Das Rohe]*—the subjective nucleus of
evil—is a priori negated by art, from which the ideal of being fully
formed is indispensable [or inseparable]: This, and not the pronounce-
ment of moral theses or the striving after moral effects, is art's participation in the moral and makes it part of a more humanly worthy society. (344, trans. 231-32)

Wissenschaft in German, unlike "science" in English, can refer to practically any systematic intellectual endeavor, any form of study or scholarship.
And when Adorno speaks of "science" *(Wissenschaft)* in this passage, I
think he means not only to include aesthetics in his reference, but to call

aesthetics specifically to our attention, if in an appropriately esoteric manner. The opposite of "crudeness"—delicacy, subtlety, nuanced conceptual differentiation—which aesthetic science and art itself have in common, places the two on the same side of the basic cultural and moral divide that is being talked about, which explains a couple of conceptual gaps in the passage's last sentences. If art is really "functionless" in society, then how is art, as itself alone, supposed to "participate" in the moral, especially where the moral is understood as a force for the betterment of society? (The untypically conciliatory comparative, "a *more* humanly worthy society," insists on these questions.) The only way to make sense of those sentences is to understand them as referring not to art alone, but to art in concert with its own science, aesthetics, a science which focuses art's critical negativity and so conceivably mediates an actual social effect.

Aesthetics has thus received its full reason for being, relative to art itself, only in the post-Nazi era. This idea is suggested again, and developed, a few pages later.

> In the culture resurrected after the catastrophe, art—regardless of its content and substance—has even taken on an ideological aspect by its mere existence. In its disproportion to the horror that has transpired and threatens, it is condemned to cynicism; even where it directly faces the horror, it diverts attention from it. Its objectivation implies insensitivity to reality. This degrades art to an accomplice of the barbarism to which it succumbs no less when it renounces objectivation and directly plays along, even when this takes the form of [oppositional?] polemical commitment. Every artwork today, the radical ones included, has its conservative aspect; its existence helps to secure the spheres of spirit and culture, whose real powerlessness and complicity with the principle of disaster becomes plainly evident. But this conservative element—which, contrary to the trend toward social integration, is stronger in advanced works than in the more moderate ones—does not simply deserve oblivion. Only insofar as spirit, in its most advanced form, survives and perseveres is any opposition to the total domination of the social totality possible. . . . Art, even as something tolerated in the administered world, embodies what does not allow itself to be managed and what total management suppresses. . . . Asociality becomes the social legitimation of art. For the sake of reconciliation, authentic works must blot out every trace of reconciliation in memory. (347-48, trans. 234)

The unavoidable "ideological" quality of recent art balances that art on a knife edge between complicity and opposition with respect to "total management"—the more "advanced" the work, the stronger the pull in *both* directions. And again, what is it if not aesthetics—who is it if not that obscure elite of true critical minds whose verdict is the sole criterion of an artwork's authenticity—that can aim to nudge the actual social operation of art toward opposition, that can aim to stabilize art's negativity and counteract the limitlessly co-optive pull of the culture industry? Not that Adorno holds out any hope of achieving these aims. But at least we chosen few, we aestheticians, can now discern some contour in our collective endeavor.

HEIDEGGER AND ADORNO: THE FINAL PAIRING

Adorno's is thus unique among aesthetic systems in being able to suggest an account, however gloomy, of its own function relative to the art it describes. Or rather: almost unique. For there is at least one other comparable case, that of Heidegger.

In his basic approach Heidegger is Adorno's diametrical opposite. If Adorno builds "aesthetic theory" on an avoidance of the millennial, Heidegger is probably the last of the fully convinced aesthetic millennialists—except that it would be a bit more accurate to call him a poetic millennialist. Harbingers of the millennium include art in media other than language—a painting of shoes by Van Gogh in *Der Ursprung des Kunstwerkes*. But mainly Heidegger counts on poetry to show him and us the way to language, the way to a condition in which "die Sterblichen wieder lernen, in der Sprache zu wohnen" [mortals learn once more to dwell in language].[18]

The trouble is that in order to operate as harbingers, poems need to be interpreted, and poetic interpretation involves risks that Heidegger is unwilling to take. But in the Trakl essay in *Unterwegs zur Sprache* he makes a suggestion that would solve both this problem and the perennial problem of finding an aesthetic function for aesthetics itself. "Die eigentliche Zwiesprache mit dem Gedicht eines Dichters," he proclaims, "ist allein die dichtende: das dichterische Gespräch zwischen Dichtern" [The authentic dialogue with the Poem of a poet must be a poetic dialogue: the poetic conversation between poets]. Surely any genuine or valid interpretation of poetry must occur in that "poetic conversation" and nowhere else. We prose-interpreters with our debatable formulations are merely wasting our time. But there is also another possible dialogue with poetry, "eine Zwiesprache des *Denkens* mit dem Dichten" [a dialogue of *thinking* with poetry], which is obviously what Heidegger now suggests his own writing is: a conversation, as far as I can see, that keeps poetry at arm's length and so avoids the problem of debatability in interpretation. And it is only this conversation, says Heidegger, that calls forth "das *Wesen* der Sprache" [the *essence* of language] and the possibility of a millennial "dwelling" in language.

Even apart from my own judgment of Heidegger, I think I have shown that he and Adorno mark something like an absolute end to aesthetics. Now the most fundamental question of all is contested: whether there shall or shall not be an aesthetic millennium. And now at last the nagging problem of the aesthetic role of aesthetics itself is incorporated into the system, but in ways that turn out not to promise much of a future. Adorno leaves us with nothing but the prospect of a sad ascetic resistance against overwhelming cultural forces. And in Heidegger, even if you regard his thought on poetry as more than a piece of terminological legerdemain, you are still excluded from any "authentic" relation to precisely those poetic initiatives by which your sense of human destiny was meant to be focused.

(This last feature of Heidegger's thought exhibits with unprecedented clarity a general characteristic of the aesthetic millennial vision: that it must somehow combine the quality of experienced immediacy with that of still-unattained ideality. In most versions of aesthetics these qualities are referred to different objects, immediacy to the present harbinger, ideality to the envisioned goal. In Schiller these would be our immediate experience of our humanity and our ideal vision of an "aesthetic polity." In Heidegger, however, the two opposed qualities belong to a single object, true poetry. Insofar as we enter into a "thinking" dialogue with it, that poetry is immediately present to us as a shaping factor in our intellectual existence from instant to instant. But as soon as we are tempted by the idea of an "authentic" dialogue, a relation on the level of the single true Poem, that same poetry is suddenly beyond our reach. What must be avoided in this situation is the hope for some insipid compromise between the opposites—which is how I think Heidegger regards the practice of serious interpretive or "philological" debate.)

Adorno and Heidegger, then, are diametrical opposites in the field of aesthetics, yet opposites that belong together. What is most important about them for the present study is that they bring to light, between them, the inevitable relation of aesthetics to the principal political manifestation of secular millennialism, twentieth-century totalitarian movements. Heidegger is of course not eager to talk about this relation in his own case. But it is certainly true, and of considerable historical importance, that a resonance between versions of secular millennialism—between aesthetics and Nazism—made it easier for him to reach whatever accommodations he did with the Nazi government, at least up to 1935.

Adorno occupies exactly the opposite relation to totalitarianism. He is fully committed to the basic aesthetic project (Schiller's or Dilthey's) of rescuing individual human particularity in an age of "total management"—by which he refers primarily to the present postwar period, but only in the sense that the totalitarian past, "the horror that has transpired and threatens," has not truly been left behind. But at the same time, he refuses absolutely to take the next step into aesthetic millennialism, a step that would compromise the basic negativity of his position and open it to being co-opted by exactly what it had been erected against, an always still potentially totalitarian system of total management. From top to bottom, his "aesthetic theory" thus retains unvaryingly its negative focus upon the totalitarian phenomenon. Here, as in Heidegger, if in the opposite sense, totalitarianism marks the end of aesthetics.

NOTES

1. For the "aestheticization of politics" see Walter Benjamin, "Das Kunstwerk im Zeitalter seiner technischen Reproduzierbarkeit," in Benjamin, *Illuminationen: Ausgewählte Schriften 1* (Frankfurt/Main: Suhrkamp, 1977), 169.

2. Martin Heidegger, *Erläuterungen zu Hölderlins Dichtung* = *Gesamtausgabe*, 4:36. Pages of the original edition, as in chap. 5 above. Heidegger quotes here from Friedrich Hölderlin, *Sämtliche Werke*, ed. Norbert von Hellingrath, 6 vols., 2nd ed. (Berlin, 1923), 4:343. Readers of my argument may recall Paul de Man's essay, "Heidegger's Exegeses of Hölderlin," in *Blindness and Insight: Essays in the Rhetoric of Contemporary Criticism*, 2nd ed. (Minneapolis, 1983), 246-66. In fact, de Man's point that "Heidegger is in need of a witness [to] the immediate presence of Being" (252) in order for his philosophy to make sense, is exactly parallel to my point about the need for harbingers of "the way to language" and its goal. But when de Man then makes the gesture of challenging Heidegger, by insisting on *"the fact that Hölderlin says exactly the opposite of what Heidegger makes him say,"* (254-55), he and I part company. It turns out that he is not really challenging Heidegger after all, but simply seeking an oblique way to pay homage to Heidegger's "level of thought," at which "it is difficult to distinguish between a proposition and that which constitutes its opposite" (255). "Heidegger and Hölderlin speak of the same thing," continues de Man. Precisely this is the proposition that needs to be tested.

3. For the best available modern reading of the passage in question, see Friedrich Hölderlin, *Sämtliche Werke: Frankfurter Ausgabe*, ed. D. E. Sattler (Frankfurt/Main, 1975ff.), 8:640, 643. For the manuscript readings that form the basis for Hellingrath's text, see 8:597, 7:155.

4. Martin Heidegger, *Einführung in die Metaphysik* = *Gesamtausgabe*, 40:47-48. Pages of the original edition.

5. *Unterwegs zur Sprache*, 12:37. Ref. in chap. 5, n19.

6. Georg Trakl, *Dichtungen und Briefe*, ed. Walther Killy and Hans Szklenar (Salzburg, 1970), 65-66, 76-77.

7. Theodor W. Adorno, *Ästhetische Theorie*, ed. Gretel Adorno and Rolf Tiedemann (Frankfurt/Main: Suhrkamp, 1973), 493; the translation used is Theodor W. Adorno, *Aesthetic Theory*, trans. Robert Hullot-Kentor (Minneapolis, 1997), 332. Pages from this translation are indicated by "trans." below. The outer quote is from Ivo Frenzel, "Ästhetik," in *Philosophie*, ed. Alwin Diemer and Ivo Frenzel, (Frankfurt/Main, 1958), 35 = Das Fischer Lexikon, Bd. 11. Diemer and Frenzel give the impression in their bibliography, 355, that they are in turn quoting Geiger from his *Zugänge zur Ästhetik* (Leipzig, 1928). In fact, the inner quote is from Geiger's essay "Ästhetik" (1921). See Moritz Geiger, *Die Bedeutung der Kunst: Zugänge zu einer materialen Wertästhetik*, ed. Klaus Berger and Wolfhart Henckmann (Munich, 1976), 85.

8. Dilthey, 5:320. See chap. 5, n12, for full reference.

9. *Sein und Zeit*, § 32, 153. See chap. 5, n13, for full reference.

10. *Werke*, 2:945. For full reference, see chap. 1, n18.

11. See e.g. Adorno, especially on "Stimmigkeit," 73-74, 211, 216-17, 252-53, 280-81, and 338, where consistency appears as an unacceptable but also unavoidable fetishism in art.

12. Erica Weitzman, *"No Fun: Aporias of Pleasure in Adorno's Aesthetic Theory,"* *GQ*, 81:2 (2008), 185-202, provides an excellent summary view, irreverent but appreciative, of the confusing multiplicity of Adorno's positions. On the question of artistic criteria, see especially 191-92, on the difficulty of distinguishing "the culture industry's mecha-

nisms of control" from the "processes of autonomous art"; 195-96, on the boundaries between "'art' and 'not art'"; 199-200, on the need for criteria that "may have to be necessarily fluid, contextual, and subjective."

13. This passage from Adorno's "Draft Introduction" is interesting for a number of reasons. In a footnote the reader is invited to compare Donald Brinkmann, *Natur und Kunst: Zur Phänomenologie des ästhetischen Gegenstandes* (Zürich and Leipzig, 1938), but without specific page references. And as far as I can see, Brinkmann never says anything from which Adorno's statement would follow logically. Brinkmann does say repeatedly that the "ästhetischer Gegenstand" is not necessarily (never more than secondarily) a "Kunstwerk," and that the "Kunstwerk," conversely, is never more than secondarily an "ästhetischer Gegenstand," which means (I think) that he would dismiss Adorno's whole project as brusquely as he dismisses Croce's (Brinkmann, 135-36). In fact it may be precisely the desire to distance himself from Croce—especially from Croce on the "expressive" origin of art (see Adorno, 480-81)—that moves Adorno to give the impression that he is aligning himself with Brinkmann. Brinkmann says: the qualities of "aesthetic object" and "artwork" have nothing fundamental to do with each other. Adorno says: those two qualities are nevertheless strictly inseparable, which produces the basic negation that he wants to find in art.

14. Stefan George, *Der Teppich des Lebens und die Lieder von Traum und Tod mit einem Vorspiel* = *Gesamt-Ausgabe der Werke: Endgültige Fassung,* vol. 5 (Berlin: Bondi, 1932), 40. George always insisted that his work be printed in a font of his own design. The font is available and I use it here.

15. Weitzman, 194.

16. For a judgment even harsher than Nietzsche's would have been, see Jost Hermand, "Die Metapher 'heile Welt': Zu Adornos Antiutopismus," in his *Orte. Irgendwo: Formen utopischen Denkens* (Königstein/Ts., 1981), where we read, "Was sich also in dieser Kunst [supposedly genuine art] als 'Protest' artikuliert, darf nur ein Protest des Subjektiven, das heißt ein cliquenhafter, formalisierter, nichtssagender sein. Was dabei ideologisch herauskommt, ist zwangsläufig das Konzept einer ästhetisch orientierten Avantgarde, die ständig die gleichen bedeutungslosen Proteste vorbringt und sich dadurch als gesellschaftliche Avantgarde—nämlich als Vertretung eines kollektiven Willens—selbst entmündigt. . . . Schließlich war Adornos Abneigung gegen alles Kollektive, Totalitäre, Sozialistische oder gar Kommunistische für die Drahtzieher der kapitalistischen Gesellschaftsordnung ein gefundenes Fressen. Doch auch seine Kunsttheorie konnte von den systemkonformen Journalisten und Publizisten der BRD ohne besondere Mühe vereinnahmt werden" (114).

17. For me at least, the reference here to Valéry is somewhat mystifying. I don't think the idea "daß . . . nur wenige [Kunstwerke] den strengen Begriff [der Kunst] erfüllen" even sounds like Valéry; it is both too definite (the "strict concept") and too equivocal ("only a few"). But Valéry does very strongly make the point: "Il était fatal, sans doute . . . que de belles réalités insoumises vinssent toujours troubler la souveraineté du Beau Idéal et la sérénité de sa définition. . . . Pureté, généralité, rigueur, logique étaient en cette matière des vertus génératrices de paradoxes, dont voici le plus admirable: l'Esthétique des métaphysiciens exigeait que l'on séparât le *Beau* des *belles choses!* . . ." (Paul Valéry, "Discours sur l'esthétique," *Oeuvres*, ed. Jean Hytier, 2 vols. [n.p.: Gallimard, 1957, 1960], 1:1301.) That is, particular instances of beauty somehow fail to be subsumed under the general concept: which is exactly the paradox that Adorno develops, with respect to the general concept "Kunst," in the paragraph we are looking at (271-72). Adorno, I think, is thus invoking Valéry without quite remembering why it had occurred to him to do so.

18. *Unterwegs zur Sprache,* 12:38.

Part II

SEVEN

Novels and the Novel

In chapter 4 I said I would bridge the nineteenth-century gap in my historical account of aesthetics by discussing the form of the novel. My argument depends on one crucial theorem: that the general idea of "the novel," while referring to actual individual novels, *does not subsume them as instances of itself.* This form of thought also characterizes Valéry's understanding of the relation between "beauty" and "beautiful things" as well as Adorno's of the relation between "art" and "artworks."[1] And the failure of the general notion to govern particular instances opens the possibility of "heteroglossia" that fascinates Bakhtin. I will argue that there are statements about "the novel" that are true, yet tell us nothing about "novels"; and that there are accurate general statements about "novels" that say nothing about "the novel." In particular, novels are as a rule realistic, whereas *the* novel, in history, is a clear instance of secular millennialism.

PECULIARITIES OF THE NOVEL

What does the phrase "the novel" refer to? An actual class of written or printed texts? The idea of a certain type of text? Or something else? The first possibility encounters obvious difficulties in the form of books about whose status as instances of "the novel" we shall never reach anything like a consensus. I mean not only *Finnegans Wake* or *Joseph und seine Brüder,* but even such less enormous works as *Orlando* or *Salammbô,* or indeed *Wilhelm Meisters Wanderjahre* or *Jacques le fataliste* or *A Sentimental Journey,* perhaps even *Don Quixote* itself.

The advantage of the second possibility, accordingly, the idea of a *type* of text, is that it leaves room for disagreement. The question of exactly which texts conform to the type or genre need never be decided once and for all, as long as the idea is clear enough to give shape to our debates on it. Especially important is that such genre-ideas offer a plausible account of how the type holds together over time, an account that will hinge ordinarily on later authors' reception of their predecessors.

And in the case of large, complex types, like the romance or the novel, the historical genre-idea has a typical shape. We agree, if only for the sake of argument, that the type is realized most completely in some particular historical version of itself: say, the genre of "romance" in French and German Arthurian poems of the twelfth and early thirteenth centuries. We then trace what now seem to us the antecedents of that perfected type, as well as the similar or cognate types that appear alongside it. And we expect, finally, to be able to describe an ensuing period of self-conscious decline, first in the form of mannered imitation or exaggeration, then in the form of mockery or satire which is usually directed against the later degenerate forms, not the type itself. Of course this scheme never works perfectly. In the case of the genre of romance, especially the later British instances cause difficulty. But our expectation of the genre's reaching an historical culmination followed by a self-conscious decline—even where it distorts facts—still has the effect of giving a certain direction and contour to our debates.

And this historical idea of genre fails utterly in the case of the novel. Some of the most extreme cases of self-conscious manipulation and criticism of the novel-form occur in the eighteenth century, when the novel as we know it was only just coming into existence: Sterne and Diderot obviously belong here, Fielding to an extent, Goethe once we learn how to read him in conjunction with such authors as Wieland, Hippel, Novalis, Jean Paul. Perhaps it will be remarked that this phenomenon is only natural, given that the form of the novel is historically rooted in the self-conscious manipulation and mockery of earlier narrative forms, especially the chivalric romance in Cervantes, and something at least cousin to romance in Rabelais. But the object of ironic manipulation in the eighteenth century is not romance or any of its cousins; it is nothing but exactly that form, the novel, in which the manipulation occurs, if it is not indeed the whole practice of story-telling. Thus the typical historical unfolding of genre appears to be reversed. For those self-conscious eighteenth-century experiments are succeeded in the nineteenth century by novels that position themselves much closer to the simple narrative representation of an imagined but plausible reality, as if the authorial posture of un-self-conscious story-telling had never been called into question.

It is well understood that the novel, when it first appears in the seventeenth and eighteenth centuries, is not only a new genre, but a new kind of genre—that it is part of a broad tendency by which the definitions and boundaries of traditional poetic genres become ever more questionable, the same tendency by which the old notion of the "poetic" is engulfed by the new concept of "literature." But this understanding alone is not enough to account for the apparent rebirth of narratorial naiveté in the nineteenth-century novel. It seems to me that only two theoretical moves are open to us here: (1) that we divide the modern novel, from the late seventeenth century down to the present, into a number of different and clearly distinct genres, each with its own historical identity; or (2) that we recognize in "the novel" not merely a new kind of genre, but an historical phenomenon that does not belong to the category of "poetic genres" in the first place. Only the second option, if we are honest with ourselves, permits us to continue speaking of "the novel" in general terms.

And since it is difficult to see how we could do without the general concept of "the novel," we shall have to explore that second option. Which means to explore the possibility of taking "the novel" not as a form or technique of writing, but as a mode of existence, a way of living. It has been suggested that Hollywood cinema—with its moralistic sentiment and sentimental morality—is not merely a reflection of American conditions and values, but also a shaping force behind them. Serious scholarly work has been done on how the life and politics of one recent president, as well as national policy under his administration, were governed by the conventions and spirit of the movies.[2] Any similar argument involving the conventions and spirit of the novel would have to operate on a much larger scale. Is such an argument possible?

REALISM IN NOVELS

Suppose we agree with Ian Watt that "realism" in novels consists mainly in an attentiveness to the strictly particular: that the "primary criterion" for novels is "truth to individual experience—individual experience which is always unique and therefore new"; that "the novelist's primary task is to convey the impression of fidelity to human experience," to "embody the individual apprehension of reality" or "the texture of daily experience"; that a novelist's skill is shown "in the closeness with which he [makes] his words correspond to their objects," in "the immediacy and closeness of the text to what is being described"; that novels—in which "the function of language is much more largely referential . . . than in other literary forms"—therefore operate "by exhaustive presentation rather than by elegant concentration."[3] It would follow that realism can be ascribed only to novels, not to *the* novel. For if realism is a quality by which each novel is focused upon the particularity of its material, a quality that is manifest only in the uniqueness or newness of each case, then we are prevented logically from carrying out any typifying or generalizing move that would enable us to speak of *the* realism of *the* novel. The particular, unlike practically any other notion, ceases to be itself in the form of a general concept. The judgment, "this or that book is realistic in

Watt's sense," is always a judgment strictly after the fact; the criteria needed to make such a judgment are simply not in one's possession until after one has read the book.

Watt's own terminology is faulty in this respect. His chapter is entitled "Realism and the Novel Form," and in it he speaks repeatedly of "the novel." But in his case this objection is only a quibble. The structure of his presentation, the manner in which his rhetoric encircles his thinking, rather than skewer it, makes clear that in effect he is always talking about novels in the plural.

The same cannot be said of Bakhtin's presentation, however much it may agree with Watt's in detail. Bakhtin's formulations are very strong and suggestive. He approaches the matter of immediacy and particularity in novels by speaking of "a living contact with unfinished, still-evolving contemporary reality (the openended present)"; he insists on a "new and peculiar zone for structuring artistic models (a zone of contact with the present in all its openendedness), a zone that was first appropriated by the novel."[4] And he is eloquent about how a novelist works:

> The novel comes into contact with the spontaneity of the inconclusive present; this is what keeps the genre from congealing. The novelist is drawn toward everything that is not yet completed. He may turn up on the field of representation in any authorial pose, he may depict real moments in his own life or make allusions to them, he may interfere in the conversations of his heroes, he may openly polemicize with his literary enemies and so forth. This is not merely a matter of the author's image appearing within his own field of representation—important here is the fact that the underlying, original formal author (the author of the authorial image) appears in a new relationship with the represented world. Both find themselves now subject to the same temporally valorized measurements, for the "depicting" authorial language now lies on the same plane as the "depicted" language of the hero, and may enter into dialogic relations and hybrid combinations with it (indeed, it cannot help but enter into such relations). (27-28)

Watt gets around to practically all these points eventually in his discussion of particular novels; but Bakhtin distills the basic critical material into a single paragraph.

In the end, Bakhtin may be too eloquent for his own good. He is talking about basically the same quality that Watt understands as the realism of novels, but he insists on imagining it as a quality of *the* novel, which entangles him in the logical difficulties I sketched above. He focuses less upon the uniqueness of novels than upon the attribute of uncompletedness or "openendedness," upon the orientation of novels toward an unknowable "future" (15). But it comes to the same thing. A fiction cannot be unique without being open-ended (thus strictly unpredictable), and cannot be truly open-ended if it does not turn out to be unique. The effect of Bakhtin's terminology is that it avoids giving the impression of simple radical differentness among novels, and enables him to emphasize the notions of change and development. "The novel is the only developing genre and therefore it reflects more deeply, more essentially, more sensitively and rapidly, reality itself in the process of its unfolding. Only that which is itself developing can comprehend development as a process" (7). But is he talking here about how the "genre" operates in history or about how each novel reflects "reality"? Or is he trying to talk about both at once?

Bakhtin's thinking is not as conceptually tidy as Watt's—always assuming we read "novels" when the latter says "the novel." But his approach has one important advantage. Watt, in avoiding conceptual confusion, denies himself the possibility of even opening the question of *the* novel—which must mean, I argued above, the question of the novel as a way of living, or indeed as an agent of historical change. And exactly this question forms the center of Bakhtin's thought, in his argument about the modern "novelization" of all literary genres.

> The novelization of literature does not imply attaching to already completed genres a generic canon that is alien to them, not theirs. The novel, after all, has no canon of its own. It is, by its very nature, not canonic. It is plasticity itself. It is a genre that is ever questing, ever examining itself and subjecting its established forms to review. Such, indeed, is the only possibility open to a genre that structures itself in a zone of direct contact with developing reality. Therefore, the novelization of other genres does not imply their subjection to an alien generic canon; on the contrary, novelization implies their liberation from all that serves as a brake on their unique development, from all that would change them along with the novel into some sort of stylization of forms that have outlived themselves. (39)

It is clear from the awkwardness of the idea of "a genre that structures itself in a zone of direct contact with developing reality" that Bakhtin is aware on some level of the difficult relation between novels and *the* novel. (The genre cannot simply *be* "in contact with reality" because such contact could exist only by way of each individual novel's "unique" contact with its own *separate,* non-generic "reality.") But he is willing to accept that difficulty for the sake of opening the question of how *the* novel, the genre, operates in a cultural range much larger than could be ascribed to the direct effect upon readers of its individual instances.

But why, then, does he restrict his discussion of this question to the domain of literature? It is true that one must be cautious about attributing historical agency to an entity like "the novel." And Bakhtin is certainly cautious enough in this regard. "In an environment where the novel is the dominant genre, the conventional languages of strictly canonical genres begin to sound in new ways, which are quite different from the ways they sounded in those eras when the novel was *not* included in "high" literature" (6). It is not as if the novel had simply burst onto the scene as a new historical player. A larger cultural "environment" had to evolve, in which the concomitantly evolving modern novel more or less naturally assumed a dominant position. (This process is the subject of Watt's chapter on "The Reading Public and the Rise of the Novel" [35-59].) And it is hard to imagine how, in such an environment, the language of even long-established poetic genres would not begin to "sound different" from earlier versions of itself. (Think of the self-consciously antiquated language of British Romantic poetry.)[5] But this point only brings us back to the same question: If understanding the novel involves understanding the larger "environment" in which it arises, why limit one's discussion of the novel's historical operancy to the strictly literary domain?

SHAPING REALITY

We cannot get into this matter except by way of the question of how language works in novels. Watt is very definite, but not very helpful, when he says that in novels "the function of language is much more largely referential . . . than in other literary forms." If novels are uniquely bound to immediate, particular reality, then referentiality will certainly belong to their manner of operating. But does this mean referentiality in the same sense as in everyday conversation, or newspapers, or history books, or the language of science? If not, then where is the difference? Does "reality" itself keep the same basic nature when it is referred to by these different types of language?

With respect to this last question, Watt is helpful after all, if we pay attention to his insistence on the ideas of individuality and experience. To put the matter into the form of a theorem: *The referentiality of novels imposes upon reality (its total referent) the shape of individual experience.* One will perhaps respond that of course reality has the shape of individual experience. How do we ever make contact with reality if not through our experience as individuals? But in the first place, such a response is characteristic precisely of the age of the novel—or we might also say, characteristic of the age of Kantian philosophy, in which an apprehensible reality (an order of representations) cannot arise except by way of transcendental apperception or the "I think." And in the second place, linguistic reference, practically by definition, operates in the direction of *common,* not individual, experience. The referentiality of language in everyday conversation, in newspapers or history books, in science, always has the effect of placing its referent out in the open, where it is in principle available to anyone. (Whereas, we recall, *individuum est ineffabile.*) Does linguistic referentiality operate differently in novels?

This question cannot help but arise in Watt's argument; but it also cannot be answered in that argument. And yet, it had already been answered more than two decades before Watt's book, by way of the question: Exactly *what* does the language of novels refer to? Again I am talking about Bakhtin, who, in "Discourse in the Novel," argues that novels are unique in that the true ultimate referent of language in them is nothing but language itself.

The basic argument of that essay is that novels refer to language by enacting, within themselves, the constitutive "heteroglossia" of language, of all language. Bakhtin insists that

> at any given moment of its historical existence, language is heteroglot from top to bottom: it represents the co-existence of socio-ideological contradictions between the present and the past, between different socio-ideological groups in the present, between tendencies, schools, circles and so forth, all given a bodily form. These "languages" of heteroglossia intersect each other in a variety of ways, forming new socially typifying "languages." . . . It might even seem that the very word "language" loses all meaning in this process—for apparently there is no single plane on which all these "languages" might be juxtaposed to one another. (291)

This idea of the limitless divisibility of any identifiable "language," into a complex system of "ideologically" differentiated component languages, reminds us of Herder's production-oriented linguistic theory. ("In the strict metaphysical sense it is never possible for there to be a single language for man and woman, for father and son, for child and codger.") But how can language in this sense become a referent of language?

Such reference cannot be carried out adequately in the form of scientific description or explanation. Language in these forms claims by definition the quality of "unitary" or maximally unambiguous language, which Bakhtin says "is not something given but is always in essence posited— and at every moment of its linguistic life it is opposed to the realities of heteroglossia" (270). The more nearly a sub-language approaches the "unitary," the more ideologically one-sided it becomes; its own operation thus automatically denies the heteroglot and cannot possibly capture it as an object.

Does it follow that the problem is insoluble, that there is no "plane" upon which heteroglossia can be surveyed and understood? Immediately after the long passage quoted above, Bakhtin continues:

> In actual fact, however, there does exist a common plane that methodologically justifies our juxtaposing [the various languages of heteroglossia]: all languages of heteroglossia, whatever the principle underlying them and making each unique, are specific points of view on the world, forms for conceptualizing the world in words, specific world views, each characterized by its own objects, meanings and values. As such they all may be juxtaposed to one another, mutually supplement one another, contradict one another and be interrelated dialogically. As such they encounter one another and co-exist in the consciousness of real people—first and foremost, in the creative consciousness of people

who write novels. As such, these languages live a real life, they struggle and evolve in an environment of social heteroglossia. Therefore
they are all able to enter into the unitary plane of the novel, which can
unite in itself parodic stylizations of generic languages, various forms
of stylizations and illustrations of professional and period-bound languages, the languages of particular generations, of social dialects and
others (as occurs, for example, in the English comic novel). They may
all be drawn in by the novelist for the orchestration of his themes and
for the refracted (indirect) expression of his intentions and values. (291-
92)

Or as I have phrased it, novels refer to heteroglossia in the only way
possible, by *enacting* it.

Heteroglossia, in other words, cannot be shown or demonstrated,
even in novels; it does not have the structure of a demonstrable object. It
exists only insofar as it *happens;* and a novel's task is therefore to give that
happening the form of an enactment, to give it a profile, to bring it to the
fore in some manner. But as it unfolds in society at large, heteroglossia
has *no* profile; it is simply the underlying nature of all language. In truth,
it can never be adequately enacted or profiled anywhere but *in individual
human consciousness,* or as Bakhtin says, "in the consciousness of real
people."

Nor is this privileged relation between individual consciousness and
heteroglossia restricted to the case of novels. On the topic of what is
experienced as "internally persuasive" discourse, Bakhtin contends:

Such discourse is of decisive significance in the evolution of an individual consciousness: consciousness awakens to independent ideological
life precisely in a world of alien discourses surrounding it, and from
which it cannot initially separate itself; the process of distinguishing
between one's own and another's discourse, between one's own and
another's thought, is activated rather late in development. . . . In the
everyday rounds of our consciousness, the internally persuasive word
is half-ours and half-someone else's. Its creativity and productiveness
consist precisely in the fact that such a word awakens new and independent words, that it organizes masses of our words from within, and
does not remain in an isolated and static condition. It is not so much
interpreted by us as it is further, that is, freely, developed, applied to
new material, new conditions; it enters into interanimating relationships with new contexts. More than that, it enters into an intense interaction, a *struggle* with other internally persuasive discourses. (345-46)

In other words, the growth of *every* normal individual consciousness is an
enactment of heteroglossia. If it were not, how could we ever recognize
the phenomenon? I think it is not too much to say that in Bakhtin's
universe, individual consciousness may be *defined* as the original and
principal arena for socio-historical heteroglossia.

Therefore it is hardly surprising when Bakhtin asserts: "The speaking person and his discourse is . . . what makes a novel a novel, the thing responsible for the uniqueness of the genre" (333). This remains the case even where a fictional character merely acts without speaking; for "such action is always highlighted by ideology, is always harnessed to the character's discourse (even if that discourse is as yet only a potential discourse), is associated with an ideological motif and occupies a definite ideological position. The action and individual act of a character in a novel are essential in order to expose—as well as to test—his ideological position, his discourse" (334). Indeed, "the speaking person in the novel need not necessarily be incarnated in a character. A character is but one of the forms a speaking person might assume (although, true, the one that is most important). Heteroglot languages may also enter the novel in [various other stylistic or parodistic guises. But still,] the images of speaking persons, clothed in the specifics of a given society at a given point in history, show through behind them" (335-36). Again, the true ultimate referent in novels is language; but language in this sense is never separated from at least the implied operation of individual consciousness.

Thus, by way of Bakhtin, we have traveled a circle and found our way back to the theorem we inferred from Watt's terminology: that the referentiality of novels imposes upon its referent the shape of individual experience. In connection with Watt we took that referent as "reality"; in Bakhtin the same idea (also called "reality" in the essay "Epic and Novel") is unmasked as "language" or linguistic "heteroglossia" in the essay "Discourse in the Novel." But it comes to the same thing. The "languages of heteroglossia," in Bakhtin's view, in effect circumscribe reality itself, by being "forms for conceptualizing the world in words . . . each characterized by its own objects, meanings and values" (291-92). And the heteroglossia of novels, by way of a "verbal-ideological decentering" of language (370), *undoes* the historically imposed "hegemony of [supposedly unitary] language over the perception and conceptualization of reality" (369), *undoes* the operation of "language . . . conceived as a sacrosanct and solitary embodiment of meaning and truth" (370), and so in a strong sense makes possible for the first time the genuinely individual experience of an immediately encountered reality. Thus the question of why Bakhtin is content to discuss the novel's effect in literature is answered. By affecting literature, novels affect all language and languages, and so liberate reality itself in an individualized form that precisely language (in its institutionalized "unitary" pretensions) had heretofore suppressed.

And to come back to Watt: Can we make sense fully of his insistence on "the closeness with which . . . words correspond to their objects" in novels, or on "the immediacy and closeness of the text to what is being described," without working through an argument like Bakhtin's? Surely something must in some sense happen to objects themselves in the process of novels' bringing words "closer" to them. Otherwise, if objects were simply waiting to be described, the same closeness could have been achieved at any time in the past and in any literary form.

Watt does not insist on the same type or degree of theoretical penetration as Bakhtin. Indeed, it is probable that he deliberately avoids theory in any comparable mode. But much of the content and structure of Bakhtin's thought is present in his work nonetheless. Like Bakhtin, he understands that the imposition upon reality of the form of individual experience is essentially a *negative* achievement, compassed not by the discovery of new verbal techniques but by the elimination of old verbal habits— of poetic or rhetorical devices by which language had earlier aimed (in Bakhtin's term) at a "unitary" version of itself. For Watt, the centralness of individual experience in a text is measured by readers' "identification" with characters, which novels promote by being "inherently *devoid* of the elements [of earlier literature] which had restricted identification" (202, my emphasis). Even the print medium has an unintended function in this respect. "The mechanically produced and therefore identical letters set with absolute uniformity on the page are, of course, much more impersonal than any manuscript, but at the same time they can be read much more automatically: ceasing to be conscious of the printed page before our eyes we surrender ourselves entirely to the world of illusion which the printed novel describes"(198). Again, it is a *lack*—here the lack of a personal presence in the medium—that promotes individualistic realism in novels.

In fact, there is one positive gap in Bakhtin's historical system that we can fill for him, practically in his own terms, by using Watt. The best Bakhtin can do with Richardson is lump him together with Rousseau and La Fayette as a writer of "Sentimental psychological novels," in which "conversational language . . . is still ordered and subjected to norms from the point of view of 'literariness'" and so "becomes a unitary language for the direct expression of authorial intentions" (396-97). What happens then is:

> In place of one conventionality . . . Sentimentalism creates another— and one similarly abstract, serving to draw attention away from other aspects of reality. A discourse made respectable by Sentimental pathos, one that attempts to replace the brute discourse of life, inevitably ends up in the same hopeless dialogic conflict with the actual heteroglossia of life, in the same unresolvable dialogized misunderstanding characteristic of the "respectable" discourse of *Amadis,* as present in the situations and dialogues of *Don Quixote.* (398)

Thus "Richardsonian language" (398, note) becomes a novelistic sidetrack, relegated to only one position vis-à-vis the many-sidedness of such true Cervanteans as "Fielding, Smollett and Sterne."

Watt approaches Richardson differently, by starting with the phenomenon of urbanization in London, which turns out to mean almost exactly what Bakhtin means by heteroglossia (minus the linguistic emphasis), in that "the citizen of eighteenth-century London had a horizon that was in many ways like that of modern urban man. The streets and places of resort in the various quarters of the town presented an infinite variety of ways of life, ways of life that anyone could observe, and yet for the most part utterly alien to any one individual's personal experience" (179). Especially important, with regard to "personal relationships," is "the fact that [that citizen] belongs to many social groups—work, worship, home, leisure—but no single person knows him in all his roles, and nor does he know anyone else in all theirs" (185). Thus individual consciousness, as in Bakhtin, is a mirror of heteroglossia; and Watt's assertion that "the world of the novel is essentially the world of the modern city" (185) differs from what Bakhtin might have said in not much more than terminology.

But Richardson's art, according to Watt, is characterized by a "recoil from this [urban] environment" (186), a recoil made possible by the fact that "there was a way out [of the city]: urbanisation provided its own antidote, the suburb, which offered an escape from the thronged streets, and whose very different mode of life symbolised the difference between the multifarious but casual relationships depicted in Defoe's novels and the fewer but more intense and introverted ones which Richardson portrayed" (186). And if we agree with Watt that the suburb is an integral component of urbanization, then it follows that what Bakhtin calls Richardson's "sentimental" limitedness in truth belongs inherently to the heteroglossia from which it "recoils," hence that that heteroglossia is as present as a force in Richardson (if differently oriented) as it is in the more obviously Cervantean novelists Bakhtin prefers. Precisely Bakhtin's argument would thus gain in simplicity, integrity, and comprehensiveness.

LIVING IN LANGUAGE

The main problem novels confront us with is not *what to say* about them, or about particular instances, but *how to talk about them*: given the unique historical situation of the type and its reliance on negative operations in language. Again: (1) The way novels emerge in history makes it unlikely that anything like a genre-idea can be applied to the form. But (2) we cannot simply dispense with the idea of *the* novel. We would sacrifice the historical insights of a Watt, the linguistic insights of a Bakhtin, and the very possibility of reasonable general statements about novels. Still, (3) even if we retain the idea of *the* novel and the ability to make general statements about novels, we must recognize that in the absence of a genre-idea, none of such statements can ever be considered authoritative. Hence (4) the importance of the question of *how to talk* about novels. And finally, (5) an answer to this question is suggested by the theorem with which we attempted to summarize the intersection of Watt's thought with Bakhtin's: that the operation of language in novels has the character of reference (as opposed to Saussurean signification), but tends to impose on its referent the shape of individual experience.

This theorem is shown to be a reasonable general statement by the discussion of actual novels in Bakhtin's essays and Watt's book—and in plenty of other critical writing. But it cannot be taken as a general statement about *the* novel. For the form such a statement would have to take— that language in *the* novel imposes on its referent the shape of individual experience—would require that there be a single intelligible shape to individual experience, which is nonsense. The very idea of individual, "ineffable" experience excludes such a possibility. Even if the statement were true of every novel ever written (and for every reader), it would still be true only case by case, in a limitless number of unaccountably different ways, and could not be considered true of *the* novel. Our theorem is therefore a reasonable statement that denies itself logically the possibility of becoming authoritative. It is thus at least a possible model for how to talk about novels.

But it is also more than that. It is the logical root of an important paradox, the single governing historical paradox that produces the system of paradoxes described by Watt as follows:

> The development of the novel's concentration on private experience and personal relationships is associated with a series of paradoxes. It is paradoxical that the most powerful vicarious identification of readers with the feelings of fictional characters that literature had seen should have been produced by exploiting the qualities of print, the most impersonal, objective and public of the media of communication. It is further paradoxical that the process of urbanisation should, in the suburb, have led to a way of life that was more secluded and less social than ever before, and, at the same time, helped to bring about a literary form which was less concerned with the public and more with the private side of life than any previous one. And finally, it is also paradoxical that these two tendencies should have combined to assist the most apparently realistic of literary genres to become capable of a more thorough subversion of psychological and social reality than any previous one. (206)

The idea of a "subversion of psychological and social reality" refers to Madame de Staël's judgment on the "evil" of novels: that they pre-empt our emotional existence and put us in the condition of experiencing even our own personal feeling as if it were the memory of reading.[6]

The governing paradox I have in mind unfolds as follows. Novels are realistic by using language referentially—it being understood that reference associates the word with an extra-linguistic reality, whereas signification takes place entirely within a universe of signs, or within a "verbal universe."[7] But the reality that language in novels refers to is not simply out there waiting to be referred to. It is created, or liberated—in the form of "ineffable" (extra-linguistic) individual experience—by a *negative* operation of language. (If it were generated by a positive linguistic operation, then the process would be signification, not reference.) Bakhtin's account of this negative operation is the best I know of: that language in novels simply learns how to stop suppressing "poetically" its own actual and inherent heteroglossia.

It is entirely crucial to understand that when we are talking about novels (plural), we must regard the referential operation of language in them as negative. With respect to a particular novel, one can never say that device X produces (or evokes or describes) reality Y. Realistic authors do employ verbal devices that have positive effects. But the reality ultimately referred to—which, as individual experience, lies beyond the formative power of language—is never itself one of those effects. Bakhtin spends much time analyzing "hybrid" linguistic constructions in *Little Dorrit* (302-308), constructions which are obviously heteroglot in character. But it would be nonsense to assert that Dickens thus produces or generates heteroglossia. What he does is set up a situation in which the actuality of heteroglossia is liberated, given room to announce itself.

But do these considerations point in the direction of a reasonable statement about *the* novel? Here the paradox arises. *What* the reality is that is liberated in novels by a negative operation of language can never be pinned down and must be assumed to vary unaccountably from novel to novel. But to say simply *that* (in novels) an operation of language liberates or sponsors an experience that lies beyond the formative range of language itself—as long as we do not attempt to specify that experience—is to make a reasonable statement (whether valid or not) that is applicable to all novels in the same way, hence a statement about *the* novel. And in its form (not in its concrete application) this statement can reasonably be taken to suggest that even our brute individual experience, at its most inexpressible, may for all we know unfold under the sponsorship or in the bosom of language.

By linguistic operations (whether understood as authorial devices or as consequences of the development of language in history), novels give us our own real individualized life. Therefore *the* novel, as an institution, embodies the message that real life, all of it, may possibly be regarded as a product of linguistic operations, that we may in truth be living our real lives inside the domain of language. It is not required by this paradox that the novel as an institution demonstrate the *actual* "hegemony of language" in our individual experience. The mere raising of such hegemony as a possibility already flatly contradicts the realistic, "ineffable," extra-linguistic experience we expect from every particular novel. The paradox here is exactly parallel to the one suggested by Mme. de Staël. Each individual novel releases powerful individual emotions in me, *my own* emotions, whence the institution of the novel gives me the impression that for all I know, my own spontaneous emotions all already exist in written form. Novels give us real individual life, beyond the generalizing force of language; but the novel as an institution takes it away again, by re-establishing the hegemony of language at least as a philosophical possibility.

This paradox, finally, helps explain the curious history of the novel. In the seventeenth and eighteenth centuries, novels not only represent a new genre, but are known to do so; and this knowledge gives rise to self-conscious experiments whose authors attempt to occupy simultaneously the perspective of the individual work and that of the supposed genre. But as the nature of the paradox emerges more clearly—the intractable opposition between novels and the institution of the novel—novelists are induced to take sides, to come down in favor of the particular and in opposition to the general or generic. Thus the maximally realistic nineteenth-century novel is born. Of course this realistic project, the attempt to free reality from an inherently conservative web of linguistic structures, is doomed to fail. The more perfectly realistic any particular novel is, the more it helps forge the philosophical link, on the level of *the* novel, between reality and language. Precisely this is the paradox.

FORMS OF THE PARADOX

The paradox of novels and the novel is clearly analogous to the paradox of Kantian and especially Schillerian aesthetics, which promises us a restoration of our own immediate individual experience but also nullifies its own aim simply by being the deliberate theoretical initiative that it inescapably was. My own inclination would be to argue that that relation is more than just an analogy, that the paradox of the nineteenth-century novel is a direct continuation of the history of eighteenth-century aesthetics. But even with the support of the analogical relation to Schiller and Mme. de Staël's contemporary testimony, the above argument on the historical operation of the novel as an institution would still be in danger of evaporating into mere speculation if it did not also reveal deep affinities with another clear-cut tendency in the intellectual nineteenth century, the tendency in linguistically oriented philosophy that eventually culminates in what the twentieth century calls its "linguistic turn."

I have pointed out that many contemporary readers, not all of them antagonistic, perceived a failure on Kant's part to deal with the linguistic aspect of his epistemological concerns: Hamann, Herder, Klopstock, Goethe, Schleiermacher are instances. Such a response is not surprising toward the end of an eighteenth century where, especially in France and Germany, much philosophical attention had been paid to questions of the origin and operation of language: Maupertuis, Condillac, Rousseau belong here, in addition to the Germans. Moreover, in the eighteenth and then increasingly in the nineteenth century, the scientific study of language was also coming into its own, especially in the fields of historical and comparative linguistics. And this combination of philosophical interest with a growing appreciation for the complexity and diversity of linguistic phenomena was bound to bring forth a certain amount of experimentation with the idea of language as a shaping or determining factor in experience, indeed in reality itself.

One manifestation of this tendency has been called "linguistic relativism" since the Sapir-Whorf controversies. It is the doctrine that the world I live in is shaped deeply by the particular language I happen to speak, that therefore speakers of widely different languages can be said to experience markedly different realities. With respect to late eighteenth- and early nineteenth-century thought, this doctrine has been associated with Wilhelm von Humboldt (more or less justly, I think), with Romanticism in general (very vaguely), and with Hamann and Herder (unjustly). The doctrine, in any case, is unsound. Apart from the obvious objections having to do with bilingualism—are Conrad and Nabokov somehow not quite native users of English? does Montaigne's claim to be more comfortable in Latin disqualify him as a native user of French?—linguistic relativism cannot ever deal adequately with the question of what precisely we mean by *a* "language." This would be Bakhtin's objection, and probably also that of the unlimitedly polyglot Hamann. As soon as we recognize that every language is divisible into an undeterminable number of sub-languages, we are constrained logically to pursue the relativist argument down to the level of each individual's personal idiolect—if not down to the idiolect spoken by each individual in a particular year or month or day—where it becomes nonsense. Herder says, "In the strict metaphysical sense it is never possible for there to be a single language for man and woman, for father and son, for child and codger." And Goethe, despite his friendship with Humboldt, carries out a parallel refutation of linguistic relativism in his discussion of translation.[8]

But it is not as easy to refute a much stronger form of linguistic determinism: the idea that our whole existence, including our most intimate experience as individuals, unfolds in the domain of language as such, regardless of which particular languages we use.[9] To be sure, it is not easy to find instances where this doctrine is directly articulated and defended, mainly because of problems in formulation. (What could I say if I were asked exactly what I mean by "the domain of language as such"?) But it is hard to deny that Georg Christoph Lichtenberg (who studiously avoids doctrinal formulation) and Herder (in his treatise on the origin of language) would have had to agree with some version of generalized linguistic determinism if pushed. And much of the early opposition to Kant's *Critiques* boils down to the idea that the concept of "language," rather than the notion of "understanding," should have been used to describe the mental or pre-mental operation by which experience is constituted as a possibility.

Then, toward the end of the nineteenth century and on into the twentieth, there is a strong reaction, as if linguistic determinism had been much more prevalent in recent European thought than in fact it was, and had represented an unworthy capitulation of serious thinking vis-à-vis its own verbal medium. Many of Nietzsche's pronouncements, both early and late, belong here, as does the "critique of language" carried out by Fritz Mauthner, plus the phenomena grouped together as a "language crisis" in German literary studies or as a poetic "revolution" by Julia Kristeva. Fredric Jameson's remarkable study of formalism and structuralism, *The Prison-House of Language,* locates the whole controversy in the twentieth century. And feminist thought seeks ways of countering an intrinsic masculine bias in language on all levels.

Even the analytic philosophers of the "linguistic turn" reflect the same general tendency—although the object of their criticism is perhaps less the corruption of thought by language than the corruption of language by what poses as thought. These critical followers of Wittgenstein are far too careful with words to be caught characterizing their activity as a doctrinal debate. But if you read through the collection of essays published by Richard Rorty as *The Linguistic Turn,* you will find it hard not to get the impression of a deep ambivalence, the simultaneous embracing and resisting of a tendency of linguistic questions to hog the space of philosophy.[10]

Thus it makes a certain amount of sense to say that the twentieth century acts as if the nineteenth had been a hotbed of linguistic determinism. And if we ask what, in the actual nineteenth century, can have provoked such a response, certainly much of our answer will have to do with the realistic novel—or rather with the paradoxical novelistic phenomenon as a whole, which comes down strongly on both sides of the issue. Particular novels, one at a time, carry out negative operations in language that liberate innumerable versions of "reality"—liberate them perhaps already from what Jameson (speaking of the twentieth century) calls "the concrete character of the social life of the so-called advanced countries today, which offer the spectacle of . . . a world saturated with messages and information, whose intricate commodity network may be seen as the very prototype of a system of signs" (viii-ix). But precisely the resulting abstract possibility of a reality dependent for its existence on operations in language (of whatever type) tends to re-establish Jameson's "systematized and disembodied nightmare" (ix) of a world entirely subject to linguistic order.

The nineteenth-century novel therefore fills an apparent gap in the history of linguistic philosophy; and the point I am principally concerned to make is that it fills a similar gap in the history of aesthetics. The difference is that in both the eighteenth and the twentieth century, linguistically oriented philosophy calls its favored object by the same name, "language," whereas I have argued that philosophical aesthetics (which does not always call itself that even in the early phase) goes by the name "hermeneutics" in its later incarnations. But the novelistic phenomenon, at both ends of itself, fits neatly into the development I am describing, and so helps mark it as a cohesive development.

The analogy between the novelistic paradox and the paradox of Kantian-Schillerian aesthetics is obvious. And for my own part, I find it hard to imagine that Dilthey, at the end of the nineteenth century, could have conceived the enormous paradox of *Geisteswissenschaften* without the support of a culture permeated by the paradox of novels and the novel. Dilthey not only understands that *individuum est ineffabile;* he takes this sentence as a constant personal motto. Yet he also insists that the most perfect and powerful instances of individuality are disclosed to us in language. How can these two positions possibly constitute a paradox, not simply a flat contradiction? How can the tension between them be sustained long enough to produce the huge metaphysical system of universal individuation which is meant to mediate it, if not with the aid of *the* novel and its suggestion of the possibility of completely individualized experience in the medium of language? Nor is the case of Heidegger much different, except that the idea of being "on the way to language" reflects a somewhat clearer recognition of the millennial dimension in its paradoxical basis.

I do not claim that these considerations complete my historical argument. They are intended only to show the direction in which the argument must now proceed. The most important piece of unfinished business is to show how the novelistic paradox operates specifically to carry forward a tradition of secular millennialism.

But at least one important connection with the ultimate form of secular millennialism, in twentieth-century totalitarian movements, can be shown even now. One of Arendt's most striking and significant points about society under totalitarianism is that it is a "mass" society composed, paradoxically, of "atomized" individuals:

> that highly cultured people were particularly attracted to mass movements and that, generally, highly differentiated individualism and sophistication did not prevent, indeed sometimes encouraged, the self-abandonment into the mass for which mass movements provided. . . . Social atomization and extreme individualization preceded the mass movements which, much more easily and earlier than they did the sociable, nonindividualistic members of the traditional parties, attracted the completely unorganized, the typical "nonjoiners" who for individualistic reasons always had refused to recognize social links or obligations.[11]

How is this paradox different from the one that characterizes the situation of a novel reader, who receives experience in a more thoroughly individualized form than even real life can offer, yet precisely as a consequence of that experience finds him- and herself engulfed in a quasi-linguistic medium that anticipates and so poisons all possible privacy?

NOTES

1. For both of these cases, see chap. 6, n17.

2. See Michael Paul Rogin, *Ronald Reagan, the Movie: and Other Episodes in Political Demonology* (Berkeley, 1987).

3. Watt, 13, 15, 22, 28-30. See chap. 4, n11.

4. *The Dialogic Imagination: Four Essays by M. M. Bakhtin*, ed. Michael Holquist (Austin, 1981), 7.

5. For an example of how the "sound" of language actually *changes*, in mid-career, with the coming of the age of the novel, see the argument on two fundamentally incommensurable readings of Goethe's poem "Auf dem See" in my *Dark Side of Literacy*, 47-57. Reference in chap. 4, n6.

6. Madame de Staël is quoted by Watt (205-6) from her *Œuvrescomplètes*, 17 vols. (Paris: Treuttel et Würtz, 1820 ff.), 11:84. The passage in question comes from pt. 2, chap. 28 ("Des Romans") of *De l'Allemagne*. For a more modern edition, see Mme. de Staël, *De l'Allemagne*, ed. La comtesse Jean de Pange, 5 vol. (Paris, 1958-1960), 3:245.

7. The idea of such a "verbal universe" is prominent not only in semiotics, but also in mainstream literary criticism, e.g. in Northrop Frye, *Anatomy of Criticism: Four Essays* (New York: Atheneum, 1966; orig. 1957), 350, from whom I quote the phrase.

8. See my essay "Histrionic Nationality: Implications of the Verse in *Faust*," *Goethe Yearbook*, 17 (2010), 21-30. As far as I can see, the "empirical" evidence that has been adduced in favor of linguistic relativism concerns experience on a level (e.g. names for colors) much too easily relearnable to make any difference.

9. I will speak here of "linguistic determinism," although this is not a term in general use. Jörn Albrecht, "Friedrich Nietzsche und das 'sprachliche Relativitätsprinzip,'" *Nietzsche-Studien*, 8 (1979), 225-44, parodies Einstein (as Whorf had before him) and differentiates between a "general" and a "special" linguistic "relativism" (227-28). But in the case of his "general" linguistic relativism, which means the dependence of thought, or indeed of all experience, on language as such, one is tempted to ask: relative to what? My term is not completely satisfactory, but I think it makes a bit more sense.

10. In the case of Nietzsche, we think of the early unpublished essay "Ueber Wahrheit und Lüge im aussermoralischen Sinne," and of the later idea of our standing "unter der Verführung der Sprache (und der in ihr versteinerten Grundirrthümer der Vernunft)," in *Zur Genealogie der Moral*, 1.13. In no. 20 of *Jenseits von Gut und Böse*, Nietzsche's criticism perhaps inclines more toward the Whorfian. Other references in the two foregoing paragraphs are to: Fritz Mauthner, *Beiträge zu einer Kritik der Sprache*, 3 vols., 3rd ed. (Hamburg, 1923; orig. 1906); Julia Kristeva, *La Révolution du langage poétique* (Paris, 1974); Richard Rorty, ed., *The Linguistic Turn: Recent Essays in Philosophical Method* (Chicago, 1967); and Fredric Jameson, *The Prison-House of Language: A Critical Account of Structuralism and Russian Formalism* (Princeton, 1972). Jameson gets his main title from a quotation that he uses as an epigraph and attributes to "Nietzsche." I cannot find that passage anywhere in Nietzsche's works or fragments or letters.

11. Hannah Arendt, *The Origins of Totalitarianism*, 316-17. See chap. 1, n4, for the reference.

EIGHT

The Millennial Novel and Its Unmasking

The main purpose of this book as a whole is to show the existence of a tradition of secular millennialism that begins in eighteenth-century aesthetics and ends in twentieth-century totalitarianism. In the previous chapter, I put together what I think will serve as a scaffolding for the argument by showing how the paradox of the realistic novel is parallel to the paradox of early aesthetics and to comparable paradoxes in the hermeneutics of Dilthey and Heidegger. But a tradition has not yet been demonstrated. The connection between the nineteenth-century novel and twentieth-century hermeneutics is perhaps especially shaky—although I still cannot imagine how Dilthey and Heidegger (and Gadamer after them) could have operated so close to the precipice of simple absurdity without feeling supported by a whole civilization of paradox. But the inclusion of hermeneutics in my historical scheme is supported by Dilthey's direct eighteenth-century connection in Kant and Schleiermacher. And the connection with hermeneutics is itself, in the end, only an ancillary point, providing background and context for the relation between novelistic society and totalitarianism. The important thing is to show that *the* novel, as an institution, is an instance of secular millennialism, for the sake of the connection with Hannah Arendt's showing that secular millennialism is the true character of totalitarian movements. The idea of a secular millennialist tradition is my attempt to go beyond Arendt by suggesting where the millennial tendency in totalitarianism came from.

THE STRUCTURE OF CONSCIOUSNESS AS A CONCEPT

In the last chapter I suggested the theorem that language in novels operates by reference, but in such a way as to impose on its referent the form of individual experience. This idea connects Watt's thought with Bakhtin's in interesting ways, and it implies the useful notion of a negative operation in language. But it is not itself conceptually anchored until we have formed a better idea of what we mean by "individual experience." Nor does it help much to invoke the concept of "consciousness," which only adds a second vague term to the equation. In connection with Bakhtin I suggested that individual consciousness might be *defined* as "the original and principal arena for socio-historical heteroglossia." I continue to be attracted to this idea, which avoids the tautologies that bedevil any attempt at a psychological definition. But it is not useful as a starting point.

Still, the concept of consciousness cannot be avoided in an analysis of the notion of experience; and I propose now to treat that concept not as the sign for a fact, but *as a concept.* Nor will I pay much attention to the history of the concept, interesting and significant as that history may be for understanding nineteenth-century thought as a whole.[1] What counts for the study of the novel in its millennial dimension is the *structure* of the concept of consciousness. And the best starting point seems to me Freud's discussion of consciousness in *The Ego and the Id:*

> "Being conscious" is in the first place a purely descriptive term, resting on perception of the most immediate and certain character. Experience goes on to show that a psychical element (for instance, an idea) is not as a rule conscious for a protracted length of time. On the contrary, a state of consciousness is characteristically very transitory; an idea that is conscious now is no longer so a moment later, although it can become so again under certain conditions that are easily brought about. In the interval the idea was—we do not know what. We can say that it was *latent,* and by this we mean that it was *capable of becoming conscious* at any time. Or, if we say that it was *unconscious,* we shall also be giving a correct description of it.[2]

That I am conscious is unquestionably a fact. But even without going into the question of gradations in how strongly one is conscious, Freud insists that the concept of a condition of conscious*ness* (as an entity cohesive enough to be named) is indefinable.

In itself this thought is not particularly profound. But it has interesting consequences, especially when the notion of consciousness is used outside the realm of psychology. Dorrit Cohn, in a book we will come back to below, describes her subject matter as "Narrative Modes for Presenting Consciousness in Fiction"; and in the course of her study she uses a number of different verbs—including "present," "represent," "portray"—to describe what narrative does with respect to consciousness. That there is always a certain amount of evasiveness here, however, appears at the very beginning, where she speaks twice of "mimesis of consciousness." For she borrows the term "mimesis" from Käte Hamburger with the proviso that it be "understood as representation, not as imitation."[3] Evidently the idea of imitation has to be avoided, since it would imply that consciousness is out there as an object to be imitated, an object with which imitations might be compared in respect of accuracy. But then how does the term "representation" help matters? How does "representation" *not* need an object?

Freud asserts not merely that consciousness is indefinable, but that it is uniquely so. The word is used in psychoanalytic theory—and *must* be used, "for the property of being conscious or not is in the last resort our one beacon-light in the darkness of depth-psychology" (*SE*, 19:18; *GW*, 13:245). But it is also a word that has no meaning in that theory's systematic view of psychical "dynamics" (*SE*, 19:14; *GW*, 13:240). (In particular, "the attribute of being conscious, which is the only characteristic of psychical processes that is directly presented to us, is in no way suited to serve as a criterion for the differentiation of systems" [*SE*, 14:192; *GW*, 10:291].) The concept of the "unconscious," by contrast, has a clear meaning in psychoanalytic theory, because it is derived from the observation-based doctrine of repression (*SE*, 19:15; *GW*, 13:241). And if we ask after the complementary concept, the concept of everything psychical that is *not* unconscious, Freud answers with the concept of the *preconscious*. The differentiation is tricky here. The boundary between the unconscious and the preconscious is permeable; and even within the preconscious there are mechanisms of censorship that prevent certain material from becoming conscious and so keep us from defining the preconscious simply as the whole of what can readily become conscious (see *SE*, 14:190-95; *GW*, 10:288-94). But still, the preconscious has the quality of a "system" in psychical dynamics, whereas "consciousness"—despite the undeniability of "being conscious" as a phenomenon and an experience—may for all we know be merely a word to which nothing but a disorganized plurality of scattered instances corresponds. In other words, there may be no justification for the *noun* "consciousness."[4]

Freud develops this point, and clarifies the quality of the unconscious *(Ucs.)* and the preconscious *(Pcs.)* as systems, when he asserts

> that the real difference between a *Ucs.* and a *Pcs.* idea (thought) consists in this: that the former is carried out on some material which remains unknown, whereas the latter (the *Pcs.*) is in addition brought into contact with word-presentations. This is the first attempt to indicate distinguishing marks for the two systems, the *Pcs.* and the *Ucs.*, other than their relation to consciousness. The question, "How does a thing become conscious?" would thus be more advantageously stated: "How does a thing become preconscious?" And the answer would be:

"Through becoming connected with the word-presentations corresponding to it."(*SE*, 19:20; *GW*, 13:247)

We must be careful not to ask too much of this idea. Above all, Freud is
not espousing even a limited form of linguistic determinism. When he
speaks of "Wortvorstellungen" — "word-presentations," but perhaps better translated as "word-ideas" — he is not referring to those potent verbal
entities that can create a whole world-view for Whorf and form the very
"house of being" for Heidegger. Words are here simply a particular class
of objects; and like other objects, they are present in the mind in the form
of "residues of memories [which] were at one time perceptions, and like
all mnemic residues . . . can become conscious again" (*SE*, 19:20; *GW*,
13:247).

It is crucial to Freud's argument that words have this object-quality —
as opposed to a strictly semiotic quality, an opening into the world as a
universe of signs. "Clinical experience," we are told, makes necessary the
conclusion that the only path into consciousness — or for thoughts and
ideas, into the preconscious — is by way of "the system *Pcpt.*" (*SE*, 19:22;
GW, 13:249-50), the system by which the mind appropriates external perceptions. But thoughts and ideas as such, as strictly internal entities, do
not have any quality that can be processed directly by the system *Pcpt.* —
unless that quality be supplied by their verbal associations, which take
the form of remembered perceptions, primarily acoustic ones (*SE*, 19:20;
GW, 13:248).

> The part played by word-presentations now becomes perfectly clear.
> By their interposition internal thought-processes are made into percep-
> tions. It is as if an attempt were being made to prove the theorem that
> all knowledge has its origin in external perception. When a hyperca-
> thexis of the process of thinking takes place, thoughts are *actually* per-
> ceived — as if they came from without — and are consequently held to be
> true. (*SE*, 19:23; *GW*, 13:250; translation modified)

It is interesting that the tone of this paragraph — which suggests a sudden
revelation breaking in on the speaker as if from outside — is a direct dra-
matization of its content. Freud does this sort of thing more often than
one might expect.

But if he deliberately avoids the theoretical route (metaphysical or
anthropological), then on what grounds does Freud assert, in the first
place, that an association with words is needed before thought can enter
the preconscious? Again the answer is: clinical experience. In this case the
experience in question had been described in detail in a 1915 essay, "The
Unconscious," to which I have already referred above. A long discussion
of various researchers' work on schizophrenia, especially on the way
schizophrenics use language (*SE*, 14:196-201; *GW*, 10:294-300), leads to
the conclusion that it is imprecise to speak of a "conscious presentation
[idea] of the object," that this notion "can now be split up into the presen-

tation of the *word* and the presentation of the *thing*" [*Wortvorstellung, Sachvorstellung*] (*SE*, 14:201; *GW*, 10:300). The crucial point about the difference between the systems *Ucs.* And *Pcs.* then follows: "The system *Ucs.* contains the thing-cathexes of the objects, the first and true object-cathexes; the system *Pcs.* comes about by this thing-presentation being hypercathected through being linked to the word-presentations corresponding to it"(*SE*, 14:201-2; *GW*, 10:300). One can object to the chain of reasoning by which these conclusions are derived from the available data. But my point concerns only the *type* of reasoning being employed. Freud understands, as well as anybody, that words are things of a special kind, that their very nature creates "relations" among them (semantic, conceptual, etymological, paradigmatic, potentially syntagmatic), relations that make up the structures we experience as conscious thought (*SE*, 19:21; *GW*, 13:248). But he scrupulously avoids using this theoretical point in the reasoning by which he shows the distinctive verbal component of the *Pcs.*

The importance of Freud's insistence on inductive argument is twofold. In the first place, "clinical experience" is still experience—though of a specially structured sort. If a fact can be derived from clinical experience, therefore, there is at least a chance that people in general can form a sense of that fact in their own personal experience. The theory that is the sum total of such derivations thus lies much closer to the domain of common sense than does, for instance, the philosophical theory of linguistic determinism, which by definition—since it holds that *all* experience is linguistically saturated—can never be supported by any specific empirical evidence.

And in the second place, the "links" between thing-ideas and word-ideas that give content to the *Pcs.* are not linguistically but *personally* determined. (Otherwise the theory would become linguistic determinism.) The words involved are not, for example, simply the names of the things. The link between a thing (or its idea or memory residue) and a word or group of words depends solely upon whether the verbal material—in *my* unique psychic development—happens to receive a "hypercathexis," a supplementary investment of the psychic energy that supports the idea or memory in question. Thus, in the Freudian theory, the possibility of what I called in the previous chapter a *negative* operation of language remains open, a possibility that is excluded by linguistic determinism in any form. In Heidegger's view, for example—as we saw specifically in his insistence on the "One" conversation to which we all belong by agreement—language cannot operate otherwise than positively, because its very nature is, precisely, to posit.

It is, in sum, as if Freud's idea of consciousness were aimed at explaining the role of consciousness in realistic novels. The possibility of a verbal communication of consciousness—as it floats or flickers atop the verbally conditioned *Pcs.*—is located in a region of experience that many readers might be expected to share; and the need, in realistic novels, for a negative operation of language, is accommodated at least in principle. To put it less fancifully: Even without corroboration from his own lost essay on "Consciousness" (see *SE*, 14:105-107), Freud's thinking documents the presence, in late nineteenth- and twentieth-century civilization, of an idea of consciousness that is at least strongly consonant with novelistic practice—and perhaps even derived from that practice.

This consonance, finally, appears even more strongly if we consider the whole structure of consciousness as a concept. That structure has two main elements: first, we know that there is a special relation between consciousness and language (mediated for Freud by the *Pcs.*); and second, we know that beyond our vague sense of that special relation, consciousness is strictly indefinable—however constant and vivid our experience of "being conscious" may seem. But the indefinability of consciousness, looked at the other way round, implies infinite room for speculation on *possible* constructions of consciousness—especially constructions carried out in a verbal medium. In other words, the number of possible verbal experiments by which consciousness might at least plausibly be represented is limitless. Which brings us back to the paradox of the realistic novel. Consciousness (like reality) is represented in only one novel (one experiment) at a time; and no controlling mechanism exists that might coordinate or compare all such experiments. But still, *the* novel—as an institution, harking back to what used to be the institution of poetic genres—is inexorably generalized into existence, and brings with it perhaps the whole idea of consciousness as a unitary phenomenon. Indeed the very process of representation—by making available in my conscious experience the conscious experience of at least one other person—is itself already an irrevocable generalizing move, pointing toward "consciousness" as such.

THE INVENTION OF CONSCIOUSNESS

It is not unreasonable to suggest, therefore, that consciousness is invented in the eighteenth and nineteenth centuries, as part of the genesis of the realistic novel. My own account of this process works backward from an analysis, developed by Freud, of the fully evolved concept of consciousness. It is supported by an account of the "discovery" of consciousness in Marshall Brown's book *Preromanticism,* an account that works in the opposite direction, beginning with eighteenth-century British poetry and reaching its first culmination in the *Critique of Pure Reason.* Brown suggests that "in Gray and Collins consciousness begins to be separated from experience. When the separation is completed by the joining of the pure forms of space and time, consciousness becomes generalized into an abstracted reverie, disembodied and out of touch with the world of sensation."[5] In both accounts Kant occupies a central position, and is perhaps the hinge that connects them. In the account I have offered, focused on the structure of the concept of consciousness, it is clear that that structure is exactly analogous not only to the paradox of the novel, but also to Kant's "millennialist invention" in the notion of transcendental apperception: the idea that what makes me uniquely myself (parallel to the strictly singular condition of "being conscious" as I experience it) is at the same time a transcendental event, the same basic event for every individual (thus parallel to the supposed general phenomenon of "consciousness"). And this pattern of analogy is reinforced if we recognize that the principal usefulness of an invention of consciousness is likely to be the same as that of both the novel and the invention of transcendental apperception: to deal with the newly emergent problem of communication, the problem that is stamped everywhere on the pre-history and birth of aesthetics.

I am fairly certain that Dorrit Cohn would not accept the idea that consciousness is invented in the genesis of the modern novel. But her own work nevertheless provides a good deal of support for that idea, especially the book that established her position in the field of narratology, *Transparent Minds*. In its opening pages she puts together an imposing list of major figures who all, in one way or another, recognize "the interdependence of narrative realism and the mimesis of consciousness" (8), hence the unique centralness of representation of consciousness in the novel. That list includes, in the order in which they are mentioned: Sterne, Proust, E. M. Forster, Thomas Mann, Ortega y Gasset, Stendhal, Henry James, Käte Hamburger, Erich Kahler, Virginia Woolf, Friedrich von Blanckenburg, Schopenhauer, Nathalie Sarraute, Leon Edel, David Daiches, Georg Lukács, Erich Auerbach, Wolfgang Kayser—"and many more voices could be cited" (9), says Cohn. Supposing this perception is correct, how could we possibly explain such an historically sudden attention to the phenomenon of consciousness, if we were to assume that the phenomenon itself had always been there waiting to be represented?

Or we might consider the structure of Cohn's work. She adopts what she calls a "typological approach to the presentation of consciousness in fiction" (9-10); and the system of types and subtypes she establishes is perspicuous, reasonable, and comprehensive. But when one gets down to the level of individual examples—which she treats, in general, without any systematic bias—it seems that the system does not control the data it refers to. The differences among instances in any one rubric are frequently much more fundamental than any similarities or parallels. For example, the discussion of "quoted monologue" includes the one section I have noticed where Cohn, in spite of her earlier reticence, uses the concept of imitation.

> Unlike fictional dialogue, which imitates a readily observable aspect of human behavior, fictional monologue purports to imitate a concealed

linguistic activity whose very existence cannot be objectively attested. This does not mean, however, that inner language is purely imaginary; writers and readers alike know it exists, even though they have heard it spoken only by their own inner voices. . . . The phenomenon that interior monologue imitates is . . . quite simply the mental activity psychologists call interior language, inner speech, or, more learnedly, endophasy. (77-78)

She then quotes the French psychologist Victor Egger who in 1881 had already associated this "phenomenon" with novelistic practice. Here, if anywhere, we should probably expect the instances of "imitation" to fit neatly into their category.

But they do not. Cohn continues by citing examples of internally mendacious and internally revelatory monologues, and summarizes: "Between the lies by which a character lives and the truths by which he dies or is revived quoted monologues run the gamut, often within a single work, and the degree of their authenticity is not always easy to determine" (82). Even the argument that at least relative authenticity is assured where inner monologue is contrasted with simultaneous outer dialogue concludes with the discussion of a "scene [that] points up that language for oneself, caught between a threatening world within and a threatening world without, is an all too precarious refuge from both worlds" (84). And all this, finally, before Cohn even begins on the matter of quoted monologues (especially in *Ulysses*) that present not organized thought but "undirected thinking patterns" (84). The category thus tends to become irrelevant with respect to the variety and complexity of examples. We have a strong sense of disjunction between the level of immediate representation, one novel at a time, and the level of *the* novel, at which "consciousness" as such, framed in a "typology" of representation, can arise. Or to phrase it differently: Consciousness is not what is represented "realistically" in novels, but is an invention that makes possible *the* novel as an overarching category.

Does this point advance our understanding of millennialism in the novel as an historical force? Suppose we agree that consciousness is invented in the growth of the realistic novel, and that the invention of consciousness is parallel to the invention of transcendental apperception. Suppose we agree further that transcendental apperception, along with its more widely recognized form as "consciousness," is a response to the problem of communication and is therefore *inherently* millennialist, because the problem of communication does not arise until after it has become insoluble. The trouble is that the millennial dimension of Kantian aesthetics is *latent,* and does not become manifest until Schiller unmasks it in the *Aesthetic Letters.* Where shall we seek a comparable unmasking with respect to the novel? As far as Kant is concerned, the problem of communication is settled by his argument that the communicability of feeling, while not demonstrable, is still assumable; and for most readers, the representation of consciousness in realistic novels probably provides a similar assurance with respect to consciousness as such, so that the inherent millennialism of the form remains latent. But a latent millennialism is not enough to support the historical project we are engaged in. The millennial component of totalitarianism is not a cultural background feature. It is asserted openly and affirmed energetically by masses of people.

THE INVENTION OF THE INDIVIDUAL

In order to argue that the history of the novel's paradox brings with it the millennialist aspect of aesthetics in a form that eventually proves useful in totalitarian politics, it is necessary to show that that millennialism lies closer to the surface, in the thinking of novels and their readers, than can be shown by way of the concept of consciousness alone. I think that such a showing can be made by way of the idea of the *individual*. For if it can be argued plausibly that consciousness is invented in the background of the realistic novel, then it can be argued at least as plausibly that the modern individual is invented there as well. Consciousness cannot happen without an individual as its vessel; and it would not occur to us to imagine an individual lacking the attribute of consciousness. But the argument with respect to the individual has a different starting point and possesses a crucial social and political dimension.

Rousseau is a key figure in discussion of both the modern individual and the modern novel. He appears, accordingly, at a central point in Nancy Armstrong's attempt to combine the two discussions, in her book *How Novels Think*. In the segment of her argument that is most relevant to the present project, Armstrong begins with Louis Althusser's notion of the "ideological state apparatus" and the idea that "the modern state creates a contradiction within the subject between the ideology of free subjectivity and the fact of social subjection."[6] Of special interest to her are Althusser's "'bad subjects' . . . who take the ideology of free subjectivity too much to heart and do not freely consent to their subjection" (29). These individualists, of whom Armstrong considers Robinson Crusoe an inaugural novelistic instance, mark one end of a spectrum. "Between the subject who freely accepts his or her subjection and the criminal or heretic, the novel introduced a whole world of possibilities without which, I believe, a modern secular state ruled chiefly by ideology could not have emerged when and how it did" (29). The magnitude of the claim being made here is considerable. It is not simply that the novel accompanies a deeper-running political and social change. Armstrong insists that the novel is an indispensable operative factor in the political development she is talking about.[7]

Especially important with respect to this claim is the case of Great Britain: "the very example of the modern nation-state," where, "during the turbulent period between 1776 and 1848," there was no "radical change in political government [to explain] how . . . ideology might have usurped the power formerly exercised by the military and the police to govern a population during turbulent times" (30). Especially in Britain, how can the contradiction between ideology and fact, between free subjectivity and social subjection, be resolved or at least suppressed? The only possible answer to this question—if it counts as an answer—is read by Armstrong out of Rousseau by way of Althusser's critique of *The Social Contract:* "To convert the early modern state into an aggregate of freely consenting individuals, [Rousseau] has to conceptualize an entirely new kind of individual, one endowed with the natural ability to understand the advantages of being a citizen" (30), an individual, in particular, who can carry out the practically impossible move of "total alienation" as part of a contractual exchange with a second party that does not yet even exist.[8]

We find ourselves in familiar intellectual territory. As in chapter 1 above, we are faced with a political impasse that appears to call for a resolution on some visionary plane. But in her discussion of Defoe, at least in its initial stages, Armstrong is not inclined to argue for a visionary or millennial dimension in the fiction.

In the first part of his story, she says, "Crusoe . . . defines himself in terms of . . . the bad subject, [not] sinful so much as naturally disinclined to respond to traditional forms of authority" (32). But his transformation, later, into "the governor of a peaceful cosmopolitan nation" (34) creates a self-conflicting structure that has great social significance. "The apparent contradiction posed by the two halves of Crusoe's stay on the island is one and the same as the contradiction enacted by the social contract itself, which demands that an individual restrain his or her individuality in exchange for the state's protection of that individuality against other forms of self-expression. To constrain his fellow individuals, Crusoe must cease to be a bad subject himself" (35). And in fact, "we are tempted to say" that by his success in organizing his island's miniature society,

> Crusoe has solved the problem implicit in the logic of the social contract, namely, how to produce individuals who want to submit to the state. But such are the wages of his success in crossing over from the one category to the other that Crusoe loses the moral energy of the misfit as he becomes the exemplary citizen, so that his successful negotiation of contractual logic is his downfall in rhetorical terms. After identifying ourselves with his excesses as an individual, it is difficult for modern readers to wish for the kind of homogeneity required of members in the new community. (36)

Precisely the novel form, therefore, precisely the applicability of "rhetorical terms," ensures that we will *not* be satisfied with Crusoe's practical success inside the fiction, that we will *not* see in the fiction a visionary resolution of social-contract contradictions.

But Armstrong is not finished. From *Robinson Crusoe* she moves on to *Moll Flanders* and *Roxana*, where the same problem becomes even more intractable. "Moll and Roxana . . . identify the entrepreneurial energy of the bad subject [Crusoe's starting point] with sexual energy: the power both to attract and to satisfy customers. In making themselves something other than docile bodies, however, these women set themselves on a course that leads not to citizenship but in the other direction, to criminality and social exclusion" (37). Which raises the question: "If Defoe cannot bring himself to sanction their sexual behavior, then we must wonder why he nevertheless authorizes these women to tell their own stories" (37).

And Armstrong's eventual answer to this question is an instance of exceptional synthetic insight, both interpretive and historical:

> If we think of [Moll's] sexuality as the additive that allows her to thrive in social terms, we must simultaneously admire her honesty and condemn her narrow mercenary interests. . . . But if, instead of sexuality, we think of writing as the additive that transforms her from a docile body into a misfit whose upward mobility, as marked by literacy, we can admire, then it suddenly becomes possible to imagine turning such a misfit into a self-governing subject. Writing can serve both purposes: to express the aspects of individuality that an unsatisfactory social position would suppress and to limit those excesses once they have found a satisfactory situation. From this perspective, the pseudonymous titles of *Moll Flanders* and *Roxana* display writing's power to express and to limit the excesses of individualism at one and the same time. (41-42)

In Crusoe's case too, we must infer, it is "his distinctive form of literacy" (35) that ultimately justifies him even "in rhetorical terms."

Armstrong thus credits Defoe with a remarkable literary feat. He develops the problem of individuality—of combining free subjectivity and social subjection—to a level of maximum intensity: first, by employing a realistic novel form in which the necessarily visionary solution cannot plausibly be imagined as part of the fiction; and second, by moving from a male to female protagonists. But then it turns out that exactly that inconvenient novel form, in its quality as writing and as first-person narration, embodies the intimation of a successfully synthesized individual after all. The novel thus develops a millennial dimension *as writing*, a vision of perfected individuality which is nowhere reflected in the realistic content of that very writing. Defoe, in this view, assumes an inaugural position with respect to the paradox of novels and *the* novel (writing as a concept) as well.

MILLENNIALISM IN THE NOVEL

There is a good deal more to Armstrong's overall argument. The transition to Richardson is fairly easy: "By converting Moll's and Roxana's sexual precocity into verbal aggression, Defoe sets the stage for discursively aggressive protagonists like Pamela and Clarissa" (42). And the next step takes her altogether beyond the self-assertion and self-limiting of first-person narration, to a point marked by the new "stylistic precision" (43) of Jane Austen's third-person, a point where

> we can observe the gap between self-expressive and self-governing subjects disappearing into the narrowing gap between Austen's plucky heroine and the narrator whose collective wisdom she must embrace in order to become mistress of Pemberly. We can . . . understand the voice of such collective wisdom as a subtler form of the same writing that allowed Moll and Roxana to defend themselves against their former excesses. We can . . . understand Austen's narrator as the expression of Elizabeth Bennet's thoroughly acculturated self, a product of her negotiation of the culture more than a product of her nature, a form of self-expression that must address the reader from outside the heroine's consciousness until it is fully incorporated within. (49-50)

From here, Armstrong follows her argument through Romantic and Victorian fiction, attentive at every step to the manner in which novels, under the pressure of varying historical circumstances, repeatedly invent individuality in its relation to "the fantasy of the liberal individual" (153) that it can never fully realize.

Can we generalize from this argument on the British novel, or from the part of it that we have looked at in detail? We cannot do so without going back to the problematics of the individual as developed by Rousseau and his later critics. If the modern political individual can be regarded as a novelistic invention, then it is not an invention that is ever fully realized—as a fully socialized individual in a fully accommodating society—in fact or in law or in customary social practice. It is a millennialist fiction, an instance of generalized particularity, which is the insoluble paradox of the novel. It is the vision of a constantly deferred future that is also constantly, tantalizingly present to us in the practices of writing and imagining that make up the novel as an institution. And my claim is that this argument situates the still inexplicit millennialist quality of the novel close enough to the surface to be available for large scale political manipulation.

The earlier argument on consciousness supports this point by bringing the problem of communication into play, with its inherent millennialist tendency. And I think it is clear that Armstrong's argument on the problematics of individuality in British novels can be paralleled in the case of German novels, from Goethe to Gottfried Keller, or French novels, from Rousseau himself to Flaubert—a problematics whose millennialist tendency, being the negative image of social alienation or ennui, is increasingly well understood as the nineteenth century unfolds. Moreover, as I have said, I do not see how Dilthey's millennialist vision of *Geisteswissenschaften,* in which the novelistic paradox of generalized particularity is hypostasized, is possible without a sense of millennialist support not only from school philosophy, but from the broader society. And we will follow below Arendt's argument on the typical form of individuality at the threshold of totalitarianism, which is in essence Althusser's and Armstrong's novelistically sensitive "bad subject."

Plenty of related arguments can be made. One with which I am particularly familiar, since I made it myself almost two decades ago, centers on the contention that Rousseau's political writings, especially *The Social Contract* and the *Discourse on Inequality,* are not really theories of society at all, but theories of the novel.[9] The idea of social experiments, the requirement that philosophical discourse shape humanity, the difficult distinction between debatable matters and matters under the authority of the general will, the self-doubling figure of the legislator, the logically questionable Assembly of the People: all these theoretical constructions, which confront crippling problems if one imagines them applied in social reality, are applicable to corresponding features of the novel—the novel as an institution—with no trouble at all. Of course the literary institution presupposed by these correspondences was only just coming into existence at the time of Rousseau's writing. But my point was (and is) that even in the process of theorizing a completed and uncorrupted individuality, Rousseau was also imagining—as a vessel to preserve that theoretical vision in a corrupt age—what we now speak of as the novel: a thoroughly visionary literary institution, visionary or millennialist not in the content or inferred doctrine of its texts, even on an allegorical level, but solely in its structure *as an institution,* as *the* novel.

Before we go on, two points need to be clarified. First, the absence or scarcity of novels that display an optimistic vision of individuality in Rousseau's sense is not an objection to my argument on millennialism in the novel form. Again, the very idea of the novel includes a bridgeless gulf between the meaning of particular novels and the character (especially the millennialism) of the novel as an institution. My contention is that that millennialism is no less present and effective for lacking direct expression. Indeed, in democratic polities, it is *more* effective for being unexpressed. When the idea of the free but fully socialized individual is brought up for explicit discussion in the presence of democratic institutions, it is ordinarily treated (deludedly) as if it referred to a simple fact or at least to an achievable goal.

And second, it must be understood that no specific value, either positive or negative, attaches to the individualistic vision as such. Rousseau's own positive valuation is undermined, in my view, by the inescapable fact that that vision belongs integrally to a history of secular millennial-ism (as aesthetics) which leads toward totalitarianism. But an unambiguously negative valuation of the vision, on these grounds, would presuppose that totalitarianism is inevitable, or ever was, which is not the case. The ascendancy of this or that totalitarian movement is always a contingent political event, an event that could just as well have turned out otherwise. And the admittedly often difficult feat of living by Rousseau-istic principles, yet still constantly trimming them to avoid a totalitarian direction, is not impossible. It is carried out by most of us every day in societies that we hope thereby to keep more or less liberal and livable.

ANTI-MILLENNIALIST NARRATIVE?

As I suggested above, one further type of evidence would be useful in marking out the novel's millennialist dimension, an instance of unmasking from within, in a novel, like Schiller's unmasking of the millennialism in Kantian aesthetics. I think there are plenty of such instances, some of which I have discussed elsewhere under the topic of reading as a "trap."[10] But the text that I have in mind here, Robert Musil's *Die Verwir-rungen des Zöglings Törleß* [The Confusions of the Schoolboy Törless], has a specially clear relation to the present argument.

Törless is a short novel set in the period around 1900. It recounts the broken-off fifth year of its protagonist at an exclusive but isolated military boarding school in the Austro-Hungarian empire, a considerable distance east of Vienna. Törless is about fifteen, certainly not more than sixteen; he is one of the younger boys in his class, two years younger than at least one of his friends. The story involves physical and sexual abuse among the boys, and rape by intimidation. The perpetrators are Törless's two older classmates, Beineberg and Reiting, who gain power over their victim, an effeminate boy named Basini, by threatening to expose him as the class thief. Basini in due course seduces Törless as well, hoping for better treatment from him and a certain degree of intimacy. Matters eventually get out of control, involving the rest of the class. Basini is sent home in disgrace for his thieving. Törless, whose involvement in any wrongdoing is never exposed, is sent home supposedly suffering from moral and psychological shock at the recent events.

The story's narrator, however, concerns himself less with the external plot than with a minutely detailed description and analysis of the inner life of his main character, a tendency that is then repeated in Törless himself, who is uninterruptedly fascinated not only with the operation of his own psyche, but with that of Basini's as well, especially with the question of how Basini "feels" in the moments of his greatest degradation, when thieving or when submitting to torture or sex. Thus a pattern is formed, a resonance between the narrator's habit of mind and that of his protagonist; and this pattern becomes increasingly interesting if we take the opportunities that are offered us to ask questions about the narrator.

Such opportunities are frequent and obvious. At the very beginning we are told retrospectively about the apparent "homesickness" Törless had experienced in his first months at the school. The narrator informs us that that suffering had been in truth "something positive, a spiritual strength, something that had blossomed and faded within him under the cover of pain." Törless's parents, however, had remained in the dark, for "They failed to see that this was their son's first unsuccessful attempt, thrown upon his own devices, to develop his own inner strength."[11]

The narrator thus nudges our attention toward Törless's *future,* toward the adult state in which his development will eventually culminate. We are asked not only to observe Törless's experience in the school—perhaps even in a sense to share it—but also to keep in mind that that experience is "now," as we read, irrevocably past, that we and the narrator are now engaged in analyzing it with a view to its place in the personal constitution of a later, "now" fully formed Törless. Only a few lines after the last passage quoted above, Törless's early friendship with "young Prince H." is introduced with the words: "One episode of this time was characteristic of what was being prepared within Törless, to develop further at a later stage" (7/10). And further on, toward the story's end—in a passage we will take up in detail—this tendency of the text is made fully explicit: "Later, once he had overcome the events of his youth, Törless became a young man with a very fine and sensitive mind" (126/111).

Narrative fiction, especially in German, is used commonly enough to explore character formation or *Bildung.* But for obvious reasons, this process is ordinarily observed from a perspective that keeps pace more or less with its unfolding, rather than from the point of view of the finished product. It seems essential to the drama of *Bildung* as experience that there be at least a suggestion of uncertainty about whether a finished personality will ever be achieved. But Musil thwarts any such uncertainty. The adult Törless unquestionably exists, and the narrator certainly knows about him—in great detail, as we will see. And if we put these facts together with what I have called the resonance between the narrator's interests and Törless's, it begins to seem at least possible that the narrator *is* that grown-up Törless, telling his own story in a third-person disguise. It would make no sense to say definitely either that this is, or that it is not, the case. We are dealing with fiction. But the effect of the textual signals we receive, and of the fairly clear flouting of narratorial convention, is to create a kind of hovering grammatical structure, as if it were halfway between the first person and the third.

Moreover, if we reflect upon this situation for a moment—keeping in mind the central idea of *Bildung*—it must occur to us that the ambiguous

grammatical person in *Törless* is perhaps an accurate emblem of the relation between past and present selves in the process of personal growth.
What I was as a schoolboy is no longer exactly what I am; it is now more
a "he" than an "I." And yet it is also a special kind of "he" that has a great
deal of "I" in it still. The psychological thinking of Ernst Mach, with
which Musil was more than just acquainted, thus perhaps plays a part in
the basic structural conception of *Törless*.

Finally, this interpretive path provides a good solution to the single
most glaring difficulty in Musil's book. Toward the end, after Basini has
gone to the school authorities to confess his thievery and seek protection
against the rest of the class, on the day when the other boys are being
brought individually before a panel of teachers for questioning, it is discovered that Törless has fled the school (151/132). The investigation goes
forward. Beineberg and Reiting see to it that Törless's flight is attributed
not to any actual guilt but to a supposed "nervous condition" and "moral
sensitivity" (152/133). Then, on the next day, Törless is brought in from a
nearby town. And we never hear anything at all, not one single fact,
about what he had done or experienced or thought or felt while running
away from school! It is true that the narrator does not always confine
himself to Törless's perspective. There are plenty of digressions in the
novel, which I will discuss later. But the narrator's obvious principal
interest throughout is the working of Törless's mind. It is therefore distinctly anomalous that at this time of maximum crisis, when Törless is
driven to an extremity beyond anything else he does in the story, we hear
nothing about it on either a factual or a psychological level. At this point
the story simply has a gap, a void.

But if we bring to this problem the understanding that two versions of
Törless are suggested, the confused schoolboy and the ostentatiously self-
assured narrator, a solution offers itself. There needs to be a hinge, a
transition, between the early and the later Törless. On the existence and
nature of that hinge depends the whole question of fulfilled individuality. The schoolboy Törless is a "bad subject" in the sense Armstrong
derives from Althusser, a subject whose differentness and intractability
are a source of moral energy and interest. And if he later simply lets
himself be reformed into a well-behaved citizen, that interest is lost. But
if—by way of a now necessarily ineffable hinge—he manages to become
a fully socialized adult without sacrificing that original confusing and
passionate differentness, then something like an embodiment of the ideal
individual of Rousseau will have been achieved. And since we are talking
about a barely imaginable ideal, we cannot expect the novel's version of
that needful hinge ever to be shown or explained to us. It must remain
what Musil lets it remain, a gap, an empty space in the account of
Törless's existence. (I will come back to the question of exactly how we
must read this apparent representation-by-absence of the unimaginable.)

We are, in any case, given the clear impression that Törless has returned from his abortive flight a changed person. Not that he has left his confusions behind. That would simply beg the question of individuality. Even the main problem he had had before Basini, his skewed manner of experiencing things, remains with him. But in a new way.

> That and everything else—he saw it as being curiously clear and pure—and small. Just as one sees things in the morning, when the first pure sunbeams have dried the perspiration of anxiety, and the table and the cupboard, and the enemy and fate, creep back to their natural dimensions. . . . But the memory that things can be otherwise, that there are fine boundaries around human beings, easily erased, that feverish dreams creep around the soul, gnawing away at solid walls and opening up strange alley-ways—that memory too had sunk deep within him and cast pale shadows.
>
> He was unable to explain a great deal of it. But that silence felt delicious, like the certainty of an impregnated body that feels in its blood the gentle pull of the future. (159-60/139-40)

There is even a relatively abstract philosophical passage—two long paragraphs on the idea of "dead and living thoughts" (155-56/136-37)—inserted right into the middle of Törless's stumbling attempt to explain himself to the teachers, but without quotation marks; and it is not at all clear whether its intellectual content belongs to Törless or to the narrator. The young Törless and the mature narrator, it appears—pursuant to whatever magical transformation is concealed from us in the invisible hinge—have now become a single realized and perfected individual.

But how exactly shall we read these signs: as a hopeful intimation of fulfilled humanity, or as a joke, a travesty, as the exposure of a hopeless and pointless millennialism in the novel form?

THE EXPOSURE OF THE NOVEL

The whole tenor of the chapter anticipates my own answer to this question. And my point now is that Musil anticipates a similar answer, a shifting of his book in the direction of travesty or satire, in the long passage I have already mentioned, where the narrator describes the character of Törless as a young man after he has "overcome the events of his youth" (126/111).

In order to understand that passage fully, one must know something about the German adjective "fein." Its basic meaning is: refined, delicate, sensitive, posh. But it often lends itself to an ironic or mocking use, especially in Austrian German, because it is the word, typically, by which a bourgeois with strong feelings of inferiority expresses his or her idea of what it means to be an aristocrat. Thus it easily becomes a sign for empty pretensions, especially when it is used over and over again.

The passage I want to focus on follows immediately the description of how Törless is drawn back repeatedly into his sexual relationship with Basini, a process that usually begins with his "feeling of ailing refinement" [Gefühl einer leidenden *Fein*heit] (126/111; my italics throughout) after each encounter. The passage itself opens:

> Later, once he had overcome the events of his youth, Törless became a young man with a very fine and sensitive mind [von sehr *fein*em und empfindsamem Geiste]. He became one of those aesthetic and intellectual characters upon whom respect for the law and, to some extent, for public morals, has a calming effect, relieving them of the need to think about anything coarse and remote from the finer things of the soul [etwas . . . von dem *fein*eren seelischen Geschehen Weitabliegendes]; but who, when asked to declare a more personal interest in the objects of morality and the law, bring to their grandiose outward show of correctness, with its hint of irony, a certain bored insensitivity. (126/111)

It almost appears that a genuine solution to the problem of individuality is being suggested here. You immerse yourself in your aesthetic otherness as a "bad subject" so completely that you find yourself automatically socialized, since you simply can't be bothered to violate either law or morals. At least we might be tempted to form this idea if it were not for the ostinato on the concept "fein," plus some other elements of vocabulary that suggest affectation — *empfindsam, gelangweilt, schöngeistig* (shortly afterward).

And what about the degrading liaison with Basini? What part does that experience play in Törless's new-found completeness? A couple of paragraphs later in the same section we read:

> And like everyone whose sole concern is the intensification of his mental abilities, Törless was not troubled by the mere presence of torrid and excessive impulses. He liked to think that the capacity for enjoyment, artistic talents, the highly refined spiritual life [das ganze ver*fei*nerte Seelenleben], was a piece of jewellery upon which one could easily injure oneself. He thought it inevitable that someone with a rich and active inner life would have certain moments about which other people could know nothing, and memories that he kept in secret drawers. And of such a person he asked only that he should know how to make refined use [sich ihrer mit *Fein*heit zu bedienen] of those moments later in life.
>
> And so, when someone to whom he had told the story of his youth asked him whether he was not sometimes ashamed of that memory, he gave the following reply with a smile: "Of course I can't deny that it was degrading. Why should I? The degradation passed. But something of it lingered for ever: that tiny quantity of poison that is needed to rid the self of its overly calm, complacent health, and instead to give it a kind of health that is more refined [eine *fein*ere], acute and understanding." (127-28/112; translation modified)

The idea is basically the same: the "bad subject" must be preserved inside oneself as a kind of salutary poison. But the element of affectation has grown clearer; and there is a direct self-contradiction as well. Surely the affair with Basini, for a truly "refined" person, would be one of those secret things "about which other people could know nothing." And yet, in the very next paragraph, we hear that Törless has told the whole story of his youth, including the Basini episode, to "someone"—not a friend or an intimate friend, just "someone." On top of which we must now ask ourselves how *we* come to be reading that story, in a novel which that operates so perilously close to the grammatical first person.

Thus, in the end, the very form of the novel, the inherently indiscreet, unrefined form of the novel, is implicated in the compulsive, affected self-overexposure that we can now infer in both persons of Törless. The novel itself is implicated in the desperate groping for inter-individual communication and contact that makes up its content—a groping that both constantly generates and also always frustrates the secular millennialist urge whose localized expression it is, the *aesthetic* urge or need for completed individuality, as Musil makes clear in describing older Törless.

Hence the importance of the narrator's digressions in the novel, by which I mean not only thoughts and perceptions that cannot be attributed to young Törless, but also pieces of detailed narration whose subject matter cannot be known even to an older Törless, pieces of text that therefore mark the narrator as a *novelist,* standing entirely outside the fictional world. Very early on, for example, we are given a short biography of Beineberg's father (17-18/18-20), including facts and perceptions that not even Beineberg himself could have contributed. And at the very end, we are made privy to the teachers' discussion of Törless after he has left the room (157-58/138). Passages of this type could have been omitted with no damage at all to the main story—as could the mention of how Törless later tells "someone" about his life at school. And if such passages had been omitted, we would have been able to read the whole book as a private meditation on Törless's experiences, a meditation on the part of either a sympathetic narrator or an older Törless. (Those novelistic passages, incidentally, do not affect by their presence the text's ambiguous grammatical person; they are just one vector in the direction of "he," balanced by others in the direction of "I.") If the offending passages had been omitted, at least the fiction of privacy could have been maintained; and the public institution of the novel would not have been implicated in a Kantian-Schillerian millennialism, in the hopeless millennial promise of restored individuality and perfected communication. It is significant in this regard that Kant himself is the single object of direct satire in the novel (94-95/84-85).

Am I suggesting that Musil wrote that whole complex narrative for the sole purpose of holding his main character up to ridicule? Of course not. There is nothing at all ridiculous about Törless (in either of his two persons) or his story. It is not a question of ridicule, it is an instance of simple realism, that Törless cannot avoid affectation in coming to grips with his past, that he fails utterly to achieve the completed and stabilized individuality he dreams of in passages like this one: "The image of a gardener occurred to him, watering his flower-beds each morning with even, expectant care. That image wouldn't let him go, its expectant certainty seemed to attract all his yearning to itself. That was the only way it could be! The only way! This was what Törless felt, and all his fear, all his reservations, were swept aside by the conviction that he must stake everything on achieving that state of mind" (146/128). This is a hopeless dream, but not a ridiculous one. We must distinguish, as always, between the level of each particular novel and the level of *the* novel as an institution. Musil, in *Törless*—however much this may conflict with the idea of an art work's unity—does two completely different things: he writes a thoroughly competent and serious and realistic novel; and at the same time, having thus elbowed his way into the novel's own domain, he contrives to unmask the institution of the novel as a principal contributor to the millennialist tendency in modern European culture, the source of hopeless wishes, that conditions his character's unresolvable "confusion" and suffering.

There is plenty of room for disagreement in detail about my reading of this particular text. But I think that its broad outlines are enough to justify my offering it as a final piece of evidence concerning the shape of a basic millennialist tendency in the novel as a form. I will try later to develop my view on this point with a parallel reading of Joyce.

NOTES

1. In Löwith, for instance, the concept of consciousness is everywhere, but without being subjected to a serious critique as a concept. For the reference, see chap. 4, n8.

2. Sigmund Freud, *The Ego and the Id*, in *The Standard Edition of the Complete Psychological Works of Sigmund Freud*, ed. and trans. James Strachey et al. (London, 1953-74), 19:13-14. The original is found in Freud, *Gesammelte Werke: Chronologisch geordnet*, 18 vols. (Frankfurt/Main, 1999; orig. 1940-52), 13:240. I will use the abbreviations *SE* and *GW* below.

3. Cohn, *Transparent Minds*, 8, 9, 10. See chap. 4, n11.

4. Freud does speak of *"Pcpt.-Cs."* (perception-consciousness) as a "system" on two occasions in *The Ego and the Id* (*SE*, 19:20, 21; *GW*, 13:247, 249). But I think it is clear that only the "system *Pcpt."*(*SE*, 19:22, 23, 24, 25; *GW*, 13:249, 250, 251, 253), the perceptual system that connects the mind with the outside world, has true systematic character. It is called *"Pcpt.-Cs."* when the emphasis is on perception as a source of conscious experience.

5. Marshall Brown, *Preromanticism* (Stanford, 1991), 58.

6. Nancy Armstrong, *How Novels Think: The Limits of British Individualism from 1719-1900* (New York, 2005), 29. Armstrong refers mainly to Louis Althusser, "Ideology and Ideological State Apparatuses (Notes towards an Investigation)," in his *Lenin and Philosophy and Other Essays*, trans. Ben Brewster (New York, 1971), 127-86; and

"Rousseau: The Social Contract (The Discrepancies)," in his *Politics and History: Montesquieu, Rousseau, Hegel and Marx*, trans. Ben Brewster (London, 1972), 111-160.

7. Lynn Hunt makes a similar claim about political efficacy in the novel form. See chap. 4, n11.

8. See Althusser, "Rousseau," 126-31.

9. See my *Beyond Theory*, 302-305. See chap. 2, n20.

10. See my *The Dark Side of Literacy*, 223-63. Chap. 3, n6.

11. Robert Musil, *The Confusions of Young Törless*, trans. Shaun Whiteside (New York: Penguin, 2001), 6-7. In the original these passages are found in Robert Musil, *Gesammelte Werke*, 2 vols., ed. Adolf Frisé (Reinbek bei Hamburg, 1978), 2:9-10. Further references will be located by page from the translation, then from the original (vol. 2), in the form, e.g. "6-7/9-10."

NINE

Aesthetic Response and Propaganda: The Invention of Simultaneity

How much remains to be done? If we agree with Hannah Arendt that the main twentieth-century totalitarian movements, in Nazi Germany and in Soviet Russia under Stalin, are not nationalist but millennialist in character; and if we agree that this fact raises the question of where the millennialist impulse and energy behind those movements comes from—it being assumed that energy as such (in the form of nationalism, Pan-Slavism, Pan-Germanism, envy and fear of the Jews, economic desperation, or whatever else) is not sufficient as an explanation: then we are looking for a tradition of secular millennialism. In Part One, I attempted to show how just such a tradition arises in the eighteenth century in philosophical aesthetics; and in chapters 7 and 8 above, I argued that the nineteenth-century novel, considered as an institution, inherits and develops that tradition.

In order to complete the argument, it is not necessary (and probably not possible) to show a direct connection between the institution of the novel and the institutional structure of totalitarian regimes. The importance of the paradox of the novel as an institution is that it enables us to understand how a millennialist habit of mind can be encouraged in large masses of people by a body of writing (novels) in which, on the level of content or attitude, there is practically nothing that is millennialist. For without this habit of mind—this persistent self-contradictory vision of the perfectibility and communicability of strict individual particularity or "consciousness"—it is difficult to imagine how the equally and similarly self-contradictory products of a totalitarian imagination could have enjoyed the enthusiastic popular support with which they were greeted.

I have made some suggestions toward fleshing out this argument. Of prime importance, in my view, is the recognition that the direction followed by mainstream nineteenth-century academic philosophy, the tendency in favor (let us say) of a Kantian over a Leibnizian approach, in favor of philosophy as system over philosophy as discussion, can be accounted for only by reference to the sort of broad social pressures (including especially the need for communication on a level recognized as impossible) that would put philosophy into the same basic category as the ever more popular form of the novel. In the present chapter I will propose a parallel argument on the question of propaganda—one of the few questions I think Arendt fails to treat adequately—in its relation to the history and conceptual habits of aesthetics.

THE MOMENT THAT MATTERS

As we follow aesthetics, in the form of secular millennialism, toward the totalitarian age, do we lose track altogether of questions of beauty and art? Does Benjamin's idea of fascism as an aestheticization of politics no longer figure in our thinking? In fact, the tradition we are talking about does maintain its connection with aesthetic matters—and not only in the attenuated sense of aesthetics in the thought of Dilthey, Heidegger, Adorno—a connection without which the political success of totalitarianism would be difficult to account for.

Let us return to Kant and to the idea of the aesthetic judgment as a judgment that is made without the application of concepts. Without doing too much violence to Kant's meaning, we can express the same idea in temporal terms: an aesthetic judgment is made in the moment *before* the object is appropriated and categorized by conceptual thought. In chapter 2, we noted that Baumgarten, in § 24 of the *Meditationes,* asserts the possibility of a moment of instantaneous self-representation, which would combine the qualities of reflection and sense-perception in a single event. Kant, in his methodological scrupulosity, would have rejected that assertion if he had noticed it. But his own notion of aesthetic judgment still implies, as a practical matter, the existence of *a special singular moment* in our experience of the beautiful, a moment of nothing but feeling, before we start thinking, a moment in which "the free play of the cognitive faculties"—as opposed to their use in thinking—can still provide a basis for judgment. We think of Schiller here, too, and of the idea of "infinite determinability" in aesthetic experience, the idea of a fleeting moment that receives value only in being quickly succeeded by moral self-determination.

I will call this special singular moment in aesthetic experience the moment of *response.* From here on I will use the word "response" only in this sense. But by discussing the idea of response, I do not mean to imply that any such moment actually exists. As readers of Part One of this book will know without being told, I am firmly of the opinion that the moment of aesthetic response has no actual existence in anyone's experience. Any assertion of the contrary—any assertion of the form, "Well, *I* certainly have had the experience of aesthetic response"—is in my view either wishful thinking or mere affectation. In this opinion, as in a number of others, I follow Goethe, who asserts in the foreword to his *Theory of Colors* that whenever we open our eyes to the world we are always already engaged in conceptual thought, in the activity he calls "theorizing" (WA, pt. 2, 1:xii).

But the non-existence of aesthetic response does not prevent it from playing a crucial role in the history of aesthetics, and eventually in the operation of totalitarian propaganda. For response becomes *necessary* as soon as one adopts an aesthetic view of art, the view that a work of art receives its proper existence *as* art only in the process of being contemplated, of being seen or heard or read, by a sensitive recipient. This view—which is suggested in Baumgarten, asserted by Moritz, and implied in Kant's refusal to discuss beauty except by way of judgment—includes the possibility of *doubting* the proper existence of the work of art, hence also of doubting its usefulness in intersubjective communication. If the work of art becomes what it truly is only in the process of my receiving it—or your receiving it—what guarantee is there that it is the same work of art for you that it is for me? And without such a guarantee, what has happened to the possibility of communication? We can, it is true, discuss the work at length, and discover that we agree on so-and-so many interpretive or appreciative ideas concerning it. But if we push the discussion hard enough, we are bound eventually to find points on which we disagree; and we have no perspective from which to judge how deeply those points affect the very nature of the work.[1]

The idea of response avoids this problem. In both your experience and mine, we now assume, there was a moment when the work of art was simply *there,* before we started thinking about it. Any disagreements or misunderstandings that arise in our discussion of it are products of that thinking, and do not call into question the unitary existence, and the continuing presence to our aesthetic sensibilities, of the object that joins us to one another in our appreciation of its value. Basically these considerations are expressed in Kant's argument that a judgment prior to the application of concepts is ipso facto imputed by me to every other human being. The moment of response is an experience we automatically have in common with every other sensitive recipient of the work; and this common experience must operate for Kantians as an intimation of the universally shared moment of transcendental apperception on which all hope of communication is founded.

The very concept of response, in other words, implies the idea of *universal uniformity of response.* This idea is perhaps not of much consequence in the eighteenth or the nineteenth century, where there is no occasion to imagine huge numbers of people responding to exactly the same quasi-artistic stimulus in exactly the same way at exactly the same time. But the situation in the first half of the twentieth century is suddenly much different. For with the advent of broadcast radio, exactly that possibility, the possibility of uniform mass response, has apparently become a reality — or has at least become persuasive enough as a possibility to assume in effect the character of a reality. The importance of this point for understanding the operation and effectiveness of totalitarian propaganda is fairly clear. We will go into the matter in detail below.

RESPONSE IN PRACTICE: THE PROBLEM

The discussion of the novel in chapters 7 and 8 above is important not only because it fills a gap in the history of aesthetics. It also forms a bridge from the secular millennialism of aesthetic theory — which is not always clearly understood even by those few writers whose work propagates it — to the sensibilities of a large European reading public. A similar bridge is required for the idea of aesthetic response. To say that this idea is a logical consequence of the aesthetic view of art is one thing. To say that it is a widespread habit of mind, capable of influencing mass movements in politics, is quite another.

Not that I think there can be any doubt that aesthetic response provided the model according to which enormous numbers of people shaped their understanding and assimilation of totalitarian propaganda. The totalitarian phenomenon as a whole, in the first half of the twentieth century, may be (as we say) unprecedented. But the idea of the "unprecedented," if we understand it too literally and broadly, entails giving up altogether on the idea of history; and I do not think even totalitarianism justifies taking such a step. If we cannot find a precedent for the phenomenon as a whole, we can certainly find precedents for its component elements. And if we isolate its propagandistic aspect: the willing acceptance, by large numbers of reasonably well-educated people, of ideas that had either (1) no actual content at all, or (2) a different content every time they were articulated, or (3) a content with which those people would normally have disagreed — I think the connection with the idea of aesthetic response, response that does not consider the art work's meaning or content, is too obvious to be denied.

But the more certain we are about this connection, the more we place ourselves under the obligation to explain it in detail. Which creates problems: for aesthetic response is at best non-verifiable, whereas the uniform mass movement of assent to totalitarian propaganda is an undeniable fact, quite apart from the thoughts and opinions of the individuals involved. How do we get from the one to the other?

The novel seems to be no help to us here. For of all art forms, surely the large prose narrative — which ordinarily takes days for a reader to get through—is as incompatible as possible with the idea of a fleeting moment of aesthetic response. Actually the novel makes its contribution to the effectiveness of totalitarian propaganda by a somewhat different path, which I have discussed in detail in my book, *The Dark Side of Literacy*. The theory or doctrine of reading that comes to be associated preferentially with the modern novel includes an idea of *the* reader, who begins the task of reading by leaving behind as much as possible of his or her unique individuality in order to become an uncontaminated vessel for the thought and imagination supposedly communicated by the book. Reading, that is, begins with a move of unthinking assent, and so cultivates "the habit of permitting one's mind to be occupied as fully as possible by the thoughts of another," which is "exactly the habit required most immediately of citizens in a totalitarian state."[2] Certainly the widespread practice of novel-reading will tend thus to support the idea of an aesthetic response uncontaminated by concepts. But how does that idea get established in the first place, as an accepted understanding of how individuals receive and assimilate works of art in general?

In the case of a photograph or a painting, we can perhaps imagine that there is an instant in which we *know of* its quality as a work of art (and therefore respond to it as such) without yet having begun to *think about* that quality. But how shall we imagine a comparable instant in our reading a poem, or watching a movie or a play, or listening to music? Does that instant occur with our reading of the poem's first line? How do we know, at that point, that the whole text will satisfy our sense of what a poem should be? And if the moment of aesthetic response has to wait until we are finished reading, how can we have prevented ourselves from thinking conceptually about the poem in aesthetic terms before then? And even supposing this problem can be solved in one way for poetry, in other ways for theater and music, will we still be justified in thinking of "response" as a single idea, a single influence upon social or political behavior?

As far as I know, no one has ever put together an argument that would satisfy all the requirements of this situation. We could perhaps extend Bakhtin's thinking on the "novelization" of poetic genres and attempt an argument on the novelization of art works in general—which might even contain a certain amount of truth, and would avoid the problem of response by universalizing the idea of reading. But it would also perpetuate a cardinal fault in Bakhtin's thinking, his failure to discriminate between novels in the plural and "the" novel.

We need to proceed more methodically; and I think a starting point for our task is provided by an important book on French art and artistic thought, Marian Hobson's *The Object of Art* (1982).

VIEWS OF ART AND THEIR HISTORY: BIMODAL AND BIPOLAR

I have concentrated so far on the development, mainly in the eighteenth century, of the *aesthetic* view of art, which takes the recipient or consumer as its starting point and imagines the effects of art upon that recipient as something comparable to physical sense experience (αἰσθητά). This type of thinking soon arrives at the conclusion that the very existence of the art work—*as* art—does not arise except in the process of its being received and appreciated.

Hobson never raises the question of the art work's existence, and sees the eighteenth-century change in views of art from a different perspective. The basic concept she works with is that of *illusion,* and she argues that the eighteenth century is strongly marked by the shift from a "bimodal" to a "bipolar" view of artistic illusion. The decisive question is that of the recipient's or spectator's relation to the "physical matter" of the art work (the canvas, the material, the artistic devices) and to its "imaginative tissue" (the content, the persuasive image, that which is imitated).[3] In the bimodal view, *"both* matter *and* tissue may be present [to the recipient] simultaneously or nearly so . . . or the representation itself may be dual" (12). Our awareness of what the work is showing us, and our awareness of the methods by which it does its showing, are aspects or modes of the same basic experience. In the bipolar view, by contrast, *"either* the physical matter *or* the imaginative tissue of the work is present to us at one time." The bipolar "account of illusion strives to exclude, not to include, consciousness" (62), meaning consciousness of the devices, materials, or machinery by which the illusion is produced. When we do become conscious of these things, in the bipolar view, the illusion is simply lost and the aim of the art work is thwarted.

Now in an absolute sense the bimodal view is clearly preferable. It does not really ever happen that one forgets completely that one is seeing or hearing a work of art. There are moments in reacting to art when we experience emotional or even bodily spasms that seem very similar to what we would experience if confronted with reality itself. But these moments pass quickly and give way to a feeling we ordinarily describe as aesthetic "pleasure"—which, as Hobson points out (49), is difficult to account for in bipolar terms. Especially striking is Hobson's treatment (56-61) of several critical texts of Diderot, in which she shows that despite their frequent insistence on a bipolar position, the shape of the thought constantly brings it back toward a bimodal view.

But recognitions of this type create a problem. Hobson concludes her argument on Diderot as follows: "Diderot's critical practice, then, in its constant play between art and nature, represents *papillotage* [bimodal experience in the form of rapid oscillation], however much his critical pronouncements may decry it. Yet his critical position was characteristic of the latter half of the century. The whole notion of the relation between art object and nature is changing from that of reference [bimodal] to that of replica [bipolar]" (61). If this historical perception is valid—and Hobson's argument on the point is extremely strong and well documented—then we are faced with the question of *how* the change she speaks of could possibly have happened. If even the committed partisans of a bipolar view are driven by their own thinking back toward the bimodal, how could a bipolar position ever have gained its ascendancy?

Hobson's answer to this question has to do with the history of epistemology, and seems to me accurate as far as it goes. But it needs to be supplemented before it can account for the establishment of bipolarity as a habit of mind beyond intellectual and academic circles. She summarizes:

> "Illusion" in the earlier part of the [eighteenth] century was an intersubjective game. . . . But by the end of the century, illusion has hardened: it has become either the designation of a private state of mind, which can be true or false, or the designation of the art object as a copy, true or false to a model. It is this movement which enables the establishment in the nineteenth century of the notion of aesthetic experience as essentially private, as having the same kind of intimate uniqueness as the experience of love or death; but it is also what sets up the modern concept of the art object. What had been a mediate area, a twilight zone between subject and object, is carved up into an experience seen as private and an object which is external. Only the greatest modern thinkers in aesthetics—Kant, Schiller, Hegel—relate these divided areas dialectically. (44)

I think the appeal to Kant (who never shows the slightest interest in "art objects") is the sign of a certain desperation. It is almost as if Kant were being invoked in order to *justify* a bipolar view of art retrospectively— where Diderot had failed. But in reality the bipolar view of art requires neither an abstract nor an historical justification. It needs only to be seen in its relation to the aesthetic view—the idea that everything important about a work of art can and should be recognized from the vantage point of a recipient who is basically as passive as one is with respect to sense-impressions.

In principle the aesthetic view can accommodate both bimodal and bipolar positions. But the historical situation ensures that it will tend more and more to favor the bipolar. For the aesthetic view is fundamentally bourgeois. It reflects a focus upon the *value* (ultimately the monetary value) of the work of art for me as an individual—rather than upon the *operation* of the work in a relatively exclusive social group to which I belong. (This tendency is seen most clearly in the new art of "literature," which supplants what had earlier been called "poetry" and calls forth especially judgments on its value as edification.) And in order for me to be as certain as possible about the work's value—starting from the basic insecurity of the bourgeois vis-à-vis a field of endeavor and appreciation that had long been the domain of the church and the court—it helps if the work is as much an "external" object or commodity as possible, and if my experience of it is as "private," as exclusively mine, as possible, an experience separated, as far as possible, from the publicly exposed artistic machinery. Whence it follows that the bipolar view, for all its deficiencies, will tend to become normal.

THE PROBLEM OF COMMUNICATION

But at this point a problem arises that goes even beyond the empirical questionableness of the bipolar view. Or at least such a problem arises if we agree that the issue of communication is as deeply involved in the developing discipline of aesthetics as I have suggested above. For the aesthetic view in its inevitable bipolar tendency creates an impassable gulf between the imaginative experience that needs to be communicable and the only possible vehicle by which it could have been communicated. The art "object" (or contrivance or artifice, in whatever sense) has been made strictly external, therefore available to every individual in exactly the same way, therefore ideally situated to serve as a basis for communication. But at the same time, it has also lost all direct contact with the newly "private" communicandum.

The result is an insoluble dilemma: Art could become truly communicative only by way of contact between the two poles whose contact (in the bipolar view) is prohibited by the very idea of art. In art viewed from a bimodal (or social) perspective, such contact is not a problem; it is simply the normal way of apprehending art. And now, in the increasingly aesthetic age of the bourgeois consumer of art, an institutional recollection of that earlier normality may be at work behind the occasional dream of renewed contact between those poles whose redefinition excludes it. At least something of the sort appears to be happening in Kant's millennialist dream of universal emotional contact by way of beauty. His idea of an aesthetically accessible *Gemeinsinn* [sense in common] is not much more than the metaphysicalization of what might otherwise have been an attempt to describe the web of social and conventional processes in which a bimodal reception of the arts arises—a metaphysicalization that is made necessary by the strict exclusion of bimodality in any theory of art that is based on an idea of private (or bourgeois) aesthetic judgment, judgment springing from "the free play of the cognitive faculties" inside an individual mind.

The advantage of Hobson's system of concepts is thus that it opens our eyes to the hugely contradictory but basically simple situation of the arts in nineteenth-century Europe, as it develops out of eighteenth-century tendencies. On one hand, the aesthetic view of art, in its bourgeois context, produces a definitive shift away from bimodality toward bipolarity in the thinking not only of critics and theorists, but of the newly forming "public" as well, those people to whom art must offer itself as a commodity with monetary value. This shift produces the insoluble dilemma we have just discussed. Art is pointless if it is not communicative; but bipolarity, in the very process of profiling a possible vehicle of communication, also excludes the possibility of communication as a fact.

And on the other hand, bipolarity is untenable as a view of real conditions. It cannot happen that consciousness of the artificiality of art is simply excluded from the receptive process. But the immediate historical consequence of this fact is not that the whole idea of bipolarity is discarded—which would be the only reasonable course in theory. Far from it. What happens is that the needful but impossible exclusion of consciousness from art appreciation is transformed from a theorem into an *imperative*—which (we have seen) is in truth what the idea of a judgment uncontaminated by concepts is for Kant. Or in another terminology, *aesthetic response* becomes an imperative. And the non-existence of response in the domain of fact (assuming I am correct on this point) only leads to its being insisted upon, as an imperative, all the more desperately; because without it the whole aesthetic view of art collapses, and art no longer has any function, any reason for existing, in bourgeois life.

One could be excused for regarding this whole situation as a kind of insanity. But it is a madness that has method in it—a method all its own, not deliberated or supervised by any human agency. In the first place, the untenable idea of response is supported by a long-established doctrine of reading that attaches itself to the age's most popular literary form. In the second place, as an imperative rather than a putative fact, aesthetic response is no longer limited to a tiny moment of time before we start thinking about the art work. Now any moment at all will serve, as long as we use it to obey the aesthetic or bipolar imperative and (by whatever contortions of self-discipline or self-forgetting) drive out conceptual thought in order to indulge ourselves in the pure presence of the beautiful. Therefore we now have no trouble associating the idea of response with works of poetry or theater or music. And in the third place, even the impossibility of communication, which follows logically from the consideration of bipolarity as a doctrine, now ceases to trouble us. For when we are in the process of responding to art as mindlessly as we have now been persuaded we should, nothing could be further from our thoughts than that logic; and if we sneak a look at the presumably rapt expression on the faces of our co-responders, it in fact becomes quite easy for us to convince ourselves that we have achieved true communication after all.

THE NINETEENTH CENTURY

The question before us is still: Can it be shown that in the nineteenth century, the imperative of aesthetic response was accepted by a segment of Europe's population sufficiently large to account for its apparent role in the success of totalitarian propaganda? But the question is now a good deal less troublesome than when we first encountered it. For in the meantime, we have understood the logical relations that connect the idea of aesthetic response with the aesthetic or reception-oriented view of art and with the doctrine of bipolarity. And we have understood the manner in which all three of these modes of thought combine to authorize a bourgeois appropriation of the world of art—or how they follow from such an appropriation, depending on how one looks at it.

In particular, we have seen that the bipolar view—the idea that art does not operate properly unless the recipient's consciousness of the artistic medium is suppressed—is theoretically and empirically untenable. Therefore, in order for such a view to hold sway in the new bourgeois age, it must be coupled with the idea of aesthetic response and sustained by something like the threefold mechanism I have sketched: the analogy with other important cultural practices such as reading; an understanding of the magical aesthetic moment as the object of a type of imperative; and a willingness to interpret the acceptance of such imperatives as a sign of communication on a level deep enough to circumvent the logic by which precisely the possibility of communication would otherwise be refuted. It follows that the idea of response, which (in its new guise as an imperative) is presupposed as part of any such mechanism, must be operative on a large scale wherever the dominant view of art is bipolar.

Hobson's argument on the growing ascendancy of bipolarity in artistic theory and practice, at the end of the eighteenth century, is therefore probably enough to establish the point we are interested in, concerning widespread acceptance of the imperative of aesthetic response. And the situation toward the end of the nineteenth century provides another kind of evidence. For it is generally recognized that early modernism orients itself by an attack on the comfortable bourgeois pleasure of submergence in artistic illusion, an attack that would be incomprehensible without the precondition of a decisively bipolar view in the broad artistic public.[4]

Or to look at the matter case by case: Even without invoking Hobson's very detailed discussion of the theater (139-208), it is clear that from the eighteenth into the early nineteenth century, the increasing use of a darkened auditorium and a stage framed by footlights encourages in spectators the attitude of a voyeur, rather than that of a social/artistic participant. And toward the end of the nineteenth century, theatrical experimentation tends to break up the illusion of sympathetic or scandalous human reality and so to destroy exactly that voyeuristic pleasure. Especially important in this connection is the cultivation of the puppet-theater and more or less kindred forms, which we will have occasion to discuss later.

The question of bipolarity in poetry and music, from the eighteenth into the nineteenth century, has complex ramifications. (See Hobson, 209-97.) But for our purposes—to assure ourselves that here too a bipolar view, including necessarily the imperative of aesthetic response, is generally prevalent—a few relatively simple considerations suffice. Here, as in the case of the novel, the imperative that I have called *the* reader assumes the function of aesthetic response, the obligation incurred by every reader or listener to de-particularize him- or herself and so to become an uncontaminated vessel for the artistic experience. And later in the nineteenth century, the expectable reaction against the imperative (or by now the bourgeois habit) of aesthetic response is not absent. The case of poetry, where the artistic medium is shared with the critical medium (on all its levels), has special complications; some very advanced Parnassian and Symbolist poetry gets assimilated to an aesthetic or bourgeois style of reading. But the general situation, the strong opposition to aesthetic response, is still clear enough, and is perhaps set forth best by critics, like Gerald L. Bruns and Julia Kristeva, who focus strongly on Mallarmé.[5]

The case of painting is made interesting by a critical paradox. If the painting is to offer a perfect replica of natural reality, as the bipolar view requires, then the painter must develop a technique to achieve this end. But the technique, if it exists, cannot avoid interfering with the illusion. Hobson points out:

> The implications of Diderot's treatment of Chardin's work are contradictory. Chardin has no art, "c'est la nature même" [it is nature herself]; Chardin is all art: "Il n'a point de manière; je me trompe, il a la sienne. Mais puisqu'il a une manière, sienne, il devroit être faux dans quelques circonstances, et il ne l'est jamais" [He has no manner; I'm wrong, he has *his* manner. But since he has a manner, *his* manner, he would have to be false in some circumstances, and he is never false].[6]

An obvious way to meet this dilemma would be to discover a technique that bodies forth, *as* technique, exactly the same nature that is meant to be imitated. Hobson mentions a number of moves in that direction (75-77).

But in reality, there is no such solution. And after a long period of groping, the decisive break with bipolarity is finally made by late-century impressionism, whose practitioners were sometimes called "scientists" by their detractors, because of their focus on the disclosure of truths—truths about the nature of color and the operation of the visual sense, and especially about painting technique. One of the best instances by which to understand this anti-bipolar shifting of technique to center stage is the comparison of the treatment of background in W. P. Frith's *Derby Day* with that in Manet's *At the Races*—a comparison suggested by Whistler and developed by E. H. Gombrich.[7] Despite the sense of much greater realistic detail in Frith's painting, his representation of the distant crowd in the grandstand relies every bit as much on the viewer's imagination as the sense of the crowd does in Manet. The difference is that Manet endows this basic fact of technique with its own strong pictorial interest, and so thrusts it before his viewer, rather than attempt to conceal it.

There is no way to decide *exactly* how widespread, in the nineteenth and early twentieth century, acceptance of the imperative of aesthetic response was. I am not even sure that the question in this form makes sense. But I think we have come far enough now to shift our attention to the question of whether the imperative of aesthetic response is *needed* to explain the operation of totalitarian propaganda, and to be confident that it is there if we do need it.

NOT QUITE UNDERSTANDING MEDIA

In theoretical discussions of political or commercial propaganda, the idea of "persuasion" often crops up.[8] It seems to me that the implications of this concept are misleading. The goal of persuasion is to induce someone to adopt a position or to form a conviction, whereas the goal of propaganda is no such thing. The propagandist is satisfied if you buy the correct product or cast the correct vote, regardless of what you happen to be thinking when you do so. Indeed, the less you think, the better; for serious interpretive thought will tend ordinarily only to complicate the choices you make. And if you do think, or are in the habit of thinking, the goal of propaganda is to establish as strict a separation as possible between your private thoughts and the choices it is interested in. Think whatever you want, as long as you toe the line where it counts. Frederick the Great is said to have said, "räsonnirt, so viel ihr wollt, und worüber ihr wollt; nur gehorcht!"[9]

Of course the supreme triumph of propaganda would be—and unfortunately, has been—to govern the actual thoughts of its audience, because the desired choices in conduct must then follow automatically. But as long as conditions are not yet ripe for that achievement, the aim of propaganda is not persuasion, but rather *unthinking assent*. This assertion is not entirely uncontroversial; but I think it holds for totalitarian propaganda in the first half of the twentieth century. And it raises the question: What exactly do we mean by "unthinking" assent?

O. W. Riegel, in 1934, wrote a "story of the new propaganda" which is concise, cogent, biting, often brilliantly prescient—and has the added advantage of being universal in scope, showing no inclination to blame all the world's troubles on Germany and Russia, or imperialist Japan. Especially striking is his understanding of the relatively new medium of broadcast radio.

> Through broadcasting channels propaganda speeds directly from the
> political fountainhead to the listener's ear without the intermediation
> of any interpreter or critic, and is not subject to the steadying influences
> of correction or reply. Radio propaganda possesses unprecedented
> force because it utilizes the persuasiveness of the human voice and the
> personal prestige of the speakers from whom it issues. It is irrespon-
> sible in the sense that it is not subject to the reconsideration and after-
> study which occur when ideas are published in cold print.[10]

There are some gaps in the logic here. Why should radio propaganda not
be subject to "reconsideration" after the speech is over? But especially in
its time, Riegel's is in my opinion surprisingly close to a definitive grasp
of the radio medium.

The only thing seriously wrong with his overall argument is that, in
effect, he takes unthinking assent to mean *uninformed* assent. Modern
propaganda, he claims, is always nationalist in intent and spirit. (In 1934
it would have been practically impossible to avoid this error.) And the
principal damage it does in the world is "the Corruption of News" (108-
68). Accurate, unbiased information is the main casualty of modern media practices; and its absence provides the main opening for a "deliberate
manipulation of public opinion" (168). In particular, "It is imperative at
this time . . . to recall the millions of human beings in the United States
and other countries who are the pawns of nationalistic thrusts and pressures, and who are dependent upon the communication facilities of the
world for the information which governs their ideas and behavior" (56).
At this point Marshall McLuhan would have sneered—and with some
justification. Surely our behavior is "governed" less by "information" or
media-content than by the medium as its own "message." Riegel himself
almost says this in the paragraph on radio quoted above.

But especially with regard to Nazi Germany, there are more concrete
objections to the idea of uninformed assent as an explanation of propagandistic success. In the first place, even in the technologically primitive
1920s and 30s, the narrow geographical confines of Europe make it practically impossible for any one state to keep its citizens significantly uninformed. Riegel mentions the notorious *Volksempfänger*, and points to "the
spectacle of Germany struggling to outdo all other nations in the power
of its sending facilities while simultaneously struggling to reduce the
power of its receiving equipment to the minimum of audibility" (105).
But there was in reality no way to stop competing sources of information
and thought at the German borders.

And in the second place, if the diagnosis of uninformed assent were
correct for Nazi Germany, it would follow that the Nazi movement, especially in its early stages, had to be carried mainly by the least-informed
strata of the population, the urban and rural lower classes. This was not
the case. The most important social precursor to the Nazi movement was
probably "the mobilization of middle-class sociability," in the form of

"cultural, athletic, and paramilitary associations."[11] And the early involvement of intellectuals with the Nazis is discussed in Arendt's section on "The Temporary Alliance Between the Mob and the Elite."[12]

But if we now skip thirty years forward to McLuhan's *Understanding Media,* in search of a better grasp of the phenomenon of unthinking assent, we are disappointed. The best McLuhan can do, in his chapter on "Radio," is the idea of *atavistic* assent.

> [Hitler's] thoughts were of very little consequence. Radio provided the first massive experience of electronic implosion, that reversal of the entire direction and meaning of literate Western civilization. For tribal peoples, for those whose entire social existence is an extension of family life, radio will continue to be a violent experience. Highly literate societies . . . have managed to absorb and to neutralize the radio implosion without revolution. Not so, those communities that have had only brief or superficial experience of literacy.[13]

And one of those only superficially literate communities turns out to be Germany.

> Just prior to 1914, the Germans had become obsessed with the menace of "encirclement." . . . Encirclement is a highly visual image that had great novelty for this newly industrialized nation. In the 1930s, by contrast, the German obsession was with *lebensraum.* This is not a visual concern, at all. It is a claustrophobia, engendered by the radio implosion and compression of space. The German defeat had thrust them back from visual obsession into brooding upon the resonating Africa within. The tribal past has never ceased to be a reality for the German psyche. (262)

Everything here is nonsense: both the idea of the insufficiently literate Germans, who receive even their visual experience in the form of an "obsession"; and the whole idea of literacy as a kind of inoculation against the insidious effects of radio propaganda (259).

Literacy is in fact part of the problem. Riegel and McLuhan—whom I choose as representing the ends of a scale of possibilities—are instances of a fascination with modernity that credits the most powerful modern innovations, like communications media, with a miraculous ability to create their own circumstances. For Riegel, modern information management creates its own stultified public of "pawns." For McLuhan, radio stirs up irrational ancestral memories that now suddenly inhabit and contaminate our thinking. But improbable conjectures of this sort are not really needed to explain the presence of unthinking assent as a common response to modern propaganda. For as I have argued at length: By the time modern propaganda and electronic media appear on the scene, unthinking assent had been accepted as an imperative for more than a century: in the form of the requirement that a reader transform himself or herself into *the* de-individualized reader, especially with novels; and in the form of the imperative of aesthetic response with respect to other artistic media. The only real question is how the habit or imperative of unthinking assent can have found its way from the artistic to the political realm. And at least part of an answer to this question is already suggested by the overwhelming popularity of realistic novels, whose content constantly brings them, and their artistically minded audience, into contact with politics.

THE INFINITE AUDIENCE

It must be understood: *Propaganda does not create the conditions of its own success.* To assert the contrary would be to suggest that propaganda cannot be successful until after it has been successful—a suggestion that is as vacuous in fact as it is silly in logic. And yet, it is a suggestion that many very intelligent people (like Riegel and McLuhan) find themselves flirting with. Even Jacques Ellul, who has been called "the doyen of propaganda theorists," insists:

> Propaganda tries to surround man by all possible routes, in the realm of feelings as well as ideas, by playing on his will or on his needs, through his conscious and his unconscious, assailing him in both his public and his private life. It furnishes him with a complete system for explaining the world, and provides immediate incentives to action. We are here in the presence of an organized myth that tries to take hold of the entire person. . . . This myth becomes so powerful that it invades every area of consciousness, leaving no faculty or motivation intact.[14]

Ellul is generally a very sensible writer. He understands clearly that "The aim of modern propaganda is no longer to modify ideas [which I have called 'persuasion'], but to provoke action. It is no longer to change adherence to a doctrine, but to make the individual cling irrationally to a process of action" (16). Yet even he cannot resist the propagandist mystique, the idea of propaganda as a kind of self-generated evil, as a sudden and complete enveloping of the individual in a fabric of lies.

The idea that propaganda provides its adherent (or victim) "with a complete system for explaining the world" is simply false. The Nazi and Soviet versions of propaganda may have been "mythical," in Ellul's sense; but they were neither complete nor systematic in any reasonable understanding of these terms. On the contrary, they were full of contradictions, reversals, slippages, times when one had no idea what tomorrow's party line was going to be. This is an important fact which Ellul himself acknowledges and even tries to explain. "Continuous propaganda exceeds the individual's capacities for attention or adaptation and thus his capabilities of resistance. This trait of continuity explains why propaganda can indulge in sudden twists and turns. It is always surprising that the content of propaganda can be so inconsistent that it can approve today what it condemned yesterday" (12). Propaganda can afford to be inconsistent (i.e., self-interrupting) because it is so continuous (i.e., uninterrupted)?

This explanation, even if one tries to accept it provisionally, also depends on an idea of "continuous" propaganda that ignores a still simpler fact than the one it supposedly explains.

> Propaganda must be continuous and lasting—continuous in that it must not leave any gaps, but must fill the citizen's whole day and all his days; lasting in that it must function over a very long period of time. Propaganda tends to make the individual live in a separate world; he must not have outside points of reference. He must not be allowed a moment of meditation or reflection . . . [Propaganda] must create a complete environment for the individual, one from which he never emerges. (11-12)

The trouble with this Orwellian vision is that it is never fulfilled in reality. As long as your victim eats, sleeps, works, walks the streets, looks at the ground or the sky, you cannot possibly enclose him or her in the kind of "environment" Ellul postulates. He or she, no matter what you do, will have at least bits of time for "meditation or reflection." The question that matters is: *What keeps the victim from making better use of that time?*

And an answer to this question cannot be provided by the study of propaganda itself. The circumstances or preconditions under which propaganda operates must be considered. The phenomenon of terror, for example, which modern totalitarianism inherited from the French Revolution, the condition of living uninterruptedly in fear of being secretly denounced, for any (or no) reason, by any of one's fellow citizens, even by one's family, may go a long way toward explaining a feeling of "uninterrupted" exposure to propaganda. But terror cannot function properly without the willingness of large numbers of otherwise harmless people to act as unofficial government spies. And this condition arises only as the *result* of a long and successful propaganda campaign. The same applies to Bruno Bettelheim's argument on the "daily tasks" by which a totalitarian regime creates psychological dependency in its subjects.[15] It is probably true in general that a population's total ideological immersion grows closer to being possible, the longer their totalitarian regime endures. But the point about propaganda is that its most important tasks must be carried out even before the movement comes to power.

I think, accordingly, that in order to account for the rise and flower and day-to-day operation of modern propaganda, we have no choice but to acknowledge the indispensability of its *aesthetic preconditions*: in the case of totalitarian propaganda, the spread of a secular millennialist habit of mind by way of philosophical aesthetics and the paradox of the realistic novel; and in the case of propaganda in general, the transfer from the artistic to the political domain of a long-established imperative of unthinking assent—an imperative that enjoins in certain situations the posi-tive *avoidance* of "meditation or reflection." My point is perhaps ultimate-ly a negative one. In order to prove it conclusively, one would have to demonstrate the complete absence of alternatives, which is impossible. But we can make a good positive argument for the way the aesthetic imperative of unthinking assent operates in modern propaganda, and the way it helps explain the impact of broadcast radio.

Let us start, once again, with Kant. His assertion that in making an aesthetic (non-conceptual) judgment, we are justified in assuming that the same judgment will be shared by every other human being, reflects two general tendencies: (1) the millennial yearning for a cultural situation in which that assumption would be a certainty; and (2) the desirability of a cultural imperative whereby I would be obligated to exclude conceptu-al thought from my response to any work of art, an imperative which, if observed consistently, would *make* the Kantian assumption a certainty with respect to art. (I have suggested above that such an imperative is reinforced by certain long-standing developments in the history of read-ing; and I have argued the relatively obvious point that that imperative is widely acknowledged in nineteenth-century Europe.) The trouble is that the very existence of an imperative of this type faces us constantly with the question of whether it can be fulfilled—can I really prevent myself from thinking?—and so engenders the craving for *evidence* of its fulfil-ment in particular cases. Hence the attraction of the theater, the opera house, the concert hall, where it seems we can actually see and hear our enthusiasm being shared by others. The mere fact that say three hundred people can be induced to keep quiet, and to refrain from smoking, for hours at a time, seems clear evidence of the aesthetic solidarity we seek.[16]

But the magic of the theater lasts only a few hours, and the people with whom one has shared it (most of whom one does not know person-ally anyway) form only a very small group relative to the mass of insuf-ferable fellow commuters by whom one is jostled the next morning. And even worse, the performance itself is now also gone—the instance of artistic beauty by which one had fulfilled one's obligation to be captivat-ed. One can struggle to remember it (and one's feelings) exactly; one can discuss it with someone claiming to be a fellow connoisseur; one can read the newspaper reviews and perhaps seem to bathe in their eloquence: but none of this makes any difference in the end. The moment that matters, the moment of aesthetic response, is now a thing of the past, gone for-ever.

This is where broadcast radio comes in. If you can be induced to situate a radio program (say, a political speech) in the aesthetic area of your experience, then suddenly you find yourself in the midst of an infinite audience—infinite in that it is as large as your imagination can make it. (And if the broadcaster is competent, your imagination will be stimulated by enthusiastic crowd noises in the background.) The trouble with the imperative of aesthetic response is that it is an imperative, not a simple fact. When you go to the theater in search of a collective experience by which to be swept away irresistibly, your sense of carrying out an imperative is sustained by the need to buy a ticket, to dress within certain limits, to obey certain rules of conduct in the auditorium. As the member of an infinite radio audience, by contrast, you can be practically anywhere at all and be doing practically anything at all. Your awareness of the imperative quality of what you now imagine to be your unwilled response is reduced to a minimum; it is as if the ultimate aesthetic goal were finally achieved in reality: *universal uniformity of response.* Even the impermanence of the experience is compensated for by its universality. The universal is practically by definition permanent.

It could now conceivably be true that everyone in the world, at least everyone who speaks the language you are listening to, is undergoing in this moment exactly the experience you are. Certainly in the United States, broadcasters were aware of this quality of their medium. I remember from my childhood (let us say, in the period 1947-1952) magazine advertisements having to do with broadcast radio, multiple-image layouts showing: a well-dressed family, with pampered dog, sitting before an expensive floor model receiver; a worker's family, with scruffy dog, huddled around a cheap radio on the kitchen table; a couple of grade-school geniuses listening to a home-made set; elegant men and women, perhaps sexually adventurous, doing their listening in a cocktail lounge; an apparently lonely man driving at night, seen obliquely from behind in the glow of the dashboard radio; and so on. What is it that unites these people? That they are all hearing exactly the same sounds from their radios, exactly the same atmospheric vibrations, is not enough to explain the sense of community that is conveyed. But it would obviously be too much to suggest that they are all thinking similar thoughts. What unites them is something somehow *between* simple sense experience and any cogitating on that experience, which is what I have called "response."

Broadcast radio could not have produced by itself the effect I have described. The presence in European culture of universal uniformity of response as an idea, as a logically inescapable aim of the whole aesthetic/ bipolar view of art, is required before broadcast radio can seem a sudden and unexpectedly complete realization of that idea. Even the idea, as such, was probably not enough. The sense of a complete realization of uniform mass response probably could not have arisen without support from the eighteenth- and nineteenth-century assumption of a level of universal uniformity in how people respond to the identical printed copies of a text—the institution of *the* reader. What we are talking about is a complicated state of affairs in which the phenomenon of broadcast radio serves particularly well as a focus. We need to understand that state of affairs as a whole.

AT THE SAME TIME

I introduced the preceding argument by saying, "If you can be induced to situate a radio program in the aesthetic area of your experience." This is an important limitation; and I have suggested a way of dealing with it, which has to do with the paradox of the realistic novel. Despite the generally liberal tendency of novels (plural), the realistic novel as an institution plays into the hand of totalitarian propaganda by creating a bridge between the aesthetic and the political as such, thus facilitating the aestheticization of political radio—as an aspect, I suppose, of Benjamin's idea of a fascist aestheticization of politics in general. Perhaps the whole phenomenon of artistic realism is involved here, including literature, theater, pictorial art, and, in due course, photography and cinema. For the immediate effect of realism in any of these arts is to create an intermixture of the domain of aesthetic experience with that of everyday experience, an intermediate domain in which the application of aesthetic categories to the new (not yet pigeonholed) experience of broadcast radio may seem entirely natural.

But it is still hard to reconcile the idea of what radio actually was, in its early days, with the idea of the aesthetic. Harry Haller, in Hesse's *Steppenwolf,* we recall, is repelled by the idea of hearing Mozart disfigured by radio interference. How much more so would he have been by the fifty or so speeches of Hitler that we are told were broadcast in 1933?[17] And yet, people did listen to those broadcasts; and a substantial number of them were influenced by what they heard. What does the general state of affairs look like that can make these things possible?

We will go into this question in detail in the next chapter, with the aid of Arendt's discussion of social conditions in Germany and in the Soviet Union. But one important point that can be made in advance has to do with the invention of *simultaneity.* As an idea or as a fact, simultaneity exists long before the twentieth century. Werther, like many lovers, worries at one point (letter of 20 January) about what his distant beloved is doing in this very moment. Or if you and I are ancient Greeks, planning to measure the circumference of the earth by comparing the length of sun-shadows at widely separated geographical points, we must be as certain as possible that our experiments are made at exactly the same time. But before broadcast radio, simultaneity exists as an *experience* only where it is combined with spatial proximity. I can have the experience of sharing a single significant moment in time with the few thousand people in a stadium; but I cannot have a comparable experience involving, for instance, the whole of the German nation. With the coming of broadcast radio, however, just such an experience becomes possible.

The notion of simultaneity even brings with it its own political dimension. Benedict Anderson, in describing the "imagined communities" that he associates with nationalism, argues that the idea of horizontal or calendar simultaneity is relatively recent, and that its importance in political history is suggested by "the basic structure of two forms of imagining which first flowered in Europe in the eighteenth century: the novel and the newspaper," a structure he reads as "a complex gloss upon the word 'meanwhile.'"[18] Especially the parallel development of connected Old-World and New-World political bodies is influential in the rise of modern nationalism (187-99)—and thence also, perhaps, in the rise of the not merely imagined but hallucinatory communities of totalitarianism. Thus from a political as well as from a cultural direction, the ground is prepared for simultaneity in its culminating form.

Nor is this culmination marked solely by the size of the experiencing group. For with broadcast radio the whole dimension of space has been removed from the experience of simultaneity, which now unfolds entirely within the dimension of time. Whenever this experience occurs, or is induced, one finds oneself sharing the same instant of time with a potentially infinite group of fellow experiencers, without benefit of any spatial buffer zone by which to maintain one's independence.[19]

We think yet once more of Kant in this connection. For at the very beginning of the *Critique of Pure Reason,* he argues that "Time is nothing other than the form of the inner sense, that is, the form of our intuition of ourselves and of our inner condition" (§ 6). And if we accept this basic thought—as practically everyone does, including (in his way) Bergson and (in his way) Heidegger—then it follows that the new kind of simultaneity made possible by broadcast radio has the effect, when I experience it, of permitting untold millions of alien human subjects to crowd into the inside of my head. Again, we must resist the temptation to attribute this whole effect to the advent of radio. But since the experience of simultaneity had long been recognized as an aesthetic desideratum, especially in the form in which it unfolds for a theater audience, it is hard to see how the transformed and magnified version of that experience could have failed to take hold once broadcast radio made its appearance.

The new experience of simultaneity brings with it an abolition of privacy—which perhaps gives us another way of understanding the impression of uninterrupted propaganda that is created under a totalitarian regime. But curiously enough, the abolition of privacy does not include an abolition of aloneness. McLuhan has a useful insight in this regard, about how "[broadcast radio creates] depth involvement for everybody. 'I live right inside radio when I listen. I more easily lose myself in radio than in a book,' said a voice from a radio poll. The power of radio to involve people in depth is manifested in its use during homework by youngsters and by many other people who carry transistor sets in order to provide a private world for themselves amidst crowds" (260). "Solitary" would have been a better word than "private" here. It is our strict inner aloneness that is invaded by the infinite audience of radio, *but without ceasing to be a condition of strict aloneness.* Arendt is often cited on the point that "totalitarian movements depended less on the structure-lessness of a mass society than on the specific conditions of an atomized and individualized mass" (318). But how can the conditions of mass submergence and atomized individuality be combined in one? The infinitely invaded but thus also intensified aloneness of the radio listener perhaps supplies at least a context for discussing this question. It is interesting that despite all the advantages the Nazis derived from radio propaganda, apparently neither Goebbels nor his ministry had any idea of exploiting the listener's aloneness. In fact, "Great emphasis was placed on the encouragement of community listening."[20] But the propaganda seems to have worked anyway.

A REMARK ON THE SOVIET UNION

In thinking about broadcast radio we cannot help thinking about the great difference between Arendt's two main examples of totalitarianism, Nazi Germany and the Soviet Union under Stalin. For while radio propaganda was extremely important to the Nazis, it was much less so to the Soviets. This is hardly a reason for putting the two movements in different categories, considering how much they had in common: a regime of terror and secret denunciation; concentration camps; willing confessions of guilt by condemned party members; the confusing duplication of party and state departments and functions; constant changes in policy and random liquidation of individuals and groups; the official denial of known facts; the sacrifice of national interests for no discernible purpose; and above all, the millennialist vision of a new world order. But the differences between these two main instances still need to be accounted for.

When Stalin took power once and for all in late 1927, much of the basic structure of the future totalitarian state was already in place, including especially the concentric distribution of authority that later also characterized Nazi government: the populace enclosing the party enclosing the Central Committee enclosing the politburo enclosing, in due course, the new leader Stalin. The struggle by which Stalin and his faction came to power was primarily an intra-party affair, not driven by its public-relations component. The Nazis, by contrast, came to power in a series of elections, and were obliged to spend much effort on forming their popular following and on maintaining it in the early years of their government. It is easy to see why broadcast radio was so much more important in their operations.

But the difficulty we started with has not been removed. For if the experience of simultaneity is as important in understanding totalitarian propaganda as I have suggested; and if that experience is first established on a national scale only by the influence of broadcast radio: then we are still unable to give as good an account of Soviet totalitarianism as of the

Nazi version. We can deal with this difficulty by anticipating here an argument that will be carried out in detail in the next chapter, on *permanent simultaneity*. Simultaneity, in the sense that I live my life simultaneously with everyone else, seems to be a simple fact—a fact, according to Benedict Anderson, that most Westerners become increasingly aware of in the nineteenth century. And when that fact is then realized as an immediate experience—particularly in broadcast radio, but also in such forms of instantaneous communication as telegraph and telephone—the character of my life is changed considerably. The quality of living in a known but abstract condition of simultaneity is replaced by the quality of living constantly on the brink or within reach of simultaneity as an immediate experience. This is what I call the condition of permanent simultaneity, and I will argue in the next chapter that it is sufficient to account for the effectiveness of totalitarian propaganda.

Once broadcast radio has had its initial effect on our sensibilities, therefore, the condition of permanent simultaneity can be expected to obtain even where radio propaganda had not been used extensively—in the Soviet Union, for instance. Which raises a further question: If permanent simultaneity is as widespread as this argument suggests, why doesn't all Europe go totalitarian in the first half of the twentieth century? I will discuss this point in the next chapter too. Briefly: Permanent simultaneity has an effect in the political sphere only in combination with certain specific social conditions, notably the "atomized and individualized mass" that Arendt speaks of. These conditions were there waiting for Hitler when he rose to power. And in the Soviet Union, essentially the same conditions were deliberately created by Stalinist policies that destroyed all forms of class or group solidarity in Soviet society: first the national Soviets, then the remnants of social classes in the cities, the countryside, and the factories, and then the bureaucracy. "Mass atomization in Soviet society," says Arendt, creates a situation where "the most elementary caution demands that one avoid all intimate contacts, if possible—not in order to prevent discovery of one's secret thoughts, but rather to eliminate, in the almost certain case of future trouble, all persons who might have not only an ordinary cheap interest in your denunciation but an irresistible need to bring about your ruin simply because they are in danger of their own lives" (323).

NOTES

1. This basic difficulty arises not only in aesthetic matters, but in all types of discussion that involve interpretation. And especially when the discussion includes very large numbers of participants (or at least readers), as in modern mass societies, one common consequence is the attachment of an unappealable value to *agreement* or *consensus* as such—a tendency which is obviously welcome in totalitarian movements.

On the relation of these matters to literature, see my *All Theater Is Revolutionary Theater*, 215-18, and my *Dark Side of Literacy*, 252-58. References chap. 4, n6.

2. *The Dark Side of Literacy*, 3.

3. Marian Hobson, *The Object of Art: The Theory of Illusion in Eighteenth-Century France* (Cambridge, 1982), 12.

4. I use the term "modernism" here despite the bad taste it leaves in my mouth. See my "It's a Word! It's a Claim! . . . Modernism and Related Instances of an Inherently Discredited Conceptual Type," *artUS*, special issue 5/6 (Jan./Feb. 2005), 10-15.

5. See Gerald L. Bruns, *Modern Poetry and the Idea of Language: A Critical and Historical Study* (New Haven, 1974), esp. 71-137; and Julia Kristeva, *Revolution in Poetic Language*, trans. Margaret Waller (New York, 1984; orig. French, 1974), esp. 226-34.

6. Hobson, 78, quoting from Denis Diderot, *Salon de 1765*, in *Les Salons de Diderot*, ed. Jean Seznec and Jean Adhémar, 3 vols. (Oxford, 1957-1963), 2:114.

7. See E. H. Gombrich, *Art and Illusion: A Study in the Psychology of Pictorial Representation* (New York: Pantheon, 1960), 216-17.

8. The classic work in this general area is Vance Packard, *The Hidden Persuaders* (New York, 1957). But even some very recent work still lumps persuasion together with propaganda: e.g., Garth S. Jowett and Victoria O'Donnell, eds., *Readings in Propaganda and Persuasion: New and Classic Essays* (Thousand Oaks, 2006); and Stanley B. Cunningham, *The Idea of Propaganda: A Reconstruction* (Westport, Conn., 2002). I do not mean that these books are not valuable; but they would be more so if their conceptual discriminations were tidier. Or one can approach the whole matter from a completely different conceptual direction, as in Christian Salmon, *Storytelling: Bewitching the Modern Mind*, trans. David Macey (London, 2010; orig. French, 2007).

9. Kant's admiring quotation of Frederick the Great, *Kants Werke*, 8:42.

10. O. W. Riegel, *Mobilizing for Chaos: The Story of the New Propaganda* (New York, 1972; reprint of New Haven: Yale University Press, 1934), 106-7.

11. Peter Fritzsche, "The NSDAP 1919-1934: from fringe politics to the seizure of power," in Jane Caplan, ed. *Nazi Germany* (Oxford, 2008), 52.

12. *The Origins of Totalitarianism*, 326-40. See chap. 1, n4.

13. Marshall McLuhan, *Understanding Media: The Extensions of Man*, 2nd ed. (New York: Signet, 1964), 262.

14. Jacques Ellul, "The Characteristics of Propaganda," in Jowett and O'Donnell, *Readings*, 7. Ellul's "essay" is an excerpt from his book, *Propaganda: The Formation of Men's Attitudes* (New York, 1965; orig. French, 1962). The characterization of Ellul as "doyen" is from Cunningham, 18.

15. Bruno Bettelheim, "Remarks on the Psychological Appeal of Totalitarianism," (orig. 1952), in his *Surviving and Other Essays* (New York, 1979), 317-32, esp. 323.

16. On public performances as supposed evidence of the validity of hermeneutics, see *All Theater Is Revolutionary Theater*,183-84. Permission to smoke was of course one of the conditions Brecht advocated, as a way of disrupting the culture of bipolarity (compelling illusion) and the concomitant ideal of aesthetic (emotional) solidarity.

17. David A. Welch, "Restructuring the Means of Communication in Nazi Germany," in Jowett/O'Donnell, 132; from his book, *The Third Reich: Politics and Propaganda* (London, 1993), chap. 3.

18. Benedict Anderson, *Imagined Communities: Reflections on the Origin and Spread of Nationalism*, rev. ed. (London, 2006), 24-25.

19. See Arendt, 465-66, on "total terror" as destruction of the dimension of space.

20. Welch, in Jowett/O'Donnell, 131.

TEN

The Totalitarian Imagination and Its Opposite

I do not claim to understand totalitarianism. I am not sure that "understanding" is an applicable category in the discussion. One common characteristic of totalitarian movements and regimes is their use of arbitrary self-revision and unashamed self-contradiction to avoid any exposure to the understanding. But this characteristic itself is very difficult to lay hold of. The best attempt to do so that I know of is the prescient allegory of totalitarian politics in Thomas Mann's "Mario and the Magician."[1]

This difficulty in understanding can be avoided by concentrating, as Arendt does, on the "origins" of totalitarianism, rather than on some idea of an essence or structure. The results of her work are indispensable, especially with regard to the ambivalent operation of the nation-state, the growth of "an atomized and individualized mass," and the evolved situation of European Jews. In the present book, while emulating her method, I have tried to complete her vision by operating in a different cultural register, where totalitarianism can be located in relation to: the secular millennialist tradition of aesthetics; the system of paradoxes that besets bipolar aesthetic thinking and the realistic novel; and especially the invention of simultaneity. One must not equate any of these concepts or phenomena with totalitarianism, or regard all of them together as a definition. They serve, rather, to *locate* totalitarianism for our thinking, by being understandable in ways that totalitarianism itself is not.

FACTUALITY AND NEGATIVITY

Even Arendt does not completely avoid the trap of misplaced under-standing. Her analysis of the structure of nested formations in the totali-tarian movement before it comes to power is instantly persuasive.

> The front organizations surround the movements' membership with a protective wall which separates them from the outside, normal world; at the same time, they form a bridge back to normalcy, without which the members in the prepower stage would feel too sharply the differ-ences between their beliefs and those of normal people, between the lying fictitiousness of their own and the reality of the normal world. . . . The world at large, on the other side, usually gets its first glimpse of a totalitarian movement through its . . . sympathizers, who are to all appearances still innocuous fellow-citizens . . . Even more striking than this relationship is that it is repeated on different levels within the movement itself. As party members are related to and separated from the fellow-travelers, so are the elite formations of the movement related to and separated from the ordinary members. . . . A definite advantage of this structure is that it blunts the impact of one of the basic totalitar-ian tenets—that the world is divided into two gigantic hostile camps, one of which is the movement, and that the movement can and must fight the whole world—a claim which prepares the way for the indis-criminate aggressiveness of totalitarian regimes in power. Through a carefully graduated hierarchy of militancy in which each rank is the higher level's image of the nontotalitarian world because it is less mili-tant and its members less totally organized, the shock of the terrifying and monstrous totalitarian dichotomy is vitiated and never full [sic] realized.[2]

Thus an answer to at least one important question is suggested: How is it possible, in the very bosom of "normal" reality, to manipulate knowledge and understanding so as to permit a thoroughly anti-normal movement to recruit and develop? Of course Arendt is talking primarily about the Nazis here; the problem in the Soviet Union was different.

And yet, although she points out that "the peculiar onion-like struc-ture" (413) is retained even after the movement comes to power, she also implies that the function of that structure with respect to factual knowl-edge has disappeared.

> Practically speaking, the paradox of totalitarianism in power is that the possession of all instruments of governmental power and violence in one country is not an unmixed blessing for a totalitarian movement. . . . Power means a direct confrontation with reality, and totalitarianism in power is constantly concerned with overcoming this challenge. Propa-ganda and organization no longer suffice to assert that the impossible is possible, that the incredible is true, that an insane consistency rules the world; the chief psychological support of totalitarian fiction—the active resentment of the status quo, which the masses refused to accept

as the only possible world—is no longer there; every bit of factual information that leaks through the iron curtain, set up against the ever-threatening flood of reality from the other, nontotalitarian side, is a greater menace to totalitarian domination than counterpropaganda has been to totalitarian movements. (391-92)

There is serious slippage here: In exactly what sense does power confront directly a "reality" beyond its power? If totalitarian movements develop in a constant interactive struggle with the factual knowledge that characterizes normality, how can that interaction suddenly disappear when a movement comes to power? And Churchill's famous metaphor notwithstanding, is there really any way to keep factual knowledge from leaking across borders, especially in the narrow confines of Europe?

These problems are related to the distinction between individual and collective knowledge, where by collective knowledge I mean simply knowledge that people employ openly in conversation. Collective knowledge, in this definition, can in fact be cut off by an iron curtain, if the secret police are efficient. But Arendt is talking about what she calls a "psychological" situation, meaning not some complicated idea of mass or crowd psychology, but the condition of an individual mind. And the idea that knowledge of facts, in this individual sense, can simply be denied to the members of large urban populations in an age of advanced communications technology, is untenable. Arendt holds fast to this idea, however, because it implies that the individual human mind, by its very existence, is a strong limiting factor with respect to totalitarianism. She couches her thought in accents of doom: "Factuality itself depends for its continued existence upon the existence of the nontotalitarian world" (388). But the converse of this proposition is that factuality, as such, is the mortal enemy of totalitarianism, that if enough of us, as individuals, simply maintain our sane grasp of fact, totalitarianism can never triumph.

This element of Arendt's thinking, in my opinion, is an instance of excessive understanding. It endows totalitarianism with something too much like an identity. Totalitarian regimes in the twentieth century, it is true, have attempted to banish certain factual knowledge by censorship. But it is probably also true that they need not have worried as much as they apparently did. Modern theory understands that the effectiveness of propaganda (in a sense that includes Arendt's "indoctrination" [341]) is measured not by how you think or what you know, but by what you do, for instance by how you vote. It does not matter what you know as long as you vote as you are meant to—or if a totalitarian regime already exists, as long as your behavior is such as to have a propaganda value of its own. Unthinking assent is what is required of you, assent without regard to any factual knowledge you might possess. My own contribution to the understanding of this point, I hope, is the recognition that aesthetic tradition—by way of the widely accepted imperative of aesthetic response—

has had the effect of training large numbers of people in exactly the unthinking assent that totalitarianism requires.

There are of course other factors in the genesis of totalitarianism. Arendt spends much time on the "front generation" (328), survivors for whom World War I had been a revelation of the utter emptiness and hypocrisy of all European institutions and values, and who now "were satisfied with blind partisanship in anything that respectable society had banned, regardless of theory or content" (331). Even Gide, later on and following their example, was moved to applaud Céline's *Bagatelles pour un massacre* (Arendt, 335). But I still doubt that the connection or passage between pure negativity and adventures in unthinking assent can be comprehended fully without taking into account the aesthetic education (to travesty Schiller) that even the front generation had received from its predecessors.

These points open a new problem, however, for both Arendt's argument and my criticism of it. How is a fundamentally negative worldview—like that of the front generation of intellectuals, or that of the disenchanted and resentful masses—transformed into a positive move of assent? And even if such a transformation occurs, how can it lead to anything but an endless multiplicity of conflicting projects and initiatives? Arendt's diagnosis of "the elite's lack of a sense of reality, together with its perverted selflessness"—characteristics that "resemble only too closely the fictitious world and the absence of self-interest among the masses" (335)—explains at most the possibility, not the actuality or even the likelihood, of a totalitarian development. And the same is true of the idea of an aesthetic training in unthinking assent that I have advanced.

PERMANENT SIMULTANEITY

I think we can get somewhere with this problem if we return to the idea of simultaneity. I have suggested that simultaneity as an experience is probably associated by large numbers of people with the experience of hearing broadcast radio. But it does not by any means follow that the experience of universal simultaneity—the sense of living in the same instant of time as everyone else—only occurs in those moments when the radio (or some comparable device) happens to be on. For no sooner does the experience of simultaneity come to be regarded as a possibility than it must also be regarded as representing a simple *fact*. Do we not all, in actual fact, always live in the same instant of time as everyone else? Is it not theoretically possible to pick a single instant and write a complete description of the world and all its inhabitants in that instant? (This possibility, interestingly enough, is denied *in theory*—by special relativity— in the same historical period in which universal simultaneity becomes important as a supposed experience.) And does it not follow that the experience of simultaneity must always be available to us, that we live our entire lives perhaps not constantly *in* that experience, but certainly at least always within reach or on the brink of it?

What difference does this state of affairs make in our ordinary lives, apart from the magic moments of radio listening? We certainly gain some tangible benefits from the invention of near-instantaneous communications media. But we also lose something. We lose *time* as what Kant calls the "inner sense"; we lose time as each individual's strictly private medium for self-contemplation and perhaps even (despite Kant) self-knowledge. We are still alone in our experience of time; but that aloneness—as I phrased it above—has now in effect been invaded by everyone else, without ceasing to be aloneness. This, it seems to me, is the condition of living constantly on the brink of the experience of simultaneity. It is a condition to which we have become so accustomed that it is difficult to articulate even the simplest description of it. It is perhaps exactly the condition that McLuhan describes as a "global village." And every now and then it betrays itself lexically, as when we speak of observing a distant event "in real time."

I am not implying (as I think McLuhan does) that modern media operate somehow to deprive us forcibly of time as a medium of reflection. My point is that in the course of the history of aesthetics, time in this sense has lost its relative value and has become something that people *willingly* sacrifice in favor of the benefits of simultaneity. For simultaneity is the only conceivable medium in which the moment of aesthetic response—whose very existence is otherwise open to doubt—might be realized as an immediate experience. And without the experience of aesthetic response, Kantian *Gemeinsinn* remains a mere speculation, that sense-in-common upon which any hope of adequate communication depends. It is possible to fulfill the imperative of response—or to convince oneself that one is fulfilling it—without using an established idea of simultaneity. But once simultaneity is established as a possibility in the culture, it becomes difficult to do without—for most people probably impossible. And the condition of living constantly at the brink of simultaneity, in this newly communicative universe, is achieved by the more or less deliberate sacrifice of time as an "inner sense," which means the sacrifice of a certain strict unbreakable privacy—perhaps the privacy Törless talks about in the very process of violating it.

The history of permanent simultaneity, since its invention in the early twentieth century, has its twists and turns, but seems in general inexorable. For some time now, neither radio nor its broadcast cousin television—its only very distant cousin, as McLuhan correctly points out[3] — has been a principal vehicle for the experience of simultaneity. Even the assurance that an event is being televised "live" no longer makes much difference to a public that has grown accustomed to taped and repeatable programs. And in the last couple of decades, broadcasting has not been needed anyway, because the experience of simultaneity is now sought—and many would say, found—in the instant availability of the whole world to users of the internet. But is this tradition sufficiently continuous—this handing of the baton from one electronic device to the next—to prove the permanent importance of simultaneity in our imaginative inventory? Isn't there, for one thing, too much historical gap between the exhaustion of broadcast media and the internet blossoming?

More attention needs to be paid here to the continuing popularity of the *novel*—in the form of printed books, or even as e-books, which do their best to mimic print artifacts in appearance and manner of manipulation. Ought the novel not by now to have become obsolete, after a full century of electric, electronic, and digital media? Assuming we agree that there is a question here, I think the answer has to do with the condition of permanent simultaneity. The trouble with most media in which the experience of universal simultaneity arises is that the illusion wears thin with time, for it is always an illusion, an experience imagined on the basis of obviously insufficient data. The broadcast media have lost power in this way. But whereas in the case of radio and its successors, the experience of the medium is used to support the idea of simultaneity, I contend that in the case of the novel, it is the established idea of permanent simultaneity that—by working backwards, as it were—endows the novelistic *medium* with a completely new experiential significance. Novels themselves, in their physical and linguistic nature, undergo no change at all. But the novel as an institution receives a completely new function.

For the principal problem with the realistic novel—the constant nagging flaw in our enjoyment of the form—arises from the paradox discussed in chapter 7 and has a strong *temporal* element. In Mme. de Staël's formulation, "On ne peut plus rien éprouver sans se souvenir presque de l'avoir lu, et tous les voiles du cœur ont été déchirés"[4] [One can no longer feel something without seeming to recall having read it, and all the veils of the heart have been torn to pieces]. The novel as an institution has the effect of suggesting that even my most intimate feelings have all been *anticipated* in the domain of writing, that I am therefore a kind of latecomer with respect to my own self.

But once the idea of universal simultaneity is established, it becomes possible for me to imagine myself—in relation to any particular novel—as one of an enormous company of simultaneous co-readers, a company joined together by the fact that all its members are engaged with exactly the same text. It is true that the supposed experience of simultaneity is much more vivid and powerful (at least for early audiences) in the case of broadcast media or the internet. But these electronically aided experiences are also more objective than the experience of reading, more literal as it were, therefore more easily opened to doubt; whereas reading unfolds entirely in the imagination, hence under my control. Moreover, novel-reading (or adopting the correct receptive attitude for such reading) is the most widespread form in our culture of obedience to the imperative of aesthetic response; and it is exactly this imperative that is answered definitively by the experience of simultaneity. Of course one is not compelled to buy into this fairly obvious link between novel-reading and universal simultaneity. But then, compulsion is not a factor in any of the cultural processes we are talking about. The question is always: What paths are open by which people may *willingly* satisfy the demands, and reap the supposed communicative rewards, of an evolved aesthetic culture?

In any event, just as the form of the novel solves the problem of finding a more or less convincingly immediate experience of simultaneity in times when no stronger medicine is available, so also the idea of permanent simultaneity solves the problem of the anticipation of personal feeling by the novel as an institution. For the feelings that attend novel-reading are now in a sense no longer strictly personal, but have themselves taken on an institutional quality, as the feelings of that total "readership" of which I imagine myself a member. Which means that the institution can no longer spoil them by anticipating them; there is no longer a quasi-historical space for them to happen in "before" they happen to me. Thus, by a paradox that supports Arendt's paradox of the "atomized mass," they become more fully and satisfyingly *mine* than they could ever have been otherwise.

I don't know if this argument demonstrates conclusively the operation of permanent simultaneity in modern Western civilization. But without an argument of this sort, I cannot see how to account for the strong popularity of novels alongside the equally strong decline in, say, newspaper-reading. In any case, the main argument of this book requires only that the point about permanent simultaneity be valid for most of the first half of the twentieth century.

THE MASSES AS A PROBLEM IN LOGIC

We can now come back to the question we started with: How can arguments like Arendt's, which explain convincingly the *possibility* of totalitarianism, be supplemented so as to provide a reasonable explanation of the *actuality* of that political development?

Arendt's argument turns on the concept of the "mass" or "masses," that social entity which emerged from the breakdown of social classes in Europe, and the breakdown of the system of political parties that had in the nineteenth century become associated with them. But this mass is neither homogeneous nor mindless. Arendt mentions secret public opinion research, conducted by the SS, showing "that mass support for totalitarianism comes neither from ignorance nor from brainwashing" (xxiii, n1). And precisely the absence of any basic homogeneity in the masses—

"whose chief characteristic is that they belong to no social or political body, and who therefore present a veritable chaos of individual interests" (Arendt, 348)—prevents traditional interest-based propaganda from having an effect on them.

But this point brings us back to the same question. How does the chaotic heterogeneity of the modern masses get mobilized behind a single movement? "Totalitarian movements are possible wherever there are masses who for one reason or another have acquired the appetite for political organization" (311), says Arendt. But where does such an appetite come from? And how does it get focused on a single movement? Arendt's actual argument moves in the other direction, from result toward cause. It can be shown that the two major totalitarian movements of the early twentieth century, under Hitler and under Stalin, both enjoyed strong "mass support." It can even be shown that the condition of "an atomized and individualized mass" (318), which had been provided for Hitler by circumstances, was deliberately created by Stalin in the Soviet Union (318-23). How can it not be true that precisely that mass is the principal enabling condition for totalitarianism, hence its cause?

The problems in this ex post facto logic appear when Arendt tries to turn it around and run it forward.

> The fall of protecting class walls transformed the slumbering majorities behind all parties into one great unorganized, structureless mass of furious individuals who had nothing in common except their vague apprehension that the hopes of party members were doomed . . . and that all the powers that be were not so much evil as they were equally stupid and fraudulent. It was of no great consequence for the birth of this new terrifying negative solidarity that the unemployed worker hated the status quo and the powers that be in the form of the Social Democratic Party, the expropriated small property owner in the form of a centrist or rightist party, and former members of the middle and upper classes in the form of the traditional extreme right. (315)

How can a "solidarity" be negative? And how can it not matter to such solidarity if everyone's negativity is directed against something different? But Arendt insists:

> In this atmosphere of the breakdown of class society the psychology of European mass man developed. The fact that with monotonous but abstract [?] uniformity the same fate had befallen a mass of individuals did not prevent their judging themselves in terms of individual failure or the world in terms of specific injustice. This self-centered bitterness, however, although repeated again and again in individual isolation, was not a common bond [i.e., not a "negative solidarity"?] despite its tendency to extinguish individual differences, because it was based on no common interest, economic or social or political. Self-centeredness, therefore, went hand in hand with a decisive weakening of the instinct for self-preservation. Selflessness in the sense that oneself does not

matter, the feeling of being expendable, was no longer the expression of individual idealism but a mass phenomenon. (315)

The quality of selflessness is what Arendt is aiming at here, because of its empirically unquestionable significance in life under the Nazis or the Soviets—in the form of a disregard for personal interest that would put most Kantian aesthetes to shame. But the "therefore" by which she makes her connection suggests that somehow the instinct for self-preservation depends on the presence of common interest.

And yet, as far as I can see, her diagnosis of the masses' need "to escape from reality" into some form of consistent fiction is entirely correct.

> The masses' escape from reality is a verdict against the world in which they are forced to live and in which they cannot exist, since coincidence has become its supreme master and human beings need the constant transformation of chaotic and accidental conditions into a man-made pattern of relative consistency. The revolt of the masses against "realism," common sense, and all "the plausibilities of the world" (Burke) was the result of their atomization, of their loss of social status along with which they lost the whole sector of communal relationships in whose framework common sense makes sense. . . . . Totalitarian propaganda can outrageously insult common sense only where common sense has lost its validity. Before the alternative of facing the anarchic growth and total arbitrariness of decay or bowing down before the most rigid, fantastically fictitious consistency of an ideology, the masses probably will always choose the latter and be ready to pay for it with individual sacrifices—and this not because they are stupid or wicked, but because in the general disaster this escape grants them a minimum of self-respect. (352)[5]

But there is still a problem here, which is a variant of the problems mentioned above. How does the "alternative" that Arendt speaks of arise in the first place? Why does the need for consistency not simply produce thousands of different fictions? Why should people who have turned away decisively from politics, in the sense of party politics, now return to the political arena in search of a visionary response to their predicament?

THE POLITICAL EMERGENCE OF SIMULTANEITY

As I have said, I do not pretend to understand totalitarianism. But I think I understand and appreciate Arendt's argument on the origins of totalitarianism, at least in its Nazi and Soviet incarnations; and I think I recognize where that argument runs into logical difficulties. My suggestion is that those logical difficulties can be dealt with by taking into account the aesthetic preconditions of totalitarianism, and probably in no other way. The argument I am proposing does not lead necessarily to an understanding of totalitarianism. The only claim I make for it is that it produces a useful reconfiguring of the concept of aesthetics. But it also offers, I hope, some untried avenues by which to approach the totalitarian phenomenon.

In particular, the difficulties in Arendt's argument can be met by adding to her presuppositions the condition of permanent universal simultaneity—by which I mean living constantly on the brink of a compelling experience of co-presence with everyone else, at least everyone in a cultural unit (e.g., all speakers of one's language) large enough to feel like a strictly supra-individual totality. This condition is a generalized form of the supposed phenomenon of aesthetic response, and so offers itself as an ultimate goal for the whole aesthetic tradition with respect to the problem of communication. The advent of broadcast radio is important because it marks the moment at which universal simultaneity is first widely regarded as a real possibility—which means, since we are not talking about objective facts here, the moment at which it in effect *is* a real possibility. And from this point on the condition of *permanent* universal simultaneity obtains, since it is now possible to interpret any one of a wide range of communicative devices, especially the novel, as entrances into the immediate experience of simultaneity.

If we agree that this condition is established in the course of the third decade of the twentieth century; and if we agree that the paradoxical combination of lonely individuality and submergence in a limitless mass belongs to its very nature: then nothing like a weakening of the instinct for self-preservation needs to be posited in order to account for the transition from self-centeredness to selflessness which Arendt correctly recognizes *must* be accounted for in any attempt to explain how totalitarian movements gain their followings. The only question is whether permanent simultaneity is a strong enough factor in people's personal lives to produce the kind of transition we are talking about.

Under more or less normal historical circumstances, the answer to this question is no. The condition of permanent simultaneity operates mainly as a vehicle or a kind of open conduit for the experience of aesthetic response, thus as a constant quiet reassurance, in the background of our cultural lives, that true intersubjective communication is available to us. And under normal circumstances the realization of this communicative potential—or to be precise, the deluded belief in such a realization—occurs under the auspices of common bonds that are much more prominent in our lives than the awareness of simultaneity because they support our individual interests: I mean mainly those political bonds that we enter into precisely for the purpose of protecting our interests, or at least sustaining our principles. But when those bonds evaporate, or when we are driven to the point of rejecting them entirely; when the condition appears that Arendt argues characterized especially Germany after World War I: then permanent simultaneity suddenly assumes a completely new level of importance, as the *only* large-scale common bond left to us, as an experience that can after all reasonably be called "negative solidarity." The otherwise practically infinite distance between self-centeredness and selflessness now suddenly becomes negligible; the two notions, in a self that has been invaded by everyone else, are close to identical; and what Arendt calls "the psychology of European mass man" can develop in earnest.

Even in such extreme historical circumstances, the condition of simultaneity cannot itself operate as a creative or formative power, forging a single communal vision out of all our individual escapist fantasies. But it is certainly true that that condition, arising as it does from a need for communication, will produce a preference for *shared* fantasies, or fantasies that can seem to be shared, if such things become available. And the business of a reasonably astute totalitarian project in politics then becomes to provide such fantasies—it being understood that the quality of the fantastic (the more egregious, the better) is crucial, since anything resembling a reasonable political program will be subject to a crippling clash of opinions. As long as the movement's publicistic apparatus is able to create the impression that its story is available to everyone, that story will be in position to offer itself as a communicative vehicle—the story, say, of a worldwide conspiracy of the Jews against "us." What matters is not whether we would ordinarily be inclined to believe the story, but rather the surge of unthinking assent in which we have learned from aesthetic tradition to recognize our last hope for communication, the experience of universal uniformity of response.

It must be kept in mind that we are talking here about exceptional circumstances. If our social situation deteriorates to the point where the permanent condition of simultaneity *can* emerge as a political force, then the blind sanction of supposed unanimity will outweigh the operation of judgment in all our political decisions. And if this political emergence of the aesthetic occurs on a large enough scale, the result will be some form of totalitarianism. (Instances on a small scale, I think, can be found practically everywhere in twentieth-century democratic politics.)

THE AGE OF IMAGINATION

Musil's Törless marks the end of his adventure into sex and torture and degradation when he declares to Reiting, the born ringleader, that he is no longer "interested": "Ich weiß jetzt nichts von Rätseln. Alles geschieht: Das ist die ganze Weisheit" [I know nothing of mysteries now. Everything happens: that is the sum of all wisdom].[6] Everything happens; nothing is excluded. David Rousset says very much the same thing apropos the incomprehensibility of the Nazi concentration camps: "Normal men do not know that everything is possible."[7] And this statement, in turn, is quoted by Arendt (436) in the last paragraphs leading up to her subchapter on the camps. The "central assumption" of totalitarianism, she had said earlier, is "that everything is possible" (427), that nothing is excluded.

For Arendt, this idea has to do with the idea of "human omnipotence" that she invokes to explain the complicity of members of the totalitarian movement who do not actually believe the assertions in their propaganda: "What binds these men together is a firm and sincere belief in human omnipotence. Their moral cynicism, their belief that everything is permitted, rests on the solid conviction that everything is possible" (387). And in Musil, a conviction of this type clearly lies behind the intention expressed by Beineberg and Reiting, each in his own way, to use Basini's abjection as the basis for experiments on the possibilities and limits of human nature.

But if we now ask where this "everything" is to be found, this inexhaustible store of possibilities, the answer, for Arendt, is given by "one of the chief characteristics of the modern masses." Namely:

> They do not believe in anything visible, in the reality of their own experience; they do not trust their eyes and ears but only their imaginations, which may be caught by anything that is at once universal and consistent in itself. . . . Before they seize power and establish a world in accordance with their doctrines, totalitarian movements conjure up a lying world of consistency which is more adequate to the needs of the human mind than reality itself; in which, through sheer imagination, uprooted masses can feel at home and are spared the never-ending shocks which real life and real experiences deal to human beings and their expectations. (351, 353)

Or in a different terminology, the age in which totalitarianism takes root, the age that is flavored culturally by the development of permanent universal simultaneity, is an *age of imagination*.

For Arendt, as for Rousset, the question of imagination arises especially in connection with the concentration camps. On one hand, what happened in the camps is strictly unimaginable.

> There are no parallels to life in the concentration camps. Its horror can never be fully embraced by the imagination for the very reason that it stands outside of life and death. It can never be fully reported for the very reason that the survivor returns to the world of the living, which makes it impossible for him to believe fully in his own past experiences. It is as though he had a story to tell of another planet, for the status of the inmates in the world of the living, where nobody is supposed to know if they are alive or dead, is such that it is as though they had never been born. (444)

But on the other hand, the camps are also manifestations of an imagination that is familiar to us.

Everything that was done in the camps is known to us [!] from the world of perverse, malignant fantasies. The difficult thing to understand is that, like such fantasies, these gruesome crimes took place in a phantom world, which, however, has materialized, as it were, into a world which is complete with all sensual data of reality but lacks that structure of consequence and responsibility without which reality remains for us a mass of incomprehensible data. The result is that a place has been established where men can be tortured and slaughtered, and yet neither the tormentors nor the tormented, and least of all the outsider, can be aware that what is happening is anything more than a cruel game or an absurd dream. (445-46)

Assuming that both these assertions make sense with respect to the phenomenon in question, how can they be reconciled with one another?

It seems to me that this paradox of imagining the unimaginable is only another version of the paradox of simultaneity, the condition of a mind that is strictly solitary yet also invaded by everyone else. The immediate experience of simultaneity would have to include the clear sense of my mind's availability for the thinking of what I cannot think, for the imagining of what I cannot imagine. Without this sense of an alien operation inside my own mind, there would be nothing to distinguish the experience of simultaneity from experience in general.

The only other possible warrant or evidence for the immediate experience of simultaneity also involves the imagination and is also connected with the concentration camp as an institution. For if universal simultaneity is actually available to me as an immediate experience, then the boundary between imagination and reality must show the effects of this situation in the form of a tendency to crumble or even disappear. Even the most outrageous products of the imagination, if they are imagined by everyone at the same time, already assume thereby a kind of reality; and the impetus to establish such imaginings as actual fact—if this should seem at all possible—is provided by the secular millennialist aspect of aesthetic tradition with its dream of human omnipotence. Thence follows one principal element of the concentration camp's importance in totalitarianism. Working from an insight of Bruno Bettelheim, Arendt points out that even for those who were directly involved with the camp as a reality, the line between reality and a nightmarish imagination was never clear.[8] And for the rest of the population, who knew of the camps' existence but were denied any basis on which to do more than vaguely imagine what happened in them, the dividing line was obscured from another direction.

It must be emphasized, again, that nothing in these arguments presupposes the actual possibility of an immediate experience of simultaneity, or even of some type of subliminally enforced belief in such a possibility. The need for adequate intersubjective communication—which arises alongside the development of lonely Cartesian individuality and then grows constantly stronger in Western culture—is already enough to account for the readiness of modern populations to take advantage of the opportunities for imagining simultaneity, for accepting the delusion, that are offered by history (especially aesthetics) and technology. Nor is it necessary to think of the idea of an age of imagination solely in terms of its more sinister implications. As I have said, there is no reason to expect that the condition of permanent universal simultaneity, on which the age of imagination is erected, will assume political influence except in times of extreme social deterioration. And in the meanwhile, there are plenty of relatively benign manifestations of the idea of a universal human imagination—especially international exhibitions (world's fairs) and the like—beginning well before the conditions for modern totalitarian propaganda had been fully established.

We have also observed, in Musil's *Törless*, a strong literary foreshadowing of the age of imagination. Musil's vision seems more focused even than Arendt's. He has his precocious adolescent say not merely that everything is possible, but that "Everything happens": that everything in the vast storehouse of the imagination must eventually find its way to some form of actuality. And if the age of imagination has its own true hero—a single inspired visionary in whom is manifest every possible positive or life-giving consequence of the collapse of the boundary between individual imagination and the mind of the millions—then surely it is the young man who, before setting out for Paris, writes in his diary: "I go to encounter for the millionth time the reality of experience and to forge in the smithy of my soul the uncreated conscience of my race."[9]

THE PARADOX OF THE NOVEL ONCE MORE

In the context of the present argument, we might be tempted to suggest that *A Portrait of the Artist as a Young Man*, historically considered, is basically a reworking of Musil's *Törless*. Both novels cause us the same type and degree of difficulty in distinguishing clearly the person and thought of the main character from those of the immediate narrator and those of the presumed author. In both plots, the main character must experience an extreme form of the sinister and violent aspect of the age of imagination—this being represented, in Stephen Dedalus's case, not by his sexual adventures but by the sermons on hell. In both novels, the impression is created that the main character eventually manages to find his way through that experience to an integrated and artistically productive form of individuality. And in both cases, we have reason to treat that impression with some suspicion.

Joyce's novel, moreover, like Musil's, directly engages the question of its own genre. But whereas this theoretical engagement emerges only gradually in *Törless*, in *Portrait* it is already emphatically present in the book's title. A "portrait of the artist," as this phrase is commonly used with reference to painting, means a *self*-portrait. And in the art of painting, "a portrait of the artist as a young man" would have to be a self-portrait painted *by* "the artist as a young man"; the person looking into a mirror is not different in age from the image he sees there. Thus a crucial difference between the art of painting and the art of writing emerges. (Shades of Lessing [*Portrait*, 186, 188].) For it is not only possible for the writer of a self-portrait to be older than the person portrayed. It is *necessary* that he be older than that person, and therefore in some degree *different* from him—as Stephen himself suggests in the last fully recorded conversation with Cranly, where we read:

> Did you believe in it [religion] when you were at school? I bet you did.
> —I did, Stephen answered.
> —And were you happier then? Cranly asked softly. Happier than you are now, for instance?
> —Often happy, Stephen said, and often unhappy. I was someone else then.
> —How someone else? What do you mean by that statement?
> —I mean, said Stephen, that I was not myself as I am now, as I had to become.
> —Not as you are now, not as you had to become, Cranly repeated. Let me ask you a question. Do you love your mother? (212)

And if Stephen is now not the schoolboy but "someone else," then surely the person of whom Stephen is a written self-portrait—wherever we might position him on the scale from narrator to author—is also "someone else" with respect to Stephen as the book shows him.

Or is he? Cranly does not directly challenge Stephen's formulation; but his meditative repetition of the words, and his changing the subject, suggest at least a certain skepticism. A skepticism we have every reason to share. It may on some level be true that in the medium of time one is always "someone else" with respect to oneself—"JE est un autre," writes Rimbaud.[10] But it will not ordinarily occur to us to formulate this truth as a "statement," like Stephen's, except when we are on the defensive against precisely our consciousness of its opposite—as Stephen is, in response to Cranly's observation: "It is a curious thing . . . how your mind is supersaturated with the religion in which you say you disbelieve" (212). And conversely, I will not ordinarily insist on the immutable sameness of my self—for Stephen, the idea of what he *"had to* become"; for Rimbaud, "JE" as the destined poet—except as a defense against the danger of losing my confidence in an integrated structure of experience.

Stephen, like most of us, attempts to occupy both sides of this paradox, to imagine himself the bearer of an unchanging destiny, yet also capable of radical self-renewal—in the form of repentance, for example. But for present purposes, it is mainly the paradox as such that matters, in its illumination of the paradoxical structure of a written "portrait of the artist," a writing whose content both is and is not identical with the writer, and both is and is not different from him. And this paradox, in turn, is important because it at least closely parallels the general paradox of the novel: the paradox of a writing that in each particular instance discloses reality in the form of individual experience—which, for me, means *my* experience—while at the same time, as an established type of writing, it also alienates that very experience by embodying the proposition that experience, as such, can be reduced to an operation of language.

The parallels among these paradoxical structures are clear enough. But how do they affect our understanding of Joyce's novel and our grasp of its historical situation? Is the autobiographical paradox merely an acknowledgment of the general paradox of the novel and thus an acceptance of the place of this particular novel in the history of aesthetics? Increasingly, as Stephen's mind develops, speculation on aesthetic matters does share space in it with the vague sense of a secular millennium: "The end he had been born to serve yet did not see" (144). And it is evidently this combination of qualities that produces Stephen's view of himself as "a priest of the eternal imagination" (195).

Must we then, in the end, regard Stephen as nothing more than a priest and prophet of the age of imagination, perhaps personally convinced of its beneficent or progressive potential, but not for that reason any less implicated in its invention of hell? Or is there a critical dimension in the novel that would complete its parallel with *Törless*?

A TEXT FULL OF BLIND SPOTS?[11]

We have heard often enough about the importance of Joyce's idea and experience of "epiphany" in the chapter-structure of *Portrait*. Part I ends, after Stephen's successful interview with the rector, with "the sound of the cricket bats: pick, pack, pock, puck: like drops of water in a fountain falling softly in the brimming bowl" (52). Part II ends with the whore's kiss, "darker than the swoon of sin, softer than sound or odour" (89). Part III ends with Stephen's making his first ecstatic communion after repenting (127). And Part IV ends with Stephen on a sandhill (151), still digesting his ecstatic vision of the girl "in midstream: alone and still, gazing out to sea" (150).

But what shall we say of Part V? Is it even clear *where* that final chapter ends? Stephen's journal, eloquent and impassioned as it may be toward its end, cannot be considered the description of an instant's epiphany, or indeed any sort of climax. The dating of the entries prevents this. Shall we then take the journal as a kind of coda and place the true chapter-end, for structural purposes, at the sentence "Cranly did not answer" (219)? If we do, then it must follow that Part V ends not in a moment of illumination or insight, but in a moment of concealment, obscurity, withdrawal.

And yet, I think that even in this case we can speak of a kind of epiphany. The final phase of the final conversation begins, from Stephen's proud declaration, as follows:

> —You made me confess the fears that I have. But I will tell you also what I do not fear. I do not fear to be alone or to be spurned for another or to leave whatever I have to leave. And I am not afraid to make a mistake, even a great mistake, a lifelong mistake and perhaps as long as eternity too.
>
> Cranly, now grave again, slowed his pace and said:
> —Alone, quite alone. You have no fear of that. And you know what that word means? Not only to be separate from all others but to have not even one friend.
> —I will take the risk, said Stephen.
> —And not to have any one person, Cranly said, who would be more than a friend, more even than the noblest and truest friend a man ever had. (218)

These are the last words of Cranly's that we are given directly; and they pique our curiosity as much as they do Stephen's:

> His words seemed to have struck some deep chord in his own nature. Had he spoken of himself, of himself as he was or wished to be? Stephen watched his face for some moments in silence. A cold sadness was there. He had spoken of himself, of his own loneliness which he feared.
> —Of whom are you speaking? Stephen asked at length.
> Cranly did not answer. (219)

"He had spoken of himself," Stephen decides. But even if we agree, we cannot possibly be satisfied; we cannot claim to have understood Cranly in any significant degree. That last sentence, "Cranly did not answer," opens a simple blind spot in the text.

The importance of this blind spot can be measured not only by its position in the text's structure, but also by Stephen's inability to let go of it. In his first journal entry, he recalls another conversation and attempts to understand Cranly by imagining his father—in an interesting parallel to Musil's treatment of Beineberg. And in the second journal entry he manages to situate Cranly as a kind of John the Baptist, presumably in relation to his own Jesus. He thus wraps Cranly up and packages him as part of his own fate, which appears to circumvent the problem of understanding him. But for us, surely—in that we recognize Stephen's stratagem—and probably also for Stephen himself on some level, the problem remains open; and as an open problem, it forms a kind of negative epiphany. For it turns the material of that last fully recorded conversation back upon itself by raising the question of aloneness from another angle. Do we perhaps never really understand *anyone?* Do we all in truth pass our entire lives in a world of nothing but blind spots, in a condition of perfect aloneness beyond the reach even of a mother's love?

And this question in turn, if we admit that it operates centrally in the book's structure, draws our attention to the obvious test question by which to approach it: To what extent and in what manner can we, the book's readers, be said to understand Stephen Dedalus?

UNDERSTANDING AND ALONENESS

The above question is not entirely unanswerable. We noted that in Musil's *Törless* there are a number of striking disruptions of the narrative perspective. Most of the fictional material is seen from the point of view of young Törless himself as the action develops. But many passages cannot be accounted for except by positing the perspective of an older Törless; and in a couple of passages, even this chronologically extended perspective does not explain how (or if) Törless can have known of facts that are recounted.

In *Portrait,* however, there are no such disruptions—even though the perspective of an older Stephen is suggested by the book's title. We are never told anything at all about the fictional world except what is available to Stephen's own mind and senses at the time of the experience being described. The book offers us a world seen exclusively through the lens of Stephen's developing mentality. And if we can make sense of that world, if we can understand it, then surely such understanding counts as an understanding of Stephen.

There are problems here. The idea that novels, by means of a negative operation of language, disclose reality in the form of individual experience, does not by any means imply that every novel must restrict itself to the perspective of a single character. But when the mental development of a single character is a novel's obvious principal focus, it seems more or less natural that that character's perspective be maintained as consistently as possible—which is why Musil's shifts in perspective strike us as disruptions. Therefore, in the sporadic tradition of what is still sometimes called the "Bildungsroman," even in third-person narratives such as *Wilhelm Meisters Lehrjahre, L'Éducation sentimentale* and *Der Zauberberg,* deviations from the main character's point of view are kept within reasonable limits as to frequency and magnitude.

But *Portrait* is not at all reasonable in this regard. On one hand, the maintenance of Stephen's perspective in the novel is absolute. There are no deviations at all, no elements of content that are not directly available to Stephen's mind or senses. But on the other hand, the book's very title insists on the presence of an older Stephen behind the text. When we think of that title, therefore, it must occur to us that the book's remarkably strict unity of perspective is not simply a natural and comfortable way of transmitting knowledge about Stephen and his world, but also a *contrivance* on the part of the immediate narrator, the older Stephen, who could just as easily have organized his material in a completely different way. This complication is not a disruption of the type we find in Musil; it does not affect what we might call the feel of the text from page to page. But it is still always there in the background as an open question, like the problem of understanding Cranly: the question of whether the object of our understanding (assuming such understanding happens) is Stephen himself, or Stephen's understanding of himself, or a self-disguised Stephen, or something else entirely.

Or let us consider the two sermons on hell (102-109, 111-117), which form a kind of centerpiece in the book. They straddle the book's actual center; and while they do not violate the principle of perspectival unity (since Stephen hears every word of them), still they stand out strongly by being easily the longest passages in the book whose language originates in a mind clearly distinct from Stephen's.

This quality is emphasized by contrast with a passage that closely precedes the sermons. The description of the second day of the retreat begins: "The next day brought death and judgment, stirring his soul slowly from its listless despair" (98). And although the tenor quickly shifts from the factual to the visionary—beginning with Stephen's imagining his own death, as he had earlier at Clongowes—the continuing use of the past tense situates the thinking in Stephen's mind, as his own personal response to the sermon he is listening to. But then, a page further on, the tense changes in mid-paragraph: "The three blasts of the angel filled all the universe. Time is, time was but time shall be no more. At the last blast the souls of universal humanity throng towards the valley of Jehoshaphat, rich and poor, gentle and simple, wise and foolish, good and wicked" (99).[12] After the sentence on time, paraphrased from Roger Bacon's brazen head, the grammatical tense shifts to the present and stays there. Henceforward we could be hearing the preacher's words directly, not Stephen's response; and by the time the sermon ends, on a rather strained coupling of Addison and Pope (100-101), the displacement of Stephen's mind by the preacher's quoted speech is obviously complete. This unobtrusive grammatical transition suggests clearly the idea of perfect continuity between the sermon itself and Stephen's feeling as he hears it.

But no such suggestion is incorporated in the two sermons on hell. Those sermons are simply given word for word, and Stephen's reaction is described afterwards. Thus a certain distance is interposed between what has to be my principal project as a reader, the assembling of a cohesive idea of the main character, and the actual words of the text. This sense of distance is reinforced by Stephen's own personal vision of hell, the "field of stiff weeds and thistles and tufted nettlebunches" (120), which follows shortly after the two sermons. For Stephen's vision has nothing whatever in common with the preacher's physical description of hell. It is as if, despite all the preacher's rhetorical skill and energy, Stephen had actually assimilated from the sermons nothing but the bare concept of hell, and had then filled it from his own imagination. It is as if he had not really been listening, as if the actual words of the sermons had somehow passed him by.

This idea is not inconsistent with what earlier chapters tell us about Stephen's character: about his feeling "that he was different from others" (56); about his instinctive self-protection from unpleasant experiences, his "silent watchful manner" (60), his "detaching himself from [what he saw] and tasting its mortifying flavour in secret" (58); about his sense of a "power" within him, capable of "divesting him of [a] sudden woven anger as easily as a fruit is divested of her soft ripe peel" (73), a power "which had often made anger or resentment fall from him" (75). It is not difficult to imagine that in the very moment of hearing the sermons—despite his later ecstasies of guilt, confession, and repentance—some part of Stephen is already detaching itself (and him) from them, some part that hears and records the description of hell, but without being involved in it, preserving that description perhaps as a concrete instance of what he will later boast to Cranly about not being afraid of.

And the interesting thing about this psychological understanding of Stephen's development, assuming it is a valid understanding, is that it is not transmitted in the text's content at the time of the sermons. (We simply hear the sermons verbatim.) I understand the contradiction within Stephen—I understand, perhaps, that precisely the violence of his reaction to the sermons on hell is a protest against the inevitable move of self-distancing that is in progress behind it—only by way of my own critical self-distancing from the text, to a point where I can speculate on relations between its content and its rhetoric. (I *read* the sermons verbatim, hence at a distance from Stephen's presumably emotional hearing, a distance which may mimic Stephen's own interior distancing.) That is to say, I understand the "power" of detachment in Stephen only by way of a corresponding power in myself, which enables me to manipulate critically my else merely emotional or imaginative engagement with the text.

Understanding Stephen, therefore, at its deepest, is a matter not of objective recognition but of sympathy or resonance with the experience of a competent critical reader, a sympathy which, in its turn, must certainly resonate with the sympathy that connects Stephen as narrator with Stephen his subject—thus enfolding in its operation the complications created by the book's title and by its insistent perspectival unity.

And if we ask now where this conclusion leaves us with respect to the question of aloneness, we arrive at two diametrically opposed possibilities. On one hand, the sympathetic relation between myself and Stephen—a sympathy which includes in its structure and thus annuls the inherent critical distance of reading—can be understood as a triumphant overcoming of aloneness. Not only has the shell of my own self-conscious aloneness (the lonely individuality of the age of Descartes) been broken through by seeing itself replicated in Stephen, but Stephen thus now also presumably serves as a medium of communication for all the book's critical readers, who now form a new kind of community, perhaps that of the "race" to whom Stephen promises a "conscience."

But on the other hand, it could also be argued that my sympathy with Stephen—including its mirroring of Stephen's with himself—has turned the book into an exercise in futility. I have undertaken a long imaginative and critical journey, at the end of which I find nothing but a replica of my own condition as a reader, nothing but a kind of mocking intensification of my original aloneness. How shall we decide between these possibilities? Is it even clear which of the two Stephen prefers? The community suggested by the idea of a "race," by the voices calling, "We are your kinsmen" (224)? Or the hopeless aloneness he has boasted of not fearing?

THE WORLD OF WORDS AND ITS OPPOSITE

We can approach the same opposition of possibilities from another direction by inquiring into our understanding not of Stephen himself so much as of his world. The crucial passage in this connection is his meditation on the phrase, "A day of dappled seaborne clouds":

> The phrase and the day and the scene harmonised in a chord. Words. Was it their colours? He allowed them to glow and fade, hue after hue: sunrise gold, the russet and green of apple orchards, azure of waves, the grey fringed fleece of clouds. No, it was not their colours: it was the poise and balance of the period itself. Did he then love the rhythmic rise and fall of words better than their associations of legend and colour? Or was it that, being as weak of sight as he was shy of mind, he drew less pleasure from the reflection of the glowing sensible world through the prism of a language many coloured and richly storied than from the contemplation of an inner world of individual emotions mirrored perfectly in a lucid supple periodic prose? (146)

If neither "the glowing sensible world" itself, nor even its reflection in language, is a matter of primary interest to Stephen, then surely it would be idle on my part to attempt to see such a world *through* either his own language or that of his self-portraitist. What the words of this book show us, I mean, is in the end nothing but themselves, a world of words and verbal relations and periods.

Language, after all, is what principally attracts Stephen's attention throughout the novel—from the monosyllables "belt" and "suck" and "kiss" at Clongowes (7, 9, 12) to the "tundish" he still cannot stop thinking of in his diary (222-23). His meditation while standing on "the trem-

bling bridge" (146) is part of what brings him soon to the ecstatic realization: "Yes! Yes! Yes! He would create proudly out of the freedom and
power of his soul, as the great artificer whose name he bore, a living
thing, new and soaring and beautiful, impalpable, imperishable" (149).
But surely this "living thing" he envisions will be made of words. And
his original meditation on the "tundish" question—still in the midst of
the conversation with the dean of studies—provides a cultural context for
this special relation to language:

> He thought:
> —The language in which we are speaking is his before it is mine. How
> different are the words *home, Christ, ale, master* on his lips and on mine!
> I cannot speak or write these words without unrest of spirit. His lan-
> guage, so familiar and so foreign, will always be for me an acquired
> speech. I have not made or accepted its words. My voice holds them at
> bay. My soul frets in the shadow of his language. (166)

Ostensibly this passage articulates a sensitive Irishman's view of English.
But in truth its content is the attitude of every sensitive individual—
especially every poet—toward language, even toward his or her "own"
language. What else is poetic sensitivity, if not this constant holding of
language at arm's length, this refusal simply to put language on like a
pair of spectacles and see the world (or pretend to see the world) *through*
it?

Thus we are brought back to essentially the same opposition of possibilities we encountered above. If we are willing to generalize from Stephen's basically poetic focus not on what language says or shows, but on
what it is and how it works; if we are willing, therefore, to operate always
on the assumption that all reality, all experience, is verbally mediated,
that reality itself is always somehow not quite as real as the language that
captures it; if, in other words, we decide to accept unreservedly the idea
of a world of words—as Paul de Man apparently wants us to at the end of
"Literary History and Literary Modernity":[13] then it becomes possible for
us to believe that we have achieved a maximally complete understanding
of *Portrait* (or of that book's world) precisely by *failing*, and insisting upon
our failure, to see beyond the words of the text. Thus, as in the case of our
sympathetic understanding of Stephen, the idea of a universal community of understanding appears to grow into the realm of the possible, a
community mediated by our understanding of just this novel. The words
of the text, after all—considered strictly as linguistic objects—are exactly
the same for all of us.

But if, on the other hand, we resist this generalizing move; or if it
occurs to us that unreserved acceptance is simply not a logically appropriate stance vis-à-vis the deduction, from the idea of poetry, of a supposed world of words: then our community of understanding vanishes
and I am again strictly alone. It is now clear to me that my inability to see

beyond the words (the *mere* words) of the text, like my discovery in Stephen of a replica of my condition as a reader, only turns me back upon myself and denies me any truly external contact or leverage.

Once the question is put in these terms, it is fairly clear that only the latter alternative makes sense. For all we know it may be true that all reality, as we experience it, is mediated or conditioned by language. It may even be true that the idea of a reality somehow subordinate to language is deducible from the idea of poetry. But these truths, if truths they are, are not truths that I can reasonably *accept*—if to accept a truth means to integrate it into my normal direct experience of the world. For the very idea of a word (in my normal direct experience of the world) includes the idea of its offering itself to be seen through in the direction of a meaning—"meaning" being understood broadly enough to include all possible speech-acts and conceptual operations, along with their consequences. Words, that is, are what they are only by always being, in some manner, *mere* words.

The meditation on language suggested in *Portrait* thus recalls the first version of our opposition of possibilities and makes clear to me that I cannot possibly be satisfied with the apparently communicative resonance between Stephen's habit of mind and my condition as a reader. I am, after all, reading a novel; and I shall merely make both personal and historical nonsense of my own activity if I deny that in the first instance I am seeking, *through* the words of the text, a disclosure of reality in the form of individual experience. Stephen himself insists, "Welcome, O life! I go to encounter for the millionth time the reality of experience" (224). And however callow this particular formula may be, it reminds me that such an encounter with reality is exactly what my reading is aimed at. It reminds me of this, moreover, precisely by way of the resonance between my condition and Stephen that had (I had thought) exempted me from the hopeless quest for an understanding in terms of personal specifics.

But this line of thought leads to an apparent contradiction. For if I approach *Portrait,* or any particular novel, as a vehicle of experience, I am automatically entangled in Mme. de Staël's paradox. The disclosure of experience in *a* novel (say, *Portrait*) implies, on the level of *the* novel, the theorem that experience as such is always anticipated in language, which is exactly the idea of language that *Portrait* (I have just argued) shows to be unacceptable. What I am suggesting, therefore, is that Joyce requires a way to break out of the paradox of the novel, which is also the inherent dilemma of aesthetics, a way to write, as Musil does, *a* novel that decisively undermines the institution of *the* novel.

The solution to this problem is easily arrived at. For the generalizing move that produces the paradox of the novel—the move from the reading of *a* novel, or novels, to the significance of *the* novel as an institution—can happen only if the experience achieved in reading is understood to be communicable. How else could the comparisons or analogies arise by which to think of it as an instance of experience in general? And precisely the quality of communicability is excluded in the type of experience that Stephen insists on: the experience of perfect aloneness, or in the term that Stephen (218) and certainly Joyce seem to prefer, the experience of *exile*, strict separation from whatever might count as one's own community. "The spell of arms and voices: the white arms of roads, their promise of close embraces and the black arms of tall ships that stand against the moon, their tale of distant nations. They are held out to say: We are alone. Come. And the voices say with them: We are your kinsmen. And the air is thick with their company as they call to me, their kinsman, making ready to go, shaking the wings of their exultant and terrible youth" (223-24). There is obviously a paradox in the statement, "We are alone." But it is no longer the timid and groping paradox of the novel. The word "We" is now not a retreat from aloneness but the "exultant" expression of an aloneness so perfect that not even the pronoun of basic human community can compromise it, an exile so remote that the "company" of those who suffer it becomes not comforting but "terrible," not an instance of community but the sum of everything that is alien.

By way of the concept of "kinsmen," moreover, the connection is made between that company of absolute exiles and the "race" Stephen imagines in his last entry but one, a race defined by the condition of perfect aloneness, hence the condition that each member forge its always still uncreated "conscience" in his or her own soul. And the content of that conscience, finally, is nothing but the resolution to pursue "the reality of experience" unfailingly to the level of strict incommunicability, to insist constantly on the perfect aloneness of the experiencing individual as the only possible opposite—especially for a poetically minded individual!—to the world of words. For the world of words is itself nothing but the phantasmal world of human omnipotence, the world as seen by a still just barely dawning age of imagination, whose more or less predictable destiny will be the founding of hell.

NOTES

1. For an interpretation in this sense, see my *Theater As Problem: Modern Drama and Its Place in Literature* (Ithaca, 1990), 164-71.

2. *The Origins of Totalitarianism*, 366-67. See chap. 1, n4 for full reference.

3. McLuhan's chapter on television, "The Timid Giant," *Understanding Media*, 268-94, especially on its captivating yet unexciting quality, is one of his best. See chap. 9, n13, for the full reference.

4. See chap. 7, n6.

5. Arendt is thinking of Edmund Burke's complaint "that rank, and office, and title, and all the solemn plausibilities of the world, have lost their reverence and effect," from *Thoughts on the Cause of the Present Discontents*, 6th ed. (London, 1784), 4.

6. Musil, 2:125. See chap. 8, n11 for the full reference. The translation, 143 (see chap. 8, n8), "Things happen, etc.," is inaccurate and misleading.

7. David Rousset, *The Other Kingdom,* trans. Ramon Guthrie (New York, 1982; orig. 1947), 168. The original French, in Rousset, *L'Univers concentrationnaire* (Paris, 1946), 181, reads, "Les hommes normaux ne savent pas que tout est possible. Même si les témoignages forcent leur intelligence à admettre, leurs muscles ne croient pas. Les concentrationnaires savent."

8. Arendt, note to 446, referring to Bruno Bettelheim's deposition on his time as a prisoner in Dachau and Buchenwald, and on his study, while there, of both prisoners and camp personnel: in *Nazi Conspiracy and Aggression,* Office of United States Chief of Counsel for Prosecution of Axis Criminality (Washington: U.S. Government, 1946), vol. 7, 818-39, esp. 824.

9. James Joyce, *A Portrait of the Artist as a Young Man,* ed. John Paul Riquelme (New York: Norton, 2007), 224.

10. Rimbaud in his letter to Georges Izambard of 13 May 1871, and again in his letter to Paul Demeny of 15 May 1871. See Arthur Rimbaud, *Œuvres* (Paris: Garnier, 1960), 344, 345.

11. I would not joke about de Man's assertion concerning Rousseau if it did not so richly deserve to be joked about. See Paul de Man, "The Rhetoric of Blindness," in his *Blindness and Insight,*139. Reference chap. 6, n2.

12. This shift has been noticed. John Paul Riquelme says, "In the middle of the sermon, although the dashes of direct discourse are absent, the past tense is replaced with a mixture of tenses, including present and future, much closer to the quotation of the later sermons as speech" (373 of the edition cited in n9). But this formulation understates the case. There is an abrupt shift—marked by the concept of "time"—from tenses that insist unequivocally on Stephen's intervening mind to tenses that are exactly those that the preacher himself would use.

13. *Blindness and Insight,* 164-65. See n11.

ELEVEN

What's Up, Doc? Resistance in Spite of Itself

This chapter deviates from the main line of argument but for that reason may be the most important chapter of all. It is a chapter about *resistance* against the historical momentum of the tradition of aesthetics, which means—if the main argument is valid—resistance against the continuing threat of totalitarian politics.

I have already mentioned a number of instances of such resistance: instances at an early stage in the tradition's unfolding, in the form of non-Kantian views of the self, and in Schleiermacher's de-millennializing of Kant; and one important instance at the tradition's culmination, in Adorno's attempt to rescue aesthetics as a discipline while rejecting absolutely its millennialist component. I have also discussed at length the paradox of the novel. Realistic novels, by resolutely turning away from a millennialist idea of human history, are by definition instances of resistance against the aesthetic tradition; but in spite of themselves, they also contribute to the elaboration of *the* novel as an institution, which is a prime repository and transmitter of the millennialist tradition of aesthetics in the nineteenth century.

Writers of novels therefore find themselves in the midst of the struggle for direction in aesthetics whether they will or no. In the field of the novel we shall therefore expect to find an especially sharp awareness of the political implications of aesthetic tradition, and perhaps some serious attempts to overcome the paradox of the form and open the possibility of conducting an effective resistance against millennialist aesthetics. I have suggested that *Törless* and *Portrait* exemplify such resistance, and I do not think they are isolated. Two chapters of my *The Dark Side of Literacy* treat devices by which narrative prose can be made unreadable in any manner that might support the paradox of the novel. And I think I could produce, and perhaps will produce, corresponding arguments on at least Flaubert, Melville, and Conrad.

But even if I were to write more on novels of the nineteenth and twentieth century, my overall project would still be incomplete. For the instances of resistance I have treated all belong in the rarefied atmosphere of philosophy, cultural criticism, and literary theory. I have discussed the more popular levels of European culture only to the extent of attempting to show how the effect of millennialist tradition was propagated and focused, for large populations, by such factors as a bourgeois-aesthetic revolution in ways of receiving art, a long-established doctrine of how to read, and the coming of broadcast radio. To leave the argument at this point would be to suggest that there is no struggle, no genuine resistance against the possibility of totalitarianism, except among intellectuals.

This picture would be wrong. I will conclude this final chapter by arguing that even in the domain of mass entertainment an instance can be found of resistance against the totalitarian tendency in aesthetic tradition. In particular, the tension between Disney and Warner Bros. in the field of animated cartoons was not merely a matter of comic style or American public taste. It was in my view a serious political struggle for which the crew at Warner Bros. were utterly unqualified, yet managed nevertheless to mount a significant resistance against aesthetic millennialist tradition during a period in which Sinclair Lewis's *It Can't Happen Here* was not the only sign of worry about the possibility of a totalitarian America.

And they managed to mount that resistance without even having an actual villain or enemy to struggle against. For Disney could never have been said to represent totalitarian thinking. Innocence became over time more and more the Disney stock in trade; and I don't know any facts or arguments to show that innocence was not about as close to an actual attribute of the Disney enterprise as could possibly be expected of a corporation—at least through the early postwar period. The views of Disney the man and Disney the machine were not socially progressive; but neither did they show a pattern that could be associated with totalitarian developments in Europe. The only connection with totalitarianism was by way of aesthetic tradition; and there is no indication that anyone at Disney had any inkling of it.

Did the Warner Bros. artists have a better idea of the political dimension of their struggle? I cannot prove that they did. But I think I can show that their relation to Disney had much more the character of a bitter struggle than is apparent on the surface, and that that struggle was a clear instance of anti-aesthetic resistance. I will argue this point by starting where Chapter 10 leaves off, with Joyce's *Portrait*, and developing the interpretation of that text toward the general idea of an anti-Kantian tendency in early twentieth-century thought, a widespread rejection of the Kantian desideratum of intersubjective communication. This idea then offers a way of situating against its cultural background the rejuvenated puppet theater of the late nineteenth and early twentieth centuries. And the final step in the argument is justified by the understanding that animated cartoons are historically not much more than an electrified mass-market puppet theater.

ANTI-AESTHETIC MODERNITY

Like Musil's *Törless*, Joyce's *Portrait* is an attempt to undo the paradox of the realistic novel; and the connection between that paradox and the basic paradox of aesthetics, its general theoretical insistence on particularity, suggests reading both novels as instances of resistance against aesthetics as an historical force, against a coming age of the imagination whose tendencies seem to have been well understood long before their realization in totalitarian politics. The historical resistance against aesthetics is fairly widespread. The large adversarial move by which modern literature and art assert themselves vis-à-vis a realist nineteenth century (see chapter 9 above) certainly includes a great deal that can be understood as anti-aesthetic resistance. And I have argued elsewhere that the whole history of the form of drama produces in the work of modern writers (even those with right-wing opinions) resistance against a conservative drift in literature as an institution.[1]

But the importance of *Törless* and *Portrait* has to do with the depth at which they engage the form of the novel and the history of a millennialist aesthetics—by contrast, for example, with the relatively simple-minded critique of realism advanced by such figures as Hermann Bahr and André Breton. And in the present chapter I will try to show the same depth of engagement in a little movement that lacks anything like Musil's or Joyce's grasp of what they were up to, a movement that seems to arise without having any idea of how: the movement—if I can show that it is one—that runs from the resurgent turn-of-the-century puppet theater to the American six- or seven-minute animated cartoon.

KANT AND COMMUNICATION ONCE MORE

I suggested in chapter 8 that the satirical reference to Kant in *Törless* reflects Musil's understanding of the basic millennialist character of Kantian aesthetics. It is probably not possible to show a comparable awareness of Kant in *Portrait*. But if we bear in mind the importance of the issue of intersubjective communication in Kantian aesthetics, I think we can find a parallel to Musil by way of Stephen's thinking on what the dean of studies calls "the esthetic question."[2]

Stephen's aesthetic theory falls into two main parts. The first, in response to Lynch's repeated urging (181-84), concerns the nature of beauty, and attempts to deal with the question of how beauty can be considered a single quality when it is judged so differently by different people—the obvious case being different cultures' preferences in women (183). This is the question that Stephen answers with an abbreviated quotation from Thomas Aquinas (186) which I will come back to in a moment.

The second part takes up the question of how works of art come into being, and leads to the idea of a progression of three "forms." "These forms are: the lyrical form, the form wherein the artist presents his image in immediate relation to himself; the epical form, the form wherein he presents his image in mediate relation to himself and to others; the dramatic form, the form wherein he presents his image in immediate relation to others" (188). Stephen then expands upon these concepts: he speaks of the "rhythmical cry" of lyric (189), and of how "[the] personality of the artist [then] passes into the narration itself, flowing round and round the persons and the action like a vital sea" and "finally refines itself out of existence, impersonalises itself." It is clear that his thinking has now become directly applicable to the book we are reading, particularly to the problems created by the title, to the relations among author, narrator, self-portraitist, protagonist, and all their fictional or factual environment. It is as if a window had opened inside the story, to guide (or challenge) our reading of it.

For present purposes it is not necessary to go into detail about how Stephen's aesthetic triad illuminates the book's narrative practice. The question I want to ask is whether the *first* part of Stephen's speculations, his argument on the nature of beauty, also possesses a significant parallel in the operation of the novel as a whole. This question is prompted by the patent sophistry of that argument. Stephen claims to be attempting a definition of beauty; but he takes as his authority a passage in which Thomas Aquinas does nothing of the kind. Thomas is concerned to show that the "essential attribute" of *species* (appearance, manifestness) is fittingly appropriated (by Hilarius) to the Son, the second person of the trinity.[3] Having discussed first the appropriation of "eternity" to the Father, he proceeds:

> *species* autem sive pulchritudo habet similitudinem cum propriis Filii. Nam ad pulchritudinem *tria* requirunter.

> [Manifestness, moreover, or beauty, has a similarity to the properties of the Son. For three things are considered necessary for beauty.]

Then follow the three concepts Stephen uses in his argument, *integritas, consonantia,* and *claritas* (186). But as far as I can see, Thomas is not equating manifestness with beauty in general. What becomes manifest in the Son, after all, is divinity itself. In this particular case, therefore, manifestness cannot be other than beauty; and Thomas is at liberty to prove his point by choosing three specific qualities of beauty (not necessarily constituting a definition) that mark its analogous relation to the Son.

But even if Stephen's citation of Thomas made more sense, and even if his translation—"*Three things are needed for beauty, wholeness, harmony and radiance*" (186)—did not disregard Thomas's own qualification and clarification of the terms, his argument would still fail in its stated aim. For what he actually offers is a non-rigorous account of how the mind arrives at a conception of any object whatever, whether beautiful or not—for instance, "a basket which a butcher's boy had slung inverted on his head" (186).[4] It is as if he were groping his way into Kantian philosophy by the back door, trying to use the idea of beauty as an opening into the structure and possibility of experience in general. But it is not the content of Stephen's speculation that must interest us primarily. Our attention is attracted by the question of what he is doing, what sort of act his thinking here represents.

And this question brings us into the vicinity of Kant from another direction. For Stephen is working, essentially, on the problem of communication by way of the idea of beauty. Starting from the undeniable fact that different people find beauty in widely differing objects (183), he asks whether, nevertheless, the basic sense of beauty is not similar in everyone and therefore communicable. Hence his "hypothesis": "that, though the same object may not seem beautiful to all people, all people who admire a beautiful object find in it certain relations which satisfy and coincide with the stages themselves of all esthetic apprehension. These relations of the sensible, visible to you through one form and to me through another, must be therefore the necessary qualities of beauty" (184). That is to say, while the specific content of my experience of beauty may not be communicable, the form of that experience, its progression in "stages," will be. This progression, Stephen suggests, must suffice us as a basis of communication.

But I argued in chapter 10 that exactly this idea of communication is embodied in the suggested relation between Stephen and the book's reader. Stephen, like every character in this novel or any other, is a "blind spot." There is no way for me to apprehend the immediate sensory or emotional details of his experience. But as a critical reader of *Portrait*, I discover in the constantly self-distancing structure of my own experience (*as* a reader) a resonance with the typical structure of Stephen's experience, a resonance that could conceivably be taken as a sympathetic understanding of Stephen the person, hence as an instance of achieved communication. I also argued in chapter 10, however, that this idea of communication is delusive, and that both Stephen and the novel eventually turn their backs on it. That argument is now reinforced by the evident inadequacy of Stephen's speculation on beauty, which turns on an exactly parallel idea of communication.

Thus we arrive again, as in chapter 10, at the idea of strict aloneness or exile as the novel's ultimate tenor—except that now we can see that idea clearly in its adversarial relation to the Kantian project of demonstrating the communicability of feeling by an analysis of beauty. It is especially interesting that Joyce in effect (if not in intent?) stands Kant's procedure on its head. By placing experience under the aegis of understanding (*Verstand*), Kant practically ensures from the outset that his system will eventually arrive at an affirmation of the communicability of feeling. But Stephen's resolve "to encounter the reality of experience" involves precisely the renunciation of any communicative relief of aloneness.

Even coupled with the parallel instance of Musil's *Törless*, this point would not justify our claiming to have shown a general anti-Kantian move in literature and thought of the late nineteenth and early twentieth centuries. But a justification of that claim emerges clearly enough when we include in our thinking the understanding: that nineteenth-century realism as a whole, to which early modernism reacts adversarially, belongs to the tradition of Kantian aesthetics; that that tradition, in turn, is not simply a natural development in European philosophy, but rather the victory—conditioned by academic and public circumstances—of a narrow philosophical position to which there were (and are) plenty of alternatives; and that alongside the initiatives in literature and art that I have mentioned, other important modern intellectual movements have the effect of attacking the very heart of Kant's system—especially Freudian psychoanalysis, which explodes definitively the idea that experience is governed by consciousness in the form of the representation "I think." This recognition of a widespread anti-Kantian tendency now provides a context in which to understand the *fin-de-siècle* resurgence of the puppet theater.

GORDON CRAIG AND THE IDEA OF A PUPPET THEATER

As far as I know, the period of the turn of the century, starting in the 1880s, is the first time in history when there has been direct competition between the puppet theater and the theater of live actors. The two types of theater had long existed side by side, usually playing to different audiences but often, nevertheless, borrowing material from one another—the Doctor Faustus story, for example. And there are plenty of other peaceable crossovers between the types. Pulcinella, of the *commedia dell'arte*, lives first in human, then in puppet form, the latter especially in his descendant, British Punch. And Walter Benjamin, in *Ursprung des deutschen Trauerspiels*, cites a number of authorities in suggesting that in seventeenth-century German drama, puppets sometimes shared the stage with live actors.[5]

Not until the period around 1900 do the two theaters develop an antagonistic relation; and it is solely by way of this antagonism that I claim for the puppet theater a role, as resistance, in the history of millennialist aesthetics. In nineteenth- and twentieth-century Europe there are any number of puppet theaters with political content, ranging from anti-Semitic to anti-fascist. But content is not my concern here. More important, in my view, is the manner in which the puppet theater mounts a resistance against totalitarianism by nothing but its quality as an alternative to the theater of live actors.

This opposition between theaters appears most clearly in the writings of Gordon Craig. The puppet theater, for Craig, is more an idea than a reality—even when he is quoting Anatole France, at length, on the puppets of Henri Signoret's Petit-Théâtre in the late 1880s.[6] And it is made necessary as an idea (for both Craig and France) by what are considered deficiencies in the live theater of the time.

The main trouble with live actors in an age of realistic theater, according to Craig, is that in their slavish, quasi-photographic imitation of a given human reality, they suppress and debase the freedom by which humanity is in truth constituted. "And so to-day we have the strange picture of a man content to give forth the thoughts of another, which that other has given form to while at the same time he exhibits his person to the public view. He does it because he is flattered; and vanity—will not reason. But all the time, and however long the world may last, the nature of man will fight for freedom, and will revolt against being made a slave or medium for the expression of another's thoughts."[7] Moreover, even if theatrical realism were a worthy project, human nature would still make it impossible to realize.

> The mind struggling and succeeding for a moment, in moving the eyes, or the muscles of the face whither it will; the mind, bringing the face for a few moments into thorough subjection, is suddenly swept aside by the emotion which has grown hot through the action of the mind. . . . Therefore the mind of the actor . . . is less powerful than his emotion, for emotion is able to win over the mind to assist in the destruction of that which the mind would produce. (56-57)

The expression is elliptical here, but the full thought is clear enough: The mind tries to shape the face into the expression of a given emotion; and this relation between an inner state (the mind's imitative effort) and an outward expression is itself by definition an emotion, but one in which the mind itself is implicated and over which it can have no control; the mind is now therefore simply overpowered by emotions it had never intended.

Art is in Craig's view always a matter of mental calculation and control. "For accident is an enemy of the artist. . . . Art arrives only by design" (55). Whence he reaches a very uncomfortable conclusion for anyone interested in theater: "The whole nature of man tends toward freedom; he therefore carries the proof in his own person that as *material* for the Theatre he is useless" (56). If theater is to become a true art, then, capable of the same controlled perfection as other arts (68), it must learn to present its plays "without actors" (80). "Do away with the actor, and you do away with the means by which a debased stage-realism is produced and flourishes. No longer would there be a living figure to confuse us into connecting actuality and art; no longer a living figure in which the weakness and tremors of the flesh were perceptible" (81).[8] And from here the conclusion is inescapable: "The actor must go, and in his place comes the inanimate figure—the Über-marionette we may call him, until he has won for himself a better name" (81). But who exactly (or what) is the "Über-marionette"? Or is this question as unanswerable as that of the *Übermensch* in Nietzsche?

First of all, the question is definitely "who," not "what." For Craig gives an exactly parallel argument earlier on. It is true, he says, that

> the Theatre will continue its growth and actors will continue for some years to hinder its development. But I see a loop-hole by which in time the actors can escape from the bondage they are in. They must create for themselves a new form of acting, consisting for the main part of symbolical gesture. To-day they *impersonate* and interpret; to-morrow they must *represent* and interpret; and the third day they must create. By this means style may return. (61)

Evidently the idea of the marionette, and that of the Über-marionette, represent metaphorically a human process by which acting must be divested of two main qualities that are fortunately absent in the marionette: the drive for emotional realism, and the force of the actor's own "bubbling" personality (75-77). "Yet even modern puppets are extraordinary things. The applause may thunder or dribble, their hearts beat no faster, no slower, their signals do not grow hurried or confused; and, though drenched in a torrent of bouquets and love, the face of the leading lady remains as solemn, as beautiful and as remote as ever" (82). The marionette, that is, is involved in no relationship that could be described (Kantianly) as the communication of feeling. The audience are offered a sympathetic relation with neither a realistically imagined character nor the actor herself.

The marionette is thus always strictly *alone* on his or her stage. And Craig's Über-marionette, as far as I can see, is nothing but the marionette in human form, the marionette whose strict aloneness is not simply built into it, but achieved as the free act of self-discipline in an actual human being. The Über-marionette, we might say, is none other than Stephen Dedalus—or perhaps, rather, what Stephen imagines as his own future. It is certainly an accident, but I think also a significant accident, that Craig's attention is arrested (77) by the same statement of Flaubert that is parodied in Stephen's idea of the artist's need to be "refined out of existence" into an invisible "God of the creation" (*Portrait*, 189).[9]

BEYOND JUDGMENT

The most important thing about the aloneness of the marionette is that it belongs to the marionette simply by virtue of its being a marionette. It does not matter whether the marionette is well made or crudely made, whether it is well manipulated or clumsily manipulated. In respect of the essential quality of aloneness, Signoret's unutterably charming little marionettes playing Maurice Bouchor[10] are no different from Jarry's homemade marionettes playing an early version of *Ubu roi*, or from the later cubist marionettes of Alexandra Exter.[11]

In other words, the faculty of judgment plays no role whatever in our appreciation of the puppets' aloneness. This point, together with the denial of communication, makes the puppet theater—whether it will or no—into an instance of anti-Kantian or anti-aesthetic resistance, hence an anti-totalitarian force. For in Kant's view, judgment based on feeling is required not only to distinguish good from bad art, but to discern the very quality of beauty by which art is defined; whereas in the puppet theater, the defining quality of aloneness—assuming it is such— cannot depend on any specific feeling in us. (If it did, then that feeling would have to be communicable, and the quality of aloneness, along with the feeling in question, would not exist in the first place.) Hence the puppet theater's character as resistance in spite of itself. Even a Nazi puppet theater celebrating the concentration camps would belong to the anti-Nazi resistance simply by being a puppet theater.

It must not be assumed, however, that the puppet theater is unique in possessing a specific political and historical meaning purely by virtue of its being the form that it is. In fact, it inherits this quality from precisely that live theater to which it tends to be opposed in the period we are concerned with. The trouble with live theater around the turn of the century, we hear, is that it had abandoned or smothered in itself that circumvention of judgment by which the puppet theater is now seen to be characterized. Anatole France writes in 1888:

> S'il faut dire toute ma pensée, les acteurs me gâtent la comédie. J'entends: les bons acteurs. Je m'accommoderais encore des autres! mais ce sont les artistes excellents, comme il s'en trouve à la Comédie-Française, que décidément je ne puis souffrir. Leur talent est trop grand: il couvre tout. Il n'y a qu'eux. . . . Je rêve de chefs-d'œuvre joués à la diable dans des granges par des comédiens nomades.[12]

> [To express myself fully, the actors ruin the comedy for me. I mean the good actors. I might still accept the others! But excellent artists, like

those at the Comédie-Française, I find simply insufferable. They have too much talent; it swamps everything. There is nothing but them. . . . I dream of masterpieces carelessly performed in barns by nomadic companies.]

And probably without knowing it, he is echoing Diderot, whose spokesman in the *Paradoxe sur le comédien* says that the only perfect dramatic performances he has ever seen were, occasionally, "mediocre plays performed by mediocre actors."[13] For France, as for Diderot, the trouble with good acting—hence with an historical age in which virtuoso acting and psychologically transparent acting are cultivated—is that it obscures the basic message that is always bodied forth by the theater as a simple fact, the unfailingly revolutionary message of the dramatic theater as an institution.[14]

Aesthetic judgment, to the extent that we are induced to exercise it, only interferes with our appreciation of the theater; and the puppet theater, as reality or idea, is employed to circumvent such judgment. This is the implied reasoning, around 1900, behind the interest of sophisticated theater artists and theoreticians in the puppet theater. Nor is the importance of this point diminished by the fact that many people, in the same period, produced and enjoyed all levels of puppet show without having any theoretical awareness or interest. The basic effect of the puppet theater—its thwarting of the processes of psychological realism and intersubjective communication, hence its disruption of the normal nineteenth-century operation of aesthetic judgment—is present whether or not one reflects on it. It is true that the puppet theater was favored by many non-theoretical factors at the time: a certain minimalist tendency in live theater, a developing urban cabaret culture, modernist primitivism in general and national and regional folk-art movements in particular.[15] But the influence of these factors is merely a happy accident from the point of view of such serious puppet advocates as Bouchor, France, Craig, or later, Schnitzler, Hofmannsthal, Ghelderode, Lorca.

The idea of a resistance in spite of itself is still problematic; and we will come back to it later. But the basic idea of a theoretical relation between puppet theater and live theater, as I have presented it, is supported by plenty of instances in which puppets are not even mentioned. For example, if "aloneness" is one reasonable designation for the defining quality of the puppet actor, then surely *opacity* is another. Its opacity, its denial of sympathetic transparency in all forms, is what constitutes the puppet's aloneness. And the idea of opaque performers in an opaque theater, in its turn, is a strong common element in the otherwise dissimilar theatrical theorizing of Artaud and Brecht, neither of whom shows a serious interest in puppets. Or there is the curious case of Samuel Beckett, all of whose theatrical works—on a scale between, say, *Act Without Words* and *Not I* (words without act, so to speak)—seem uniquely adapted to performance by mechanical actors. That Beckett never entertains the possibility of any but human actors, therefore, suggests again, as it were by the back door, the theoretical equivalence of live theater and puppet theater.[16] And I have argued that the gap between a corrupt "real theater" and what Pirandello imagines as a "true theater" can be traversed by a proper understanding of the strict opaque physicality of the stage, or in effect, by viewing the real theater as if it were a puppet theater.[17]

But two Viennese friends, Arthur Schnitzler and Hugo von Hofmannsthal, probably show the most complete grasp, in their time, of the puppet theater's theoretical significance. Schnitzler's *Zum großen Wurstel* of 1906, subtitled "Burleske in einem Akt," is a live play within which a puppet play is performed, and in the course of which the boundary between the live action and the puppet action is violated. Then, at the end, a mysterious figure in a blue cloak appears, wielding a large sword with which he first cuts the puppets' strings, then cuts the invisible strings over the heads of the live actors, causing them to fall to the ground just as the puppets had. And finally, he threatens to do the same for us, in the audience, thus to unmask the supposed free human "reality" of our lives as a delusion.[18] As far as I know, this scene has never been understood as anything but a philosophical comment on the superficiality of human pretentions. But it is also obviously a comment upon the theater, suggesting that the puppet theater, by its nature, represents with maximum exactitude the truth about its audience and therefore shadows forth the direction in which a well-conceived live theater must develop.

Hofmannsthal, finally, also in 1906, published a little "Prelude for a Puppet Theater" which turns on the idea that the theater can never serve as the vehicle for a poet's meaning, that the theater is in truth never transparent to the supposed human interiority that writes for it or acts in it or is depicted by it, but only ever expresses its own generically given meaning.[19] Thus the whole theoretical force of the puppet theater, in the decades around 1900, is compressed into a single short sketch. Hofmannsthal, as it happens, never tried to work with actual puppets. But toward the end of his life, he had moments when it seemed to him that his whole career had been a struggle with Heinrich von Kleist—specifically, Kleist as the author of an essay, "Über das Marionettentheater," that has made him the acknowledged predecessor of all modern puppet-theater advocacy.[20]

REAL PUPPETS AND EARLY CARTOONS

Generally speaking, even for theoretically sophisticated modern authors, the real puppet theater tends more toward farce and comical violence than toward theoretical reflection. And when it leaves the realm of the farcical, it often veers into something like an opposite extreme, as in

Bouchor's Christian and pagan mysteries or the Christian mysteries of
Ghelderode—the mystery play being a type in which there are obvious
reasons for excluding the personality of live actors. But still, the norm is
farce, for the modern puppet theater as for its antecedents—on a scale,
say, from Lorca's relatively simple variations on the Don Cristóbal figure
to things like Ghelderode's *Le Siège d'Ostende,* which is so enormous that
its very farcicality takes on a programmatic or quasi-theoretical character.

And the tendency toward farce, in turn, helps establish a connection
between modern puppet theater and the twentieth-century American
version of theater with other than live human actors, the animated cartoon. Interestingly enough, the cartoon comes to meet the modern puppet theater halfway—by having, from its earliest silent days, a strong self-
reflexive, thus essentially theoretical component. The Fleischers' "Out of
the Inkwell" hybrids of animation and live action spring to mind—including the hybrid-within-a-hybrid of rotoscoping. But perhaps more
significant for the connection with puppet theater is Otto Messmer's Felix
the Cat, of whom Norman M. Klein writes:

> When Felix the Cat uses the horizon as a laundry cord and walks on it,
> going forward and backward simultaneously into a non-existent dis-
> tance, the audience is reminded of the flat screen. To paraphrase Re-
> snais, if we ask how far back the castle is in *Felix in Fairyland,* the
> answer might be: about five feet from the bottom, along the surface of
> the screen.
>
> The silent cartoon, like all animation, was supposed to defy per-
> spective or plausibility. . . . Felix is inventive purely within the re-
> straints (or freedom) of the flat screen. Every object he transforms is flat
> ink.[21]

Just as the puppet theater makes use, crucially, of its *inability* to attract
direct human empathy, so also, according to Klein, the cartoon employs
expressively what must at first seem its disadvantage vis-à-vis photo-
graphic media, its inability to show depth—although that limitation was
later overcome.

But how deep does the relation between puppet theater and animated
cartoon go? The political and historical importance of the modern puppet
theater depended on its constantly implied critique of the live theater.
That critique, in turn, would have had no political bite if the live theater
itself had not been, in its uncorrupted form, the guardian of a revolutionary political perspective in modern Western societies. But the self-reflex-
ivity of the early animated cartoon seems to be not much more than a
reveling in its own innovative technical and artistic sophistication. It is
true that especially in early cartoons, human transparency and empathy
are blocked every bit as effectively as in the puppet theater. But where is
the standard against which to measure the political significance of this
anti-aesthetic stance? And as the history of animation develops, opposi-

tion to the aesthetic tradition seems to fade into the background. New forms of realism are constantly introduced; the focus on gags is gradually replaced by a focus on personality and story; the industry makes more money from feature-length works. And Disney's adaptation of *Pinocchio,* the story of a puppet who becomes a real, emotionally transparent human, can reasonably be taken as the animated cartoon's attempt to retract everything the modern puppet theater had hoped to accomplish.

AESTHETICS AND INFANTILE POLITICS

With the mention of Disney, we have answered one important question before even asking it: the question of where and how the animated cartoon becomes politicized. Except that with Disney, the process of politicization seems to be headed in the wrong direction.

The conservative political opinions of Disney (the man and the organization) are not what I have in mind. The crucial political fact is that it is primarily with Disney that the animated cartoon comes to be understood as a form of children's entertainment. There were plenty of cartoons made alongside Disney, by others, that were viewed and enjoyed by children. But most of the significant work was not meant for that audience. Certainly Betty Boop requires adult experience in her viewers; Tex Avery and Chuck Jones both insist emphatically that they were always aiming at adults in their best efforts;[22] and no mother in her right mind would accuse Bob Clampett of having a child-friendly imagination.

But despite the supposed rough edges of early Mickey Mouse, Disney was always thinking of children, more and more so as time went on. Which is to say that as a producer of entertainment, he always did his best to think apolitically. But for Disney, as for most others who have attempted the same trick, the apolitical intention produces a strongly political tendency, which cannot avoid showing its face from time to time. In 1933, for example, after Hitler had found occasion to attack Mickey Mouse, Walt responded: "Mr. A. Hitler, the Nazi old thing, says that Mickey's silly. Imagine that! Well, Mickey is going to save Mr. A. Hitler from drowning or something some day. Just wait and see if he doesn't. Then won't Mr. A. Hitler be ashamed!"[23] I do not mean that Walt was a Nazi sympathizer. He wasn't. But I am also not sure that he was wrong in what he said about Mickey and Hitler; I am not sure that the Disney enterprise is not, in spite of itself, part of what keeps afloat, or preserves and develops, the historical tendency in European and American politics of which Nazism was a characteristic phase.

A principal contention of the present book is that that historical tendency exists and that the aesthetic tradition from Kant and Moritz and Schiller is an important component of it. Disney does not merely conform to that tradition; without intending to, he makes a major contribution to it by adding the element of childhood innocence. The factual non-existence of childhood innocence (as Disney imagines it) makes no more difference to its operation in aesthetic tradition than the factual non-existence of judgment uncontaminated by personal interest had made at an earlier stage. And just as the Kantian idea of judgment makes possible a complicated structure of reasoning that supposedly entitles us to assume the intersubjective communicability of feeling, so the Disney version of innocence makes available to large middle-class audiences the delusive certainty that merely by having once been children (even if, in years, they still are) they are automatically qualified to participate in the great emotional unanimity of American virtue. They need only wish it. Like Kant, but armed now with the hypnotic technology of cinema and the increasingly realistic craft of animation, Disney solves triumphantly a problem he himself had first insisted upon. And as with Kant, it is now once again the insistence upon the problem, the stoking of a desperate hunger for communication, that energizes aesthetic tradition and propels it in the direction of totalitarian politics.

Moreover, if one has any lingering doubts about the secular millennialist character of aesthetic tradition, one has only to go to Disneyland, where the millennial goal is actually constructed, in the form of an idealized (and in scale, infantilized) "Main Street, U.S.A.," through which all the suckers are funneled. Thus all the significant elements of the aesthetic tradition are taken up by Disney and magnified like parade floats—including, inevitably, the dream of human omnipotence, now in an infantile form, as the strenuous attempt to believe that imagination (or "imagineering" in Disneyese) makes all things possible. It is difficult not to believe that there is some connection between Disneyism and an increasingly infantile politics in America, a politics of imagineering, of absurd promises, ridiculous visions, and idiotic planning, with general agreement upon nothing but the resolve to ignore simple facts. But it is not clear whether we must think of Disney as a symptom or as a causal factor in this situation.

Many people have taken critical or concerned positions with respect to Disney and the supposed Disney influence. And as far as I can see, the Disney discussion is remarkably free of paranoid tendencies, even after being confronted with the enormity of Disneyland. From Louis Marin on "Disneyland: A Degenerate Utopia," in *Glyph 1*, and Umberto Eco's remarks in *Travels in Hyperreality*, to Richard Schickel's *The Disney Version* and Scott Bukatman, "There's Always Tomorrowland: Disney and the Hypercinematic Experience," as well as in the writings of Laurence A. Rickels and in Norman M. Klein's recent *The Vatican to Vegas*: the tone is generally calm, the apocalypse absent.[24] But even here it is hard to read without getting the sense that more is going on in Disney products, and in their relation to their public, than is capturable by even a very sophisticated social and semiotic analysis.

I think this sense of mystery is dangerous. There may be much going on in the land or world of Disney that I do not understand. But there is one thing that I think I do understand, and that I think is more important politically than anything else connected with Disney: a thing that Disney cannot be blamed for, but of which Disneyism is a kind of signal. I mean the possibility of a new form of totalitarian politics. In neither Nazi Germany nor Stalin's Soviet Union could one have spoken reasonably of an infantile politics. But Disney's place in the aesthetic tradition shows that a totalitarian development of infantile politics is not at all inconceivable.

WORLD WAR 2½: BUGS VS. DONALD

For present purposes, however, the important thing about Disney's politicizing of the animated cartoon—of the cartoon *as a type,* not as the expression of political meanings—is that it places Warner Bros., Disney's natural and constant antagonist, in the position of being an element of anti-aesthetic resistance in spite of itself. Disney and his people were exceptionally adept and far-sighted in taking advantage of sound when it arrived; and by the beginning of the 1930s, the Disney enterprise was dominant in the animation business. All the other studios scrambled for advantage; but in the early war years—thanks to a fortunate infusion of talent and the enormous popularity of Bugs Bunny—Warner Bros. emerged as Disney's principal competitor. And at Christmas 1942, the polar antagonism of Disney and Warner was cemented by Bob Clampett's thrust at the very heart of Disneyism in *Coal Black and de Sebben Dwarfs.*

Only a few days later—it was pure coincidence—on New Year's Day 1943, Disney in effect acknowledged this competitive situation by bringing out a Donald Duck cartoon called *Der Fuehrer's Face,* which attempts to match Warner's trademark vulgarity with a song that turns on the idea of farting in Hitler's face. The song, also recorded by Spike Jones, was a hit; and the cartoon won what was certainly one of the least deserved Academy Awards of all time. Entertaining and vulgar as the song may be in itself, it is completely unmotivated in the cartoon—sung, inexplicably, by a chorus of Nazis and their allies—and conflicts awkwardly with the film's basic idea of Nazism as a form of irresistible mind control.

The war and the war period tend in general to bring into focus the opposition between Disney and Warner Bros. A little more than two years after Disney's experiment in uncharacteristic vulgarity, the title of that cartoon is quoted in *Herr Meets Hare,* when Hermann Goering attempts slobberingly to kiss "der Fuehrer's face," which happens to be Bugs Bunny's face hastily made up to resemble Hitler. Sander H. Lee has written an excellent essay comparing the two cartoons. With reference to the Disney cartoon, he argues:

By showing us the notoriously combative Donald Duck meekly submitting to Nazi oppression without even a hint of resistance, the cartoon suggests that the Nazi governmental structure is so powerful that
mere individuals, no matter how naturally rebellious, are unable to do
anything but comply. . . . But if individual citizens are powerless to act
against the all-powerful Nazi state, what hope is there? The ending of
the cartoon [in which Donald awakens from his nightmare in a world
filled with American national symbols] suggests that the only weapon
powerful enough to destroy Nazism is another all-powerful state, the
United States of America. . . . State power, first fetishized as the swasti-
ka and fascist salute, is now replaced with the equally fetishistic forms
of the Statue of Liberty and the American flag.[25]

Or to put it a bit more broadly: Disney, the consummate corporate art-
producer, understands very deeply the corporate aspect of the Nazi menace and is terrified. Only a similarly corporatized America (presumably
with Disney in the forefront) can protect us.

But in *Herr Meets Hare* there is no attempt whatever to understand the
Nazis. Warner Bros. (or at least Friz Freleng on their behalf) exercise
resistance against Nazism simply by refusing to budge from their accustomed method of gags—sometimes gags with a geopolitical component,
as when Bugs emerges in the final scene disguised as Stalin, but gags
nonetheless. Lee probably goes too far toward moralizing when he says
that "Bugs . . . goes ahead and punctures the Nazis' pretensions and
reveals them as the cowardly bullies and conmen they really are" (75).
The point is that it doesn't matter what Goering and Hitler may "really"
be; when they get into a Bugs Bunny cartoon, they have no choice but to
accommodate themselves to the culture of gags. Whereas in Disney it is
the cartoon that accommodates itself to the Nazis—"realistically," one
might say—in a curious somnambulistic manner that Lee explicates very
clearly.

The same basic difference applies to cartoons set on the home front. In
Sky Trooper (1942) Private Donald Duck gets into all sorts of violent conflict with Sergeant Black Pete. But at the end we see the two of them on
KP, being punished together, and although they are still gruff with each
other, they and we all know that they (and we) are on the same side. In
Super Rabbit (1943), by contrast, Bugs uses the superpowers he receives
from special carrots to commit all sorts of mayhem ("deviltry," he calls it)
on an anti-rabbit fanatic (and his horse) in Deepinahearta, Texas. But then
things go wrong. He loses his carrots, his opponents get the superpowers,
and he takes refuge in a phone booth, managing to survive only by
emerging in the uniform of a U.S. Marine and marching off to war. Com-
mentators, for some reason, regard this as a patriotic ending. It is nothing
of the kind. The obvious lesson suggested by the ending is: Need to make
yourself scarce? People after you? Maybe trouble with the law? Join the

Marines and they can't touch you. Again the serious business of war is trumped by gags.

And if it is asked how these differences make Warner Bros. into a relatively progressive agent of anti-totalitarian resistance, the answer is, again: only by making WB the implacable polar opposite of Disney, hence of Disney's naïve and patriotic resuscitation of aesthetic tradition, with its political dangers, in the very bosom of what had been otherwise a promising anti-aesthetic successor to the puppet theater.

A JEW, A MURDERER, AND BLACKS

And yet, perhaps there is after all something going on behind the fabric of gags in WB cartoons. One extremely important point made by Lee—which I can find no hint of anywhere else—is that Bugs Bunny is a Jew. The arguments that Lee advances on this point (74-75) are not particularly convincing, which makes the accuracy of his perception all the more admirable. For an argument is available that seems to me practically irrefutable. It involves, obviously, the accent given Bugs by Mel Blanc, which has to be described as "lower-class New York." The only other possible description would be "Brooklyn." But if Bugs were really a Brooklynite, there would have to be some indication of this in the *content* of his speech and his imagination. For example, he would have to make at least one of his wrong turns not at Albuquerque but perhaps at Flatbush Avenue or in Canarsie. When he first pops up in *Herr Meets Hare*, he is on his way to Las Vegas, which would make him more familiar with Frank Sinatra than with, say, Pete Reiser.

Bugs's accent, then, is not Brooklyn but lower-class New York. The trouble is that at the time of Bugs's conception and in his heyday, there was no such thing as a lower-class New Yorker. The concept "New Yorker" referred only to the magazine, to the city's upper class, and perhaps to a somewhat larger group of people with the all-American sophistication that is presupposed in the song "Manhattan" (Rodgers/Hart, 1925). (The great big city's a wondrous toy / Just made for a girl and boy.) It did not apply to people who talked like Bugs Bunny—and who, like Bugs, were not far from illiterate (see *Falling Hare* [1943]). Not until John Lindsay's first campaign for the mayoralty in 1965—when he called New York "fun city," an even stupider idea than the designation "Big Apple" which eventually took hold—was a serious attempt made to get all classes of "New Yorker" to feel like a single huge family.

Until that time, the lower and lower-middle classes in the city were understood to consist of four main groups: Irish, Italians, blacks, and Jews, with the Puerto Ricans coming along fast. (The Chinese were outsiders, and other nationalities were mostly disregarded.) But Bugs is not Irish or Italian or black. He would have to have specific preferences and mannerisms if he belonged to any of those categories, which is not true in the same way of Jews, because of the enormous variety of Jewish types and national origins in New York: from Hasidim in Brooklyn to lawyers in Reform congregations to sellers of stolen goods on Delancey St. and jewelers on Canal St. and notoriously exploited garment workers and commune dwellers in the Bronx who spoke Yiddish as a principal language but had never heard of Yom Kippur.

It follows that Bugs is Jewish, as it were by default, which definitely adds a level of meaning to his encounter with the Nazis, but not a level of menace. It is one thing to entangle enemy politicians and generals in a web of gags. It is quite another thing—and to say the least, questionable—to do the same with the exterminators of all Europe's Jews, as Hitler and Goering are surely seen in a cartoon from 1945. And how does Bugs get to be a Jew in the first place? Lee mentions (74) the fact that both Friz Freleng and Mel Blanc were Jews. But Blanc, as far as I know, was a Californian from birth to death; and Freleng was an ex-Kansas City Californian. Would either of them have been familiar enough with New York to know how Bugs's accent would position him? Certainly Tex Avery would not have been. Is the figure of Bugsy Siegel, the New York mobster turned Californian, a factor in Bugs's background? As far as I know, not a word on any of these questions, or on the whole matter of Bugs's Jewishness, was ever uttered by any of the people involved.

Another curious silence obtains in the case of Elmer Fudd. The facts are these: (1) Elmer's name suggests "fuddy-duddy," which means both "conservative" or "old-fashioned" and "fussy in non-essential matters of detail"; if he were in a supervisory position, he would insist that his subordinates conform to prescribed values and practices. (2) He is a human being who lives in a world of cartoon animals. (3) He has a number of pronounced infantile characteristics, especially his inability to pronounce the consonant -r- and his obsessiveness. And (4) he has a nasty temper and is apparently serious in his intention to kill Bugs Bunny.

A final touch to this portrait is provided by Chuck Jones in his masterpiece *What's Opera, Doc?* (1957). This parody of Wagnerian opera starts out with a traditional nod to Elmer's silliness, hence his supposedly infantile character, when he faces the audience and asks them to be "vewy quiet" while he hunts rabbit. But then he discovers a rabbit-hole and begins singing "Kill the wabbit" in a mock-operatic voice which is recognizably his but now neither silly nor infantile. It is an angry, grating, somewhat asthmatic adult male voice marred by a speech impediment. Jones thus unmasks Elmer's infantile traits as at best superficial, in all probability an affectation put on to cover a ruthless resolve that will move heaven and earth to achieve its ends—as Elmer does literally in the opera. And what all this adds up to, unless my mathematics is completely screwy—indeed, what the original list of characteristics by itself should have added up to—is "Walt Disney": the human being who lives among cartoon animals and makes a highly competitive business out of being self-consciously infantile; who is notoriously particular about rules for his work and his workers to adhere to; and whose worst enemy, the single most powerful force favoring his competitors, is Bugs Bunny. But again, as with Bugs's Jewishness, no word is ever breathed about what seems to me this obvious identification. At least as far as I know.[26]

I have an idea about these silences, which may make better sense if it is situated first with respect to *Coal Black and de Sebben Dwarfs* (1942). Cartoon aficionados regard this piece as one of the best ever made; but writers on racism in animation regard it as one of the worst. "Unlike many other cartoons of this period, which also included negative images of blacks, this cartoon appears to be intentionally malicious in its treatment of black characters in general and black women in particular. For example, the character Queenie combines all of the stereotypes that have been applied to black women in feature films and in animated short subjects — fat, ugly, immoral, hedonistic, stupid."[27] And defenses against this view tend to be rather ineffectual. We read: "A critical difference between Warner Bros.' hepcat portrayals of race in Clampett's cartoons and the Jim Crow cartoons of Columbia's Heckle and Jeckle was this very celebration of the hot urban music of the emerging black culture. In fact, key black nightclub performers contributed their talents to *Coal Black* and supplied exuberant performances that are unequaled in vitality and comic energy."[28] You can buy into this thinking if you want to. But many readers will find in it not only an exploitation of supposed "key" blacks against the rank and file, but also a patronizing of "the emerging black culture."

In fact *Coal Black* is offensive, every bit as much so as making gags about a Jewish rabbit's effortless discomfiting of the perpetrators of the shoah. Especially puzzling is the thinly motivated sequence in which So White, the black heroine, apparently enjoys being gang-raped by thugs in a van and then thanks them for the ride. There is no way to make excuses here. The whole plot of the cartoon, Queenie's attempt to get rid of her younger, sexier rival, is nothing but a frame for that van-ride. One must either condemn the cartoon or else read it *entirely* the other way round, as nothing but parody, nothing but an unmasking of the hidden racial hatred (white is pure, black is the opposite) in Disney's *Snow White.* This possibility cannot be established by argument, any more than the possibility of reading *Herr Meets Hare* as an unmasking of political capitulation in *Der Fuehrer's Face.* But it still seems to me that the choice is offered, the choice of seeing in practically all of WB animation a much more concentrated attack on Disney than ever appeared on the surface, including the personal attack on Walt that had always been there in Elmer Fudd and is finally brought to the fore in a Wagnerian parody.

If there is really that much animus toward Disney at WB, then why not attack him more directly? This question has several answers. An obvious one is commercial and economic. Disney was too much a power in the field to be attacked openly with the kind of venom that at least some of the work from WB seems to harbor. And the movement of personnel among the studios was extensive enough to make an open attack on any of them personally risky. Next year, for all you knew, you might need a job with Disney.

But there is another answer that is both artistic and political. You cannot attack innocence openly, at least not with the violence of a *Coal Black* or a *Herr Meets Hare*. And Disney, as far as anyone could reasonably maintain, was genuinely innocent in the war period and the ten or fifteen years following. There was no overt sign of malice to latch onto. To attack him openly one would have had to attack him absurdly, as Georg Bendemann, in Kafka, is attacked by his father: "You were really an innocent child, but still more really you were a diabolical person." (Bugs would have said, "di-a-bo-*lick*-le.") And precisely Disney's innocence was what needed attacking, which was the innocence of the aesthetic, of judgment uncontaminated by personal interest, that innocence of perfect communicative openness which opens an easy path to totalitarian politics. Hence the need for genuinely offensive attacks. There is no moral high ground with respect to innocence.

But again, if this sort of thinking really operates behind WB cartoons, who is the person, or who are the people, who thought that thinking? This question is impossible to answer. No one admits anything. As far as we can tell—at least as far as I can tell—those thoughts managed to get thought without anyone's thinking them. Which means that here, as with the puppet theater, we are constrained to speak of a resistance in spite of itself.

A KIND OF CONCLUSION

However difficult they are to figure exactly, the cartoons of the WB resistance need to be remembered, because Disney won in the end. How can innocence lose? Warner Bros., now Time Warner, became just another corporate version of Disney; and what has been done to Bugs Bunny, in *Space Jam* for instance, would have exceeded the imagination of a Mengele. Those cartoons, moreover, need to be remembered as what they really were. Not nostalgically, not as memories of a supposedly better time when our creative energies were not inhibited by political correctness and constantly yapped at by family values. (Paul A. Cantor has shown, on the example of *The Simpsons*, that family values [and he might have included political correctness] are not at all incompatible with an allusive and often vulgar cartoon wit in the WB tradition.)[29] WB in their heyday need to be remembered as a resistance that eventually failed—a resistance against the aesthetic tradition and its political consequences—

and perhaps also as the distinctly weird model for a resistance of the future.

But a resistance against exactly what? How shall we know exactly what we are up against—or even *that* there is something for us to be up against? It is easy to understand a great deal about Disney in retrospect. But at the time—when workers frequently moved back and forth between Disney and the other studios, including WB—would we have recognized in him the kind of adversary that several of the best and subtlest cartoons make of him? Arendt speaks of "the politically most important yardstick for judging events in our time, namely: whether they serve totalitarian domination or not."[30] But given the enormous differences between her two main examples, Nazi Germany and the Soviet Union under Stalin, how do we know what we are looking for? Especially if the practically unchallengeable innocence of Disneyism counts as a significant tendency in that direction. Do we have to wait until we can see concentration camps before making a decision? When do we ever "see" concentration camps anyway, except either after the fact, or from inside?

I have tried to make some progress on these questions by arguing: first, that totalitarianism (essentially as Arendt understands it) can be thought of as the emergence of secular millennialism in the form of a political program or movement; and second, that secular millennialism is the main characteristic of an intellectual tradition ("aesthetic" tradition in my terminology) from Kant down to the present day—a discontinuous tradition, but also an *ineradicable* tradition because of its connection with the insoluble problem of intersubjective communication. And if I have made it a bit easier for us to orient ourselves politically in Arendt's sense, I think we must also pay for this advantage with a clearer recognition than ever that resistance is all we have, that victory is out of the question.

NOTES

1. See my *All Theater Is Revolutionary Theater*. Reference in chap. 4, n6.
2. *Portrait of the Artist*, 163. See chap. 10, n9.
3. Thomas Aquinas, *Summa theologica*, Pt. 1, Q. 39, A. 8.
4. There may even be a little joke here, at Stephen's expense. For Thomas concludes, a bit further on, in expanding on *consonantia*, "Unde videmus quod aliqua imago dicitur esse pulchra, si perfecte repræsentat rem, quamvis turpem."
5. Walter Benjamin, *Ursprung des deutschen Trauerspiels*, 2nd ed. (Frankfurt/Main: Suhrkamp, 1982), 105-6.
6. See Edward Gordon Craig, "The Perishable Theatre" (1921), in *Craig on Theatre*, ed. J. Michael Walton (London, 1983), 19. Craig quotes from Anatole France, "Les Marionettes de M. Signoret," "La Tempête," and "Hrotswitha aux Marionettes," all of which appeared in *Le Temps* in 1888 and 1889. See Anatole France, *Œuvres complètes illustrées*, 25 vols. (Paris, 1925-35), 6:466, 595; 7:23-24.
7. Edward Gordon Craig, "The Actor and the Über-marionette" (1907), in his *On the Art of the Theatre* (Chicago, 1911), 54-94, here 60. Page numbers in the running text refer to this essay.

8. The words "weakness and tremors of the flesh" are quoted supposedly from Napoleon (80). I do not know the source of this attribution.

9. See Gustave Flaubert, letter of 18 March 1857 to Mlle. Leroyer de Chantepie, in Flaubert, *Correspondance*, 5 vols., ed. Jean Bruneau (Paris: Gallimard, 1973-2007), 2:691.

10. In the opinion of Anatole France. See n6, and also the essay "M. Maurice Bouchor et l'histoire de Tobie," where France speaks rhapsodically of "ces petites marionettes, charmantes comme des figurines de Tanagra," playing Bouchor's delicate mysteries before "paysages de rêve" (7:220).

11. On Exter in particular, and on modern puppets in general, see Harold B. Segel, *Pinocchio's Progeny: Puppets, Marionettes, Automatons, and Robots in Modernist and Avant-Garde Drama* (Baltimore, 1995). Exter is discussed, with illustrations of her work, on 243-50.

12. "Les Marionettes de M. Signoret," *Œuvres*, 6:466-67.

13. Denis Diderot, *Œuvres Esthétiques*, ed. Paul Vernière (Paris, 1968), 373.

14. See my *All Theater Is Revolutionary Theater*. The argument on Diderot is found on pages 136-57.

15. On all of these matters, see Segel, *Pinocchio's Progeny*.

16. On these points, see *All Theater Is Revolutionary Theater*, 78-83, 164-67.

17. See my *Theater As Problem: Modern Drama and Its Place in Literature* (Ithaca, 1990), 208-213.

18. Arthur Schnitzler, *Die Dramatischen Werke*, 2 vols. (Frankfurt/Main, 1962), 1:894.

19. See *All Theater Is Revolutionary Theater*, 117-19.

20. See my *Hugo von Hofmannsthal: The Theaters of Consciousness* (Cambridge, 1988), 3-18, 348-50.

21. Norman M. Klein, *Seven Minutes: The Life and Death of the American Animated Cartoon* (London, 1993), 5.

22. Statements by Avery and Jones are quoted in Kevin S. Sandler's "Introduction: *Looney Tunes and Merry Metonyms*," in his edited volume *Reading the Rabbit: Explorations in Warner Bros. Animation* (New Brunswick, NJ, 1998), 14.

23. Walt Disney, "The Cartoon's Contribution to Children," *Overland Monthly and Out West Magazine*, 91, no. 8 (Oct. 1933), 138.

24. See Louis Marin, "Disneyland: A Degenerate Utopia," in *Glyph: Johns Hopkins Textual Studies*, vol. 1 (1977), 50-66; Umberto Eco, *Travels in Hyperreality*, trans. William Weaver (San Diego: Harvest, 1990), 39-48; Scott Bukatman, "There's Always . . . Tomorrowland: Disney and the Hypercinematic Experience" (orig, 1991), in his *Matters of Gravity: Special Effects and Supermen in the 20th Century* (Durham, 2003), 13-31; Richard Schickel, *The Disney Version: The Life, Times, Art and Commerce of Walt Disney* (New York, 1985); Laurence A. Rickels, *The Case of California* (Baltimore, 1991), and parts of *Nazi Psychoanalysis*, 3 vols. (Minneapolis, 2002); Norman M. Klein, *The Vatican to Vegas: A History of Special Effects* (New York, 2004). On Klein, see also my review piece, "Attack of the Kleins," *artUS*, 8 (May/June, 2005), 50-51.

25. Sander H. Lee, "Herr Meets Hare: Donald and Bugs Fight Hitler," *artUS*, 26 (2009/1), 72.

26. There is, to be sure, a direct Disney connection to Elmer in Charlie Thorson's contribution to his making; and there is good evidence that the WB directors made Elmer as "cute" as possible, "cute" being of course the quintessential Disney quality, as opposed to WB's "funny." See Gene Walz, "Charlie Thorson and the Temporary Disneyfication of Warner Bros. Cartoons," in *Reading the Rabbit*, 63-65. Full reference in n22.

27. Henry T. Sampson, *That's Enough, Folks: Black Images in Animated Cartoons, 1900-1960* (Lanham, MD, 1998), 147.

28. Terry Lindvall and Ben Fraser, "Darker Shades of Animation: African-American Images in the Warner Bros. Cartoon," in *Reading the Rabbit*, 131. See n22.

29. Paul A. Cantor, "The Simpsons: Atomistic Politics and the Nuclear Family," *Political Theory*, 27 (1999), 734-49.

30. *The Origins of Totalitarianism*, 442. See chap. 1, n4.

Bibliography

Abrams, M. H. *Natural Supernaturalism: Tradition and Revolution in Romantic Literature.* New York: Norton Library, 1971.
———. "Kant and the Theology of Art."*Notre Dame English Journal* 13 (1981): 75-106.
Adelung, J. C. *Grammatisch-kritisches Wörterbuch.*Vienna: Pichler, 1807-8; orig. 1774-86.
Adorno, Theodor W. *Ästhetische Theorie.* Edited by Gretel Adorno and Rolf Tiedemann. Frankfurt/Main: Suhrkamp, 1973.
———. *Aesthetic Theory.* Translated by Robert Hullot-Kentor. Minneapolis: University of Minnesota Press, 1997.
Albrecht, Jörn. "Friedrich Nietzsche und das 'sprachliche Relativitätsprinzip.'" *Nietzsche-Studien* 8 (1979): 225-44.
Althusser, Louis. *Lenin and Philosophy and Other Essays.* Translated by Ben Brewster. New York: Monthly Review Books, 1971.
———. *Politics and History: Montesquieu, Rousseau, Hegel and Marx.* Translated by Ben Brewster. London: NLB, 1972.
Anderson, Benedict. *Imagined Communities: Reflections on the Origin and Spread of Nationalism,* rev. ed. London: Verso, 2006.
Arendt, Hannah. *Lectures on Kant's Political Philosophy.* Edited by Ronald Beiner. Chicago: University of Chicago Press, 1982.
———. *The Origins of Totalitarianism,* new edition with added prefaces. San Diego: Harvest Books, 1985.
Armstrong, Nancy. *How Novels Think: The Limits of British Individualism from 1719-1900.* New York: Columbia University Press, 2005.
Arnold, Matthew. *The Works of Matthew Arnold,* 15 vols. New York: AMS Press, 1970, rpt. of London, 1903-4.
Arnsperger, Walther. *Christian Wolff's Verhältnis zu Leibniz.* Weimar: Emil Felber, 1897.
Bakhtin, M. M. *The Dialogic Imagination: Four Essays by M. M. Bakhtin.* Edited by Michael Holquist. Austin: University of Texas Press, 1981.
Baumgarten, Alexander Gottlieb. *Reflections on Poetry: Alexander Gottlieb Baumgarten's Meditationes philosophicae de nonnullis ad poema pertinentibus.* Translated by Karl Aschenbrenner and William B. Holther. Berkeley: University of California Press, 1954.
———. *Meditationes philosophicae de nonnullis ad poema pertinentibus: Philosophische Betrachtungen übereinige Bedingungen des Gedichtes.* Edited and translated byHeinz Paetzold. Hamburg: Felix Meiner, 1983.
———. *Theoretische Ästhetik: Die grundlegenden Abschnitte aus der "Aesthetica" (1750/58).* Edited by Hans Rudolf Schweizer, 2nd ed. Hamburg: Felix Meiner, 1988.
Becker, Eva D. "'Klassiker' in der deutschen Literaturgeschichtsschreibung zwischen 1780 und 1860." In *Zur Literatur der Restaurationsepoche 1815-1848.* Edited by Jost Hermand and Manfred Windfuhr, 349-70. Stuttgart: Metzler, 1970.
Bellah, Robert N. "Civil Religion in America." *Dædalus: Journal of the American Academy of Arts and Sciences* 96, no. 1 (Winter, 1967): 1-21.
Benjamin,Walter. *Illuminationen: Ausgewählte Schriften 1.* Frankfurt/Main: Suhrkamp, 1977.
———. *Ursprung des deutschen Trauerspiels,* 2nd ed. Frankfurt/Main: Suhrkamp, 1982.
Bettelheim, Bruno. *Surviving and Other Essays.* New York: Knopf, 1979.
Betti, Emilio. *Die Hermeneutik als allgemeine Methodik der Geisteswissenschaften.* Tübingen: Mohr, 1962.

Bowie, Andrew. *Aesthetics and Subjectivity: from Kant to Nietzsche.* Manchester: Manchester University Press, 1990.

Brinkmann, Donald. *Natur und Kunst: Zur Phänomenologie des ästhetischen Gegenstandes.* Zürich and Leipzig: Rascher Verlag, 1938.

Brown, Marshall. *Preromanticism.* Stanford: Stanford University Press, 1991.

Bruns, Gerald L. *Modern Poetry and the Idea of Language: A Critical and Historical Study.* New Haven: Yale University Press, 1974.

Bukatman, Scott. *Matters of Gravity: Special Effects and Supermen in the 20th Century.* Durham: Duke University Press, 2003.

Burke, Edmund. *Thoughts on the Cause of the Present Discontents,* 6th ed. London: J. Dodsley, 1784.

Cantor, Paul A. "*The Simpsons:* Atomistic Politics and the Nuclear Family." *Political Theory* 27, no. 6 (December 1999): 734-49.

Cassirer, Ernst. *Die Philosophie der Aufklärung,* 2nd ed.Tübingen: Mohr, 1932.

————. *An Essay on Man: An Introduction to a Philosophy of Human Culture.* Garden City, NY: Doubleday Anchor Books, n.d.; orig. 1944.

————. *The Philosophy of the Enlightenment.* Translated by Fritz C. A. Koelln and James P. Pettegrove. Princeton: Princeton University Press, 1951.

Cohn, Dorrit. *Transparent Minds: Narrative Modes for Presenting Consciousness in Fiction.* Princeton: Princeton University Press, 1978.

Craig, Edward Gordon. *On the Art of the Theatre.* Chicago: Browne's Bookstore, 1911.

————. *Craig on Theatre.* Edited by J. Michael Walton. London: Methuen, 1983.

Cunningham, Stanley B. *The Idea of Propaganda: A Reconstruction.* Westport, CT: Praeger, 2002.

De Man, Paul. *Blindness and Insight: Essays in the Rhetoric of Contemporary Criticism,* 2nd ed. Minneapolis: University of Minnesota Press, 1983.

Diderot, Denis. *Les Salons de Diderot.* Edited by Jean Seznec and Jean Adhémar, 3 vols. Oxford: Clarendon Press, 1957-1963.

Diemer, Alwin, and Ivo Frenzel, eds. *Philosophie. Das Fischer Lexikon,* vol. 11. Frankfurt/Main: Fischer, 1958.

Dilthey, Wilhelm. *Gesammelte Schriften.* Edited by Bernhard Groethuysen et al. Stuttgart: Teubner and Göttingen: Vandenhoeck & Ruprecht, 1966ff.

Disney, Walt. "The Cartoon's Contribution to Children," *Overland Monthly and Out West Magazine* 91, no. 8 (October 1933): 138.

DuBos, Abbé Jean-Baptiste. *Réflexions critiques sur la poésie et sur la peinture,* rpt. of 1755. Paris: Pierre-Jean Mariette, 1993.

Eagleton, Terry. *The Ideology of the Aesthetic.* Oxford: Blackwell, 1990.

Eco, Umberto. *Travels in Hyperreality,* translated by William Weaver. San Diego: Harvest, 1990.

Ellul, Jacques. *Propaganda: The Formation of Men's Attitudes.* New York: Vintage, 1965; orig. French, 1962.

Erasmus, Desiderius. *Desiderii Erasmi Roterodami Opera omnia.* Leiden, 1703-06.

Flaubert, Gustave. *Correspondance.* Edited by Jean Bruneau. 5 vols. Paris: Gallimard, 1973-2007.

France, Anatole. *Œuvres complètes illustrées,* 25 vols. Paris: Calmann-Lévy, 1925-35.

Frank, Manfred. *Das individuelle Allgemeine: Textstrukturierung und –interpretation nach Schleiermacher.* Frankfurt/Main: Suhrkamp, 1977.

————. *Einführung in die frühromantische Ästhetik: Vorlesungen.* Frankfurt/Main: Suhrkamp, 1989.

Franke, Ursula. *Kunst als Erkenntnis: Die Rolle der Sinnlichkeit in der Ästhetik des Alexander Gottlieb Baumgarten.*Wiesbaden: Steiner, 1972.

Freud, Sigmund. *The Standard Edition of the Complete Psychological Works of Sigmund Freud.* Edited and translated by James Strachey et al. London: Hogarth Press, 1953-74.

————. *Gesammelte Werke: Chronologisch geordnet,* 18 vols. Frankfurt/Main: S. Fischer, 1999; orig. 1940-52.

Fritzsche, Peter. "The NSDAP 1919-1934: From Fringe Politics to the Seizure of Power." In *Nazi Germany*. Edited by Jane Caplan. Oxford: Oxford University Press, 2008.
Frye, Northrop. *Anatomy of Criticism: Four Essays*. New York: Atheneum, 1966; orig. 1957.
Gadamer, Hans-Georg. *Gesammelte Werke*, 10 vols. Tübingen: Mohr, 1985-1995.
Geiger, Moritz. *Die Bedeutung der Kunst: Zugänge zu einer materialen Wertästhetik*. Edited by Klaus Berger and Wolfhart Henckmann. Munich: Wilhelm Fink Verlag, 1976.
George, Stefan. *Der Teppich des Lebens und die Lieder von Traum und Tod mit einem Vorspiel = Gesamt-Ausgabe der Werke: Endgültige Fassung*, vol. 5. Berlin: Bondi, 1932.
Goethe, Johann Wolfgang von. *Goethes Werke*, "Weimarer Ausgabe," 143 vols. Weimar: H. Böhlau, 1887-1918.
Gombrich, E. H. *Art and Illusion: A Study in the Psychology of Pictorial Representation*. New York: Pantheon, 1960.
Grimm, Reinhold, and Jost Hermand, eds. *Die Klassik-Legende*. Frankfurt/Main: Athenäum, 1971.
Habermas, Jürgen. *Strukturwandel der Öffentlichkeit: Untersuchungen zu einer Kategorie der bürgerlichen Gesellschaft*. Frankfurt/Main: Suhrkamp, 1990; orig. 1962.
———. *The Structural Transformation of the Public Sphere: An Inquiry into a Category of Bourgeois Society*. Translated by Thomas Bürger and Frederick Lawrence. Cambridge, MA: MIT Press, 1989.
Hamann, Johann Georg. *Sämtliche Werke*. Edited by Josef Nadler, 6 vols. Vienna: Verlag Herder, 1949-1957.
———. *Sokratische Denkwürdigkeiten. Aesthetica in nuce*. Stuttgart: Reclam, 1958.
Hegel, Georg Wilhelm Friedrich. *Sämtliche Werke. Jubiläumsausgabe*. Edited by Hermann Glockner. 27 vols. Stuttgart: F. Frommann, 1927.
Heidegger, Martin. *Gesamtausgabe*. Frankfurt/Main: Klostermann, 1975ff.
Herder, Johann Gottfried. *Werke*, 11 vols. Frankfurt/Main: Deutscher Klassiker Verlag, 1985-2000.
Hermand, Jost. *Orte. Irgendwo: Formen utopischen Denkens*. Königstein im Taunus: Athenäum, 1981.
Hess, Jonathan M. *Reconstituting the Body Politic: Enlightenment, Public Culture and the Invention of Aesthetic Autonomy*. Detroit: Wayne State University Press, 1999.
Hirsch, E. D., Jr. *Validity in Interpretation*. New Haven: Yale University Press, 1967.
Hobson, Marian. *The Object of Art: The Theory of Illusion in Eighteenth-Century France*. Cambridge: Cambridge University Press, 1982.
Hölderlin, Friedrich. *Sämtliche Werke*. Edited by Norbert von Hellingrath, 6 vols., 2nd ed. Berlin: G. Müller, 1923.
———. *Sämtliche Werke: Frankfurter Ausgabe*. Edited by D. E. Sattler. Frankfurt/Main: Verlag Roter Stern, 1975ff.
Hunt, Lynn. *Inventing Human Rights: A History*. New York: W.W. Norton, 2007.
Hutcheson, Francis. *Collected Works*, facsimile ed., 7 vols. Hildesheim: Georg Olms Verlagsbuchhandlung, 1969-71.
Jameson, Fredric. *The Prison-House of Language: A Critical Account of Structuralism and Russian Formalism*. Princeton: Princeton University Press, 1972.
Jantz, Harold. *Goethe's Faust as a Renaissance Man: Parallels and Prototypes*. Princeton: Princeton University Press, 1951.
Jolley, Nicholas, ed. *The Cambridge Companion to Leibniz*. Cambridge: Cambridge University Press, 1995.
Jowett, Garth S., and Victoria O'Donnell, eds. *Readings in Propaganda and Persuasion: New and Classic Essays*. Thousand Oaks, CA: Sage Publications, 2006.
Joyce, James. *A Portrait of the Artist as a Young Man*. Edited by John Paul Riquelme.New York: W.W. Norton, 2007.
Kant, Immanuel. *Kants Werke*, Akademie-Textausgabe, 9 vols. Berlin: de Gruyter, 1968; rpt. of 1902ff.
———. *On History*. Edited by Lewis White Beck and translated by Lewis White Beck, Robert E. Anchor, and Emil L. Fackenheim. Indianapolis: Bobbs-Merrill, 1963.

————. *Kant's Political Writings*. Edited by Hans Reiss and translated by H. B. Nisbet. Cambridge: Cambridge University Press, 1970.

Kaufmann, Walter. *Hegel: A Reinterpretation*. Garden City, NY: Anchor, 1966.

Klein, Norman M. *Seven Minutes: The Life and Death of the American Animated Cartoon*. London: Verso, 1993.

————. *The Vatican to Vegas: A History of Special Effects*. New York: New Press, 2004.

Klopstock, Friedrich Gottlieb. *Klopstocks sämmtliche Werke*, 10 vols. Leipzig: G. J. Göschen, 1854-5.

Kluge, Friedrich. *Etymologisches Wörterbuch der deutschen Sprache*, 18th ed., rev. Walther Mitzka. Berlin: de Gruyter, 1960.

Kristeva, Julia. *La Révolution du langage poétique*. Paris: Editions du Seuil, 1974.

————. *Revolution in Poetic Language*. Translated by Margaret Waller. New York: Columbia University Press, 1984; orig. French, 1974.

Lee, Sander H. "Herr Meets Hare: Donald and Bugs Fight Hitler." *artUS* 26 (2009/1): 70-75.

Leibniz, Gottfried Wilhelm. *Die philosophischen Schriften von Gottfried Wilhelm Leibniz*. Edited byC. J. Gerhardt, 7 vols. Berlin: Weidmann, 1875-90.

————. *Philosophical Writings*. Edited by G. H. R. Parkinson. London: Everyman, 1995.

Lessing, Gotthold Ephraim. *Werke*. Edited by Herbert G. Göpfert, 8 vols. Munich, 1970-79.

Löwith, Karl. *From Hegel to Nietzsche: The Revolution in Nineteenth-Century Thought*. Garden City, NY: Anchor, 1967; orig. German, Zürich, 1941.

Marin, Louis. "Disneyland: A Degenerate Utopia." In *Glyph: Johns Hopkins Textual Studies*, vol. 1 (1977), 50-66.

Mauthner, Fritz. *Beiträge zu einer Kritik der Sprache*, 3 vols., 3rd ed. Hamburg, 1923; orig. 1906.

McLuhan, Marshall. *Understanding Media: The Extensions of Man*, 2nd ed. New York: Signet, 1964.

Meier, Georg Friedrich. *Anfangsgründe aller schönen Wissenschaften*, 3 vols., 2nd ed. Halle im Magdeburgischen, 1754-59; reprint Hildesheim: Olms, 1976.

Moritz, Karl Philipp. *Schriften zur Ästhetik und Poetik*. Edited by Hans Joachim Schrimpf. Tübingen: M. Niemeyer, 1962.

————. *Werke*. Edited by Heide Hollmer and Albert Meier, 2 vols. Frankfurt/Main: Deutscher Klassiker Verlag, 1997-99.

Musil, Robert. *Gesammelte Werke*. Edited by Adolf Frisé, 2 vols. Reinbek bei Hamburg: Rowohlt, 1978.

————. *The Confusions of Young Törless*. Translated by Shaun Whiteside. New York: Penguin, 2001.

Nazi Conspiracy and Aggression, Office of United States Chief of Counsel for Prosecution of Axis Criminality. Washington D.C.: U.S. Government, Printing Office, 1946.

Nieraad, Jürgen. *Standpunktbewußtsein und Weltzusammenhang: Das Bild vom lebendigen Spiegel bei Leibniz und seine Bedeutung für das Alterswerk Goethes*. Wiesbaden: Franz Steiner Verlag, 1970.

Nietzsche, Friedrich. *Sämtliche Werke: Kritische Studienausgabe*. Edited by Giorgio Colli and Mazzino Montinari, 15 vols. Munich: Deutscher Taschenbuch Verlag, 1980.

Packard, Vance. *The Hidden Persuaders*. New York: D. McKay Co., 1957.

Plato. *The Collected Dialogues of Plato Including the Letters*. Edited by Edith Hamilton and Huntington Cairns. New York: Pantheon, 1961.

Rasch, Wolfdietrich. "Schein, Spiel und Kunst in der Anschauung Schillers." *Wirkendes Wort* 10 (1960): 2-13.

Rickels, Laurence A. *The Case of California*. Baltimore: Johns Hopkins University Press, 1991.

————. *Nazi Psychoanalysis*, 3 vols. Minneapolis: University of Minnesota Press, 2002.

Riegel, Oscar W. *Mobilizing for Chaos: The Story of the New Propaganda*. New York: Arno Press: 1972; reprint of New Haven: Yale University Press, 1934.

Rimbaud, Arthur. *Œuvres*. Paris: Garnier, 1960.

Rogin, Michael Paul. *Ronald Reagan, the Movie and Other Episodes in Political Demonology*. Berkeley: University of California Press, 1987.

Rorty, Richard, ed. *The Linguistic Turn: Recent Essays in Philosophical Method*. Chicago: University of Chicago Press, 1967.

Rousset, David. *L'Univers concentrationnaire*. Paris: Editions du Pavois, 1946.

———. *The Other Kingdom*. Translated by Ramon Guthrie. New York: Reynal and Hitchcock, 1982; orig. 1947.

Salmon, Christian. *Storytelling: Bewitching the Modern Mind*. Translated by David Macey. London; New York: Verso, 2010; orig. French, 2007.

Sampson, Henry T. *That's Enough, Folks: Black Images in Animated Cartoons, 1900-1960*. Lanham, MD: Scarecrow Press, 1998.

Sandler, Kevin S., ed. *Reading the Rabbit: Explorations in Warner Bros. Animation*. New Brunswick, NJ: Rutgers University Press, 1998.

Schickel, Richard. *The Disney Version: The Life, Times, Art and Commerce of Walt Disney*. New York: Simon and Schuster, 1985.

Schiller, Friedrich. *Schillers Sämtliche Werke: Säkular-Ausgabe*. Edited by Eduard von der Hellen et al, 16 vols. Stuttgart and Berlin: J. G. Cotta'sche Buchhandlung Nachfolger, 1904.

———. *Sämtliche Werke*. Edited by Gerhard Fricke and Herbert G. Göpfert, 5 vols. Munich: Hanser, 1959.

———. *Essays*, ed. Walter Hinderer and Daniel O. Dahlstrom. New York: Continuum, 1995.

Schleiermacher, Friedrich. *Hermeneutik*. Edited by Heinz Kimmerle, 2nd ed. Heidelberg: Carl Winter, 1974.

———. *Schriften*. Edited by Andreas Arndt. Frankfurt/Main: Deutscher Klassiker Verlag, 1996.

Schnitzler, Arthur. *Die Dramatischen Werke*, 2 vols. Frankfurt/Main: S. Fischer, 1962.

Segel, Harold B. *Pinocchio's Progeny: Puppets, Marionettes, Automatons, and Robots in Modernist and Avant-Garde Drama*. Baltimore: Johns Hopkins University Press, 1995.

Solms, Friedhelm. *Disciplina aesthetica: Zur Frühgeschichte der ästhetischen Theorie bei Baumgarten und Herder*. Stuttgart: Klett-Cotta, 1990.

Staël, Madame de. *Œuvres complètes*, 17 vols. Paris: Treuttel et Würtz, 1820 ff.

———. *De l'Allemagne*. Edited by La comtesse Jean de Pange, 5 vols. Paris: Hachette, 1958-1960.

Taylor, Charles. *A Secular Age*. Cambridge, MA: Harvard University Press, 2007.

Trakl, Georg. *Dichtungen und Briefe*. Edited by Walther Killy and Hans Szklenar. Salzburg: O. Müller, 1970.

Valéry, Paul. *Oeuvres*. Edited by Jean Hytier, 2 vols. n.p.: Gallimard, 1957, 1960.

Watt, Ian. *The Rise of the Novel: Studies in Defoe, Richardson and Fielding*. Berkeley: University of California Press, 1964; orig. 1957.

Weitzman, Erica. "No Fun: Aporias of Pleasure in Adorno's *Aesthetic Theory*." *The German Quarterly* 81 (2008): 185–202.

Welch, David A. *The Third Reich: Politics and Propaganda*. London: Routledge, 1993.

Wellek, René. "Das Wort und der Begriff 'Klassizismus' in der Literaturgeschichte." *Schweizer Monatshefte* 45 (1965-1969), 154-73.

Wilson, W. Daniel. *Das Goethe-Tabu: Protest und Menschenrechte im klassischen Weimar*. Munich: Deutscher Taschenbuch Verlag, 1999.

Woodmansee, Martha. "The Interests of Disinterestedness: Karl Philipp Moritz and the Emergence of the Theory of Aesthetic Autonomy in Eighteenth-Century Germany." *Modern Language Quarterly* 45 (1984): 22-47.

———. *The Author, Art, and the Market: Rereading the History of Aesthetics*. New York: Columbia University Press 1994.

Yates, Frances A. *Astraea: The Imperial Theme in the Sixteenth Century*. London: Ark Paperback, 1985; orig. 1975.

Subject Guide by Subchapter

Three: The Irrelevance of Aesthetics as Discovered in "Classical" Weimar

Four: Kant and His Shadow: The Persistence of Philosophical Aesthetics

Five: Aesthetics and Hermeneutics

Index of Names

About the Author

Benjamin Bennett is William R. Kenan, Jr. Professor of German and Comparative Literature at the University of Virginia. He is known mainly as a Goethe scholar and an expert on the history and theory of the dramatic theater. But his most recent books, *Goethe as Woman* (2001), *All Theater Is Revolutionary Theater* (2005), and *The Dark Side of Literacy* (2008), have moved toward a focus on political questions, especially the question of the structure and genesis of totalitarianism. The present book develops this tendency, and will be succeeded in its turn by a book on Freud and the original psychoanalytic movement as an anti-totalitarian force in the domain of literature and culture.